Tradition Transformed

THE AMERICAN MOMENT

STANLEY I. KUTLER,

SERIES EDITOR

TRADITION TRANSFORMED

The Jewish Experience in America

GERALD SORIN

THE JOHNS HOPKINS
UNIVERSITY PRESS
Baltimore and London

© 1997 The Johns Hopkins University Press
All rights reserved. Published 1997
Printed in the United States of America on acid-free paper
06 05 04 03 02 01 00 99 98 97   5 4 3 2 1

The Johns Hopkins University Press
2715 North Charles Street
Baltimore, Maryland 21218-4319
The Johns Hopkins Press Ltd., London

Library of Congress Cataloging-in-Publication Data and a list of books in the American Moment series will be found at the end of this book.
A catalog record for this book is available from the British Library.
Title page: Hester Street. Library of Congress

ISBN 0-8018-5446-6
ISBN 0-8018-5447-4 pbk.

FOR SOL COHEN

1911–1994

In Loving Memory

Contents

Series Editor's Foreword

Celebrations of ethnicity are currently fashionable in the United States, particularly as we descend to third-, fourth-, and fifth- generation Americans, desperately seeking roots and a special identity. Older traditions, once muted or scorned, have been revived, in some measure reflecting a greater sense of security and self-confidence. For most Jews, however, even in the relative safety and security of America, there never could be any doubt as to who and what they were. If they desperately sought to disassociate, the world about them nevertheless usually perceived their identity. "Ethnicity" in all its manifestations always has been very much a part of one's Jewishness in America.

In the twentieth century, America became the largest homeland for Jews, and here they have enjoyed an unprecedented degree of freedom, mobility, security, and prosperity. The American Jewish experience was largely fragmented, isolated, and inconsequential until the great waves of migration, first, from central European Jews in the mid-nineteenth century and then with the larger numbers from eastern Europe in the late nineteenth and early twentieth centuries. Since then, Jews have played a vital, very visible role in American life. The result has been a new synthesis of Jewry, yet one still largely rooted in its traditional faith. The "tradition" has been "transformed," as Gerald Sorin acutely observes in this volume, yet he wisely notes that the experience has been one of "acculturation" not "assimilation." Jews, he notes, have "become American" in their allegiance and outlook, yet most eagerly have maintained their particular ethnic identity.

Except for brief interludes, the Jewish European experience was precarious, marked by oppression, persecution, and finally, the catastrophe of the Holocaust. America, however, was different. George Washington, that most quintessential of Americans, bestowed a specific blessing for tolerance of Jews in the eighteenth century. Certainly, such burdens as employment discrimination, educational barriers or quotas, and instances of incendiary "hate speech" have been part of Jewish history in America. Primitive anti-Semitism always has been among us; even today, prominent leaders of the Christian right hint darkly at sinister, malevolent Jewish conspiratorial forces that threaten American economic and social life. But since the Holocaust of the 1940s, anti-Semitism has lost whatever legitimacy and "respectability" it once had. Furthermore, American pluralism, sanctioned by the Constitution and spurred by reality, has prevented any hint of pogroms or forced conversions that throughout history had tested both the very being and the faith of Jews. For that and other reasons, of course, America has been a "wonderment," an unbelievable marvel, as the Yiddish expression goes.

The joys of the Jewish encounter with America have been a mixed blessing, particularly as the "New Zion" tempered Jewish traditions and distinctiveness. Yet this is hardly new in Jewish history. The Diaspora was a diverse experience, resulting in sharp internal differences such as, for example, those between Ashkenazic and Sephardic Jews, or the vast gulf that separated central from eastern European Jews. The openness of America, with its boundless opportunities, has resulted in a success story for the Jews totally out of proportion to their small representation in the general population. The irony is that American Jewish survival now is most threatened by that precious freedom and mobility that has characterized life in the United States. They have moved beyond their self-made ghettoes and dispersed themselves more widely throughout the land, they have intermarried, and many have decreased their adherence to rituals and religious practices. Yet Sorin optimistically notes that Judaism "continues to be reconfigured rather than attenuated." This has been apparent in the liberation of women from doctrinal restraints, the emphasis on the social and moral justice aspects of the prophetic tradition, and the migration of American Reform Judaism back to older articles of faith and practice. Meanwhile, traditional Orthodox groups grow and prosper. The traditions of *tsedakah* expressed through philanthropy happily combine religious and secular impulses that otherwise might create enormous tensions. The "ever-disappearing people" once again seem to have confounded the ever-present doomsayers, pessimists, and skeptics.

Stanley I. Kutler

Preface and
Acknowledgments

In his classic work *Assimilation in American Life,* Milton Gordon drew clear and useful distinctions between *acculturation*—accommodation to the larger society without total loss of ethnic distinctiveness—and *assimilation*—complete or nearly complete disappearance of traditional cultural traits. The Jewish experience in the United States is a powerful example of successful acculturation: Jews have been able both to maintain their own particular ethnic identity and at the same time to become American and middle class.

Despite decades of predictions by historians and sociologists that assimilation was inevitable and that wholesale Americanization was in store for the children or grandchildren of the immigrants, Jews did not assimilate. Over a period of more than two hundred years, Jews acculturated and became proud, loyal, and contributing Americans, but they did not assimilate; they did not "melt."

The American Jewish community was the first truly voluntary Jewish community in the modern world in the sense that Jews could choose to live here as Jews, and as equals to gentiles. In a long history of transient residence in other societies, Jews had been allowed only two options: isolation or assimilation. In the United States there was a much wider spectrum of choice, and Jews were clearly enticed by the openness and opportunities of the American environment.

This was true in the colonial era and in the period before the Civil War, but the attractiveness of America to Jews was never more pronounced than between 1880 and 1920, when economic and social possibilities flourished here and degenerated in Europe. More than two million Jewish immigrants came to the United States during these years, increasing the American Jewish population more than tenfold and making America home to 23 percent of world Jewry.

The religious, social, and cultural baggage the immigrants brought with them from Eastern Europe, and earlier from Central Europe, constituted the traditional civilization that would be transformed in the United States. Jewish tradition, of course, was not always as stable as it has sometimes been portrayed, and certainly in the eighteenth and nineteenth centuries, Judaism and Jewish culture were already very much in flux well before the mass migration to the New World. Nevertheless, parts of the tradition were still powerfully in place for many Jews. Even as they uprooted and transplanted themselves, Jews continued to pay attention to many scripturally ordained *mitzvot* (moral and ritual obligations), as well as to the ethical vision and injunctions of the prophets, especially *tsedakah* (righteousness, charity, and social justice). They also remained committed to communal responsibility, mutuality, interdependence, and *tikn olam* (the commandment to repair or improve the world). Above all, they continued to acknowledge a real God, who wielded awesome power and held out the possibility of human salvation.

This tradition—or more accurately, this set of traditions—was challenged by American mobility, individualism, and secularism even more than it was by European modernization. But tradition would be transformed rather than destroyed. For, while Jewish immigrants and especially their children acculturated, and relatively rapidly, they did it largely on their own terms. Inspired by the American ideals of democracy and pluralism, Jews, like many other immigrant groups, became Americans gladly, but in the process, which was not without its strains and stresses, they reshaped and thereby made it possible to retain many of their distinctive traditions and characteristics.

American Jews, although notably mobile, economically and socially, remain Jews right through the 1990s. Conservative and Reform synagogues, beginning mainly in the 1920s and increasingly outnumbering the traditional Orthodox houses of worship, represented a significant transformation of Jewish religious practice and belief; and part of the Orthodox world itself underwent an Americanization process. It is true, too, that by the end of the nineteenth century and throughout most of the twentieth, Jewish religion, or Judaism, gave way in significant part to "Jewishness," which took a variety of forms. Many of these expressions of Jewishness, however, including Zionism (support for a Jewish homeland in Palestine), philanthropy, political liberalism, and even the fight against anti-Semitism, although described as secular, contained important elements of ritual and a sense, if not of the sacred, at least of religious sensibility and moral content. In this way tradition was transformed and thereby at least partially salvaged rather than wholly destroyed.

Jews in the United States became manifestly American in a period of nearly two hundred years. Yet they also distinguished themselves significantly from the American norm. As the demographer Barry Kosmin observed, "The Jews are . . . too well-educated, too liberal, too secular, too metropolitan, too wealthy, too egalitarian, too civic-minded to be normal Americans when compared to the overall U.S. population."

The liberal, egalitarian, civic-minded Jewish American community faces future challenges from within and without. But at least into the 1990s that community, the vast majority of which is fully integrated into American national life, continues to help satisfy the need for greater authenticity and more intimate social affiliation, and it continues to help meet the need for continuity and meaning.

I owe thanks to the many historians of the American Jewish experience whose names and works appear in the bibliographical essay. Librarians and archivists in the following institutions were very helpful and professional, and their cooperation was indispensable: State University of New York, New Paltz; YIVO; Hebrew Union College–Jewish Institute of Religion in New York and Cincinnati; William Weiner Oral History Collection at the American Jewish Committee; Columbia University Oral History Collection; Tamiment Library at New York University; New York Public Library Jewish Division; Brooklyn Public Library Manuscript Division, Grand Army Plaza; and the American Jewish Historical Society, on the campus of Brandeis University.

Several of my colleagues in history, urban and immigration studies, women's studies, and Jewish studies read and commented upon one or more chapters. Special thanks are due to Richard Varbero, David Krikun, Carole Levin, and William Strongin. Copy editor Irma Garlick was extraordinarily thorough in all respects and made a number of very good suggestions. Stanley Kutler and Henry Y. K. Tom of the Johns Hopkins University Press also made valuable suggestions. Once again I am especially grateful to my wife, Myra, for her perceptive reading and probing questions, and most for her love and patient support.

I

Perspectives
and Prospects

The Jewish experience in modern America, which contains the largest Jewish community in the world after 1945, has been remarkably positive and, overall, enriching for Jews and non-Jews alike. Indeed, in terms of mobility and achievement, the experience has been stunning. Jewish Americans—less than 2.5 percent of the general population in the 1990s— are, for example, overrepresented relative to other ethnic groups and native-born Americans in all of the following categories: college graduates, doctors, lawyers, university professors, publishers, editors, television producers, advertising executives, investment bankers, computer scientists, Nobel Prize winners, and millionaires. Moreover, despite the continuing belief on the part of many Jews that anti-Semitism is a serious problem in America, there has been since World War II a sharp decline in negative feelings about and discrimination against Jews. In fact, by the 1970s overt anti-Semitism was simply no longer significant in the United States, and the few vocal Jew-haters were to be found only on the lunatic fringe.

Throughout American history, even in the colonial and revolutionary periods, when they were virtually excluded from politics, Jews, unlike Blacks and Indians and later Asians and Latinos, have found America generally hospitable. Yet, in this relatively receptive country, which essentially replaced Israel as the new promised land, there were from the beginning vexing questions—questions about the costs of freedom and mobility, especially in regard to the erosion of Jewish tradition and distinctiveness.

As early as the revolutionary era, when the Jewish population numbered fewer than fifteen hundred primarily Spanish- and Portuguese-speaking Sephardic Jews with roots in the Iberian Peninsula, a German mercenary in New York City found that it was difficult to distinguish Jews from the surrounding Christian majority. According to this reflective soldier, Jews "enjoy all the rights of citizenship" and "are not like the ones we have in Europe and Germany, who are recognizable by their beards and their clothes, for these are dressed like other citizens, get shaved regularly, and also eat pork. . . . The women also go about with curled hair and in French finery such as is worn by the ladies of other religions."

Later, in the 1850s, after several decades of Central European Jewish immigration to the United States, a number of Jewish leaders, including Rabbi Isaac M. Wise of Cincinnati, were known to ask "whether the Jewish people," now some 150,000 strong and generally prospering, "could survive the emancipation and openness of American civilization." And in 1907, in the midst of a massive immigration of relatively traditional Eastern European Jews (which would help push the American Jewish population from 1.8 million to nearly 3.4 million by 1920), Israel Friedlander, a Zionist and a biblical scholar at the Jewish Theological Seminary in New York City, warned that "the more emancipated, the more prosperous, the more successful the Jew becomes, the more impoverished, the more defenseless, and the more threatened becomes Judaism." Almost fifty years later, Hayim Greenberg, a leading Jewish journalist and lecturer, continued to predict, in the Labor Zionist monthly *Jewish Frontier,* that the majority of the nearly 5.3 million Jews in America were "in grave danger of becoming merely an ethnic group in the conventional sense of the term . . . no more the Congregation of Israel, but only a group with a long and heroic history, with [proud] memories . . . but without the consciousness of the specific drama and tension in its life."

Despite these observations and dire prophecies, the Jews who emigrated from Central and Eastern Europe between 1820 and 1920 and settled mainly in the urban centers of the United States grew in number and did maintain a strong sense of Jewish identity. And even the children of these immigrants, their departure from strict religious observance and their acculturation to American ways notwithstanding, remained manifestly Jewish. This was true, too, for the refugees from various parts of Nazi-occupied Europe—German middle-class professionals and the ultra-Orthodox Jews —who came to the United States in the 1930s and 1940s. The refugees added a heterogeneous new dimension to an already diverse American Jewish population, which included descendants of the earlier German and Eastern European immigrations (Ashkenazim), as well as smaller numbers of Sephardim. Although the variety of cultural and social backgrounds strained the ties of community, the countervailing force of a venerable and sacred heritage provided an important sense of shared Jewish identity.

American Jewish life in every era, including the colonial period, when Jewish communities waxed, waned, and sometimes withered, was characterized and shaped by economic and physical mobility and by the rhythms of the great American balancing act—the need for integration or acculturation, on the one side, and the need to retain something of a Jewish world, on the other. With the notable exception of the small minority of ultra-Orthodox Jewish refugees bent on transplanting closed sectarian communities to the United States in the mid-twentieth century, this dynamic process of synthesizing values and behaviors from the world of tradition with those of modern American civilization was a central and defining experience for Jews, whatever their regional origins and whenever and wherever they settled in the United States.

Although never faced with the virulent and sometimes murderous racism elicited by the presence of Blacks, Indians, and Asians or the violent anti-Catholicism directed at Italian and Irish immigrants, Jews were kept from being fully absorbed into the surrounding society by powerful forces, including gentile hostility. Moreover, second-generation Jews in America were still emotionally attached to their parents, whose traditions and world continued to provide meaning and community. The American Jewish community, however, was the first diaspora Jewish community to experience choices that went beyond isolation or assimilation. The openness and freedom of the American environment meant that Jews would discover a variety of ways of becoming fully American while remaining distinguishably Jewish. Inspired by the American ideals of democracy, pluralism, and equality of opportunity, Jews became Americans relatively rapidly, but by transforming parts of their tradition, they reshaped, and thereby enabled themselves to retain much of, their cultural distinctiveness.

Although Central European or "German" Jews in the nineteenth century substituted English for Hebrew in their American prayer books and services and eliminated particular rituals, among other changes, this did not mean they assimilated or that they rejected Jewishness as a group identity. On the contrary, their emphasis on the social justice dimensions of prophetic Judaism, their extraordinary philanthropic activity, and their consistent concern for the welfare of Jews overseas strongly suggest that many of these nineteenth-century Jewish Americans continued to perceive themselves as an organic part of the Jewish people. Eastern European Jews in the twentieth century also retained their identity with Jewish civilization, and as a religious community they, like their German cousins before them, attempted to fashion a group identity that would be distinctively Jewish at the same time that it enhanced their integration into American life. They established synagogues and other distinctively Jewish religious institutions including *mikvot* (ritual baths), Hebrew schools, and rabbinical councils. And some of them invented an *American* Orthodoxy, with more orderly religious services, more English, fewer beards and sidecurls, and fewer old-country-style clothes. Still others moved toward a religious transformation, a "scientific" Judaism, with an "evolving theology" constructed in part to attract the American-born or American socialized children of the immigrants. And all segments of the Eastern European Jewish community created educational, self-help, philanthropic, and group defense agencies meant to reinforce Jewish identity and solidarity and to protect and advance Jewish interests in the competitive American system. In short, Jewish immigrants, at least since 1820, integrated themselves into American society, but they sustained Jewish community, and they did not "melt."

By the end of the nineteenth century and throughout most of the twentieth, the nucleus of Jewish communal consciousness was not so much Jewish religion or Judaism, which no longer commanded a widespread intensity of commitment, but Jewishness, which manifested itself in many forms. Several of these, including Zionism (support for a Jewish homeland in Palestine), philanthropy, and political liberalism, although described as secular, contained important elements of ritual and a sense of the sacred, or at least of religious sensibility and moral content. As the persuasive Jewish historian Yosef Yerushalmi has said, "the blandly generic term secular Jew gives no indication of the richly nuanced variety within the species."

Yet there are many in the late twentieth century who are pessimistic about a Jewish American future. Citing declining affiliation, low levels of participation in Jewish education, and increasingly high intermarriage rates, the assimilationists or survivalists, as they are sometimes called, contend that Jewish life in America cannot survive without the nourishment of classical Judaism, that the substance and form of American Jewish identity has been too severed from Jewish tradition to be sustained—and even if sustained, to be authentically Jewish.

Transformationists, on the other side, argue that Judaism continues to be reconfigured rather than attenuated. They optimistically emphasize the social cohesion of Jews and point to imaginative reformulations of Jewish observance, as in modernized Passover seders and Hanukkah celebrations.

They are impressed as well with Jewish reengagement with *halakha* (law—literally, "the way"). In Reform Judaism, for example, there has been a radical departure from viewing ritual *mitzvot* or commandments (as opposed to ethical commandments) as optional or even superfluous, to an emphasis on ritual as a vehicle for confronting God and Jewish history, a way to shape and energize one's ethical impulses. Furthermore, they predict that a redefined, enriched relationship between Jewish Americans and Israelis, as well as the revitalization of Judaism brought by the increasing participation of women liberated from doctrinal restraints, will promote continuity. Transformationists also contend that a pervasive, ritualized, and even sanctified philanthropy and a persistent liberalism will mean the survival of a religiously authenticated Jewish ethnic identity in pluralistic America.

Despite the predictions of social scientists in the first half of the twentieth century, ethnic identity hangs on, if it does not quite thrive, in modern America. The prevailing interpretation in American historiography and in American nationalist ideology had emphasized, until recently, relatively rapid mobility and inevitable assimilation. Various theories, including those about Anglo-conformity and the melting pot, predicted that the cultures of the immigrants and their children would yield increasingly to "class concerns" and within a generation or two to a "homogenized human brew." The experience of Americans since the 1950s, however, and the watershed work of sociologist Milton Gordon and the work of social historian Rudolph J. Vecoli, among others, have made us recognize and re-examine the persistence of ethnicity in modern American society. Now many scholars, including John Bodnar, Kathleen Niels Conzen, and Deborah Dash Moore, increasingly emphasize the conscious resistance of immigrants to wholesale Americanization and highlight their vigorous attempts to maintain a variety of cultural traditions.

Even for descendants of early-twentieth-century immigrants, including Jews, Greeks, Poles, and Italians, Old World ways persisted, and the children and grandchildren of immigrants manifested a powerful attachment to selected ethnic traditions. Among second- and third-generation Italians, for example, 80 percent of the men and almost all of the women married Italian Americans, and into the 1990s, Italian remained one of the most widely spoken second languages in the United States. Eastern European Catholics—Slovenes, Czechs, and Lithuanians, for example—in order to maintain kinship ties and religious loyalty sacrificed social and geographic mobility to stay together. Second- and third-generation Jews took advantage of opportunities for geographic mobility as their class status changed, but they also continued,

in a process of "concentrated dispersion," to cluster in their new areas of settlement. In the 1950s, when some Italians joined the exodus to the suburbs
in the northeastern and middle Atlantic states, they moved with the extended
family in the spirit of *campanilismo* (primary loyalty to the group within the
sound of the village church bell), and Little Italy communities flowered in
places such as Long Island, New York, and Silver Spring, Maryland. Similarly,
60 percent of all Germans continue to live in the German triangle, between
St. Louis, Cincinnati, and Milwaukee, and the German belt of the North and
Midwest; and almost 75 percent of the Irish live in northern cities.

Most of the immigrants, at least initially, were members of the working class, but they and their children remained tied to a variety of ethnic symbols, institutions, and values that tended to dilute strictly class concerns.
Jewish immigrants were very much part of this process of interaction between class and culture. Jews brought with them from the old countries a
complex economic history and some commercial and industrial experience,
which temporarily defined their class status; but they also brought a deeply
embedded religious culture, a longstanding commitment to community, and
a centuries-old tradition of mutual aid.

The culture persisted, but that persistence was neither total nor linear.
In the first place, Jewish culture was not monolithic. All immigrant groups,
including the Jews, were divided by varying combinations of geographical
origin, class, dialect, politics, and degree of adherence to traditional religion.
Moreover, interactions with changing conditions in the Old World, and particularly in the new one, produced distinct adjustments that redefined the
ethnic and religious dimensions of Jewish culture. The adjustments, or negotiations with the culture of the host society, produced reformulated ethical
injunctions, remodeled self-help institutions, and a progressive politics. In an
ever changing American context, the children and grandchildren of Jewish
immigrants, tied to capitalism and urbanization but simultaneously tied to
their Jewish traditions, households, and community, constructed over time
an American Jewish ethnic identity.

In the late twentieth century, widespread intermarriage among whites,
including Jews, signified and promoted the erosion and for some persons,
perhaps, the virtual elimination of any meaningful sense of ethnicity. But
"national identities" or at least awarenesses persisted. And for many Jews,
perhaps even for a sizeable majority, ethnic identity—or cultural identity,
which some preferred to call it—continued to be important. The enduring
appeal of ethnic identity to many "national groups," including the Jews, was

partly instrumental; it could serve as a vehicle for political mobilization in the struggle over the distribution of wealth, power, and status, and in the defense of the group and its cultural values. The appeal of ethnic identity was also partly primordial, as a vehicle for adaptation and reinforcement of communal solidarities and historical memories for their own sake. It was also likely that the tenacious vitality of Orthodox Judaism and the durability of the religious dimensions of Jewish philanthropy, liberal political activism, and concern for fellow Jews abroad were indications that Jewish Americans were getting, in both their transformed and their traditional Judaism, "goods" they could not secure elsewhere in the modern consumer society: chiefly community and meaning.

Ethnic attachment, including Jewish attachment to a particular, religiously authenticated ethnic identity, was also promoted and reinforced by the increasing heterogeneity of the American population and the increasing acceptance of the idea of pluralism. As early as 1945 the United States had become the most heterogeneous society in the world. Of some 150 million inhabitants, perhaps 110 million (nearly 75%)—including 20 million Germans, 16 million Blacks, 13 million Irish, 6 million Italians, 6 million Jews, 3 million Mexican Americans in the rural Southwest and in urban barrios, a half-million Native Americans living on reservations, and a half-million Asians in New York City, on the West Coast, and in Hawaii—consciously identified with an ethnic community, either as racial minorities or foreign-born immigrants and their descendants. Moreover, none of the so-called non-white peoples saw themselves as single races or ethnic groups; instead, by the 1990s Americans were claiming membership in nearly three hundred ethnic and racial classifications and six hundred Native American tribes. Hispanics had seventy categories of their own.

Such diversity posed a challenge to the ideal of a common civic culture. But the concept of American pluralism, which was partly shaped by such Jewish thinkers as Horace Kallen and Louis Brandeis, had always implied a powerful obligation on the part of groups to reject too exclusive a particularism, to reject ethnic rigidity, and to participate fully in society so that society might benefit from their diverse contributions. And as Blacks, Asians, and Latinos made America more culturally and racially pluralistic, the potential for the acculturation of these groups, even as they remained relatively distinct, increased over time because the similarities between the host society and the diverse newcomers also increased. The relevant metaphor was no longer Anglo-conformity or the melting pot. These were neither desir-

able nor possible outcomes for the extraordinarily rich immigrant and ethnic experience of the United States. Instead, America could be seen as a
"stew pot," in which ideally all the ingredients, simmering in the same stock,
retained something of their distinctive textures and tastes even as they contributed to one another's flavor and to the overall savor of the stew.

Beginning in the 1960s and on into the 1990s, the growing self-awareness
and assertiveness of ethnic groups, including the new immigrants from Asia
and Africa and the Latinos of the Western Hemisphere, ultimately helped
reinforce the idea of an American stew pot, a vision of a society in which universalism and a moderated particularism could be more and more compatible and beneficial. It is true that many ethnic advocates, especially during the
Vietnam War and the Black Power movement, promoted a view of America
as incorrigibly racist and encouraged group rights over individual rights, as
well as an anti-integrationist ideology. But many members of ethnic groups
came to see, especially in the face of interethnic competition and violence,
that their own chauvinism and racial separatism were just as reactionary and
counterproductive as the "100 percent Americanism," or Anglo-conformity,
which denied them inclusion and privileges. They discovered, as had the
immigrants and the descendants of immigrants before them, that to begin to
tap the full range of opportunities in American society, they had to focus less
on ethnic differences and loyalties and more on commonalities, or at least
compatibilities, with other ethnic groups and the larger society generally.

By the mid-1990s increasing numbers of ethnic leaders and their constituencies, including many Blacks, Mexican Americans, Puerto Ricans, and
Asian Americans, while bearing their national heritages proudly, nonetheless
reflected a broad consensus of opinion in harmony with American values and
ideals and participated in political action to fulfill and extend, rather than reject, the American promise.

In their struggle for inclusion and equality, racial and religious minority groups (especially African Americans and Jewish Americans who had been
at it with varying degrees of success since the nineteenth century) helped to
preserve and advance the very privileges that were denied to them, including access to housing, jobs, and voting rights, and they thereby helped further democratize the nation for the benefit of all Americans. Even some of
the racial minority leaders who emphasized particularist protection, for
"fixed" group interests, separate from "white interests," in the form of employment and college admissions quotas, for example, also enunciated a more
universal rationale for empowering minority groups: they would serve as a
check on the political system, ensuring, it was hoped, that prejudice and dis-

crimination as general social ills would be counteracted for the sake of the larger good.

It is clear that for a democracy to endure, the people of a society made up of many cultures must be willing, indeed must desire, to participate in a common civic culture, even as they extend and reshape that culture by infusing it with adaptations of their own traditions and values. And for multiculturalism to endure, it is necessary to sustain democracy. Pluralism in the United States can flourish only with a common commitment to core political and moral values, including the recognition that all citizens, apart from whatever group loyalties they claim, are entitled as individuals to liberty, equal opportunity, and equality under the law.

These political ideals at the center of our democratic civic culture are indeed ideals and not quite yet a description of social reality. As David Hollinger, an intellectual historian, has said: "A truly postethnic America would be one in which the ethno-racial component in identity would loom less large than it now does and in which affiliation by shared descent would be more voluntary than prescribed. . . . The United States is a long way from achieving this ideal." American history is unfortunately filled with distressing and sometimes shocking examples of oppression of minorities and painful and sometimes bloody episodes in the long struggle to make social practice conform to our own widely announced noble goals. Indeed, in the matter of racial equality, and particularly in regard to African Americans, the wounds—disproportionate infant mortality, poverty, and violent crime, for example—remain open and bleeding. But the democratic ideals still provide the path to social and economic justice and to the unity within which a mutually enriching diversity can flourish.

In *The American Dilemma*, his classic study of race relations, Gunnar Myrdal emphasized the blatant hypocrisy of a democracy that would not extend equal rights to Jews, Blacks, and other "outsiders." At the same time, however, the Swedish sociologist recognized that the disadvantaged minorities "could not possibly have invented a system of political ideals which better corresponded to their interest" than the American system. Many individuals in many groups, including Cubans, Japanese, and African Americans, understood this. Jews, to whom we pay the most attention in this history, also understood this. From the beginning, despite initial rebuff, Jews were anxious to participate in American society, and they were ready, even delighted, to accept America's ideals, norms, and obligations (many of which paralleled Jewish values and aspirations) while at the same time they wished to keep, and succeeded in keeping, important albeit reshaped elements of their Jewish culture. In this way Jews and American society changed and enriched each other, and in this way, too, Jews and many other groups contributed, and continue to contribute, to a process of fusion in which some dimensions of ethnic culture and identity were incorporated into changing definitions of what was American and what it meant to be American.

2

The Threshold
of Liberation,
1654–1820

In 1654 a group of twenty-three Jewish refugees fled
Brazil, which had been reconquered from the tolerant Dutch by the Inquisitional Portuguese. When they arrived in Dutch New Amsterdam, the Jews
received a chilly reception from Governor Peter Stuyvesant. Indeed, he and
at least one other Calvinist colleague went so far as to ask their employers,
the West India Company of Amsterdam, to prohibit "the Jewish nation" from
settling in the community. After all, it was argued, "as we have . . . Papists,
Mennonites, and Lutherans . . . Puritans . . . and many Atheists and various
other servants of Baal, . . . it would create still greater confusion if the obstinate and immovable Jews came to settle here." The company, however, some
of whose stockholders were Jewish, did not agree to exclude Jews from New
Netherlands, and it was not long before the Jewish refugees and those who
came after them recognized that Stuyvesant's negative attitude, though hardly
unique, was not to remain the norm in the New World.

Despite some constraints on their residential and economic mobility
and despite sporadic public denunciations, the Jewish settlers, now numbering about fifty, gradually began circumventing the restrictions. Increasing
acceptance, beginning as early as 1656, resulted from the recognition that
Jews were white people, after all, and subjects of the Dutch crown in a vulnerable outpost affected by Indian raids, economic shortages, and British
competition. And after the British conquest of New Netherlands in 1667, the
rights of Jews were extended. As the most aggressive empire builders in the

late seventeenth century, the British were prepared to tolerate and even encourage increases in Jewish manpower and capital for their overseas possessions. In disembarking in North America, the Jews had crossed an important threshold. The relative tolerance and sense of liberation they would experience in the New World from the late seventeenth century onward was all the more remarkable in contrast to the generally oppressive history of Jews in Europe.

Although there had been some periods of mutually beneficial interchange between Jews and non-Jews, especially in Spain from the tenth to the fourteenth centuries (the Jewish golden age), isolation, most often externally imposed, was the more frequent and pervasive Jewish experience. Governmental repression of Jews reached its height in the walled ghettos and expulsions of the late Middle Ages. Jews in France and Germany, and later in Eastern Europe, were forced to live in segregated communities, which became centers of demanding but intellectually and spiritually vital rabbinic Judaism. These were communities of faith, built upon a religious culture rooted in Hebrew Scriptures, ritual, Talmudic law (*halakha*), and age-old customs. The *kehillah,* or governing body of the community, run by lay and rabbinical figures of influence, administered the law, collected taxes, and generally exercised authority over the everyday life of the Jews. In this way, and through the regulations of *halakha* and traditional ritual, Jewish communities developed the cohesion and discipline needed to face the hostility of the larger alien world that surrounded them.

Seen as a pariah people and stigmatized as "killers of Christ," Jews lived on the periphery of European Christian society, maintaining a precarious existence. Prohibited from landholding and circumscribed in their choice of occupation by craft guilds, Jews were channeled into enterprises generally considered insecure, demeaning, or sinful by Christians—commerce, money-lending, and tax collecting. Jewish concentration in these areas not only led to further stigmatization and even demonization but also exposed Jews to sporadic murderous attacks by poor peasants and to the violent anger of indebted aristocrats. For the great bulk of European Jewry, the late Middle Ages were a time of persecution and massacre. And in thirteenth-century England, fourteenth-century France, and fifteenth-century Spain and Portugal, the Jews faced exile, forced conversion, or death.

The expulsions from Inquisitional Spain and Portugal in the fifteenth and sixteenth centuries created an Iberian Jewish diaspora that included the Sephardic Jews, who settled in the Netherlands, England, and the West Indies and on the South and North American continents during the colonial period.

In New Netherlands (later New York and New Jersey), Pennsylvania, and South Carolina, Jews almost immediately established religious congregations, cemeteries, ritual baths, schools, and a system of charities. In addition to administering religious services, the first congregations also supervised the supply and distribution of kosher meat and provided matzo (unleavened bread) for Passover. The port city congregational communities located in New York (1656), Newport, Rhode Island (1677), Savannah, Georgia (1733), Philadelphia (1745), and Charleston, South Carolina (1750) were dominated by the Sephardim, and all contained a component of compulsion. New York's Shearith Israel, for example, the city's only congregation until 1825, claimed for itself a universal authority like the European *kehillah*. Not joining could mean ostracism in life and even, with no Jewish burial rights, in death. However, the mobility and generally unrestricted rules of settlement in the New World made this claim dubious, and synagogue and community leadership, though autocratic in intent ended up permissive in practice. Every Jewish male was needed, often desperately, for a *minyan*—ten men, the minimum required for communal religious services. Not having this quorum meant no services; no services meant no Judaism; and no Judaism meant, in colonial America, no survival of a Jewish community.

Congregations had to make concessions in order to hold members. As late as the 1750s, leaders of Shearith Israel threatened to expel from the synagogue, built in 1730, and even to bar from burial in the congregation's cemetery any who engaged in commerce on the Sabbath, ate forbidden meat, or otherwise violated religious laws. But inevitably and almost from the start, there were compromises on the dietary laws, circumcision, and Sabbath observance from New York to New Orleans. In Baltimore those who married outside the faith could remain in the congregation, but without a vote. In America's open port cities and on the nearby frontier, compromise was the only way to maintain a Jewish community in the eighteenth century. An American Judaism, distinguishable from traditional European Judaism, was beginning to emerge in several Jewish communities.

These Jewish communities were sustained and even extended beyond the immediate localities on the Atlantic coast. To construct their synagogues and other structures, for example, less prosperous Jewish communities had to rely on the resources of individuals and congregations in other cities, as well as on kindred Sephardic congregations in Europe and South America. Moreover, although the great majority of Jews were craftsmen and small shopkeepers, mercantile aspirations were powerful and pervasive. Jews had early won their way into the fur and retail trades, and eventually a significant minority traded widely, reinforcing the connections between scattered Jewish settlements of the colonial world and, indeed, the entire transatlantic world. In addition, the colonial merchant families, such as Lopez, Gomez, and Rivera, were related through marriage, with branches stretching from Rhode Island to Georgia. Aaron Lopez, Jacob Rivera, and a small number of other Jews were involved in a cluster of economic activities including whaling, shipbuilding, international commerce, and the slave trade.

Given the attention paid in the 1990s to the unfounded claim by some African American racial separatists that Jews dominated the slave trade, a word or two is in order here about the relationship of Jews to slavery in the New World. To be sure, the Brazilian sugar industry owed much to Marrano (secret Jews) and Dutch Sephardic initiative; in Surinam, Dutch Jews constituted something of a planter class. And small numbers of Marrano, Sephardic, and even Ashkenazic Jews owned slaves in Curaçao and Guiana, though proportionately fewer than their Protestant neighbors. But by 1700 the British supplanted all other nations including the Spanish as the primary importers of slaves; and in the British West Indies, Jews did not emerge as prominent slave traders or slaveholders. They managed retail shops and engaged in moneylending, and they were hardly on a level of affluence with the great planters.

In colonial America a very small number of Jewish families, along with their vastly more numerous gentile neighbors, in Newport, Rhode Island, New York City, Philadelphia, and Charleston, South Carolina, imported slaves as well as other "commodities." But everywhere in what was to become the United States, Jews played only a minor role in the slave trade. Most Jews, even in the international trading center of Newport, were shopkeepers and craftsmen, many specializing in candlemaking. Lopez and Rivera traded in slaves, but the great majority of slave traders in Newport were non-Jews. The most prominent were: Philip Wilkinson; Stephen d'Ayrault Jr.; Christopher, George, and Robert Champlin; the Wanton family; Esek Hopkins; and John, Joseph, and Nicholas Brown. The slave sales of all Jewish traders taken together did not equal that of the one gentile firm dominant in the business. Whatever small role the Jewish refugees from the Old World and Portuguese Brazil may have played in the expansion of the trade in sugar and slaves northwestward, it is clear, as David Brion Davis and most other reputable scholars have shown, that "Jews had no major or continuing impact on the history of New World slavery."

Ashkenazic Jews, too, were very much part of the colonial Jewish economy and community. Jews from Poland and Germany had organized a congregation in Amsterdam by 1635, and from there several had joined the Iberian Jews in the move to North America via Brazil. As early as 1654, then, representatives of the two great subdivisions of the Jewish people were brought together on Manhattan Island. More Ashkenazic Jews from widely dispersed points in Central and Eastern Europe followed in the eighteenth century, and they generally joined the larger Sephardic communities already established.

There were tensions between Sephardic and Ashkenazic Jews. Their rituals, liturgies, and Hebrew pronunciations differed, as did their vernaculars, Ladino and Yiddish. The Sephardim also had some pretensions to cultural superiority, and the Ashkenazim were wont occasionally to accuse their Iberian cousins of religious laxity. But differences in rites and customs and mutual prejudices did not divide North American Jewry during the colonial and early national periods. After all, unlike Catholics and various Protestant sects whose falling out over basic religious tenets ravaged Europe, the Sephardim and Ashkenazim shared a religious heritage that coincided in virtually all the essentials.

This shared heritage promoted an actual fusion of the Ashkenazim and Sephardim within the Jewish congregational communities. Despite the dominance of the Sephardim and their rites, Ashkenazim were among the leaders and main financial supporters of the colonial congregations. In fact, Jacob Franks (1688–1769), an Ashkenazi and probably colonial New York's most successful Jewish merchant, presided over the New York Jewish community in 1729 on the eve of the building of the first synagogue in the city, popularly known as the Spanish and Portuguese Synagogue of New York. Marriage between the two groups occurred with increasing frequency, especially after the Sephardim, with the end of the Inquisition in 1720, virtually stopped immigrating to America. Business ties also brought the Ashkenazim and Sephardim together, and the acculturation of both groups in the same American social environment reinforced the alliance.

Acculturation was very much the order of the day by the mid-eighteenth century, and it was reflected in imitation as well as synthesis. In New York City in the 1760s, for example, Gershon Mendes Seixas (1746–1816), the *hazzan* or reader for Congregation Shearith Israel, imitated the Protestant practice of preaching sermons, and he even used Christian theological terms, including *original sin, grace,* and *regeneration.* In the same era, when the New York Jewish community needed new schoolmasters, it sought men who synthesized Old World and New World skills, men who had facility with the Hebrew language but who could also teach English, reading, writing, and "cyphering." Abigail Franks also tried to be both American and Jewish. Despite the evident relish with which she mingled freely in Christian society, participated in New York's culture, and read contemporary literature, her commitment to her distinctive identity as a Jew remained primary. She persisted in being observant along with her husband Jacob.

Synthesis was also apparent in synagogue building. In Rhode Island, the Newport Jewish community in 1759 built its Touro Synagogue in the latest Colonial American style, with an exterior very different from the synagogue exteriors of Europe. But its interior, based on that of the Sephardic congregation of London, was traditional. In South Carolina, Charleston's synagogue also symbolized the amalgam of Jewish tradition and modern Western style. Built in 1794, it looked very much like an English village church and was topped by a spire, but the interior was very familiar to Jews from the Old World. Eighteenth-century synagogue architecture apparently could be taken as a metaphor for colonial Jewry's adherence to the integrative concept and practice of "Jewish on the inside, American on the outside."

This does not mean that colonial and post–Revolutionary era Jews kept their Jewishness entirely invisible in public life. On 4 July 1788, the *hazzan* of the Jewish congregation in Philadelphia, for example, joined in the celebration of Pennsylvania's ratification of the constitution. And Benjamin Rush was delighted by the sight of "the Rabbi [sic] of the Jews locked in arms of two ministers of the gospel." In 1798, during a commercial voyage from New York to Madras, Isaac Levy celebrated the Fourth of July in the company of another American Jew, "as was becoming American citizens." But Levy and companion, as he indicated in his correspondence, did not shrink during the same voyage from celebrating Passover openly "with strictness, as much so as was possible on board a ship." He added, "God send we may spend the next one in New York." We cannot be certain that Levy was playing with the traditional closing of the Passover seder, "Next year in Jerusalem," but surely he was reflecting, consciously or otherwise, his pleasure in discovering Zion in America.

Even before the American Revolution and the Declaration of Independence, which pointedly articulated and reinforced the ideal of equality, the Jews of colonial America enjoyed a tolerance and inclusiveness with regard to residence, trade, and religious practice unknown to other Jewish communities. Unquestionably, by 1776 the two thousand Jews in colonial America were the freest in the world. But with the exception of New York, which granted individual Jews citizenship and allowed them to vote and hold minor appointive offices, that freedom and tolerance, in the eighteenth century did not generally extend to political life. Although Parliament declared as early as 1740 that Jewish aliens in the colonies had the right to be naturalized after seven years of residence and were exempted from taking oaths "upon the true faith of a Christian," Englishmen restricted the franchise and public office to males, property owners, and Protestants.

The American Revolution was a turning point for Jews, as it was for other groups in the society, including Blacks. In the face of the persistent enunciation and deeper internalization of the principles of freedom in the Revolutionary era, every northern state, between 1776 and 1804, had put the institution of slavery on the road to gradual abolition. And between 1780 and 1820, Jews gradually won the right to vote and hold office almost everywhere. Some Black slaves in the North were freed in recognition of their service in the patriot cause. Jews, too, had served with distinction, and their suppliers, merchants, and financiers had had significant contact with government officials throughout the war. In each case the demonstrated loyalty of the group in combination with the growing pervasiveness of egalitarianism loosened shackles. As late as 1840 there were still five states, four in the Northeast, which had not yet accorded Jews full political equality. But the religious equality inherent in the Northwest Ordinance of 1787 and the principles of the Revolution embodied in the Federal Constitution of 1789 prohibited Congress from interfering with the free exercise of religion and from making laws respecting the establishment of religion. These principles also prohibited religious tests as a qualification for holding national office, and ultimately they made Americans the people who, in the words of the historian Jacob Rader Marcus, "dared for the first time in Christian history to give Jews equal privileges and immunities."

The changing condition of Jews in eighteenth-century America is evidenced by two very different actions. First, although Jews had won significant personal freedom by 1759, those in Newport still believed it was necessary to design Touro Synagogue in that year with a trap door that led to an escape tunnel. Second, George Washington's letter to the same congregation in 1790 assured it that the "government of the United States . . . gives to bigotry no sanction, to persecution no assistance." The Jews were promised religious freedom and citizenship for the first time anywhere by a head of state.

Jews had dared in the context of the Revolution to make the case for civic equality, and as part of the larger story of American egalitarianism, they proved that the outsider could achieve a substantial degree of justice. Although stereotypical anti-Jewish remarks occasionally appeared in the press or were heard from the lectern and a residue of actual rejection and discrimination persisted, gentile hostility by the late eighteenth century did not

constitute grave social mistreatment of Jews in America. There were no man-
dated ghettos, no anti-Jewish guilds, and instances of physical molestation
were rare. There was also nothing quite analogous to the situation in the 1770s
which saw Baptists in Virginia jailed for their religious convictions. And no
laws were ever enacted in British North America explicitly to disable Jews,
unlike Catholics. Constitutional guarantees and ideological promises, the separation of church and state, and the presence of other targets of antipathy—
for example, Blacks, Indians, Catholics—meant that Jews, ultimately, were
more easily accepted by their new compatriots.

The relatively high incidence of intermarriage in the eighteenth and
early nineteenth centuries is partial testimony to Jewish acceptability. Esti-
mates of Jewish intermarriage range from more than 20 percent for America generally, to 50 percent for wide-open boom towns such as New Orleans.
The daughter of the wealthy and observant Abigail and Jacob Franks married
Oliver DeLancey and into one of New York's leading Christian families. Their
son did the same with a Philadelphia Evans. Jewish community and synagogue leaders were convinced that intermarriage threatened the very existence of the American Jewish world. Their worry was not without a rational
foundation, for when Jews married gentiles, very few lived as Jews. The overwhelming majority—indeed, nearly 90 percent of those who married outside the faith—appear to have assimilated entirely within the Christian population.

Intermarriage, however, did not destroy the Jewish community; it
merely "diluted" it. Most Jews continued to marry other Jews. And if those
Jews refused to be strictly observant, they were just as stubborn in refusing
to convert to Christianity. Part of the "acceptability" of Jews lay in the Christian hope for their conversion, which was seen as a giant step toward the millennium. Ezra Stiles, a minister, astronomer, and bibliophile, wrote in his
diary of his Jewish friend Aaron Lopez, the great Newport merchant, "How
often I wished that sincere, pious, candid mind could have perceived the evi-
dences of Christianity, perceived the truth as it is in Jesus Christ, known that
Jesus was the Messiah predicted by Moses and the prophets!" Stiles hoped
that decent people of all religions "notwithstanding their delusions may be
brought together in Paradise in the Christian system." Jews continued to dis-
appoint this hope. Even as they became less tied to the commandments of
Hebrew Scripture and to the synagogue, they firmly resisted the New Testa-
ment and the church. In this, too, they were not so different from their fellow Americans, fewer than 7 percent of whom were church affiliated by 1800.

It was increasingly clear by the early nineteenth century that one could be both American and Jewish. It was not, as Hector St. John De Crevecouer would have it, that "Here individuals of all nations are melted into a new race of men" but that the integration of the two identities was made easier by important confluences of Jewish and American values and institutions. For example, the relatively liberal values of the new democratic republic, themselves partly founded on scriptural precepts, meshed well with the Hebraic tradition of the covenant and its emphasis on the pursuit of justice. Also, the American idea of progress was compatible with the Jewish injunction to repair and perfect the world in an ongoing partnership with God. And in addition, the rational, secular American pursuit of individual happiness within an orderly community was in consonance with modern Jewish aspiration for personal achievement and communal fulfillment in "this" world.

The high degree of integration reinforced a vexing question, one that became a perennial concern: would Jews be able to survive as a distinct group in America? Intermarriage levels were high, synagogue attendance low. The Newport congregation had virtually dissolved by the end of the eighteenth century, and by 1822 there were no Jews left in the city. Only one new synagogue had been built in the United States—in Richmond, Virginia—in the fifty years since the Revolution. And when the leader of New York's Shearith Israel synagogue died in 1816 after forty-eight years of service, he was replaced by a merchant who filled in part-time. Yet, despite some periods of shrinkage in numbers and some decline in commitment, the push toward assimilation was persistently counteracted by the many substantial advantages of Jewish community and its meaningful belief system, as well as the "comforting psychological haven" of Jewish identification. And in the first decades of the nineteenth century, though Jewish Americans felt some tension between ethnic group loyalty and the preservation of distinctiveness, on the one hand, and identification with American society and assimilation, on the other, they appear to have been relatively confident about the future.

In the post–Revolutionary period, there was among the Jewish merchants, as among merchants generally, a drift away from Atlantic commerce. The war had disrupted trade networks. So did the conflict between Britain and France on the high seas and our own undeclared naval war with France from 1798 to 1800. But Jews continued to be moderately prosperous in the more modest domestic commercial arena. Myer Moses, a state legislator from Charleston, citing the economic opportunity, freedom, civic equality, and respect his country accorded Jews and describing the United States as a promised land, said in 1806, somewhat presciently, "Collect together thy long scattered people of Israel, and let the gathering place be in *this land* of milk and honey." Though Moses could not have known it, the Jewish community of America, numbering some two thousand at the start of the nineteenth century (approximately 0.03% of the American population) would indeed, in the not so distant future, receive a new infusion of health from abroad. It would not be the last time that immigration would help revivify the growth and group distinctiveness of the American Jewish community.

3

The Age of Reform, 1820–1880

The status of Jews in Central and Western Europe was significantly altered in the late eighteenth and nineteenth centuries by the Enlightenment and the French Revolution. New modes of thought opened the way for the rise of secular, religiously "neutral" societies. Secularism did not mean the end of religion but rather, a decline in the power of religious ideas and institutions to control whole areas of modern life—political, economic, or personal.

In such an intellectual and social context, Jews of "rationalist" persuasion were more likely to find acceptability. Jewish emancipation, however, granted first by France in 1790, came slowly and in fits and starts to the rest of Western and Central Europe: Prussia in 1850, Britain in 1858, and Austria-Hungary in 1867. In all these places, including France, Jews were expected to dissolve their relatively autonomous communities and renounce the idea of Jewish peoplehood or nationality. The new nation-states viewed Jews as alien and backward and promoted an emancipation that they hoped would bring ultimate assimilation or total absorption of the Jews by native populations.

In Central Europe, especially in those independent political entities with German-speaking populations or linked to German culture, the "emancipation" took the form of repressive legislation limiting Jews to a narrow range of trades and occupations. At the same time, anti-Semitism, so often with emerging nationalism, was increasingly becoming a feature of everyday life. Jews from Bavaria, Baden, Wurtemberg, and Posen, that part of Poland under German influence, faced bleak prospects if they stayed in place. This became even more apparent as early industrialization hastened the disintegration of the peasant economies in which they had served as petty traders, middlemen, and cattle dealers.

Young, mostly single Jewish men began leaving Central Europe in 1820. The better-off and more modern Jews were more likely to move to cities nearby, but those who went to the United States were also ambitious and courageous entrepreneurs searching for better opportunity. Relatively quickly they expanded across the American continent, forming a configuration of distinctive Jewish communities that has essentially remained intact to the present.

Few groups chose a more fortunate moment to come to America than these Jews of Central Europe. The frontier was still open and moving, and the economy was expanding. At the same time, however, the transportation system of the country was relatively undeveloped. Despite the railroad speculation, turnpike construction, and rapid canal building in the 1840s and 1850s, huge areas in the interior of the country had few stores or links either to factories that produced goods or to port cities that received goods. The German Jews helped fill this merchandising vacuum, and in less than a generation they came to dominate the men's and women's clothing trades, in both manufacturing and retailing. Jewish entrepreneurs were attracted to the soft goods industry because it was a low-capitalization, labor-intensive enterprise. It also entailed significant risk, which the more established investors in mining and hard goods manufacturing preferred to avoid. In any case, names such as Hart, Schaffner and Marx, and Florsheim still serve as reminders of the early Jewish initiative in the world of wearing apparel.

Many German Jewish immigrants started as mere peddlers. We do not know precisely how many, but memoirs and historical studies suggest significant percentages. One analysis, for example, demonstrated that considerably more than half of the adult Jewish males in Easton, Pennsylvania, from 1845 to 1855 were peddlers. The pack carriers everywhere needed little initial inventory and paid no rent for storage. Often they initiated their businesses on borrowed funds, "risk capital" acquired from family, fraternal orders, and other social institutions including religious congregations. The early development of an intragroup credit system was a major ingredient in the extraordinary business success of the German Jews. In response to the growing system of distribution, a mutually beneficial network developed, strongly marked by family ties. It connected peddler, creditor-supplier, retailer, wholesaler, clerk, bookkeeper, skilled worker, clothing manufacturer, and importer.

The expansion of this system, particularly from east to west, shaped the grid of Jewish settlement, and the primary routes to the interior became dotted with sites of new Jewish communities. Inland cities such as Albany and Rochester, New York, and Cleveland, Milwaukee, and St. Louis witnessed the clustering of Jewish peddlers in the 1830s and 1840s. Some of these men, dreaming of one day becoming "businessmen," failed, their backs breaking under the weight of their 150-pound packs. But an important number graduated from carriers to "wagon barons" and finally to owners of retail stores or peddler supply depots. The occurrence was common enough that the legend of peddler–to–department store owner, reinforced by names such as Adam Gimbel (New York, Philadelphia, and Milwaukee), Benjamin Bloomingdale (New York), Edward Filene (Boston), A. L. Neiman and Herbert and Carrie Marcus (Dallas), Benjamin Altman (New York), Gerson Fox (Boston), Nathan and Oscar Lazar Straus (Macy's and Abraham and Straus), Julius Rosenwald (Sears, Roebuck), and many others, became a credible part of American Jewish history.

Between 1850 and 1880 the inland cities filled with significant enough numbers of Jews and Jewish institutions to stimulate the development of satellite communities. Cincinnati is a good example of this process. An inland port serving the Ohio River system and an area with a sizeable German population, Cincinnati attracted thousands of German Jewish immigrants. By the 1850s, Jewish peddlers in the city had moved up to the retail clothing trade and had turned Cincinnati into a center for the manufacture of garments. Growing factories, stores, depots, supply routes, and credit operations required additional family members and countrymen, many of whom settled in towns surrounding the greater Cincinnati area.

By 1855 there were five synagogues in Cincinnati and two prominent rabbis. Isaac Mayer Wise (1819–1900), the renowned founder of the Reform movement in America, and Max Lilienthal (1815–82), the first person with both a rabbinic and a university degree to settle in the United States, held pulpits in the city. Cincinnati soon became the religious center for the smaller Jewish communities in Indiana, Illinois, Tennessee, Kentucky, and Missouri.

Jewish settlers, connected in one way or another to the ever expanding merchandising network, also penetrated the South and Far West. By 1880, Mobile and Montgomery, Alabama, had Jewish populations of 530 and 600, respectively, while Jews in New Orleans in that year numbered 5,000. San Francisco, which experienced rapid growth following the California gold rush, had more than 16,000 Jews by 1880. Jewish peddlers trailed prospectors into mining towns, supplied clothes and tools, and eventually established stores. Small communities developed around these stores in Sacramento and

Stockton, as well as in mining areas in Arizona, Colorado, and Nevada. Typical is the story of Alexander Ritmaster, who arrived in Central City, Colorado, and proceeded to peddle notions and essential merchandise to miners' wives from a pack strapped to his back. Ritmaster's trips up and down the mountainsides of Black Hawk and Nevadaville brought him enough prosperity to open his own store and employ other young immigrants.

Throughout the country, Jewish immigrants found roles to play in retailing, ranching, real estate, agriculture, and other enterprises, through initiative and imaginative innovation and simply by responding to local or regional needs. In the West, Jewish entrepreneurs provided specialized clothing such as the famous riveted Levis denim trousers. They encouraged Black customership in the South, and everywhere Jews introduced smaller profits, lower prices, direct selling, bargain basements, and time purchasing.

In isolated areas of the country, some Jews even became local bankers. I. E. Solomon, for example, a retailer in Arizona Territory, started out by keeping his customers' valuables in his safe. Soon he was making "handshake" loans to his friends, and then he began dealing in drafts and checks. In 1899 he and a group of Arizona businessmen opened the Gila Valley Bank in a corner of the Solomon Commercial Company store. From this seed sprang the Valley National Bank of Arizona, and Solomonville was on the map.

Similar stories could be told for dozens of other towns, including Sutro, Nevada; Goldtree (named for Morris Goldbaum), California; Ehrenberg, Arizona; and Jewtown, Georgia. By 1880 across America there were nearly one thousand points of significant Jewish settlement in at least thirty-two of the thirty-eight states, four territories, and Washington, D.C., and Jewish newspapers reached readers in 1,250 different locations.

Successful Jewish businessmen accumulated wealth, and some were ready, as early as the 1850s, to enter the capital market. Mobility and capital accumulation, however, were not necessarily marks of successful integration into the general American business system. Despite the open economy, there was discrimination against Jews in a number of areas, particularly banking. Ironically, this barrier helped stimulate the establishment of separate Jewish banking houses in America. To some degree this was a product of an already established Jewish banking group in Europe, which sent its agents to the United States. But ultimately it was the ambitious risk taking and the religious, family, and social networks of the German Jewish settlers that supplied the bond of trust so necessary for the banking business, and that substituted for the lack of experience.

The Seligmans, beginning as peddlers in Pennsylvania, Alabama, and

Missouri, went on to become wholesale clothiers in New York and gold merchants in California. With capital accumulated in these states, they established the banking firm of J. and W. Seligman and Company, opening offices in leading cities in the United States and Europe. The company helped finance innumerable industrial enterprises, including railroads, public utilities, and the Panama Canal. The Goldmans, Kuhns, Loebs, and Lehmans also started with little help from old-country financiers, but once established in banking, they soon developed connections with the Europeans to facilitate overseas business.

From the combination of American economic needs and the industriousness, commercial experience, and cultural attributes of the Jewish peddler and shopkeeper came many business success stories, some modest, some sensational. Not all of these prosperous Jewish families—the department store owners, the manufacturers, the financiers—were desperately poor when they began; nor did their collective fortunes ultimately match the wealth and economic power of the gentile American oligarchy that controlled heavy industry and directed the flow of investment capital in the late nineteenth and early twentieth centuries. "Rags to riches," then, is perhaps too extreme a description of their histories. But there was impressive mobility. In numerous quantitative accounts by urban historians of Jews in nineteenth-century Atlanta, Boston, Columbus, Omaha, Poughkeepsie, Los Angeles, and San Francisco, similar conclusions were reached: Jews outpaced non-Jews in occupational and social mobility. In fact, the German Jews did well enough to allow the careful historian John Higham to conclude that, "proportionately speaking, in no other immigrant group have so many men ever risen so rapidly." It is important to point out here that affluent merchants were far outnumbered by less prosperous craftspeople and laborers and that even the more pervasive small shopkeeper economy was made possible in good part by "self-exploitation" and by the labor contributed by family members, especially wives and daughters.

Jewish women brought with them a tradition of employment in a family economy. In the old countries most wives and daughters of craftspeople and merchants had participated actively in production and sales. And in the United States the smaller the enterprise, the more likely it was for female family members to work. Indeed, such work often meant the difference between success and failure. Hannah Dernburg Horner, for example, labored in the family grocery store on Chicago's West Side. She not only supplemented the work of her husband, however. From the beginning, according to her son, Hannah was also "the guiding force in the business, the pusher." And the wife of butcher Bernard Nordlinger in Washington, D.C., "could cut up a forequarter of beef just as well as any man."

Non-Jews typically portrayed Jewish men as successful capitalists and their wives and daughters as pampered women who had never felt deprivation and the need to work hard. However, not only was the hard and skillful work of Jewish women crucial to small business viablity, there was also poverty at the very base of the Jewish social pyramid. Records indicate sporadic massive appeals, in community after community, for assistance to the Jewish poor and widows and for interest-free loans to impoverished peddlers. Although the centuries-old stereotype of the rich Jew failed to depict anything like reality, moderate prosperity was widespread in the Jewish community, and it had a relatively sizeable commercial elite.

The commercial elite was part of a growing Jewish community (50,000 in 1850; 150,000 in 1860; and 250,000 in 1880; see table 1); the vast majority of whom by 1880 lived in urban centers with populations of five thousand or more. At a time when such centers were home to only 25 percent of all Americans, 83 percent of the Jews in the United States lived there. Although innumerable individual Jews lived in relative isolation from their coreligionists as itinerant peddlers or merchants in hundreds of villages and towns with fewer than twenty Jewish inhabitants, American Jewry generally was already highly concentrated in a relatively limited number of communities, large and small.

German culture was an important unifying force for Jews in these communities. Jewish immigration from Germany was partly connected to the general German immigration of the period, and in the United States, German Jews and German Christians settled in some of the same places, such as Milwaukee, Cincinnati, and St. Louis. Many German Jews subscribed to the German-language press and were patrons of the German-language theater. In the relatively tolerant German American community, the Jews, religious differences notwithstanding, were also members of German clubs and participated in German benevolent and recreational institutions. Beginning in the 1850s, however, increasing numbers of German Jews more clearly identified as American and Jewish.

That Jews could be found on both sides of the conflict leading to the Civil War partly reflected their growing American identity. For example, there were few if any Jews in the American Antislavery Society or the antislavery Liberty Party, and one northern rabbi even gave something of a proslavery speech in New York City in 1860. But Rabbi David Einhorn of Baltimore was an abolitionist; several Jews served in the Pennsylvania Society for

Table 1.   JEWISH POPULATION IN THE UNITED STATES

	U.S. Population	Jews	% of U.S. Population	% of World Jewry
1790	3,930,000	1,350	0.03	
1800	5,310,000	1,600	0.03	0.06
1810	7,340,000	2,000	0.03	
1820	9,640,000	2,700	0.03	
1830	12,866,000	4,500	0.03	
1840	17,070,000	15,000	0.09	
1850	23,192,000	50,000	0.22	1.05
1860	31,443,000	150,000	0.48	
1870	38,558,000	200,000	0.52	
1880	50,156,000	250,000	0.50	3.27
1890	62,947,715	450,000	0.71	
1900	75,994,575	1,050,000	1.38	9.91
1910	91,972,265	2,043,000	2.22	15.91
1920	105,710,630	3,600,000	3.41	22.86
1930	122,775,046	4,400,000	3.58	29.23
1940	131,670,000	4,700,000	3.65	30.46
1950	150,698,000	5,000,000	3.32	43.48
1960	179,323,000	5,400,000	3.00	42.97
1970	203,253,000	5,691,000	2.80	40.94
1980	243,801,650	5,900,000	2.42	40.75
1990	252,174,910	5,800,000	2.30	45.00

Sources: U.S. Bureau of the Census, Historical Statistics of the United States to 1957 (Washington, D.C.: Government Printing Office, 1976); American Jewish Year Book (1901–93).

the Promotion of the Abolition of Slavery and in the New York Manumission Society; Joseph and Isaac Friedman ran stations on the underground railroad; and three Jews rode with John Brown on his antislavery guerilla raids in the 1850s. An even more important reflection of Jewish "Americanness" is that approximately ten thousand Jews served in the armies of the Civil War, a number far out of proportion to their percentage of the general population. Seven thousand served in the Union forces, three thousand in the Confederate, and more than five hundred, another overrepresentation, lost their lives.

German Jews were not only Americanizing but, at the same time, were also moving into an increasingly Jewish, less German orbit. This is partly reflected in the fact that by 1880, *Jewish* organizations of one kind or another existed in 90 percent of the 160 communities with one hundred or more

Jews. And nearly seventy towns with fewer than one hundred Jewish residents hosted a number of Jewish institutions, which more often than not
were organized religious congregations.

By 1868, Jewish hospitals could be found in Cincinnati, New York,
Philadelphia, and Chicago. New York City by 1880 was home to some fifty
Jewish charitable and educational institutions. Philadelphia boasted twenty,
Cincinnati a dozen or more. B'nai B'rith chapters, dedicated to "uniting
Israelites in the work of promoting their highest interests and those of hu-
manity," and Young Men's Hebrew Associations increasingly appeared in the
larger cities. Jewish societies for poor relief, free loans, mutual aid, and literary pursuits were founded in at least eleven major cities of the South, as
well as in San Francisco, Los Angeles, San Diego, and Sacramento. The German Jews' reputation for philanthropy in the nineteenth century was not
only impressive but also well earned.

In creating their visibly Jewish institutions, the Germans were demonstrating that Jews did more than pray differently from other Americans, that
they were not merely religious Jews or just "Americans of Hebrew persuasion." The B'nai B'rith and the Young Men's Hebrew Association, for example, were not simply Jewish imitations of Christian associations. In each organization there was significant Jewish content including Hebrew classes and
lectures on Jewish history. In creating the Hebrew Ladies Benevolent Societies, German Jewish women were probably influenced to some degree by
the *Frauenverein* of the German American community and most certainly by
what their neighbors were doing in their churches, but the benevolent societies were explicitly Jewish organizations. They had been formed first and
foremost as Jewish women's burial societies, and they concentrated heavily
on *tsedakah*—philanthropy and social justice for the sick, the poor, and the
unemployed.

The German Jews combined American and Jewish ideals and identities, but it is clear that they did not shy away from creating associations and
other structures that deviated from the larger American—gentile—society.
After 1860, German Jews often chose a Moorish style for synagogues. This
was very different from the style used for building churches, and it signified
a link with a historical people outside the American mainstream. The link
was reinforced as German Jews continued to chose Hebrew names for their
synagogues—Beth Elohim in Charleston, South Carolina, and Kehilat Ko-
desh B'nai Yeshurun in Cincinnati, for example—names they chiseled in
stone on the entranceways.

If the expanding philanthropic network provided some Jews with both a substitute for religion and a secular framework for the preservation of their ethnic identity, the growing number of religious congregations was nonetheless also impressive. Well over two hundred, many with their own synagogue buildings, were constituted in more than one hundred cities and towns by 1880. Most congregations, aside from a small number established by newly arriving East Europeans, were Reform congregations, in practice at least, if not in name. Congregations and synagogues established by American Jews before 1820 had already undergone some transformation from Old World style and content and had even adopted a number of Protestant forms. Some of the early German Jewish arrivals in Savannah, Georgia, for example, may have seen at the dedication of the synagogue, Torah scrolls carried around the speaker's platform seven times in Orthodox mode. At the same service, however, they also saw a choir performance accompanied by an organ played by the music director of one of the city's churches. But from as early as the 1820s, and accelerating in the 1840s, demands were made for more innovations or "reforms" in the conduct of religious services. The first attempt to organize a Reform synagogue took place in Charleston, South Carolina in 1824. Young acculturated Jews, many of Sephardic descent, who knew little if anything about the Reform movement in Europe, petitioned the board of Congregation Beth Elohim to make changes. When the synagogue trustees refused even to discuss the group's requests, the dissidents organized an independent Reformed Society of Israelites. Many influences combined to spur the movement for Reform Judaism. The liberal spirit of the United States, the desire to reformulate a Jewish ritual in the idiom of the times, and a desire to Americanize the synagogue with a more decorous English-language service were important. So was the absence of a vigorous, traditional Jewry to oppose changes. Finally, the arrival of authoritative, ordained Reform rabbis steeped in philosophical rationalism and the idea of progressive revelation provided leadership for the movement.

Some of what we call the Reform movement or the Americanization of Judaism was an outgrowth of the larger process of Jewish secularization based in Europe's nineteenth-century challenge to all religious tradition and authority. Indeed, in America the Reform movement added little new to the system of liberal religious ideas that had already surfaced in Europe. But in the wide-open United States in the mid-nineteenth century, an era marked by the ideal of democratic egalitarianism, by social reform movements, and by religious revivals, the ideas were developed and transformed in a radically different historical context. Some change in women's legal status, for example, had already been promulgated in the Reform movement in Germany, but women's traditional role in the synagogue remained virtually unaltered. In America, in contrast, most Reform synagogues permitted women to sit with men in family pews and to sing in a mixed choir. Confirmations were introduced for girls as well as boys. The Reform prayer book excised the male benediction thanking God "that I am not a woman," and women were counted as part of the *minyan*. Moreover, through Reform synagogue sisterhoods, women administered charitable and other social services and tended to temple maintenance and to the religious education of children.

I. M. Wise of Cincinnati, a moderate Reform Jew, stands out as the figure who, through diligent compromise and improvisation, shaped an American Judaism (a term he preferred to *Reform*) which enabled nineteenth-century German Jews to maintain their religious allegiance at the same time that they took their place in American society. Wise did not seek to be a sectarian, but his activities, along with those of the more radical Reformer, David Einhorn (1809–79) of Baltimore, resulted in the evolution and crystallization of a Reform denomination. Wise's hope for unity was reflected in his establishment of both the Union of American Hebrew Congregations in 1873, and Hebrew Union College, a rabbinical seminary, in 1875. That hope, however, foundered on a variety of obstacles including American mobility and individualism as well as Jewish sectarianism. Not the least of the obstacles to unification under the Reform umbrella, however, was the arrival of masses of poorer, less modernized East European Jews wedded to a greater traditionalism, if not to theological Orthodoxy or rigorous ritual observance.

But German Jewry in America remained preeminent in 1880. It is true that as early as 1852, New York's Beth Hamidrash synagogue had a membership consisting largely of Russian and Polish Jews, and by 1872 there were nearly thirty additional East European congregations in New York City. On the other side of the continent, in San Francisco, Los Angeles, Sacramento, and San Jose, Polish and East European Jews, though relatively few, outnumbered German Jews as early as the 1860s. But by 1880 the German Jewish community had built a network of viable institutions and organizations crossing the entire continent, had established a multilingual press and attracted a body of able, European-ordained rabbis, and were supporting a seminary to train an American rabbinate. The flow of immigrants from Eastern Europe, though growing (only 7,500 between 1820 and 1870, but more than 30,000 between 1870 and 1880), was still small. Moreover, Jews of Polish, Silesian, Bohemian, and Slovakian background, in California and New York, and in a growing number of points of settlement in between, desired to become "respectable" American Jews. This required not only Americanization; it also required acculturation to German Jewish standards.

The German Jews became relatively affluent and influential, and even as they created more of a public Jewish world than they had found here in the 1820s, they also became more acceptable to their fellow Americans. In the 1840s Jews served in the state legislatures of Indiana, North Carolina, South Carolina, Georgia, and New York. And Jewish mayors led at least nineteen towns in New Mexico Territory and in eight states from Kansas to Oregon and from Idaho to Texas. But in the status-hungry years following the Civil War, German Jews who aspired to social acceptance were rejected nearly everywhere, and especially by leading social clubs in large cities. The rapid mobility of the Jews contributed to the erection of social barriers such as "restricted hotels" and exclusive clubs. Gentiles in the scramble for prestige could use these noneconomic status markers in their competition with the Jews, and social discrimination was intensified. By the late 1870s the German Jewish *nouveaux riches* found themselves increasingly excluded from upper-crust private schools, college fraternities, and desirable neighborhoods.

In the decade's most prominent exclusionary incident, the Grand Union Hotel in Saratoga Springs, owned by Judge Henry Hilton, refused accommodations to Joseph Seligman, a long-time patron, whose name meant wealth and status in the Jewish community. Leading Jewish merchants, incensed by this public insult boycotted Hilton's wholesale firm, the A. T. Stewart Company. The company was forced into bankruptcy, but general social exclusion against Jews continued and increased. San Francisco's *Elite Directory* for 1879 included Jews, but on a separate list from Christians. The New York *Social Register* closed its lists to Jews entirely, and in 1893 the prestigious Union League Club, which Jews had helped establish, barred Jews, giving a determined finality to Jewish exclusion from socially prestigious associations.

Yet snubs such as these paled into insignificance compared to the violence Jews experienced in the Deep South during the 1890s. Farmers, burdened by debt, sacked the stores of Jewish merchants in several states, including Louisiana and Georgia, and in their attempts to drive Jewish merchants out of southern Mississippi, marauding horsemen in 1893 burned dozens of farmhouses belonging to Jews.

In the late nineteenth century, the United States was being further transformed from a relatively rural society into an industrial nation, more marked by urbanization, ethnic and class heterogeneity, and mobility. These radical changes of the 1880s and 1890s produced economic grievance, fear of dis-

placement, and social insecurities. These in turn contributed significantly to
the strength of nativism and anti-Semitism. It is important to remember, however, that Jew-hatred, although in evidence even earlier than the 1890s—
indeed, visible as early as the birth of the nation itself—never became part
of the national political agenda; and prejudice and discrimination against Jews
have been mild compared to the violent and government-sanctioned anti-
Semitism of the Old World. It was mild, too, compared to mob violence
against Blacks throughout the South in the nineteenth and early twentieth
centuries and against the Chinese in California in the 1870s and 1880s. And
it never matched in ferocity the anti-Catholic rampages that led to deaths in
Butte, Montana, and Kansas City, Missouri, to lynchings of Italians in West
Virginia, Pennsylvania, Massachusetts, and Illinois, or to the genocidal war-
fare waged against Native Americans in the nineteenth century. This does not
make anti-Semitism unimportant, however, and Jews in America whose property was attacked, who were physically assaulted, or who were closed out of
social acceptability and locked out of enterprises at the upper reaches of the
U.S. economy suffered in varying degrees.

When anti-Semitism intensified in the United States in the last quarter
of the nineteenth century, the German Jews were more ready to blame the
new immigrants from Eastern Europe than to recognize that their own conspicuous success also played a role in the unfortunate turn of events. Fearing
an even greater anti-Semitism as the numbers of immigrants increased expo-
nentially in the 1880s and anxious over the potential burden of masses of
poor dependents, German Jews, in their cultural and class arrogance, initially took an anti-immigration position. But ultimately—indeed, relatively
quickly, as we shall see in later chapters—the stance of the German Jews
changed, and they played an important role in the fight against immigration
restriction. They also provided, despite a strained, often bitter relationship
with the East European Jews, significant aid, including jobs, social welfare
philanthropy, and political support. The new, more positive attitude, which
combined condescension and empathy, was reflected in the columns of the
American Hebrew. From May to December of 1881, the editors insisted that
every effort be made "to rescue our own and give them a space wherein they
may breath the air of peace." There is "plenty of room for them all in this
'haven of the oppressed,'" the *American Hebrew* argued, and it went on to
remind readers that "All of us should be sensible of what we owe not only to
these . . . coreligionists but to ourselves, who will be looked upon by our
Gentile neighbors as the natural sponsors for these our brethren."

By the 1880s the German Jews had become significantly acculturated. This was reflected in their rapid economic and social mobility, the growth of Reform Judaism, and their pride in identifying as Americans and Jews. The Germans had some trouble with the second of these identifications as they faced the flood of East Europeans. They feared, with some reason, that the distinction between "the better class of Jews" and the "vulgar Jews" would collapse and that everything they had worked for would be destroyed.

Though they never relinquished significant influence—which they maintained particularly through their philanthropy—the Germans did witness, between 1890 and 1920, the end of their total dominance of the American Jewish scene. But everything they had worked for was not destroyed. They had created the institutional framework and even many of the modes of behavior and values that, with some important qualifications, continue to mark the American Jewish world today. The East Europeans, after all, established no new communities; they followed the Germans to their points of settlement, the largest of which remained the more important centers of Jewish population, organizational activity, and cultural continuity throughout the era of massive East European immigration.

Like the German Jews before them, the East European immigrants and their children became Americanized, even if not with the same remarkable rapidity. Many also achieved relatively rapid economic and occupational mobility, sometimes, as in the garment business, by displacing the Germans. And like their German predecessors, the East Europeans retained and reshaped a distinctive, if somewhat transformed, ethnoreligious Jewish culture. Indeed, if the Germans set the stage for the new immigrants, the East Europeans supplied the biological and cultural reinforcements needed to save American Jewry from assimilation or at least from becoming a virtually invisible remnant. German Jewish population increases in the nineteenth century were notable, but they did not keep pace with even greater increases in the general American population. It is at least arguable that without the East Europeans a viable, visible, distinctively Jewish culture would have become increasingly unlikely in America and might have disappeared.

4

The Eastern European Cultural Heritage and Mass Migration to the United States, 1880–1920

In 1880 close to 6 million of the world's 7.7 million Jews, or about 75 percent, lived in Eastern Europe, and only 3 percent lived in the United States. By 1920, however, after a series of large-scale migrations, more than 23 percent of world Jewry called America home. In order to understand what produced this massive uprooting and transplanting of Jews and the social and cultural baggage the immigrants carried with them to the United States, we need to examine briefly the traditional world of the East European Jews, the physical wretchedness they increasingly suffered, and the forces for cultural renewal and spiritual hope they experienced there.

The great bulk, more than 73 percent, of the Jewish immigrants to the United States between 1880 and 1920 came from the Russian Empire, particularly from the Pale of Settlement, which consisted of the fifteen western provinces of European Russia and the ten provinces of Russian-held Poland. Nearly four million Jews, considered by the Russians a pariah people, were confined to the Pale, and for more than two centuries, to pervasively Jewish *shtetlekh* (small towns) therein. Although Jews rarely constituted more than 5 percent of the population of the Russian Empire, they were often close to

15 percent of the population of the Pale; even more often they constituted the majority, if not all, of the inhabitants of their *shtetlekh*.

Most Jewish towns provided surrounding agricultural villages with commercial services, especially marketing and milling. Since Jews, the least-favored minority in Eastern Europe, were mostly forbidden to own land and were limited to a small base of occupational and economic operations, they earned their livelihoods by trade and artisanship, thereby filling an important need in the underdeveloped agrarian economies of the Russian Empire, Galicia (Austria-Hungary) and Rumania.

At the center of the *shtetl* was the marketplace, to which peasants from many miles around brought livestock, fish, hides, and wagonloads of grain, fruits, and vegetables. In exchange they bought produce, which the Jews imported from the city, dry goods, clothing, lamps, and tools. Despite the Jews' virtual monopoly of business life in the Pale, poverty was the general condition in the *shtetl* from at least the 1650s, and the condition deteriorated in the late eighteenth and nineteenth centuries. Outside the *shtetl* some Jews—a small number of factory owners, grain merchants, cattle dealers, stewards, and estate administrators—were relatively well off, but their general economic position was increasingly precarious. The great mass of Jews in the *shtetlekh* and in Eastern Europe generally were the *proste yidn*—the common people.

Hand in hand with poverty went fear. A Jew in Eastern Europe, often marked by distinctive dress and speech, was fair game for all, from schoolchildren to government officials. Jews who ventured outside the *shtetl* to peddle considered themselves lucky if they were not set upon and beaten. Even within the town they were vulnerable to the invasions and excesses of the occasional drunken mob or of discontented peasants intent on violence.

Despite the fear of attack on person and property, and despite the pervasive poverty, the *shtetl* eked out a subsistence. But it was not only an economic entity; it was at its heart a community of faith encompassed in a long-standing, deeply rooted religious culture. The community acknowledged an overwhelmingly real God who wielded awesome power and held out the possibility of human salvation.

Scholarship was one of the important pathways to God and to the future, and every *shtetl* maintained at least one *heder* (elementary school) and a *khevre* (society or committee) for the purpose of providing poor boys with religious education through their thirteenth year. Sometimes there was a yeshiva, a school for advanced Jewish learning, which was chiefly, but not exclusively, for students preparing for the rabbinate.

On an individual level study fulfilled the critically important religious value of *takhles,* an orientation to ultimate outcomes rather than to immediate benefits. And study was a *mitzvah,* a scripturally ordained obligation whose fulfillment not only brought honor and status in the community but also was pleasing to God. Religious education was formally the domain of boys and men, who often spent ten hours a day at it. Girls did often receive a year or two of instruction in reading and writing Yiddish, the so-called *mama-loshen* (mother's tongue), and they learned to recite, but not translate, Hebrew prayers.

By their own piety, however, older women provided models and an informal religious education for their daughters, with whom they spent a good part of the day. Girls and women worked together often, baking items to peddle, sewing clothing to sell (independently or through small contractors), caring for smaller children, or simply doing the innumerable, seemingly unending domestic chores. Although the picture of the scholarly husband, spending all his time in the *bet hamidrash* (house of study) and the *shul* (synagogue), leaving his wife and daughters slaving away at home or market, has been significantly overdrawn in Jewish historical literature and memory, Jewish women did indeed play an extraordinarily time-consuming part in providing for their families. Some worked in factories, but most employed women were involved in small commercial enterprises of one kind or another, selling food and dry goods from stalls in the local marketplace. Or they went from house to house selling bread they had baked or tea and beans and potato pancakes.

The tasks were performed within the overarching context of religious duty, ritual, regulation, and spirit. Mothers "set important examples of service and self-sacrifice." Although learning these traditional values did not bring to girls the status that scholarly achievement brought to boys, daughters were highly valued and were part of an important educational dynamic.

In addition to education, formal and informal, there were many other communal institutions that helped transmit values. Every *shtetl* had a *mikvah* (ritual bath), a *shokhet* (ritual slaughterer), and at least one *shul,* where the daily prayers were recited and on *shabos* (the Sabbath) the Torah was read and studied.

Even though most *shtetl* Jews were poor, there was in *shul* a rigid separation not only of men and women, but also of the *shayna yidn* (refined or gentlepeople) and the *proste yidn* (common people). Scholarship was the most important determination of *yikhes* (status), but wealth and family background also clearly counted. Whatever the tensions between poor and well-to-do, however, all Jews in the towns of Eastern Europe up to the nineteenth century could be classified in relative terms as *kleine menschn* (little people) rather than be divided into fully formed rival classes. And all shared in the embrace of personal and communal ties, as well as powerful family loyalties.

Well-off Jews were obligated to give, to perform *tsedakah* (charity as justice and righteousness), and to participate in the *khevrot,* committees of the *kehillah* (Jewish community council), which provided loans, dowries, supplies, and free education for the less well off. Ideally, as the historian Elias Tcherikower has pointed out, "recipients of aid were in no way beholden to donors: it was their due. The word for benefice—tzedakah—derives from the word for justice. In fact the donor owed thanks to the recipient for the opportunity to do a mitzvah." If reality deviated at times from the ideals, if the not-so-poor lorded it over the very poor, if the scholars behaved arrogantly toward the untutored, or if wealthy merchants were too openly proud and condescending in their charitable giving, still the ideals established the moral tone. The Jews were responsible for one another; their conception of human relations, reinforced by religious philosophy, generally promoted mutuality and interdependence.

The life of East European Jews, with its isolation, provincialism, poverty, and sporadic violence, was anything but ideal. But Jews were at least spared the brutality and indifference that consistently attended the world of lord and peasant. In the face of oppression they were sustained by their belief in a common destiny, buoyed by their feeling of moral superiority, and strengthened by their sense of community.

The *shtetl* was never so stable as it has sometimes been portrayed, and it had already begun to experience the decline of the authority of the rabbis and the *kehillot* by the middle of the eighteenth century. Hasidism, an enthusiastic, pietistic movement of religious renewal which emerged in the 1750s, temporarily challenged an encrusted rabbinic traditionalism. In demanding spontaneity and rejecting overly formal ritual and rote, the Hasidim appealed to and brightened the spiritual life of many Jews, particularly the numerous *proste yidn*, even as they upset their critics.

A more enduring challenge and split became manifest, however, when the Jewish community councils were forced to increase taxes significantly. The Polish and Russian governments forced Jewish community leaders not only to tax more heavily but also to supply significant numbers of men for the army. Until 1827 only peasants had to face the draft and twenty-five years of military service. Under Czar Nicholas I, Jewish men aged eighteen to twenty-five were called up, and younger recruits of twelve to seventeen were given preparatory military training as "cantonists." The high draft quotas, as many as thirty Jewish boys for every thousand Jews, moved community leaders to conscript Jews as punishment for failure to pay taxes and to hire *khapers*—professional kidnappers—to ferret young boys out of hiding. At the same time members of the *kehillah* and Jews of means bought exemption for their own sons.

By the middle of the nineteenth century, it was clear that czarist Jewish policy was designed to promote conversion and assimilation. Young Jews were to be recruited either for the "crown schools," which were by czarist decree dedicated to the "eradication of the superstitions and harmful prejudices instilled by the study of the Talmud," or for extremely long service in the military, where, if explicit conversion pressures did not work, time and distance would. The experiences of the cantonist period, which lasted until the middle of the 1850s, were a source of enduring and divisive resentment in the Jewish community

The leaders of the community never regained their prestige or influence, and communal solidarity was even further undermined by new and complex economic forces surrounding and penetrating Jewish populations. In many areas in the late nineteenth century, the peasant-based economies of Eastern Europe were slowly eroding. For Jews this meant increased poverty, intensified competition among themselves, and the further disintegration of communal cohesiveness. The modernization of agriculture and the very beginnings of industrialization, particularly in the Pale, where Jews in the 1890s constituted approximately 70 percent of those engaged in commerce and 30 percent of those engaged in crafts, led to the displacement of petty merchants, peddlers, and artisans, as well as teamsters and innkeepers.

Other effects of modernization were felt as well. Railroads and peasant cooperatives changed the functional role played by large numbers of Jews in the small market towns, virtually eliminating local fairs. By 1880 some sections of Eastern Europe had one Jewish peddler for every ten peasant customers. And the emancipation of the serfs (1861–62) left the peasants with heavy, long-term mortgages, unable to afford the services of Jewish middlemen. Nobles, too, bereft of wealth by the freeing of the serfs, needed fewer stewards and administrators for their diminished estates.

The Russian economy was experiencing long periods of instability, and as the need for scapegoats intensified in the face of Russian restlessness in the 1860s and 1870s, the government did not hesitate to promote anti-Semitism by focusing on the Jews' preeminence as middlemen. Native middlemen organized boycotts of Jewish merchants, and the government offered loans to a nascent class of Russian commercial men waiting for businesses to be abandoned by Jews.

These pressures on Jews were great and were exacerbated after Russian terrorists assassinated Alexander II in 1881. Confusion reigned and victimization was intensified. Murderous violence took place against Jews in pogroms that erupted in 225 cities and towns between 1881 and 1882. In addition, the draconian May Laws (1882) were promulgated, prohibiting Jewish settlement in villages. This meant expulsion of five hundred thousand Jews from rural areas. An additional seven hundred thousand including twenty thousand Jews expelled from Moscow in chains, were driven into the Pale by 1891.

Between 1894 and 1898 the number of Jewish paupers increased by 30 percent, and in many communities the number of families of *luftmenshn*, people without marketable skills or capital (literally a people who live on air), approached 40 percent of the entire Jewish population. The numbers moving from *shtetl* to urban concentrations within the Pale increased significantly from 1885 to 1915; by 1897 almost half the Jewish population of the Russian Empire lived in larger towns or cities. *Shtetl* life, however, through powerful spiritual ties, through the common language of Yiddish and the sacred language of Hebrew, and through a sense of shared history had firmly molded Jewish values and behavior. Even when they left their small towns, therefore, Jews carried with them much of their *shtetl* culture, which they reformulated and transplanted in new locales.

Economic dislocation and government policy changed the geography of Jewish life in Eastern Europe. But the cities such as Warsaw, Lodz, and Bialystock, which became increasingly Jewish, also offered only a precarious existence. Victims of Russian paranoia and xenophobia, Jews continued to be excluded from many branches of the economy. All of this was aggravated by high Jewish birth rates, which caused the Jewish population of Eastern Europe to continue to grow at a steady rate between 1800 (1,250,000) and 1900 (6,500,000) despite considerable emigration.

In the major urban centers of the northwest region, including Vilna, Minsk, Bialystok, Grodno, Vitebsk, and Kovno, the material condition of Jews, who were mostly craftsmen and artisans rather than factory workers, continued to decline. And it was here primarily that a Jewish working class developed. The small shop Jewish proletariat found it increasingly difficult to compete with the factories or with the handcraft enterprises of the masses of emancipated peasants. And Jewish employers, themselves squeezed, felt

compelled to intensify their exploitation of Jewish workers, thereby harden-
ing class feeling. The new Jewish proletariat participated in a series of strikes
in the 1870s and 1880s which were spontaneous, sporadic, and at first generally uninfluenced by Jewish socialists. An organized movement developed
only after the Jewish socialist intelligentsia established significant contact with
the Jewish working masses.

Russian schools and universities, which were centers of revolutionary
ferment, particularly in the last third of the nineteenth century, helped mold
that intelligentsia. Between 1884 and 1890, Jews, approximately 4.5 percent
of the general population of the Russian Empire and only little more than that
of the university population, provided more than 13 percent of those who
stood trial for subversive activities. By 1901-3 that figure rose to 29 percent
and included increasing and disproportionate numbers of young, unmarried
Jewish women. The outside influences on and internal changes within *shtetl*
culture were raising aspirations for all, perhaps most for previously hemmed-
in girls.

Numerous Jewish student radicals and intellectuals, men and women,
were, at least until the pogroms of 1881-82, convinced assimilationists. Greg-
ory Weinstein admitted later in his *Reminscences* that "like zealots of a new religion, we discarded everything—valuable as well as valueless—of the old
teachings." But Jewish youth developed new self-awareness when they were
confronted by personal rebuff within the socialist movement and when, after
the pogroms, they encountered the stunning indifference of Russian radicals
to violence against the Jews. Abraham Cahan reported that in the wake of more
than two hundred anti-Jewish uprisings that spread across southern Russia and
into Poland from 1881 to 1882, some young people finally went to synagogues
to demonstrate their solidarity. In Kiev, one speaker, according to Cahan, confessed to the assembled worshippers: "We are your brethren. We are Jews like
you. We regret that we have up to now considered ourselves as Russians and
not Jews. Events of the last weeks . . . including the pogroms . . . have shown
us how grievously mistaken we have been. Yes, we are Jews."

Undoubtedly conflicts with regard to their own Jewishness continued
to exist for many Jews attracted to socialism, and some even became hostile
or indifferent to Jewish culture. Lev Deutsch, one of the early revolutionaries who stayed active in Russian radical circles even after the pogroms "wanted
the Jews to assimilate as quickly as possible; everything that smelled of Jewishness," Deutsch said, "called forth among us a feeling of contempt." But
most of the Jewish radicals chose to be active within the Jewish mainstream,

and they helped develop class-conscious socialists among Jewish artisans and craftsmen, whose numbers, unions, and strikes grew during the 1890s.

It was clear not only that a Jewish proletariat had developed but that it was conscious of both its class interest and its cultural identity. Organizers and strikers often took oaths on the holy Torah or swore by a pair of phylacteries that they would never break a strike. The cultural dimension was even more evident in 1897, when many of the local organizations of workers and intelligentsia united to form the first and most important *Jewish* social democratic party—the *Bund.* A revolutionary party with a mass labor base, the *Bund,* or General Jewish Workers' Union, which spread throughout Russia and Poland, moved slowly toward the idea of an autonomous Jewish movement, combining class war with loyalty to the Jewish people—indeed, to Jewish peoplehood.

Jewish socialism was one among several movements through which Jews in the throes of social change tried to redefine their identities by drawing on the traditional as well as the modern. Zionism, the quest to make Palestine a haven or a home for Jews, was another. Like Bundism, Zionism, which emerged as a tiny movement after the pogroms of 1881–82, emphasized Jewish peoplehood. But in contrast to the Bundists, the early Zionists held the entire Jewish diaspora in disdain. They rejected the Yiddish language and its rich folk culture as well as the inflexibility of religious tradition. They strove not to remake a Russia more hospitable to Jews and workers, but to revolutionize their own Jewish society, to "normalize" the Jewish people, to make it like all other peoples, and in its own land. But as Zionism began to grow into a mass movement and to win adherents among even the middle classes and the Orthodox, it, like the *Bund,* drew on and moved toward a deeper national-religious identity.

The same cannot be said, however, for the *Haskalah* (enlightenment) movement. As early as the 1850s, the Haskalah, originally a product of West European Jewry, had gained a foothold among some secularly educated Jews living in the more urbanized areas of Eastern Europe. By 1870 the Haskalah began to penetrate *shtetl* society. Most of the *maskilim* (enlightened ones) did seek a path that would preserve something of the national-religious identity of the Jews, but they strove toward a complete emancipation, increased secularization, full Jewish citizenship, and the virtual elimination of the *kehillah* as an intermediary between Jews and the state.

The activities of the *maskilim,* the liberalization of Jewish educational policy by Alexander II (1855–81), and the general draft law of 1874, which

granted exemption to students in Russian secondary schools, resulted in a
massive increase of Jewish youth in Russian educational institutions. Even
young girls pressured their parents, often successfully, into sending them to
the gymnasia. Russian secular education reinforced the growing alienation of
the Jewish intellectual youth from the Jewish people in general. This was a
serious blow to the nationalist wing of the *maskilim,* but it was they who had
helped unleash forces over which they now had little control. Secularization
and acculturation, if not assimilation and conversion, made incremental inroads into the Jewish world, particularly in the cities.

In Western Europe, Jews had achieved, at least temporarily, some individual liberties in return for the communal autonomy and corporate rights
that the respective European states had abolished. In Russia, however, where
neither individual nor corporate rights had ever been guaranteed, the process of integrating the Jews tended to take on a repressive character. This led
in the last quarter of the nineteenth century not only to great turmoil but
also to important political movements, such as socialism and Zionism, which
developed new definitions of Jewishness.

As with the socialists and Zionists, a dynamic of redefinition took place
among the devotees of secular *yiddishkayt* (Yiddish-based culture). Primarily
artists and writers, the "Yiddishists," still nourished by traditional religion
but alienated by ritual excess, worked to develop a Yiddish culture combining a Jewish national identity with a dedication "to a humanitarian, perhaps
even universalist present." The Yiddishists were well aware of the difficulties,
but they worked indefatigably to promote a seeming paradox, a modern culture resting mainly on the Yiddish language.

Many movements in Jewish life, including socialism, came to Yiddish
through expedience. Leaders saw the language as a tool with which to reach
the masses; but then they stayed with it out of love. For true Yiddishists,
however, the love of the language and culture was first and paramount. At
the heart of the movement were writers like Sholom Aleichem, Mendele
Mokher Sforim, and Isaac Lieb Peretz. These men, especially Peretz, tried to
rediscover Jewish tradition and to reformulate it and somehow link it to the
worldly culture of modern Europe. *Yiddishkayt* took on an increasingly secular character, but like so many cultural forms in Jewish history, it retained
strong ties to the tradition. We make distinctions, as Irving Howe has said,
"between religious and secular ideologies, and we are right to make them;
but in the heated actuality of East European Jewish life, the two had a way of
becoming intertwined."

The political renewal of the late nineteenth century, particularly socialism, Zionism, and the new cultural emphasis on secular *yiddishkayt,* stirred the Jews in city and *shtetl* to a greater awareness of their condition and aroused in them a new sense of the potential of their unused energies. But without means to fulfill the new aspirations, Jews were simultaneously made aware of how intolerable their life remained. This became even clearer in the context of the vicious anti-Semitism that at first reinforced the new political and cultural movements but which after 1881 threatened to overwhelm the Jews of Eastern Europe.

Immediately following the assassination of Alexander II in 1881, the Russian government, in order to deflect peasant discontent and to defend itself against revolutionary criticism and attack, stepped up the accusation that Jews were responsible for the misfortunes of the nation. There followed hundreds of pogroms in southern Russian towns and cities involving physical violence and rape and the sack of thousands of shops and synagogues. In the immediate aftermath of violence in 1881, thirteen thousand Jews, desirous of escaping the physical threat, emigrated from Russia to the United States. This was almost half the number that had gone to America during the entire decade of the 1870s. And Jewish emigration increased even more significantly in 1882.

Russian commissions investigating the causes of pogroms concluded that "Jewish exploitation" was at the root of the violence. On the basis of this finding, the government published the "Temporary Laws" (May Laws, 1882), which, as I have already noted, led to wholesale prohibitions and expulsions. In 1884, though pogroms were temporarily halted, there was serious administrative harassment of Jews, including restrictive educational quotas. In 1886, reacting to the virtual flood of Jews seeking entry to secondary schools and universities, the government limited the number of Jewish students to 10 percent of the student body in the Pale and 3–5 percent outside it. In 1887 over twenty-three thousand Russian Jews, many in response to the *numerus clausus* (quota system) and other restrictions, emigrated to the United States. This was the highest total emigration for a single year up to that point.

By 1891 previously privileged Jews were subject to wholesale expulsion from several Russian cities, and hundreds of thousands living east of the Pale were forced into the area of confinement. The press continued a campaign of unbridled anti-Semitic propaganda, and Konstantin Pobedonostev, the head of the governing body of the Russian Orthodox Church and a major instigator of pogroms, clarified the goals of the government when he predicted that "one-third of the Jews will convert, one-third will die, and one-third will flee the country." More than 107,000 Jews left Russia for the United States between 1891 and 1892.

After a short interval (1893–98) the strict application of the discriminatory laws continued under Nicholas II (1894–1918). His government subsidized close to three thousand anti-Semitic publications including the classic forgery *Protocols of the Elders of Zion*. Free reign was given to anti-Jewish agitation, particularly in reaction to the growth of the revolutionary movement, in which a disproportionate number of Jewish youth took part. An explosion of pogroms filled the years from 1903 to 1906. In contrast to those which took place between 1881 and 1884, the new programs involved a steep escalation of personal violence and murder. "At our door four Jews were hanged, and I saw that with my own eyes," said Marsha Farbman, who fled in 1904. "The gentiles were running and yelling, 'Beat the Jews. Kill them!'"

In 1906 pogroms became practically uncountable, with many hundreds dead, robbed, raped, and mutilated. The pogroms in the beginning of the twentieth century, like those in the 1880s, were followed by steep jumps in the rate of emigration from Russia to the United States. In 1900, some 37,000 Jews emigrated; by 1904, the number had risen to 77,500. More than 92,400 left in 1905, and 125,200 followed in 1906. A total of 672,000 Jews entered the United States as immigrants between 1904 and 1908, the vast majority from the Russian Empire.

Emigration, of course, was not the only response to anti-Jewish violence. Nearly two-thirds of East European Jewry chose to remain in the old countries. Some stayed because they had a strong vested interest in the world of tradition and feared the potentially corrosive effects of life in a *treyfe medina* (unkosher land); others stayed because they were too old or too poor to make the voyage.

A small group, mainly Bundists, remained because they thought that Russia could be transformed by revolution into an egalitarian society. In the meantime they were determined to defend themselves, and in the face of the new wave of pogroms in 1903, the Bundists formed defense societies in every Jewish town. They were joined by Zionists and Socialist-Zionists. Attackers now met with the armed resistance of Jewish youth, who were not only attempting to protect life and property but were also acting to "assert the honor of the Jewish nation." Many of these young people would leave after the aborted Russian Revolution of 1905 and the repressive violence that followed. Their aspirations, raised by a combination of oppressive material conditions and cultural renewal, would have to be fulfilled elsewhere.

Pogroms alone do not explain the extraordinary movement of the Jewish population between 1881 and 1920, although they were a major factor. The highest rate of emigration was experienced in Galicia, where there were economic hardship and some local repression, but virtually no pogroms. Likewise, Lithuania, with relatively few pogroms, had a very high emigration rate. Yet the Ukraine, the heartland of pogroms in the Russian Empire, produced a relatively low rate of emigration before World War I. Also, concurrent with increasing Jewish emigration was an expanded emigration from the Russian Empire of non-Jewish Poles, Lithuanians, Finns, and even Russians. Jewish emigration in this context can be seen as directly related to economic strains and dislocations of Eastern Europe and particularly of pre-revolutionary Russia.

Jews, however, constituting only about 5 percent of the population of the Russian Empire, made up close to 50 percent of the Russian emigrant stream, 60 percent of the emigrants from Galicia, and an astounding 90 percent of the Rumanian exodus between 1881 and 1910. These figures, when added to the high correlation between pogroms and Jewish mass exodus, continue to suggest strongly that fear of violent persecution, while not the only or primary cause, was critical in moving an extraordinary 33 percent of East European Jews to leave their countries between 1881 and 1920.

Mass Jewish migration had been gathering momentum throughout the 1870s. After 1881, however, Jews had to face anti-Semitism in their homelands not simply as a permanent inconvenience but as a threat to their very existence. Increasing numbers of leaders, including M. L. Lilienblum (1843–1910), a former *maskil* and now a Zionist, and Leon Pinsker (1821–91), an Odessa physician once a fervent assimilationist and now a Jewish nationalist, were perceiving anti-Semitism as a deeply rooted disease, incurable in the foreseeable future. And after the late nineteenth century pogroms, more and more believed that emancipation for Jews was not possible within the intolerable conditions of the Russian Empire or for that matter anywhere in Eastern Europe.

Although fear and poverty had clearly become central in Jewish life, cultural ferment and renewal had also become important. The new ideologies and cultural forms, Bundist socialism, Zionism, and Yiddish secularism were products of modernity, fashioned mostly by people alienated from traditional Judaism, but all the new "belief-systems" and thought patterns drew upon authentic sources in the Jewish past.

"To become, to achieve," whether in the collective version of messianism or in the individual version of *takhles* was always central to Jewish culture. Modernization redirected and intensified that desire, and increasing East European anti-Semitism frustrated it. The combination of spiritual hope and physical fear and wretchedness provided the requisites for emigration. For large numbers uprooting and resettlement seemed the only answer.

Millions of Jews left the *shtetlekh* and cities in which they had built their lives. Artisans, stewards, and peddlers, faced with obsolescence and dislocation; merchants, faced with legal disabilities and discriminations; socialist militants, faced with repression from outside their movements and Jew-hatred within them; students and the religiously committed, faced with grave uncertainties; and above all, the innumerable ordinary Jews faced with impoverishment and persecution—all of these made the decision to leave Eastern Europe in the late nineteenth and early twentieth centuries. They did not merely flee. With a strength born of cultural renewal, they aspired also to accomplish something. The United States, with its reputation as a land of opportunity and fortunately enjoying a period of extensive industrial expansion and economic growth, provided the context for potential fulfillment.

The motives of Jews leaving Eastern Europe—to escape the hardships of life under the czar or to fulfill new hopes forged in the Old-World Jewish communities—were similar to those of many other emigrants who yearned for change. But unlike the movement of members of other national groups, the Jewish migration to America, beginning in earnest in the 1880s, constituted a momentous and for the most part irreversible decision of a whole people. Greeks, non-Jewish Russians, Slavs, Hungarians, and Italians were certainly in motion during these years, and significant numbers of them came to the United States. This influx occurred because late in the nineteenth century, countries in Southern and Eastern Europe were integrated into the Atlantic economy at the same time that industrialization was creating millions of jobs in America. As large commercial farms in Europe converted to capital-intensive agriculture in order to compete with American producers, peasant society deteriorated, uprooting large numbers of people.

But none of these other national groups migrated as a people. There were, of course, important similarities between the movement of Jews and the migrations of other groups. Like the Quakers and the French Huguenots, for example, the Jews left Europe in part to escape religious persecution. Like the Poles and Rumanians of the 1890s, the Jews were caught up in the disintegration of a peasant economy and suffered the same traumas of uprooting and transplantation. And like the Italians, Irish, and Chinese, the Jews ended up in ghettos and experienced nativist resentment and discrimination.

But the Jewish experience had unique elements. No other group possessed their degree of historical consciousness as a "nation." Only Jews, after all, left the ghettos of Europe for the ghettos of America. Most non-Jewish immigrants came from independent nations in which they had been citizens, or at least unsegregated subjects. In addition, they represented only a small percentage of the societies they left behind. Moreover, large numbers of these non-Jewish migrants, approximately 30 percent, returned to their homelands after sojourning here. Jews, on the other hand, left their old countries at a stunningly high rate; 33 percent of the Jewish population left Eastern Europe between 1880 and 1920, and after 1905 only small numbers, ranging between 5 and 8 percent, returned.

Although the collective movement of the Jewish people was an extraordinary if not wholly unprecedented event, only a tiny minority left Eastern Europe in organized groups or with ideological intent. A small number of Biluim, Zionist pioneers who departed for the ancient homeland of the Jewish people, constitute one example. The members of the Am olam movement, who also sought new soil in which to replant and re-form Jewish life through socialist agriculture, were another. More frequent, however, were the thousands, ultimately millions of uprootings and departures based on individual and family struggles and decisions. Yet the unorganized mass of Jews who left resembled in important ways the dedicated members of the much smaller Am olam and Zionist movements, for theirs too was a collective enterprise filled with hope. And "every emigrating Jew," insisted Abraham Cahan, soon "realized he was involved in something more than a personal expedition . . . [that] he was part of an historical event in the life of the Jewish people . . . .Even Jewish workers and small tradesmen . . . joined . . . the move westward to start a new Jewish life. They did so with religious fervor and often with inspiring self-sacrifice."

The powerful combination of physical wretchedness and spiritual hope pushed the Jews out of Eastern Europe; the lure of openness and tolerance, economic opportunity, and the possibilities for new modes of living pulled them toward America. They were responding to visions of their own making, but also, as with other immigrant groups, to American realities. The United States in the late nineteenth century was undergoing an economic revolution. Since its beginnings in the 1870s, the increasing rationalization of agricultural production was already significantly changing the nature of the U.S. economy. In 1880 about 50 percent of the work force was in agriculture; by 1920 little more than 25 percent remained tied to the land. The completion of a number of transcontinental railroads in the 1880s contributed to the phenomenal growth of the economy, as did an unprecedented level of industrial mechanization and capital investment between 1870 and 1890. In these years, the United States experienced a 28 percent growth in the number of its industries and a net increase of 168 percent in the value of production. Between 1880 and 1920 this rapidly expanding industrial economy created tens of millions of jobs for immigrants to fill.

Though some cautious, old-country periodicals warned that "there is no land which devours its lazy inhabitants and those not suited to physical labor like the land of America," few paid heed. Between 1881 and 1910, 1,562,800 Eastern European Jewish immigrants, 73 percent of whom were from the Russian Empire, arrived in the United States. The two million mark was surpassed in 1914, and another quarter of a million Jews arrived before 1924.

Letters containing information about job opportunities, wages, and depressions acted as stimuli or brakes. The cost of transportation also affected the numbers who would come. But modest changes in the rate of Jewish immigration pale in the face of the overall numbers for 1881–1924. Moreover, and in strikingly higher proportion than for other migrating groups, the *goldene medine* (golden land) remained the destination of choice for Jews. More than three million of them crossed borders in Eastern Europe in these years. Seven percent went to Western Europe; between 10 and 13 percent to Canada, Australia, Argentina, South Africa, and Palestine; but more than 80 percent ended up in the United States.

Leaving was not particularly easy. Numerous obstacles stood in the way, not the least of which was the lengthy, circuitous expedition out of Russia, Rumania, and Galicia. There was the thirty-four dollars (by 1903) to pay for a steamship ticket, and more money was necessary for passports and various bribes along the way. Somehow vast numbers of Jews scraped together the money. One young mother in a story by Anzia Yezierska said, after listening to a letter from America filled with good news, "Sell my red quilted petticoat." Her children immediately suggested the feather beds and the samovar. "Sure," the mother said, "we can sell everything." Families often did sell everything, which brought them just enough money to get to Western Europe, where they reembarked to arrive finally in the New World, penniless and bereft of possessions.

In Western Europe the emigrants' difficulties did not quite disappear. They even faced being sent back by Jewish organizations anxious to help the victims of the pogroms but afraid that the refugees might engulf their countries. Trouble was especially intense in the pogrom-ridden years of 1881–83 and 1903–6, when Jewish migration resembled mass flight. But in the face of growing numbers of refugees who refused to be repatriated and who steadfastly resisted being sent to the United States without their families, the Westerners began to accept the reality of mass Jewish migration from Eastern Europe.

Between 1905 and 1914, 700,000 East European Jews passed through Germany, and 210,000 were directly aided by the Hilfsverein der Deutschen Juden, a group of German Jewish associations. Baron Maurice de Hirsch, heir of financiers to the Bavarian royal court, who made several fortunes in banking and railway finance, contributed large amounts to improve the condition of East European Jews. In the late 1880s, however, after the pogroms and mass expulsions from Russian cities, the baron encouraged emigration, and in 1891 he set up the Jewish Colonization Society with vast programs for international resettlement.

While organized efforts at resettlement were important, they played a small part compared to the migration of the vast majority of individuals and families who came to America on their own resources. The journey of these people, as well as those who were directly aided in the immigration process, continued to be filled with tribulation even at ports of departure such as Hamburg, Bremen, and Antwerp. All travelers, even those with legal passports, had to deal with conmen and thieves, not to mention the bewildering confusion of various bureaucracies and the officious manner of German authorities, who, fearful of plague and other diseases, conducted innumerable inspections before allowing passengers to embark. There were questions upon questions, disinfections, and the constant fear of being sent back or quarantined for "medical reasons."

Even after successfully negotiating all the hurdles of boarding, the emigrants faced the grueling transatlantic passage, a thirteen- to twenty-day voyage in the primitive conditions of steerage class. A steerage berth was an iron bunk with a straw mattress and no pillow. Only two water closets were available in steerage, and both were used by both sexes at the same time. There was a shortage of receptacles to use in case of seasickness, and as the voyage progressed, conditions became filthy and unbearable.

The end of the voyage did not mean the end of bewilderment. Still to be negotiated were the admissions procedures at Castle Garden and later, at Ellis Island. Authorities in New York had failed to anticipate the massive wave of immigration, which led to overcrowding and its attendant ills. In addition, corruption added to the problems. Some immigrants were overcharged for the shipment of baggage, and many were bilked by moneychangers who hung

about the Battery looking for easy prey. Complaints mounted, and the federal government took over the supervision of incoming aliens, opening Ellis
Island as a modern immigration center in 1892.

As with many reforms, this one was inadequate. New York, the United
States' most active port, received approximately 70 percent of newcomers
from all nations. An estimated 5,000 immigrants per day were inspected at
Ellis Island, and on April 17, 1907, the busiest day in the island's history,
11,745 immigrants were processed. Between 1899 and 1910, 86 percent of
the Jews heading for the United States landed in the North Atlantic states,
the vast majority in New York City. The overworked and often insensitive
immigration officials checked the new arrivals for tuberculosis (considered
"the Jewish disease"), "dull-wittedness," eye and scalp problems, contagious
and "loathsome" diseases, and other "defects." Squeezed into massive halls in
dozens of lines, the newcomers underwent incessant pushing, prying, and
poking. Whenever suspicions were aroused, immigrants had their clothes
marked with chalk and were isolated. Approximately one out of six underwent further medical checking.

Women traveling alone were a special problem because immigration
officials feared they would fall into the hands of the white slave traders who
operated around the docks and frequented Ellis Island looking for young
prospects. The women were interrogated more intensely and often detained
until relatives or husbands came to escort them from the processing center.

Whereas the average immigrant passed through Ellis Island in a matter
of hours, detainees could be there for as long as two weeks. And for those
(between 1% and 2.5%) "diagnosed" as having "loathsome and dangerous
contagious diseases" or judged so deficient either physically or mentally that
they were seen as "likely to become a public charge," there was no admit-
tance, only the ordeal of a return trip to Europe.

Jewish immigrant aid societies tried to help, and the German Jews
extended a hand, but it was not until the East European Jews on their own
established the Hebrew Sheltering and Immigrant Aid Society (HIAS) in 1892
that substantial relief was achieved. By 1897, the society had grown into an
organization that combined under one roof facilities for skills training, interpreters, legal aid, temporary housing, and an employment agency.

Leaders of the German Jewish community had admitted in the 1880s,
mostly in the pages of the *American Hebrew,* that "immigration was not popular among our people" and claimed that the "mode of life" of the Russian Jew
"has stamped upon them the ineffaceable marks of permanent pauperism."
Nothing but "disgrace and a lowering of the opinion in which American Is-

raelites are held . . . can result from the continued residence among us of these wretches." Even prior to the flight from the first widespread Russian pogroms (1881–83), which appeared to threaten the Germans with a significantly increased burden of impoverished Eastern newcomers, many of the philanthropic agencies cautioned against open immigration. Indeed, in 1880 the United Hebrew Charities of New York and the newspaper *American Hebrew* urged the passage of restrictive immigration laws.

High cost was often cited as the reason for reluctance to welcome masses of immigrants from Eastern Europe. The Union of American Hebrew Congregations, suspecting that West European Jewish organizations were "dumping" Eastern immigrants on American Jewry, stated early that it "no longer assumes any charge of . . . material aid for the immigrants arriving in the United States."

But the opposition by German Jews to the unrestricted immigration of East European Jews was more directly tied to class and cultural differences and to social insecurity than to the economic burden they might become. A representative of the United Charities of Rochester called the Yiddish-speaking Russian Jews "a bane to the country and a curse to all Jews" and warned that the "enviable reputation" German Jews had earned in the United States was being "undermined by the influx of thousands who are not ripe for enjoyment of liberty." All "who mean well for the Jewish name should prevent them as much as possible from coming here."

From as early as the 1870s, when the Eastern Europeans were few in number, German Jews in America and in Europe alike, though generous materially, shunned their less acculturated coreligionists. Though there were few visible reminders of their peddler origins, the German Jews in the 1880s were apparently too insecure to feel comfortable with the poverty, the Yiddish, the Orthodoxy, and the socialism of the new arrivals.

In the last three decades of the nineteenth century, the discomfort of the German Jews was significantly increased by two important simultaneous changes: the immigration from Eastern Europe became massive, and anti-Semitism in America intensified. Anti-Jewish feeling in the late nineteenth century was the product of a complex constellation of forces. It was tied to general nativism, rooted mainly in agrarian regions, and was reinforced by urban elites who perceived their own displacement in a rapidly changing society. Anti-Jewish feeling was also promoted by the *nouveaux riches*. Raised to believe in the ideal of a traditional, stable, nonacquisitive social order, Protestant strivers were troubled by their own materialistic pursuits. The newly wealthy, however, could find in the classic stereotype of the grasping, rootless Jew, rather than in their own behavior, the "reason" for the decline of stability and "community" and for the rise of the new individualistic world of commercial exploitation.

In an era of rapid industrial and demographic change and of increasing mobility and heterogeneity, many people demanded a simple explanation for increasingly complex conditions that they no longer controlled. Farmers, for example, were confused and angered by the frequent whiplashing they took from market forces and by their precipitous decline in status. In the 1870s and into the 1880s, farmers mostly blamed the railroads and the middlemen, upon whom they had become more and more dependent. By the mid-1880s the farmers, almost always debtors, found themselves caught in a deflationary cycle. Not only was the money they owed worth more than the money they had borrowed, but the prices for their products were seriously declining. Many came to believe in the existence of a conspiracy designed to cheat them of the fruits of their labor through the curtailment of the quantity of money and through other forms of currency manipulation, and they increasingly turned their wrath toward the banking system and government fiscal policy. With stereotypes long held and images deeply embedded in Christian tradition, it was but a short jump from banks and government to polemics about "money changers in the temple" or city Jews heading up a worldwide system of money control.

Prejudice against Jews is diffused in the United States because of the absence of a national church and because anti-Semitism has had to compete here with other forms of animus, particularly anti-Black and anti-Indian racism and anti-Catholicism. Also, Jews in newly formed, relatively modern America did not, as they did in Europe, have to go through any process of "emancipation" from medieval bonds. For these reasons, American anti-Semitism has been milder than the European versions. But an important measure of Jew-hatred was carried to the United States at the very birth of the nation; and it found a reception here through long-nourished myths that portrayed Jews as a people "eternally alien" to Christendom and as unscrupulous moneylenders. These myths were reinforced by the works of patrician intellectuals, writers, and political polemicists such as Henry Adams, William Harvey, and Populist Ignatius Donnelly. America's money difficulties and her social and cultural decline were traced to Jews such as Hartbeest Schneidekoupon (coupon clipper) in Adams's novel *Democracy* (1880) or to rapacious Jews in total political and financial control in Donnelly's futuristic book *Caesar's Column* (1890), as well as to the ruthless, anti-American, pro-

British Jew, Baron Rothe, in William Harvey's "historical fiction" *A Tale of Two Nations* (1894).

Rude economic wrenchings in the 1890s provided the context for an even greater intensification of negative feelings about Jews. A depression beginning early in 1893 was deepened by a stock market panic in May, and by mid-1894 the economy appeared exhausted. Farmers reeled at the collapse of wheat and cotton prices. Banks and businesses failed at astonishing rates. Joblessness mounted, reaching as high as 20 percent, and Coxey's "army of the unemployed" was marching in protest on Washington. The violent Pullman strike followed thereafter, soon to be crushed by federal troops sent to Illinois by President Cleveland. And by the end of 1894, the Populist Party, with its monetary planks and demands for inflation, was making an important challenge to the strength of the Democratic and Republican parties in the West and South. People worried about how far the crisis would carry the nation from "its old ways" or how many institutions were still fated to fall.

Victims, and those who perceived themselves as victims, of the crisis cried for a quick and simple solution, and the understandable confusion over the complexity of causes only increased the dogmatism about the cure. Political rhetoric was filled with images of money conspiracies implicitly and sometimes explicitly tied to Jews. When William Jennings Bryan, campaigning for the presidency in 1896, peppered his diatribes against the gold standard with Christian images, he simply—even if inadvertently—added fuel to the fires of conspiracy theories which had been burning for more than two decades. These theories, in the historian Richard Hofstadter's words, did not exceed a kind of "rhetorical vulgarity" since no explicit action was urged against Jews as such, but writing and rhetoric filled with anti-Semitic allusions and phrases such as "crucifixion upon a cross of gold" or "put all moneylenders to death" made Jews, especially the conspicuously successful German Jews, wary.

Moreover, from the late 1870s through the 1890s, anti-Semitism went beyond the printed page and the speeches of politicians. As was noted in Chapter 3, there was in these years significant widespread social discrimination against Jews as well as sporadic anti-Semitic harassment and violence, particularly in the South.

The objective members of the more established German Jewish community in the United States admitted that the arrival of the new breed of Jews from Eastern Europe did not cause the anti-Semitism; nevertheless, many believed the immigrant presence promised only to intensify it. And at

Table 2. GENERAL AND JEWISH IMMIGRATION FROM EASTERN EUROPE TO THE UNITED STATES, 1871–1920

	General	Jewish	% Jewish
1871–80	2,810,000	15,000	0.5
1881–84	2,580,340	74,310	2.9
1885	395,350	19,610	4.9
1886	334,200	29,660	8.8
1887	490,110	27,470	5.6
1888	547,000	31,360	5.7
1889	444,430	24,000	5.4
1890	455,300	34,300	7.5
1891	560,320	69,140	12.3
1892	579,660	60,325	10.4
1893	440,000	33,000	7.5
1894	285,630	22,110	7.7
1895	258,540	32,080	12.4
1896	343,270	28,120	8.2
1897	330,830	20,685	6.25
1898	229,300	27,410	11.9
1899	311,715	37,415	12.0
1900	448,570	60,475	13.5
1901	488,000	58,100	11.9
1902	648,745	57,670	8.9
1903	857,050	76,205	8.9
1904	812,870	106,240	13.1
1905	1,026,500	129,910	12.7
1906	1,100,735	153,750	14.0
1907	1,285,350	149,180	11.6
1908	782,870	103,390	13.2
1909	751,790	57,550	7.7
1910	1,041,570	84,260	8.1
1911	878,590	91,225	10.4
1912	838,170	80,595	9.6
1913	1,197,890	101,330	8.5
1914	1,218,480	138,050	11.3
1915	326,700	26,500	8.1
1916	298,825	15,110	5.1
1917	295,405	17,340	5.9
1918	110,620	3,670	3.3
1919	141,130	3,055	2.2
1920	430,000	14,290	3.3

first the German Jews fought open immigration or sought to disperse the immigrants to rural areas. After 1891, however, the desperate straits of Russian Jews under the reign of Nicholas II transcended considerations of material comfort among the established American Jews and even worry over the rise of anti-Semitism. Indeed, at the same time that Americans generally inclined toward restriction, leaders of the German Jewish community committed themselves to open immigration as well as to aiding the East Europeans materially. And while occasionally warning against the possibility of millions of Eastern Jews pouring "pell-mell . . . into the country," the editors of the *American Hebrew* and several older German Jewish organizations such as the B'nai B'rith vehemently resisted all legislative efforts to curtail Jewish immigration.

The united effort to beat back the restrictionists was necessary to counteract nativist pressure, which in the last two decades of the nineteenth century moved Congress toward curtailing immigration. From the end of the Civil War to the early 1880s, a relatively optimistic period in U.S. history, Americans were generally tolerant of immigration; and industrial manufacturers seeking cheap labor were positively encouraging, as were state governments. Beginning in the 1880s, however, a series of challenges to the national confidence brought nativism to the center of American thought and behavior.

The rapidly changing society of the 1880s and 1890s, though often celebrated in terms of "progress," was also feared for its power to destabilize and complicate life. During this same period the number of immigrants entering the United States markedly increased; there were more than 2.5 million new arrivals between 1881 and 1884, equaling total immigration for the entire decade of the 1870s. Another 5.5 million arrived by 1898, and a stunning 15 million more by 1920 (see table 2).

As important as the increasing numbers between 1880 and 1920 was the visible shift in the geographic origins of the foreign born. In 1880, 82 percent of foreign-born persons residing in the United States had emigrated from Germany, Ireland, or elsewhere in Northwestern Europe. Another 11 percent came from Canada, and only 4 percent were from Southern and East-

---

Table 2 *(Continued)*

Sources: U.S. Bureau of the Census, *Historical Statistics of the United States to 1957* (Washington, D.C.: Government Printing Office, 1976); Samuel Joseph, *Jewish Immigration to the United States from 1881 to 1910* (New York: Arno Press, 1969); Simon Kuznets, "Immigration of Russian Jews to the United States: Background and Structure," *Perspectives in American History* 9 (1975): 35–124.

ern Europe. In stark contrast, by 1920, 46 percent of America's foreign born had come from Southern and Eastern Europe. Not only were the "new immigrants," according to historian John Higham, disproportionately Catholic and Jewish relative to the majority of the American population, but they were also seen as disproportionately radical, and "they had an exotic look about them for ethnological as well as cultural reasons." The "thought of European immigration [after 1881] suggested strange images of Mediterranean, Slavic and Jewish types."

Advocates of an "Anglo-Saxon" America argued for the need to decrease radically the number of immigrants and to be more selective. Restrictionist pressures against the "menace" of open immigration bore fruit. From as early as 1882, with the Chinese Exclusion Act, Congress began to pass a series of laws to regulate and limit immigration. Up to World War I most of the bills for radically restricting the number of immigrants were defeated. But several that did pass caused problems for Jewish immigrants, including an 1891 act that called for the exclusion of persons with a "loathsome or dangerous contagious disease." Although deportations rarely exceeded 1 percent of arrivals, the proportion of those rejected on medical grounds increased significantly between 1895 and 1914.

The "new" immigrants were no less healthy than the "old"; increased deportations were mostly the product of prejudice, new biomedical thinking, and the bureaucratic zeal of Public Health Service officers. Responding to the dire needs of Russian refugees and to the increase in subjective exclusions, several major national Jewish bodies—including the B'nai B'rith, the Union of American Hebrew Congregations, HIAS, and the American Jewish Committee, newly formed in 1906 to defend Jewish interests—joined in protest against restriction and the anti-Semitism inherent in it.

Any ambivalence on the part of German Jewish leadership regarding the mass influx of Russian Jews disappeared in the face of the horrors of the pogroms in Russia between 1903 and 1906. Not only were these years a peak period of mass murderous violence against Jews in Eastern Europe, but they were also the peak years of Jewish immigration to America. The German Jewish organizations, responding to the depredations in Russia, dedicated themselves to a full-scale campaign to defeat the efforts of the restrictionists. There were already clear signs in the first decade of the twentieth century that the direction in U.S. politics was toward curtailment of immigration. In 1909, congressmen leaning strongly in the direction of restriction began an investigation of immigration. They concluded their work in late 1910 with a forty-volume report recommending a basic shift in government policy from regulation to limitation.

In the immigration struggle the German Jews sharpened their skills in the art of quiet diplomacy. Louis Marshall, a brilliant attorney and for many years the president of the American Jewish Committee, played a crucial role here. Along with men such as attornies Max Kohler and Simon Wolf and philanthropist Cyrus Sulzberger, Marshall opposed the restrictionists in print, in legislative battles, and in private meetings with political leaders. In the hope of eroding anti-immigration and anti-Semitic sentiment and forestalling restrictionist action, they also encouraged and helped organize the dispersal of East European Jews from the urban centers of the American Northeast to the interior of the country. In non-Jewish circles the German Jews insisted that the immigrant newcomers actually enriched the northeastern cities in which they resided. The Germans challenged the negative stereotypes of the Jewish immigrants publicly and head on, pointing with pride to the East Europeans' admirable qualities—their virtuous home life, healthy ambition, drive for education, and low level of crime and disease. Paradoxically, at the same time, they feverishly engaged in plans to empty ghettos and direct newcomers to other areas.

The Germans consistently coaxed and prodded the immigrants to Americanize as well as to disperse. The established Jews, often mirroring values current in the Progressive era (c. 1900–1917), wanted their Old-World coreligionists to discard "alien" social habits that made the newcomers embarrassingly visible and stood in the way of rational, efficient adaptation. From the beginning, Yiddish was targeted as an "anachronistic jargon," and Orthodoxy as an "irrational set of superstitions." The German Jewish philanthropists also called for an unquestioning compliance with U.S. law and a repudiation of radical political ideologies such as socialism and anarchism.

Dispersal and Americanization were connected in the minds of established Jews and reflected the environmentalist ideology of the Progressive era. The areas of urban Jewish concentration were viewed by the German Jewish community as ghettos that tended to perpetuate a distinctively foreign life style. Relocated to the interior of the country, the East European immigrant, it was thought, would be unable to depend on a Yiddish-speaking environment and would be forced to acculturate more rapidly.

The East Europeans were indeed crowded into the great cities of the East and Midwest. Of nearly 1.5 million Jews who arrived in New York between 1881 and 1911, more than 73 percent remained there. Moreover, as

many as 60 percent of the Jews in the nation were located in the northeastern corridor from Boston to Baltimore, with another 30 percent in Cleveland, Pittsburgh, Chicago, and other urban centers of the Midwest. Like other
urban newcomers in the period from 1880 to 1920, Eastern European Jews
massed together in ethnic enclaves, including Chicago's West Side, Boston's
North End, South Philadelphia, and New York's Lower East Side.

By 1900, in response to growing worry about Jewish congestion in the
cities, the dispersal idea began to receive even more serious consideration.
B'nai B'rith, now a major national organization, joined those advocating dispersion, and the Baron de Hirsch Fund brought the Jewish Colonization
Society, renamed the Jewish Agricultural and Industrial Aid Society, to the
United States. Interested mainly in creating a class of American Jewish farmers, the society helped finance more than 160 agricultural settlements.

In 1901 the society also created the Industrial Removal Office, whose
job it was to relocate Jewish immigrants individually to smaller Jewish communities throughout the United States. Centered in New York but with
dozens of local committees, usually organized by B'nai B'rith lodges, the
office extended across the entire country and operated as a nonprofit employment agency. The committees kept the main branch informed about the availability of jobs in their cities and towns and committed themselves to accepting a monthly quota of immigrants.

The New York Industrial Removal Office placed advertisements in the
Yiddish newspapers, and by the end of the first year, over fifteen hundred
persons had been relocated. By 1917 the organization, after more than a
decade and a half of activity—mostly under the able and devoted direction
of David Bressler, a young lawyer who became general manager in 1903—
had relocated more than seventy-five thousand persons to 1,670 cities and
towns in all forty-eight states and Canada.

But it soon became clear that the vast majority of Jews who came to
New York City or Boston or Philadelphia would never leave. A number who
came directly from the *shtetlekh* of Eastern Europe disliked cites and went on
to small towns. But the seventy-five thousand who did relocate under the
auspices of the Industrial Removal Office between 1901 and 1917 represented only 6 percent of the Jewish newcomers to the United States. The
German enthusiasm for social engineering was not generally shared by the
potential beneficiaries. The ethnic enclaves or voluntary ghettos of the great
cities provided anchors for the newly uprooted. The urban Jewish neighborhoods supplied familiarity, friends, relatives, synagogues, kosher meat and
Hebrew teachers. The ghetto meant *yiddishkayt*.

The absence of a wider Jewish fellowship and the limited cultural opportunities of the small towns discouraged immigrants from relocating to the hinterlands. Indeed, even the newest arrivals, not yet directly familiar with New York but aware of the promise of the great city, were reluctant to choose the American interior. An experiment undertaken by the Industrial Removal Office in 1902 to persuade newcomers being processed at Ellis Island to settle in the interior was an abysmal failure and was abandoned after less than two years of operation.

And still the flood of immigrants continued. In 1903 and on through 1906, new waves of pogroms broke out in Russia. With Congress in these years coming closer and closer to serious immigration restriction, it appeared to many American Jewish leaders, particularly the noted banker and German-born philanthropist Jacob Schiff, that something more effective had to be devised to distribute the Russian Jewish refugees throughout the United States. In a private letter he asked Judge Mayer Sulzberger of Philadelphia to think about what could be done "not only to divert the stream of [Eastern] immigrants into the American 'Hinterland,' but even to promote a considerably larger immigration than we now receive." Clearly, Schiff not only was concerned with the deflection and dispersal of immigrants; he also wanted, as he told the *New York Times,* to "take every one of our persecuted people out of Russia and bring them to the United States."

The German Jewish leaders continued to believe that the most effective way to defuse popular support for restriction legislation was to distribute the Eastern immigrants throughout America. And by 1904 they reached the conclusion that only by rerouting the immigrant stream to new ports could newcomers be induced to settle in areas other than the northeastern and large midwestern cities. In 1906 a bill establishing an entry station for immigrants in Galveston, Texas, was being debated in Congress. Jacob Schiff and others, including Oscar Straus, secretary of commerce and labor, under whose jurisdiction immigration lay, used their influence to secure passage of the bill. Schiff, like Louis Marshall and Simon Wolf, saw himself as a steward, obligated along the lines set forth in Andrew Carnegie's famous "Gospel of Wealth" essay to take on the burdens of the community. Once again, however, the philanthropists took little account of economic realities and immigrant preferences. By 1914, after seven years of operation, the Galveston Plan had deflected no more than 10,000 immigrants (about 1.2%) from the ports of the Northeast.

Another suggested solution to the problem of impending restriction was to create a class of Jewish farmers. The stewards, including the Baron de

Hirsch, hoped by the Galveston Plan both to achieve distribution of immigrants and to "exterminate peddling and petty trading"—the allegedly unproductive, "abnormal" pursuits of the Eastern Jews. But the largest number of Jewish farm families in America, 3,040 (reached in 1909), contained a total of fifteen thousand people, less than 1 percent of the Jewish population.

The meager impact of farming ought not to come as a surprise. Jewish farmers were not the only agriculturalists who failed in this era. The attempt to "return Jews to the soil" ran counter to the worldwide advance of industrialization as well as the prevailing economic trends in the United States. Despite the country's rise to the position of the world's largest agricultural producer, the number of male workers in agriculture dropped from 39.6 to 35.8 percent of all gainfully employed men in the United States between 1900 and 1910.

The economic opportunities for Jews, as well as the cultural familiarities in cities, large and small, were simply unmatched in the hinterland. The vast majority of East European Jews recognized this early and either refused to leave the urban areas or soon returned to them. Agricultural colonization as a vehicle for significant dispersion was quickly given up. And as early as 1907 the Industrial Removal Office also admitted that "no wholesale solution to our problem is possible." By 1910 it was clear also that the Galveston experiment, although beneficial in many individual cases, was a failure in terms of large-scale deflection and distribution. The transplantation of Jews to America's cities and larger towns, however, proved increasingly successful.

5

Transplanted
in America:
The Urban Experience

East European Jews forged a unique transitional culture in the cities of the United States for almost four decades. Fashioned out of Old World tradition and New World experience, the immigrant culture of the Lower East Side of New York, the West Side of Chicago, South Philadelphia, and other Jewish urban neighborhoods helped ease the pain of accommodation for a people whose recent experience combined several kinds of dramatic change. Jews had been physically uprooted from the familiar small-town world of Eastern Europe, through its cities, and on to the bewildering vastness of America. They underwent a radical shift in class status, mainly from artisan, craftsman, and petty merchant to proletarian; and despite major links of continuity, they suffered a separation from the longstanding moral context supportive of Jewish tradition. Furthermore, they often experienced the breakup or at least the temporary disruption of family as sons and daughters left older parents behind and husbands preceded wives and children to the United States.

The immigrants ultimately experienced the Lower East Side of New York, as well as the North End of Boston and East Baltimore as fertile ground for cultural sustenance and renewal. But they initially confronted the ghettos of urban America as a stark, concrete reality of congested streets, poor housing, and cramped and dangerous work spaces. New York was America's largest city; it was also the most densely populated and the most cosmopolitan. With many of its neighborhoods crowded with immigrants from many different parts of the world, who by 1900 constituted more than 75 percent of the city's constantly growing population, New York represented most closely the simmering American stew pot.

Of the twenty-three million immigrants to the United States between 1880 and 1920, seventeen million came through the port of New York, and many stayed in that city. But no one, not even the Italians, outdid the Jews. Practically all East European Jewish immigrants arriving after 1870 initially found their way to the Lower East Side, and the vast majority, from Russia, Hungary, Galicia, Rumania, and a smaller number of Sephardic Jews (who had fled Turkey, Greece, and Syria in the wake of the Turkish Revolt of 1908, the Balkan Wars of 1912–13, and World War I) remained within its nucleus, a twenty-square-block area south of Houston Street and east of the Bowery.

By 1892, 75 percent of the city's Jews lived on the Lower East Side. The percentage declined with time, but the absolute number continued to climb until it reached its peak of 542,000 in 1910. Already by the turn of the century, some blocks of the Lower East Side approached the astounding population of 1,000 inhabitants per acre. Only Bombay and Calcutta had higher densities.

Jews in New York enjoyed the luxury of numbers and diversity. More than 1.5 million strong by 1920, they were the city's largest single ethnic group. But whether in New York on Hester and Orchard streets, in Chicago on Halstead and Maxwell streets, or in Philadelphia on William Street, the scene was crowded and unkempt. Indeed, in Chicago, Philadelphia, Boston, Baltimore, and a dozen other cities, early East European Jewish neighborhoods were most often located in the older, deteriorating sections. A 1901 housing survey noted that nearly half the dwellings in the heart of Chicago's Jewish neighborhoods were dangerous, ill-ventilated tenements with poor drainage, little light, and no baths. In the Jewish sections of Philadelphia, Gaskell and Kater streets were especially notorious for their decaying wooden "bandbox" houses, animal excrement encrusted in the cobblestone alleyways, and visible evidence of crime and prostitution. These streets were not very different from those dominated by immigrant Jews in other cities such as Newark, Minneapolis, and Buffalo, in every region of the United States. Atlanta's Decatur Street, for example, a main commercial thoroughfare and more than 50 percent Jewish, was lined with dilapidated buildings and stores intermixed with saloons and pool halls, which together with the houses of prostitution nearby gave the neighborhood an offensive reputation.

Still, the condition of the streets was often preferable to the constriction of the tiny living quarters. One immigrant boarding with the family of a cantor remembered that his two-room apartment on Allen Street on the Lower East Side of New York contained the parents, six children, and five other boarders. Two daughters took in dresses to sew at home, and one boarder plied his shoemaking craft in the apartment as well. The "cantor rehearses, a train passes, the shoemaker bangs, ten brats run around like goats, the wife putters in her 'kosher restaurant.' At night we all try to get some sleep in the stifling roach-infested two rooms."

Only a small number of Lower East Side apartments had hot running water, and there was often only one hallway toilet for every ten people. There were also few fire escapes in the crowded buildings. These conditions persisted despite remedial legislation in the late nineteenth century. Even after the building construction reforms of 1903 and as late as 1908, there were still three hundred thousand dark, unventilated interior rooms south of Houston Street, and between 1902 and 1909, the Lower East Side, with less than 20 percent of the population, suffered 38 percent of the fire fatalities for all of Manhattan.

Despite the dangers and lack of amenities, new immigrant Jews continued to pour into the Lower East Side and to a lesser degree into Chicago's West End and other Jewish population centers in Philadelphia and Boston. Indeed, by 1920 more than 72 percent of Jewish Americans resided in major cities: New York contained 45 percent; Chicago and Philadelphia together accounted for 13 percent; and seven other large or mid-size cities in the East and Midwest accounted for an additional 14 percent (see table 3). In these cities as early as the 1880s, immigrants were recreating, reweaving, and transplanting *yiddishkayt*, their Yiddish-based culture, as well as a Jewish communal existence, which helped them gain some measure of control over the process of Americanization.

Equally important to providing *yiddishkayt*, the ghettos, particularly the largest one on New York's Lower East Side, offered the possibility of employment for Jews. At the time the masses of East European Jews were coming to America, the garment industry, for example, was undergoing rapid expansion, and New York City was central to this development. Between 1899 and 1914 nearly 67 percent of the gainfully employed Jewish immigrants— a much higher proportion than any other incoming national group—possessed industrial skills, many in garment work, one of the few occupations open to Jews in nineteenth-century Europe. By 1897 approximately 60 percent of the New York Jewish labor force was employed in the apparel field, and 75 percent of the workers in the industry were Jewish. Jewish concentration in the clothing field was evident outside New York as well. A plural-

Table 3.   Cities with the Largest Jewish Population, in Rank Order

	1878		1907	
New York	60,000		600,000	(33.0)
Chicago	10,000		100,000	(5.6)
Philadelphia	12,000		100,000	(5.6)
Baltimore	10,000		40,000	(2.2)
Boston	7,000		60,000	(3.3)
Cleveland	3,500		40,000	(2.2)
Newark	3,500		30,000	(1.7)
Detroit	2,000		10,000	
Pittsburgh	2,000		25,000	(1.4)
Los Angeles	330		7,000	

	1927		1948	
New York	1,765,000	(44.0)	2,000,000	(40.0)
Chicago	325,000	(8.0)	300,000	(6.0)
Philadelphia	270,000	(6.7)	245,000	(4.9)
Boston	90,000	(2.3)	137,350	(2.7)
Cleveland	85,000	(2.1)	80,000	(1.6)
Detroit	75,000	(1.9)	90,000	(1.8)
Newark	65,000	(1.6)	56,800	(1.1)
Los Angeles	65,000	(1.6)	225,000	(4.5)
Pittsburgh	53,000	(1.3)	54,000	(1.8)
Baltimore	48,000	(1.2)	75,000	(1.5)

	1977		1992	
New York	1,998,000	(34.6)	1,450,000	(25.0)
Los Angeles	455,000	(7.9)	500,870	(8.6)
Miami/Ft.Lauderdale	225,000	(3.9)	330,000	(5.7)
Chicago	253,000	(4.4)	261,008	(4.5)
Philadelphia	350,000	(6.0)	250,008	(4.3)
Bergen/Essex, NJ	195,000	(3.3)	160,008	(2.7)
Boston	170,000	(3.0)	228,000	(3.9)
Washington, DC	120,000	(2.0)	165,000	(2.8)
Baltimore	92,000	(1.6)	94,500	(1.6)
San Francisco	75,000	(1.2)	210,000	(3.6)

Sources: Lee Shai Weissbach, "The Jewish Communities of the United States on the Eve of Mass Migration: Some Comments on Geography and Bibliography," *American Jewish History* 78:1 (September 1988): 79–108; Arthur Goren, *The American Jews* (Cambridge: Harvard University Press, 1982); Jacob Rader Marcus, *United States Jewry, 1776–1985* (Detroit: Wayne State University Press, 1993), 4:744; *American Jewish Year Book* (1977), (1993). Numbers in parentheses represent percentage of U.S. Jewry.

ity of Philadelphia's Jews—40 percent in the 1890s—and significant percentages of those in Baltimore and Boston found skilled and semiskilled employment in the garment industry, sometimes in the factories but at least as
often in the contracting or sweatshop systems.

Contracting utilized section work, which encouraged a minute division
of labor. The contractor, usually an immigrant who had been in America
somewhat longer than the newest arrivals or "greenhorns," picked up cut,
unsewn garments from the manufacturer and then supervised in his own
home or in a loft or tenement room converted to a shop, a group of opera-
tors, basters, pressers, finishers, buttonholers, and pocket makers. Some
section and finishing work was given to a subcontractor who found people
willing to take that work into their own apartments.

Exploitation, including exploitation of one's self (as the contractors
and subcontractors and their family members often worked alongside the
employees), was more intense in the sweatshop tenement rooms, lofts, and
apartments, than in factories or "inside shops." The contractor's profit margin was low and so therefore was pay. The sweatshop, in addition, demanded
extremely long hours in terribly close quarters. In 1894 state investigators
visited the Chicago garment establishments and described the "shops over
sheds or stables, in basements or on upper floors of tenement houses," as "not
fit working places for men, women, and children."

The worst conditions of the factory and the tenement had come together in one place. Yet to the newly arrived immigrants there were advantages to the sweatshop system. The workers could communicate in their own
language. The work, however arduous, did not prevent the performance of
religious duties, the observance of the Sabbath, or the celebration of religious festivals. Moreover, working together in small units, the immigrants
thought they could preserve the integrity of their families.

Nonetheless, nearly 25 percent of Jewish breadwinners moved out of
sweatshop and factory work and into self-employment in small businesses at
the earliest opportunity. In New York's virtually all-Jewish Eighth Assembly
District, there were 144 groceries, 131 butcher shops, 62 candy stores, 36
bakeries, numerous bookbinders and watchmakers, and 2,440 peddlers and
pushcart vendors. In Chicago on the blocks surrounding the intersection of
Halsted and Maxwell streets were found the kosher meat markets and chicken
stores, matzo bakeries, tailor shops, bathhouses, pushcarts, and peddler stalls.
"Every Jew in this quarter," according to an account in the Chicago Tribune in
1891, "is engaged in business of some sort. The favorite occupation, proba-

bly on account of the small capital required, is fruit and vegetable peddling."
There were also peddlers of rags, clothing, scrap iron, and old furniture.

Peddling was enervating, often backbreaking work, with long hours
and low profits. But it was a way of avoiding the oppressive discipline and
monotony of factory and sweatshop labor; and many observant Jews chose to
become pushcart vendors in order to avoid breaking the Sabbath prohibition
on work. Women and even some children, mirroring old-country patterns,
were often involved in the trade as part of the family economy. The New
York City Mayor's Pushcart Commission in 1906 reported that men owners
often had "other occupations [and] regularly . . . let their wives and children
attend to the pushcarts."

In the heart of every pushcart vendor was the hope of becoming the
owner of a "real store." In turn, those who already owned stores dreamed of
expansion. The goal of the peddlers and vendors, then, was not simply to
remain independent of the restrictive environment of the factory; it was also
to take advantage of the market opportunities presented by the ethnic and
religious needs of the East European Jewish community, particularly its food
preferences.

Jewish dietary habits and preferences were determined by a complex
amalgam of regional custom, historical circumstance, and religious law.
Knishes, blintzes, bagels, and bialys, as well as herring and seltzer, were regional food and drink that had become part of the ethnic diet and were
strongly desired. And peddlers, pushcart vendors, and other Jewish entrepreneurs knew how to provide the "cultural symbols" that East Siders craved.

Religious ritual, particularly kashrut (observance of the dietary laws),
was even more important in creating openings in the ethnic economy of the
Lower East Side of New York, in South Philadelphia, and in almost every
other Jewish urban concentration. As only domestic herbivorous animals
that have been humanely slaughtered may be eaten by observant Jews, there
was a need for kosher butchers and shokhetim, or slaughterers, who needed
special training and religious piety to perform what was a sacred ritual.

The mixing of meat and milk products is also prohibited in the kosher
kitchen, to the extent that separate kitchen utensils and dinnerware are required for milk and meat dishes. All of this meant that those who produced
food, sold it, or served it in bakeries, restaurants, and cafes had to take care
to observe the dairy/meat distinctions. Jews would rarely trust anyone but
other Jews in these matters.

In addition, almost every religious holiday celebrated by the Jews involved a special food or beverage: matzo (unleavened bread) and gefilte fish

on Passover, *hamantash* (three-cornered pastry filled with fruit or poppy seeds) at Purim, challah (egg bread) for the traditional Sabbath meal on Friday evenings. In all, about 20 percent of the Jewish community, with their carts, wagons, retail stores, cafés, bakeries, and lunchrooms, were able to survive—some even to prosper—by catering to the remaining 80 percent.

Jewish pushcart vendors and peddlers also sold non-food items. In addition, they extended credit, promoted their wares, and soon introduced high-quality goods. Quick to assess the needs of customers and willing to operate on the lowest margins of profit, Jewish street merchants soon turned the peripheral business of itinerant peddling into a vital retail institution.

Like the Japanese and Chinese in San Francisco and Oakland, California, at the turn of the century, the Jews, with the same Old World cohesion and penchant for small-business enterprise and with similar credit associations, created an ethnic economy in many American cities which provided wide opportunities for Jews seeking employment. But since most immigrants were poor, children often had to be included in the family economy. In future songwriter Irving Berlin's basement apartment on Cherry Street in New York, the four youngest girls were daily "bent over [in] bead work" while the middle brothers worked in a sweatshop. Young Irving brought home the coins he occasionally earned singing songs on corners and in taverns, and at times all the siblings sold papers on the street.

The immigrants knew, mainly from the Yiddish-language press, that by American standards their living conditions were abominable, but they also remembered the outrages of the Old World, where many of them had lived in rundown hovels, fearful of drunken peasants, increasing economic dislocation, oppressive czarist decrees, and government-sponsored pogroms. The vast majority of Jewish immigrants were persuaded and relieved that no matter what else, they had escaped the czars and the *pogromchiks*. Although they continued to suffer separation, poverty, and confusion in the United States, the transplanted Jews could begin to entertain notions of a better life for their sons and daughters, and even for themselves. These visions, combined with cultural memory and the willingness to adapt, promoted a strategy of survival. Jewish immigrants responded to both the American present and the European past in dealing as best they could with their daily burdens. Many determined to escape as quickly as possible, and in the meantime they found solace in small improvements: a fire escape perhaps, a lighted hallway, an apartment free of boarders, a private toilet, or windows on the street. They could even eat during the week what would have been considered in the Old World "holiday" and Sabbath foods.

Despite the generally congested and airless living and working conditions—conditions that normally promote disease—the physical health of the
Jews was surprisingly good in comparison to that of both non-Jewish immigrants and native-born Americans. Personal cleanliness was at times strictly
compelled by Jewish law, and at least one day in the week, in preparation for
the Sabbath, the apartments were thoroughly cleaned.

Jews also may have remained comparatively healthier because of their
sobriety. Jews rarely drank to excess, preferring seltzer to intoxicants. The
comparative death rates from diseases of the liver—diseases linked to consumption of alcohol—are instructive. For East European Jews the rate was
five per one hundred thousand; for immigrants from Germany it was thirty-
two, and for those from Ireland, seventy-one. Even for the native born the
fatality rate from alcoholism was nearly three times the Jewish rate.

While Jews were relatively healthy physically, they were not spared a
large share of maladies associated with nervous stress. The rupture with tradition and the pain of dislocation produced a significant measure of family
instability, neuroses, and mental breakdown, and there was in addition juvenile delinquency and adult criminality. Jewish marital and generational relationships were marked by the strain and struggle of adjustment to new ways
of life; and in the early years of the twentieth century, desertion by Jewish
husbands became disturbingly evident on the Lower East Side of New York,
in the North End of Boston, and in other large cities in the Northeast and
Midwest.

Husbands and wives often adjusted to the new environment at different rates. The husband who preceded wife and family to the United States
sometimes became so Americanized that he felt estranged from the greenhorns when they finally arrived, and some men were tempted to leave. For
some men such as Yekl (Jake, in the New World) in Abe Cahan's novel of the
same name, divorce, rather than desertion, was the way out, and the traditionally close-knit Jewish family on the Lower East Side, for a few years at
least, produced one of the highest divorce rates in the city. The various Jewish charities in New York made some efforts to deal with this problem. Several organizations sponsored "workrooms," which provided job training. They
also supplied day care for unskilled divorced, widowed, and deserted mothers of young children. But most of these workrooms were short lived and
could, in any case, only afford to employ a small proportion of the needy
women.

The problems created by divorce and desertion were acute. In Boston's
North End, for example, there was enough desertion and crime to prompt

the formation of both a Jewish Prisoner Aid Society and a special committee of the National Council of Jewish Women to deal with the situation. In East Baltimore delinquency was described as common, and the absence of fathers compelled the Federation of Jewish Charities to establish a Big Brothers League. In 1913 as many as 20 percent of the Jewish children housed by municipal institutions in New York City were from deserted families, and one of every two Jewish inmates of juvenile reformatories was from a broken home. Even those children who remained with their mothers and siblings suffered from neglect and from the need to help supplement decreased family income.

The memoir literature suggests that among the great majority of fathers who stayed with their families, significant numbers struggled with the temptation to leave and were made tense and irritable in the process. Others, poorly paid and holding jobs lower in status than those they had held in the old countries, appear to have experienced a measure of bewilderment and loss of hope. The problems were intensified by the difficulties of transplanting to America the authority and obedience inherent in the Jewish religious culture of Eastern Europe. The resulting family destabilization made it more likely that some children would go astray and that some young troublemakers would grow up in the ghetto to be adult criminals.

Crime was one route out of the ethnic slums. The Irish were first to dominate the gambling, liquor, and prostitution rackets in the United States. But as they moved into and took over the Democratic Party and machine politics in several northeastern cities, the Irish gained new status and power from control of construction, public utilities, and the docks; and Italians and Jews moved into the rackets.

In an article published in the *North American Review* in 1908, New York City Police Commissioner Theodore A. Bingham claimed that "alien" Jews amounting to only 25 percent of the population furnished 50 percent of all the city's criminals. The claim was soon withdrawn as unfounded, but it continued to rankle, especially as it was reinforced by other articles and government reports. For several years before these articles were published, concerned discussion about East Side delinquency and vice had filled many columns in the Yiddish papers. Moreover, there are enough accounts from Jewish and non-Jewish sources to indicate that prostitution, gambling, and extortion rackets did indeed thrive in the Jewish district, as in every poor district in the city. Although the statistics reported by the police commissioner were greatly exaggerated, crimes and criminals sullied the life of the East Side. The names of Jewish gangsters such as Dopey Benny (Benjamin

Fein), Gyp the Blood (Harry Horowitz), and Kid Dropper (Nathan Kaplan) were well known in the community; and as Mike Gold, in *Jews without Money,* reported, it was hard not to trip over the prostitutes who "sprawled indolently, their legs taking up half the pavement" on Allen Street.

No one was more disturbed by the revelations of Jewish crime in the downtown ghetto than the established, uptown German Jews. Distressed by their political radicalism and religious Orthodoxy and repelled by their "strange ways and speech," the Germans saw the immorality and vice of the East Europeans as a great threat to themselves. "If there should grow up in our midst a class of people abnormal and objectionable to our fellow citizens," read the proceedings of the nineteenth annual convention of the Union of American Hebrew Congregations, "all of us will suffer. . . , the question is largely one of self-preservation."

The uptowners were very taken with Israel Zangwill's 1908 play *The Melting Pot* because they thought they saw in it a reinforcement of their own proposed solution for the problems of downtown: the sooner the immigrants from Eastern Europe gave up their cultural distinctiveness and "melted" into the homogenized mass, the sooner anti-Semitism would also melt.

One of the major social and educational vehicles for melting and remaking the East Europeans was the Educational Alliance. It was for several decades an important source of help to the East European immigrants, as well as a major source of friction and hostility between uptown and downtown Jews. The German Jews poured money, time, and energy into the alliance's Americanization programs. But the sincerity of their efforts continued to be accompanied by cultural arrogance. From 9 A.M. to 10 P.M., a wide range of social, cultural, and educational activities were held in classrooms, meeting rooms, the library, and an auditorium seating seven hundred. A roof garden, and a well-equipped gymnasium installed to overcome the Eastern Jew's "lack of courage and repugnance to physical work" were also in use a good part of the day. While adults were instructed on the "privileges and duties of American citizenship," youngsters were exposed to vocational training, courses in English and English literature, and lectures on American and ancient history. These classes were augmented by training in hygiene, sermons on virtue, and flag-waving exercises on national holidays.

The German effort to Americanize the East Europeans was strongly parallel to the efforts of the Irish, who, as leaders of the American Catholic Church, devoted vast energies and resources to the Americanization of other Catholic ethnics, particularly Italians and Poles. These efforts immediately promoted resistance and in the longer run, an enduring intergroup hostility and conflict. But the Irish had feared that if the greenhorn Italians and Poles did not acculturate quickly, the Catholic Church, which was a target of Protestant nativists, would continue to be regarded as alien, inferior, and un-American. Leaders of the Education Alliance in their *Report of the Committee on Moral Culture,* expressed similar fear over the "medieval Orthodoxy and anarchistic license . . . struggling for mastery [of the East Europeans], a people . . . apt to . . . become a moral menace." And apt, no doubt, to tar the uptowner with the brush of the ghetto.

Things began to change after the directorship of the alliance was assumed by David Blaustein in 1898. While the formal, stated objective of the organization remained rapid Americanization, the daily programs became more responsive to immigrants' needs. Blaustein, himself an acculturated East European immigrant who had made his way through Harvard, was sensitive to the immigrants' desire to retain in the New World the cultural supports of language and folkways and religious rites and rituals.

Blaustein and a handful of others eventually came to feel that the more established Jews might even learn something from their "clients." Indeed, by 1905 it was clear that the uptown Americanizers, more than the ghetto dwellers, had been reeducated. Louis Marshall, the prominent German-Jewish attorney and philanthropist, admitted in a letter to a friend that the German Jews had "held themselves aloof . . . bringing gifts to people who did not seek [them]. . . . The work was done in such a manner as not only to give offense, but to arouse suspicion of the motives." Marshall taught himself Yiddish to understand and communicate with the immigrants better, and the Educational Alliance lifted its ban on the language in order to help East Europeans become Americans in terms of their own Yiddish culture.

Other institutions were created by the Jewish establishment to serve the needs of the ghetto, including Mount Sinai Hospital, which admitted 90 percent of its patients without charge, the Hebrew Orphan Asylum, and— sponsored by the Baron de Hirsch Fund—the Hebrew Technical Institute for boys and a school to teach domestic arts to girls. By 1895, in the heart of the depression that started in 1893, the budget of the United Hebrew Charities in New York, reflecting increased services for the newcomers, had reached the then astronomical sum of $116,000.

The Clara de Hirsch Home, endowed by the baroness in 1897 to provide recreational facilities and vocational training for immigrant girls, soon took on the task of "uprooting the evil" of prostitution by providing young women, Jews and non-Jews, with decent living arrangements, opportunities for employment, and, occasionally, matchmaking. An even more important philanthropic and "protective" agency was the National Council of Jewish Women, founded in 1893. Female agents of the New York branch were stationed at the port armed with pamphlets printed in English, German, and Yiddish, warning immigrant girls of dangers and informing them of addresses in sixty cities where they could apply in case of need. The women helped new arrivals find residences in more than 250 towns and cities and made follow-up inquiries.

In addition to aid rendered by German Jewish organizations, there were significant efforts by German Jewish individuals to improve conditions in the ghetto. In New York, for example, Isaac Seligman designed and funded the building of a model tenement on Cherry Street, and Felix Adler founded a kindergarten on the Lower East Side, the city's first.

In creating their philanthropic organizations and agencies, particularly the Educational Alliance, the German Jews were very much influenced by the American settlement house movement of the late 1880s and by the sincere and devoted settlement house workers, such as Charles Stover and Jane Addams, who hoped to provide the poor with the social and cultural wherewithal to help themselves. By 1898 "a picket line of settlements" on the Lower East Side including the Henry Street Settlement (formerly the Nurses' Settlement), the Educational Alliance, and the Madison Street Settlement House, were a familiar sight to ghetto dwellers. Later, the Neighborhood House was created by the sisterhood of the Spanish-Portuguese synagogue, Shearith Israel, primarily for the Sephardic Jews from Turkey, Greece, and Syria. The Sephardim had all the problems of newcomers and several additional ones: they spoke Ladino, not Yiddish, and most existing Jewish organizations hardly recognized them as Jews.

Although some settlement workers, drawn from patrician and middle-class families, were paternalistic and judgmental toward the poor and the immigrants, most were genuinely sympathetic. Moreover, many of these workers were astute Progressives, convinced that the ameliorative work in which they were engaged would be less effective if not accompanied by structural change in the society. As Jane Addams put it in her autobiography, *Twenty Years at Hull House*, settlement workers had to "arouse and interpret the public opinion of neighborhoods, . . . furnish data for legislation and even use their influence to secure it." It was no accident that many political activists, Jews and non-Jews, in favor of Progressive change at state and national levels in the 1920s and 1930s—such as Herbert Lehman, Belle and Henry Moskowitz, Eleanor Roosevelt, and Frances Perkins—had earlier been connected to the settlement house movement.

The settlement house workers were role models and undoubtedly powerful forces for Americanization. But one of the settlement movement's greatest contributions lay in its insisting that immigrants maintain the viable traditions of the old country. Workers assured immigrants that it was not necessary to reject their pasts entirely to become American. They also tried to lessen the alienation between parents and their children by reinforcing cultural self-respect through festival pageants and folk art.

One of the most notable settlement house social workers was the Cincinnati-born German Jew Lillian Wald (1867–1940). A nurse who founded the Henry Street Settlement, she grew to be "a figure of legend, known and adored on every street" on the Lower East Side. In 1893, Lillian Wald, the daughter of a comfortable bourgeois family, moved with another nurse into a small East Side apartment on Jefferson Street. The two young women made themselves available to anyone asking for aid whether or not they were able to pay. Needless to say, their tasks were endless. Help in defraying costs came from Jacob Schiff, a German Jewish philanthropist; and a growing number of nurses came to volunteer their services or to work for nominal pay. Larger quarters were soon necessary and the Nurses' Settlement was founded in 1895.

As her work proved successful, Lillian Wald's reputation grew, and she used it to persuade the city to start a program of public nursing and to hire nurses in the public schools. In addition, she actively opposed child labor, supported the playground movement, lined up with the striking cloak makers in 1910, and was a committed pacifist during World War I. Even as she became a figure of wide renown, Lillian Wald remained dedicated to her East Side neighbors. One of the most genuine and respected liberals of the Progressive era, Wald, within the narrower Jewish world, was expert at creating links between the Germans and the East Europeans.

Some attempts to forge links between the two groups were not so successful. The uptowners and downtowners were often able to put aside some of their mutual hostility in order to cooperate to good effect. But a measure of misunderstanding and antagonism continued to mark the German–East European relationship and stood in the way of an effort undertaken in 1908 to create a highly centralized Jewish community in New York.

In response to New York City Police Commissioner Theodore Bingham's accusations in 1908 about the extent of criminality on the Lower East Side, a movement emerged to establish Jewish communal self-government in New York. Called Kehillah in an effort to emulate the more successful attempts at communal self-government in sixteenth- through eighteenth-

century Russia and Poland, the New York experiment brought hundreds of
organizations together in a loosely knit confederation, and it lasted from 1908
to 1922. But it never matched its historical namesake in reach or power.

While the Kehillah did useful work, notably in the fields of philanthropy
and Jewish education, it failed to fulfill its founders' goal, which, according
to the movement's foremost historian, Arthur Goren, was to *control* the unruly ghetto by "molding New York Jewry into a single, integrated community." Conflicting ideologies—Orthodoxy, Reform, Zionism, and socialism
—contributed to the undoing of the centralized organization. But ultimately
the Kehillah did not matter much in the life of the immigrant Jews. It was not
their own; it was a "Jewish social pacifier" that came from on high rather than
from immigrant experience and vision.

The Kehillah failed to endure not because the immigrants were incorrigibly unruly but because too many established Jews—Germans and acculturated East Europeans—exaggerated the need for order and self-discipline
in the ghetto and insisted that the solution to disorder lay in a monolithic hier-
archy. The Kehillah was too distant and abstract, and it threatened to bring
the shackles of too much organization compared to the more familiar institutions, formal and informal, that the immigrants had built for themselves.

The dynamics of the relationship between the Germans and the Russians—the strains, misunderstandings, and contempt, as well as the philanthropy and the eventual cooperation—were similar in locations beyond New
York City. The established, prosperous German Jews of Chicago's "Golden
Ghetto" on the South Side, for example, were embarrassed by the poverty,
"radicalism," and Old World ways of the newly arrived East European Jews of
the West Side; and in the beginning they resisted their influx. Typically, however, the Germans came to accept the inevitability of mass immigration and
ultimately responded with programs of philanthropy and Americanization.

Julius Rosenwald (1862–1932), the president of Sears, Roebuck and
Company, was a generous German Jewish benefactor who gave great sums
to Jewish charities, as well as to education for Blacks, housing, the University of Chicago, and the Museum of Science and Industry. Rosenwald also
helped found the Chicago Hebrew Institute, later the Jewish People's Institute, which resembled New York's Educational Alliance at its progressive
best. German Jews were also crucial in funding the Jewish Training School,
one of the first vocational schools in the United States; the Mandel Clinic,
which provided free medical care for poor immigrants; and the Chicago Ma-
ternity Center. The Jewish establishment also founded the Maxwell Street

Settlement, the Jewish counterpart to Jane Addams' Hull House on Halsted Street, and it too was often hailed as the "university of good will, good English, [and] good citizenship."

German Jewish volunteer women were particularly active in organizing and raising funds for social welfare programs. In response to the needs of the new arrivals from Eastern Europe, Hannah Solomon worked effectively with American institutions such as the Chicago Women's Club and Hull House, but in 1896 she created the Bureau of Personal Service, an institution to be staffed and administered by Jewish women. The bureau investigated financial needs of immigrants for the Women's Loan Society, studied tenement conditions for industrial reports, directed parents with "troubled" children to the appropriate agencies, and cooperated regularly with the settlement houses.

The Chicago chapter of the National Council of Jewish Women, which Hannah Solomon had helped establish in 1893, created a Sabbath school for girls, as traditional Talmud Torahs did not provide religious education for young women. Council members in Chicago, like their sisters in New York, were also largely responsible for the establishment of a juvenile court. These women began as inexperienced volunteers but soon became expert in the field of judicial procedures and juvenile delinquency. Several became unpaid probation officers of the court.

Hannah Solomon and other prosperous German Jewish women from Chicago, including Esther Loeb Kohn and Rosa Sonneschein, while using Jewish social service as a way to redefine acceptable behavior for women, were equally committed to their work as a religious duty—an obligation to repair or improve the world. But they also viewed the tasks of "uplift" and "social housekeeping" as a responsibility of their class. And the patronizing attitudes that occasionally surfaced among them were often resented by the Russian and Polish immigrants.

The newcomers accepted the help extended to them because Chicago ghetto life was hard, but as soon as they could, they created their own self-help agencies. A similar dynamic marked almost every Jewish community in the United States. In Baltimore, for example, the German Jews had established a Federation of Jewish Charities, a chapter of the National Council of Jewish Women, and a Federation of Jewish Women encompassing together thirty-eight philanthropic societies and involving more than ten thousand volunteers. But the East Europeans soon created parallel and/or complementary organizations and institutions to provide shelter for immigrants and the aged, as well as burial societies, relief and loan associations, and orphanages.

In Chicago, Orthodox Jewish immigrants established Maimonides Hospital, later called Mount Sinai, rather than use the unkosher Michael Reese Hospital founded by the Germans, whose Reform Judaism did not require them to follow the dietary laws; they also created their own orphanage, sheltering society, and old-age home, where traditional East European Jews felt more comfortable. Despite the discomfort and suspicion in the relationship of Germans and East Europeans in Chicago, there was over time increasing cooperation, and by 1920 the philanthropic and mutual aid organizations of the East European Jewish community and the German Jewish community merged.

In Philadelphia the German Jews were an old and well-established community, and they worried in the era of mass immigration about how the Yiddish-speaking East European Jews, with their Old World ways and their radicalism, would affect German Jewish status in the city. For several decades, Philadelphia's Protestant establishment had been relatively tolerant. But in the status-conscious 1880s, the gentile elite quietly built an inviolable caste system that closed many "proper" resorts, clubs, and neighborhoods to Jews, no matter how prominent.

Fearful of an even more intensified anti-Semitism, some German Jews at first attempted to limit or at least to deflect the flow of East European immigration. But by the late 1880s, recognizing that the East Europeans were destined to be "representative of the race of Israel in the United States," the Germans, who had always been actively benevolent, entered a particularly creative period of community development and philanthropy. Relief expenditures were increased from twelve thousand dollars in 1880 to forty-two thousand dollars by 1892, and large groups of German Jewish women in Philadelphia, as in most cities, did the valuable, day-to-day work of communal philanthropy, even if sometimes in a patronizing manner. The Jewish elite also established the Hebrew Emigrant Society, a settlement house opened in 1891 at Tenth and Carpenter streets, in the very heart of the immigrant quarter. In addition, the German benefactors doubled the size of the Jewish Foster Home and founded the Federation of Jewish Charities in 1901.

The leading Philadelphia Jews, predominantly intellectuals and scholars, such as Sabato Morais, Cyrus Adler, Solomon Solis-Cohen, Mayer Sulzberger, and Joseph Krauskopf, were not as wealthy as the businessmen and lawyers who led New York Jewry. But along with New Yorkers Jacob Schiff, Oscar S. Straus, and Louis Marshall, the Philadelphians were committed to both Americanizing the newcomers and keeping them attached to Jewish life. Like the New York leadership, they were concerned that unmodified Orthodoxy would alienate the American-born children of immigrants. But they also understood that radical Reform Judaism, so alien to newly arrived traditional Jews, would not be an effective vehicle in the ghetto. They worked, therefore, to build institutions for a new American Judaism. Recognizing the centrality of New York in the evolving pattern of the Jewish community in America, the Philadelphia group often worked with and through the New Yorkers. But the Philadelphians were important in the building and running of many of the central institutions of American Jewish life, including the Jewish Theological Seminary, the Jewish Publication Society, the American Jewish Historical Society, the American Jewish Committee, and the Baron de Hirsch Fund.

In Boston, too, the "Russian invasion," struck fear into the hearts of Germans lest the non-Jewish community associate them with the "uncouth" immigrants. When historian Frederick Jackson Turner visited the Jewish North End, the arrogant patrician was filled with revulsion at streets filled with "oriental noise and squalor," and "fairly packed with swarthy sons and daughters of the tribe of Israel . . . some of the latter pretty—as you sometimes see a lily in the green muddy slime." The Germans' fear of being tainted by association was understandable in post–Civil War America. And Brahmin Boston was no exception to the era's nativism and anti-Semitism. A bill "to keep Chinese, Negroes, and Jews from neighborhoods where they are not wanted" was hotly debated in the city, and even such prominent Jews as Louis Brandeis and Edward Filene met rebuff.

In the early 1880s the Boston Hebrew Emigrant Aid Society refused to accept responsibility for several hundred Russian Jewish refugees and sent them back to New York. But by 1883 the desperate needs of some East European immigrants already in the city were increasingly obvious, and the Boston German Jewish community, embarrassed by its prior failure "to take care of its own" and its compassion now aroused, accepted—and by 1889 even sought out—full responsibility for Jewish immigrants. They formed a Federation of Jewish Charities and a branch of the American Committee for Ameliorating the Condition of the Russian Refugees, which operated as an employment agency and a vocational training school. And from 1880 to 1914, Jewish philanthropy in Boston went from being a paternalistic, loosely organized, and relatively inexpensive effort to being a well-financed and highly coordinated enterprise.

Boston's East European Jews in need of aid also continued to help themselves by establishing several mutual aid and philanthropic associations. By 1895, "Russian" and "German" charitable and self-help agencies were able to coordinate efforts, and by 1914, although there remained two clearly distinguishable groups of Jews in Boston, there was movement, as in Chicago, Philadelphia, Baltimore, and New York, toward integration in common institutions including hospitals, orphanages, loan societies, and industrial training schools.

The established, prosperous German Jews everywhere supported their coreligionists by funding relief efforts, providing temporary shelter, and procuring employment especially in the early years before a substantial, more self-sufficient Jewish community had become rooted on the Lower East Side of New York and in Jewish sections of other large cities. But from the start, East European Jewish immigrants created a web of their own voluntary organizations and improvised a viable, decentralized pattern for their collective existence. The family, the *shul,* and the *landsmanshaft,* the club, and the mutual aid society, the café, the union, and even many workplaces were arenas of genuine interaction and psychological sustenance. And in spite of disturbing new influences and internal stresses of crime, prostitution, desertion, and divorce, the Jewish immigrants maintained general tranquility and order in the ghetto.

The primary association remained the family, which had already been challenged in the old country and was seriously beleaguered in the ghetto. Yet it demonstrated remarkable resilience. Jewish emigration was preeminently a family emigration. The great mass made the journey with relatives or came to kin already in the United States; and Jewish families continued to be instruments of mutual support once they reconstituted themselves in their new world.

Families also influenced the nature of the workplace. Garment workers often brought relatives into the factory, instructed them in work routines, and sustained them during slack seasons. Sam Rubin, who came to America in 1908, remembered: "My brother-in-law was an operator and he took me into his shop and he taught me how to be an operator. . . . [He] tried to give me a few dollars more than I was able to earn. . . . My sister gave me food and drink. And when it got slack, she even gave me a few dollars in my pocket."

At the heart of the family were the immigrant parents, who, within the cramped apartments, loved, ruled, and tried to protect. The mother, especially in the early years of a family's life in the United States, appears to have coped best with the strange new world of the tumultuous American city and, by her scrappiness and strength, frequently was able to hold things together. Zalmen Yoffeh tenderly recalled in the *Menorah Journal* (1929) that with "one dollar a day [our mother] fed and clothed an ever-growing family. She made all our clothes. She walked blocks to reach a place where meat was a penny cheaper. . . . There was always bread and butter in the house."

For the immigrant mother and her family, food remained a central concern. So central was food in fact that Jewish wives and mothers occasionally picketed, boycotted, and even used physical coercion in the face of rising food costs. In early May 1902, for example, when the retail price of kosher meat soared from twelve cents to eighteen cents a pound and butchers ignored the ensuing protests, immigrant Jewish women organized the Ladies Anti-Beef Trust Association and took to the streets. They staged a successful three-week boycott of kosher meat shops throughout the Lower East Side and parts of upper Manhattan, the Bronx, and Brooklyn. The boycott at points led to violent scuffles, the breaking of butcher shop windows, and the dousing of meat with kerosene, but there was no looting. When one "ringleader" was arrested and charged with riot, she responded: "We don't riot. But if all we did was weep at home, nobody would notice it. We have to do something to help ourselves."

During the course of the boycott, the Jewish housewives addressed themselves to the labor movement and to socialists, as well as to the constituencies of the *shuln* and *landsmanshaftn*. They won enduring sympathy and support from both the *Jewish Daily Forward*, a socialist paper, and the *Yiddishe Tageblatt*, an Orthodox religious daily. The organizational behavior of these women activists and their strategies of mobilization gave evidence of a modern political mentality. That mentality was in evidence again during the depression of 1907–8, when, in response to rent increases, Lower East Side women staged rent strikes and mobilized hundreds of others to join them. Jewish women also organized a kosher meat boycott in Cleveland in 1906 and one in Detroit in 1910.

The boycotting and striking women had begun to understand and to wield their power as consumers and homemakers, and in the issue of high-priced food and shelter, they temporarily found a vehicle for political organization. Many Jewish women (see ch. 7) organized and participated in other, larger social and political movements. But the majority stayed close to home, and particularly to the kitchen, except for occasional forays such as the kosher meat riots and rent strikes.

It was from the kitchen that the Jewish housewife, although later the butt of jokes and the target of her children's anger, became a figure that

would inspire generations of sons and daughters. Alfred Kazin, in his won-
derfully evocative memoir of Brownsville, *A Walker in the City,* wrote:

> The kitchen gave a special character to our lives, my mother's character. All
> my memories of that kitchen are dominated by the nearness of my mother
> sitting all day long at her sewing machine. . . . The kitchen was her life.
> Year by year, as I began to take in her fantastic capacity for labor and her
> anxious zeal, I realized it was ourselves she kept stitching together.

Several other Jewish sons, particularly the novelist Henry Roth, have
given us intimate, complex portraits of mothers in kitchens, nourishing families with food and love. For daughters, in contrast, the kitchen was often
unremitting drudgery. Whether or not they had paying jobs, girls were expected to help with the housework. Cooking, cleaning, ironing, helping with
the younger children, and assisting in the piecework that was the mainstay of
so many households meant long hours of toil in the kitchen. Yet it was in the
same kitchen that deep psychological and emotional attachments were made
between mothers and daughters.

This was possible because Jewish immigrant mothers, even when they
worked, usually stayed at home. The number of married Jewish women
working in factories or shops was very small. Only 2 percent of East European Jewish households in America reported working wives in 1880 and
only 1 percent by 1905. These figures undoubtedly omitted all those women
who were partners in small businesses or who took up pushcart operations.
Also, many wives were gainfully employed at home, where they kept boarders, looked after other women's children, took in laundry, and did piecework. Moreover, because many immigrant families lived behind or above
their stores, women could often shuttle between minding the store and ful-
filling the more domestic and nurturing roles.

One of those roles was preparing for the Sabbath. It was necessary to
have the apartment clean, the best meal of the week prepared, the challah
baked or bought, and the wine and candles ready. Although transplantation
to the United States accelerated the fragmentation of Jewish religious culture, a process that had begun earlier in Eastern Europe, many Jews tried to
hold fast. And some succeeded. "I could hardly believe I was in America,"
wrote Zvi Hirsh Masliansky about his visit to the North End of Boston. "The
streets of Boston remind me of those of Vilna. Large synagogues, with truly
orthodox rabbis. Talmudic study groups . . . Hebrew schools in the old style
[and] almost all the stores are closed on Saturdays."

But in the 1880s and 1890s, the religious community in the ghettos of Boston, New York, and Philadelphia could not really provide the organization or environment for sustaining Orthodox Judaism. The busy city and "the busy season" made it difficult to pray three times a day, to obey the dietary laws with any strictness, or to adhere to numerous other religious regulations. Old World *rebbes,* men with some learning but not ordained as rabbis, who acted as teachers, offered no inspiring model for the children, and religious education was sadly neglected. The question of religious observance became the heart of the conflict between the pious immigrants and their children, as secular America increasingly beckoned to the young.

By the second decade of the twentieth century, however, many traditional Jews recognized that in order not to lose their children to secularism entirely, they would have to make some accommodation. "We seek," one explained, "to deal effectively and happily with the great task of Americanization . . . in such a way that [it] will not mean the alienation from the principles and practices of traditional Judaism." The Young Israel movement, established on the Lower East Side in 1912, also aimed to develop what would later come to be called Modern Orthodoxy. Within a few years several thousand members were attracted to the movement, where, according to the *Hebrew Standard* (1918) one could feel "thoroughly American and at the same time a true, whole-hearted and loyal . . . Jew."

Although the religious life of observant Jews did not show many signs of vitality on the Lower East Side before 1910, the ghetto's six hundred religious congregations demonstrated that Jews were still responding to "the Jewish religious imperative to worship." The congregations also clearly responded to the imperative "to care for one's own." Many of the *shuln* had developed around *landslayt,* groups of Jews from the same East European towns, and these *shuln* often operated as mutual aid societies.

As early as 1892 there were eighty-seven East European *landsmanshaftn,* some independent, but most connected to synagogues, unions, or extended family circles. By 1910 there were more than two thousand *landsmanshaftn* in New York City, six hundred in Chicago, and several hundred in other locations, representing nearly one thousand European cities and towns, and embracing virtually every Jewish family in urban America. All *landsmanshaftn* maintained a link to the old country location, particularly in times of crisis when the *shtetlekh* from which they sprang were in need of material relief. All maintained a continuation of important communal services, such as burial arrangements and poor relief, as well as a context for a shared expression of nostalgia.

Equally important, the *landsmanshaft* was a context for reconciling American Jewish and East European identity. It served as a sanctuary from the excessive strains of acculturation, ambition, and even ideology, and it gave the immigrants a breathing space, a place to be themselves, to continue the tradition of *tsedakah* and self-help but a place also to settle into a game of pinochle. At the same time it resembled an American fraternal order, with its rites and constitutions, its camaraderie, and its opportunity for "doing a little business."

The world of the *landsmanshaft* very much reflected the broader themes of American Jewish life and clearly was not a mere nostalgic "brotherhood of memory." The *landsmanshaft* was a vehicle for mutual aid, philanthropy, health services, insurance, credit, and relaxation; and it was a way station, an ingenious social improvisation, from which immigrants could go on to confront the new society around them.

The strong ethnic and religious ties and the need for mutual aid that gave birth to the *landsmanshaftn* also promoted the creation of other institutions. Many hospitals, orphanages, and nursing homes, which observed dietary laws and had Yiddish-speaking doctors, were founded by the East Europeans in New York City, including Beth Israel Hospital in 1890. This facility was specifically designed to meet the peculiar needs of the sick poor among the Jewish immigrant population, and by 1910 nearly all neighborhoods in larger cities where Jews lived had their own Jewish hospitals. In addition, there were so many new synagogues, political organizations, labor union locals, philanthropic organizations, loan societies, credit unions, and educational institutions that the East European Jews, by the second decade of the twentieth century, possessed a more elaborate organizational structure than any other ethnic group in the United States.

Many of the institutions created by the East European Jews became vital elements in the new transitional culture. Outstanding in this respect was the Yiddish theater, which arrived in New York City in the 1880s in its infancy and was nurtured there at the turn of the century by its greatest audience, the largest, most heterogeneous aggregation of Jews in the world. In the early years in America, the Yiddish theater overflowed with corrupt and mindless versions of the European repertoire, as well as flamboyant "trash" and crude talent. It took hold in the public mind only after many trials. But with the emergence of playwrights such as Jacob Gordin, stars such as Jacob Adler and Boris and Bessie Tomashevsky, larger and larger audiences were attracted. By 1900 there were three major theater troupes in New York City and numerous smaller endeavors in other Jewish population centers.

The Yiddish theater provided a collective experience for the entire community. It was also a powerful vehicle for fund-raising. Philanthropic, mutual aid, and labor organizations often sponsored benefit performances. Ticket prices ranged from twenty-five cents to a dollar, not a small outlay for the stretched budgets of immigrant laborers, but somehow thousands managed it. By 1918 New York City boasted twenty Yiddish theaters, which in a single year, before the inroads of movies, attracted two million patrons to eleven hundred performances. New York troupes also made regular appearances in the Yiddish theaters on Roosevelt Road in Chicago and on Arch Street in Philadelphia.

The involvement of the audiences in all the cities was total and fervently enthusiastic. Crying, always part of an evening at the Yiddish theater, was cathartic for the bone-weary workers who made up most of the house. Laughter, at characters with familiar problems, was just as prevalent, and the comic as well as the tragic stories and situations helped immigrants recognize their own strength and motivation to hold on, even to succeed. Patrons ate and drank, exchanged loud remarks, and unabashedly cheered or hissed when they felt moved to do so.

Family life with all its problems preoccupied the Jewish playwrights. Leon Kobrin's comedy *The Next Door Neighbors* dealt with the difficulties faced by a couple who did not immigrate together, and Gordin's *Mirele Efros* (also known as the Jewish *Queen Lear*), a melodrama about a self-sacrificing mother, "instructed" members of the audience to respect their parents. These plays, as well as those of David Pinski, Sholem Aleichem, I. L. Peretz, Sholem Asch, and others, were performed innumerable times over several decades and remained enormously popular with parents and children.

Popularity was largely a result of the similarity of the problems of stage characters to those of every immigrant: How to be both an American and a Jew? How to protect the family and religious tradition from disintegration in a secular, seemingly normless society? How to enjoy the opportunities for material success in the United States without giving up the spiritual values of Judaism? These were the questions that befuddled people who were still very much part of two worlds, and the Yiddish theater, like many other transitional East Side Jewish institutions, helped newcomers deal with those questions, in this case by portraying them on stage.

The Yiddish theater also directly encouraged members of the audience to feel connected to both the American and the Jewish worlds. Patrons felt pride in their Jewishness as the Jewish playwrights and actors consistently expressed the immigrants' own exuberant vitality. And they shared a patriotic enthusiasm with the general American public, when, for example, they cheered Boris Tomashevsky in *Der Yidsher Yenki dudl.*

Although the plays were always performed in Yiddish, it was possible, as Lincoln Steffens observed, to enjoy the Yiddish theater without knowing the language. But virtually all the East European immigrants spoke it. Although the Galicians, the Poles, and the Rumanians spoke with different vowels from the Lithuanians, and the Hungarians spoke a variant that was closer to German, Yiddish was the lingua franca of New York's East Side, and its growth and development there in the 1880s and 1890s helped Jews of various nationalities feel more like one people.

The Lithuanians came to outnumber the other Yiddish-speaking groups in the 1880s and inspired the initial attempts to mold a more uniform language. The Lithuanian scholar Alexander Harkavy developed a very successful English-Yiddish dictionary that ran through a dozen editions. Fellow Lithuanian Abraham Cahan and other journalists and writers from the region were widely popular and reinforced the dominance of the Lithuanian idiom.

Jewish intellectuals and radicals also had an important role to play in the creation of a revitalized Yiddish in America. Unlike the poets, writers, and activists of many other nationalities, Jewish intellectuals and political activists came to the United States along with the masses and helped enrich the Yiddish culture that ordinary immigrants built here. Yiddish eventually became a vehicle for Americanization and ultimately, and ironically, for its own demise. But the continuing mass immigration, the momentum of Yiddish literary activity, and the involvement of Yiddish in the progressive social and political movements of the early twentieth century invigorated the language beyond all expectation.

As Abe Cahan pointed out in 1898, "the five million Jews living under the czar had not a single Yiddish daily paper even when the government allowed such publication, while [Russian Jews] in America publish six dailies . . . countless Yiddish weeklies and monthlies, and [enough] books [to make] New York the largest Yiddish book market in the world." In New York City, the hub of the Yiddish American universe, over 150 Yiddish dailies, weeklies, monthlies, quarterlies, festival journals, and yearbooks appeared between 1885 and 1914. Some 20 dailies came into existence during that period, and for a time, at the turn of the century, as many as 6 competed simultaneously for readers. The *Tageblatt,* founded in 1885, represented the Orthodox religious point of view. The *Morgen Journal* was also Orthodox and was the first (1901) truly successful Yiddish morning paper. The 1890s saw the beginning of the *Forvarts (Jewish Daily Forward)*, a socialist paper that under the guiding hand of Cahan became the largest Yiddish newspaper in the world. In the same decade the *Freie Arbeiter Shtime,* representing the anarchists, was born. Even the weekly *La America* (1910–25), a Ladino paper for Sephardic readers, printed a Yiddish column to attract advertisers in the greater East European community.

Although it promoted a serious modern Yiddish literature, the press was also a powerful agent of acculturation, nourishing the process of Americanization for the Jewish masses in their own language. Even Abe Cahan's *Forward,* which was dedicated to the propagation of socialism, was equally dedicated to Americanization. The paper consistently emphasized the acquisition or development of "desirable" qualities and manners, "taught" American history and geography, and made untiring efforts to explain American ways. As early as 1903, Cahan advised immigrant parents to let Jewish "boys play baseball and become excellent at the game." After all, he admonished, we ought not to "raise the children to grow up foreigners in their own birthplace." Cahan was a moderate socialist whose anticapitalist views were tempered by American conditions. His paper, which excluded theoretical pieces and instead presented the class struggle in the form of stories and news from the marketplace, home, and factory, remained attractive to nonsocialist Jews. At its height the *Forward* published twelve metropolitan editions from Boston to Los Angeles, with a circulation of 500,000 (more than 250,000 in New York City alone).

One of the *Forward*'s best-read innovations was the Bintl Brief (bundle of letters) section, started in 1906. Letters from readers about poverty and sickness, love and divorce, unemployment, intermarriage, socialism, generational conflicts, and declining religious observance were printed daily. The responses, written by Cahan in the early years, then increasingly by his staff as well, tried to suggest that the immigrants should not make excessive demands on themselves, that they should even enjoy life a little. The editors did not advise immigrants to give up their religious or ideological preconceptions entirely, but they did encourage the newcomers to make the needs of everyday life in America primary.

The Yiddish papers, as part of the Americanization process, also tried to acquaint their readers with English. Cahan, opening himself to the charge of corrupting the Yiddish language, encouraged his writers to follow the general custom of incorporating English words into their Yiddish articles. The *Tageblatt* went further; it began printing a full English page in 1897. These practices no doubt both reflected and influenced ghetto conversation. By 1900 the immigrants were mingling an estimated one hundred English words in their daily speech. "Politzman," "never mind," "alle right," and other idioms slipped readily from the tongue.

At the same time that the Yiddish press acted as an Americanizing agent, it was, along with the Yiddish theater, the *landsmanshaft*, and so many other Jewish immigrant institutions, an important part of the transitional religiously based ethnic culture of the Lower East Side. This culture, sustained by the largest, freest, and most heterogeneous Jewish community in the world, became a Yiddish culture richer and greater than any achieved in Eastern Europe.

Producers and disseminators of the vibrant Yiddish culture of the ghetto —the writers, playwrights, and journalists—often met in small restaurants and cafés to eat, talk, and argue. Hutchins Hapgood, a sensitive gentile journalist, correctly sensed the dominant "socialistic feeling . . . in these cafes," but Jewish writer Harry Roskolenko, who sold papers there, astutely observed in his memoir, *The Time That Was Then,* that his tea-sipping patrons were not ideological purists: "Ideas about God, the synagogue, the union, intermeshed. It was like a chess game—with no rules. . . . Who was not at least two or three separate spiritual and physical entities on the Lower East Side? My father managed socialism, Orthodoxy and Zionism, quite easily, and so did the kibitzers and the serious."

To most immigrants the cafés probably seemed exotic, perhaps even frivolous. But what many workers did take seriously was the endless stream of lectures and public meetings sponsored by the socialists, the Zionists, the unions, the New York City Board of Education, the People's Institute at Cooper Union, and the Educational Alliance. In Philadelphia they flocked to the Hebrew Literary Society. A "certain grandeur of aspiration" was to be found in these people, who toiled long hours in the shops and then somehow mustered the energy to drag themselves to evening lectures in pursuit of learning. On the Lower East Side and in many other urban Jewish concentrations, learning for its own sake or for the sake of future generations and learning for the social revolution all merged into one explosion of self-discovery.

Those who had already mastered the rudiments of English often attended the public night schools. In 1906, Jews constituted a majority of the one hundred thousand students enrolled in New York City evening classes. Almost 40 percent of the students were women, some of whom were mothers. "I admit that I cannot be satisfied to be just a wife and mother," one woman wrote to the *Forward*. "I am still young and I want to learn and enjoy life. My children and my home are not neglected, but I go to evening high school twice a week."

The same passion for learning that adults displayed was instilled in the children. According to Mary Antin, an immigrant writer, and repeated in virtually every Jewish autobiography, Jewish parents brought their boys and girls to the first day of school "as if it were an act of consecration," and parental encouragement was sustained throughout the child's school career.

Education and mobility will warrant further attention, but it should be said here that the respect and drive for education does partly explain Jewish economic and occupational mobility, and it can help us understand why a disproportionate number of immigrants achieved professional status relatively early. There was no large-scale social ascent to the professions in the immigrant generation or even in the second generation. But by 1907 the number of Jewish doctors making a living on the Lower East Side had doubled to 200 since the 1880s, and the number of lawyers increased almost as fast. There were also 115 Jewish pharmacists and 175 Jewish dentists serving the ghetto. Similar proportions obtained in several other cities including Cleveland and Chicago.

Success in small business actually played a more important role than education in the relatively rapid mobility of the Jewish immigrant generation. This was especially true in Jewish communities of the American interior, where the newcomers were less dependent on the garment industry. But it was also the case in New York. It has already been pointed out that thousands of East Siders were involved in the pushcart trade and in subcontracting, and hundreds more had groceries, butcher shops, candy stores, and bakeries. Many of these businesses remained marginally profitable, but some entrepreneurs advanced enough to constitute the beginning of a middle class.

As early as the 1890s the apparel trade and the real estate business also became arenas for immigrant energy and aspiration. By 1905, German Jewish manufacturers and landlords were virtually replaced by East European Jews. It is the "Russian-Jewish employer" now who hires the "Russian-Jewish laborer," I. M. Rubinow, an immigrant economist and statistician, wrote in 1905; and it is the "Russian-Jewish landlord" now who collects "his exorbitant rent" from the "Russian-Jewish tenement dweller." The vast majority of gainfully employed Jews on the Lower East Side did not become manufacturers or property owners; they remained proletarians for at least one generation, but the Jewish middle class was clearly growing.

Consumption patterns on the Lower East Side reflected this growing affluence of the immigrant generation as well as their desire to Americanize.

Impoverished newcomers of all ethnic backgrounds responded positively to the symbolic as well as physical aspects of American abundance. But Jews, in seeking and creating new identities, pursued the "American standard of living" with special vigor. The most obvious symbol of acculturation and ambition was the new suit of clothes. Most immigrants, Jewish or not, seemed bent on proving the axiom that clothes make the man, and they quickly adopted the attitude of American workers toward clothing: dressing well meant respectability, even equality. But Jews again were outstanding in this respect. Their great involvement in the garment business and retail trade of New York City reinforced an interest in clothing, but Jewish sensitivity to American appearance stemmed as much or more from the powerful desire for acculturation. Unlike most newcomers, Jews intended at the outset to make a permanent home in American society; and the quickest way they could gain a sense of the social membership they desired was as consumers. And consume they did, despite the Jewish reputation for delayed gratification through "ruthless underconsumption."

Beyond fashionable clothing, Jews identified several other components of the American life style as especially meaningful building blocks of an American identity: a summer vacation in the mountains or at the seashore, which East European Jewish immigrants virtually invented as a matter of course for ordinary people; and they looked upon the parlor and the piano as potent symbols of the ideal of social equality, the dignity of ordinary families, and the sanctification of the home.

The role of Jewish women in the home played a crucial role in helping newcomers adapt to American abundance. Jewish wives and mothers had more commercial experience, had more scope and authority within the household, and were present in America in greater proportion than the women of other immigrant groups. In the context of the comparative domesticity of Jewish social life and the increasing prospects for consumption in urban America, Jewish women, already market wise in the Old World, sharpened their skills as consumers in the new one. Between 1900 and 1920 they extended their control over domestic consumption and facilitated Jewish adoption of American habits.

Acculturation through consumption, however, did not mean assimilation. For example, although Jews were alone among immigrant groups adopting the full-fledged *American* vacation, they had developed, in the process, the distinctively *Jewish* resort. Moreover, in the words of Andrew Heinze, a social historian, the parlor and the luxuries it contained, particularly the piano, "provided a secular outlet for the traditional Jewish belief in dignifying the individual through the creation of a Sabbatical atmosphere in the home."

The inspirational capacity of material luxury had always been part of the Jewish experience. Festivals and Holy Days, particularly the Sabbath, were marked materially by the use of one's "best things," specially reserved for the occasion. This was one way of distinguishing the sacred from the profane and of dignifying the humblest of Jews with a foretaste of God's splendor. American abundance and democratic secular ideas embodied in mass-marketed luxuries tended to erode the distinction between the holy and the mundane, as with the ability to eat holiday foods during the normal week. But abundance also added a dimension to the holidays that rooted Jewish identities in a new world.

The celebration of Passover, for example, perhaps the most popular, conscious manifestation of Jewish identity in America, was also reformulated to reflect the anticipation of ever higher living standards in the New World as well as remembrance of ancient captivity and liberation. The pulse of retail commerce in Jewish urban neighborhoods rose in anticipation of all the holidays and festivals, but the intensity of shopping for Passover, when sometimes whole households were refurbished, was extraordinary.

Significant numbers of families, pursuing both the "sanctification" of the home, by making it a place of comfort and mutual support, and the American ideal of social equality, installed gas ovens, turned bedrooms into "parlors" for daytime use, and bought pianos on the installment plan. At the same time a much smaller number of immigrants actually grew rich. Harry Fischel, who arrived penniless in New York, became a millionaire in the building industry. Israel Lebowitz who started as a peddler, graduated to a men's apparel shop on Orchard Street and by 1907 was among the largest shirt manufacturers in New York City. After a brief stay in New York City, the seventeen-year-old Bernard Hourwich was told he would find conditions more to his liking in Chicago, the "second America." He arrived there in 1880, started peddling, and rose over time to become the president of two banks and a prominent figure in Jewish philanthropic circles. There were dramatic instances of social mobility in Philadelphia as well, where Jews parlayed small businesses into major new enterprises. Sam Paley, for example, built a thirty-million-dollar cigar business from a storefront workshop, and Albert M. Greenfield, who started as an office boy, opened a small real estate business and eventually amassed a vast commercial empire encompassing retail stores, banks, hotels, and transportation companies.

This was impressive, but the very thin crust of East European wealth remained unimportant in comparison with the wealth of the German Jews or the American elite. The East Europeans were not involved at the centers of American economic power. Nor, for that matter, were the Germans. The major heavy industries, Wall Street, and banking and insurance, remained closed to them. They were primarily confined to economic mobility in the fields of real estate, merchandising, and light manufacturing.

Between 1890 and 1910 great numbers of Jewish immigrants remained in the old neighborhoods, and more continued to arrive. A considerable proportion continued to be petty tradesmen, and a large majority remained shop and factory laborers throughout their working lives, about half of them in the garment industry. The real earnings of these workers did show a rise— at an annual average rate of 1.3 percent between 1890 and 1914. Life was often hard during these years, especially during the depression of 1893–95, but working and living conditions, general amenities, and incomes did improve slowly for many immigrants. This enabled them to sustain a modest increase in standard of living and to underwrite education and economic mobility for their children.

Economic mobility often meant residential mobility. By 1910, Jews were leaving the Maxwell Street area of Chicago for Greater Lawndale, and the North End of Boston for Roxbury and Dorchester. For more than thirty years immigrant Jews from Eastern Europe had sustained in their old neighborhoods—and especially in the Lower East Side ghetto and in its satellites in Brooklyn, the Bronx, and upper Manhattan—a vibrant transitional culture laced with elaborate institutional arrangements. But South Philadelphia, East Baltimore, the West Side of Chicago, and the Lower East Side Jewish communities and their spinoffs were not destined to be permanent communities. After 1910 the process of moving up and out meant lower population density, declining membership in the United Hebrew Trades, decreasing attendance at the Yiddish theater, and diminishing circulation of the Yiddish press. As among Western European Protestants, European Catholics, Asians, and even Native Americans, English among second-generation Jews was becoming the language of home, school, and commerce.

Acculturation and mobility and their attendant challenges and opportunities also characterized Jewish communities outside the larger metropolitan areas, and it is to these we now turn.

6

Transplanted in America: Smaller Cities and Towns

Outside New York, in the other great American cities at the turn of the century, immigrant Jews mirrored in microcosm the communal life of the Lower East Side. The North End of Boston, South Philadelphia, East Baltimore, and the West Side of Chicago sheltered dense enclaves of East European Jews steeped in a transitional culture built on a combination of new American experiences and the deeply internalized values and habits of *yiddishkayt*.

But even in the smaller cities and towns, there were large enough pluralities of Jews on significant numbers of adjacent streets and large enough clusters of Jewish businesses in relatively small areas for neighborhoods, and parts of neighborhoods, to become known as Jewish; and more importantly, to become public spaces in which Jews interacted with familiarity and in which they transplanted modified versions of Old World cultural forms.

Cities and towns all over the United States received Jewish newcomers, some of whom—approximately seventy-nine thousand—were assisted in the dispersal and resettlement process by the Industrial Removal Office and a vast network of cooperating branches which stretched from Hartford, Connecticut, through Atlanta, to El Paso, Texas, and from Providence, Rhode Island through Kansas City, Missouri, and Denver to Portland, Oregon and San Francisco.

A much smaller number of immigrants, some ten thousand, were deflected after 1907 through the port of Galveston, Texas, to interior cities including Fort Worth, Oklahoma City, Omaha, Minneapolis, and as far west as Los Angeles. But the vast majority of Eastern European immigrants who ended up outside New York and the major port cities left the crowded ghettos under their own steam, some of them following relatives who had been assisted by the Industrial Removal Office or the Galveston Plan.

The immigrant who worked six months in a New York sweatshop to save enough train fare to go to Minneapolis, where his two brothers had already settled, was not unusual among those who left the East, nor was the peddler who forsook Boston to join relatives in Cleveland. But several things besides ties of kinship guided the voluntary secondary migration. Immigrants were often drawn to new locations by a *landslayt* connection. For example, Portland, Oregon, attracted a disproportionate number of people from Chartoriysk, a town on the ever changing border between Poland and Russia; Lithuanian Jews, often from the same old-country districts and towns, dominated the Jewish communities in Atlanta and Milwaukee; and by 1914, Seattle was home to six hundred Sephardic Jews, the largest concentration outside New York City.

Immigrant Jews who settled or resettled outside the large Eastern or Midwestern cities saw in places like Cincinnati, St. Louis, and Los Angeles better opportunity to enter into or expand small business. As many as 35 percent of that small portion of Jews who decided to strike out anew had had entrepreneurial experience; most of the rest were ready to take the risks involved in leaving a known environment to start over, convinced that their skills would enable them to begin careers in trade in new places such as Columbus, Ohio, Johnstown, Pennsylvania, Atlanta, or Denver.

Just as with the German Jews, peddling and other commercial occupations played a much more important role than industrial labor in the work life of East European Jews in the smaller cities and towns. Rarely were Jewish immigrants employed in the principal industries of these places. The breweries and iron foundries of Milwaukee, the steel plants of Pittsburgh, the stone quarries and railroads of Columbus, and the textile mills of Malden, Massachusetts, hired few Jews. This was partly the result of discrimination by employers, but it was also the consequence of the petit-bourgeois motivation of the Jews themselves. In Providence, Rhode Island, for example, Jews were seven times more likely to be peddlers than any other ethnic group, and an extraordinary 65 percent ran small businesses or were self-employed.

Similar proportions of Jewish peddlers, merchants, and self-employed craftsmen were to be found in Springfield, Massachusetts, and Hartford, Connecticut. In Portland, Oregon, Columbus, Milwaukee, and Minneapolis, too, innovative East Europeans followed the paths of the German Jews who preceded them and borrowed capital from friends, relatives, and cooperative loan societies to pursue the often risky process of building small businesses. Many of the businesses were marginal, but Jews were willing to make short-term sacrifices in order to remain linked to the long-term potentialities inherent in the world of commerce.

Los Angeles, with its appealing climate, attracted some Jewish health seekers, but here as well it was business opportunity that accounted for the remarkable surge in the city's Jewish population from about four hundred in 1880 to seven thousand in 1907 and sixty-five thousand by 1927. With its agricultural potential, warmth, easy access, and availability of land, the Los Angeles area experienced the celebrated economic "boom of the eighties." Peaking in 1886–87, the boom spawned dozens of new west coast towns and attracted thousands of new settlers, including businessmen and aspiring entrepreneurs anxious to serve the new arrivals.

There were dramatic success stories throughout the West, an area that according to historian Moses Rischin, promoted greater social mobility for Jews than the older regions of the country. The story of the Madanic family is a case in point. Hyman Madanic and his son Ben emigrated to the United States in 1889. They took jobs in the sweatshops of St. Louis and saved enough money to bring the rest of the family from Russia in 1893. The Madanics opened their own fairly successful clothing store in Fairfield, Illinois, but in 1908 they moved to the boom town of Tulsa, Oklahoma, where their business proved so successful that they opened branches in several nearby towns. They changed their name to May following World War I, and their stores continued to spread across the continent.

Perhaps the most sensational set of examples of the rise from rags to riches in the West is the story of the "Hollywood Eight"—Jewish immigrants who seized the opportunities inherent in a marginal moviemaking business and by the 1920s created eight major companies in complete control of the production, distribution, and exhibition of moving pictures. Dozens of Jews, on their way to "inventing Hollywood," began like Louis B. Mayer, Harry Cohn, and the Warner brothers, with nickelodeon storefronts in their own East Coast neighborhoods and soon graduated to small theater ownership.

As late as 1912, moviemaking was still a fledgling industry. Most American films were produced by approximately one hundred small firms owned mainly by gentiles, some of whom thought they were involved in little more than a passing fad. The Jewish theater owners, however, who were outsiders conditioned to working on the fringes of commercial enterprise, sought new opportunities. They became attuned to the tastes of their audiences and to the developing revolution in manners, morals, and popular culture and determined to make their own films.

Louis B. Mayer, who arrived in Boston at age nineteen without enough money for a sandwich, Samuel (Goldfish) Goldwyn, a traveling glove salesman, and several others with great ambition and little capital borrowed money and persuaded their families, friends, and *landslayt* to pool resources. The new moviemakers produced funny, patriotic, egalitarian, sensual, and opulent films, and they built palatial theaters to show them in. The combination attracted large audiences of all classes and made the filmmakers wealthy.

Nicholas Schenck, the head of United Artists, said perceptively, "It is not always greatness that takes a man to the top, it is a gambling spirit." The willingness to take risks was significant: along with a strong sense of group cohesion, a desire to Americanize rapidly, and to rise, "the gambling spirit" enabled the Hollywood Eight to build a major new multimillion-dollar industry that catapulted them to the status of commercial barons, or moguls, as they were sometimes disparagingly called.

Few East European immigrants became barons in any field of endeavor in the West or in any other region. But most, often after at least one initial entrepreneurial failure, gambled again and pulled themselves out of poverty to lives of relative comfort. Indeed, for Jews living in communities beyond the east coast cities, there are striking analogies in mobility and occupational patterns. Commerce predominated, whether in the form of peddling and storekeeping in Omaha, Patchogue, New York, Phoenix, Columbus, and Sioux City, Iowa, or in the form of wholesaling and light manufacturing in Portland, Oregon, junk scavenging in Cleveland, and the slaughter and sale of meat in Kansas City, Missouri.

Even in those cities where the majority of gainfully employed Jews were laborers, as in St. Louis, Louisville, Kentucky, and Rochester, New York, or where significant proportions (40% or more) worked in industry, as in Pittsburgh, Cincinnati, Syracuse, New York, Toledo, Ohio, and Worcester, Massachusetts, as many as 25–40 percent were peddlers, merchants, or dealers.

In all these places the extended Jewish family played a critical role as an economic unit or network. From instances of peddlers to moviemakers, relatives deployed collective resources, borrowed from one another, hired, trained, sustained, and encouraged one another. In Cleveland, one young scavenger recalled protesting when the uncle who was "training" him picked unattractive, seemingly worthless junk out of backyards. The older man re-torted: "That's business! . . . Everything goes into the wagon. If you're too finicky, you'll never make a living." Relatives and *landslayt* were also trained and employed by small store owners in Eastport and Setauket, Long Island, as well as by Jewish wholesalers in San Francisco, who extended family busi-ness networks to other towns. And in Hollywood, Louis B. Mayer hired so many of his relatives that Metro-Goldwyn-Mayer (MGM), came to be known as "Mayer's ganza mishpoche" (Mayer's entire extended family).

Like Hollywood, the Catskill Mountain resort hotels in Sullivan and Ulster counties in New York State were an invention of the immigrant Jews and their social networks of relatives and *landslayt*. East European Jews who tried to make a living in mixed farming in the relatively inhospitable soil of the Catskills found, like their gentile neighbors, that it was often necessary to take in boarders to make ends meet. For Jewish innkeepers the early board-ers were friends and kin. They came for the clean mountain air, the sun, and to be in the country. Returning one hundred miles south to New York City, Jewish vacationers told other associates and relatives the news of the bucolic pleasures to be had "in the mountains."

In response to rising demand, reinforced by the refusal of many gentile-owned Catskill and Adirondack resorts to rent accommodations to "He-brews," Jewish farmhouses were converted to rooming houses, and Jewish farmers, seeing the profitability of taking in boarders, spent less time farm-ing. It should be pointed out that during the time they did farm, Jews were as successful as their gentile counterparts in New York State. Moreover, with the help of the Jewish Agricultural Society, Jews were instrumental in estab-lishing rural credit unions, agrarian sanitation reform, and farmers' cooper-atives that became models for American agriculture.

It was not long, however, before Jewish bungalow colonies, boarding-houses, and hotels dotted the Catskill landscape. Between 1900 and 1910, one thousand farms in a ten-mile strip near Ellenville were sold to Jews mi-grating from New York City. "Nearly every one of the purchased farm houses," according to the *Ellenville Journal* "is used as a summer boarding house." Resentment over the invasion of "Israelites" from the big city was modified some when native farmers realized profits from the sale of untill-able lands to prospective Jewish innkeepers.

The string of Jewish hostelries eventually became the borscht belt, with its impresarios and hotel magnates whose families, like the Grossingers and the Browns, were often engaged in the enterprise, season after season and generation after generation. Like the Jewish resorts on the south New Jersey

shore and in Atlantic City, "the mountains" became an important feature of
Jewish life and a fixture on the Catskill landscape. Before the general collapse
of the Catskills in the 1960s, hastened by acculturation, affluence, and jet
travel, thousands of hotels, bungalow colonies, and rooming houses accommodated more than a million mostly Jewish vacationers annually, and several
resorts rose from shacks to conglomerates with their own post offices, air-
ports, and tinted snow.

In the Catskills, in Hollywood, and in the American interior generally,
Jews established family businesses and utilized innovative techniques that promoted a remarkable mobility. A not dissimilar pattern was discernable in the
South as well. The "Jew peddlers" became a fixture, their growing businesses
sometimes becoming the nuclei of small towns. Jews were also attracted to
the business opportunities of southern cities, such as Atlanta, which was the
terminus for five different railway lines. Whether in small towns or in cities,
Jewish entrepreneurs broke into the commercial networks by filling needs.
Like their German Jewish predecessors, who had established the great southern department stores—Goldsmith's in Memphis, Sakowitz's in Houston,
Godstraux's in New Orleans, Rich's in Atlanta, and Cohen Brothers in Jack-
sonville—the East European Jews sold on credit and often cultivated a Black
clientele.

This last could lead to trouble, but more often it simply meant more
customers. Jewish businessmen were more interested in customers than
in the customs of racial discrimination, and they generally followed the pro-
fessed philosophy of the owners of Neiman Marcus, who early on announced, "Anyone alive should be considered a prospect."

Because of the social and cultural comforts of the east coast ghettos and
the selective influences of inertia and fear, only a small portion of Jewish
immigrants left the northern cities for the American hinterlands in the West
and South. Most of those who did were likely to have been more adventurous, independent, and acculturated than the millions who remained in the
North. These traits partly account for the risk taking and rapid economic
mobility of the Hollywood producers, the Catskill hoteliers, the San Francisco wholesalers, the Kansas City meat slaughterers, and the Southern Jews
who extended credit to Blacks.

But did independence and acculturation mean that Jewish immigrants
in the smaller cities and towns also assimilated more rapidly? It is true that in
Los Angeles, and in a very small number of other places where Jews settled,
a Jewish immigrant milieu hardly came into being. It is also true that Jewish
immigrants outside the largest cities were less densely concentrated and even

more likely than Jews in Boston, Chicago, and Philadelphia to share neighborhoods and streets with other ethnic groups—Italians, Irish, Poles, and
Blacks. Indeed, in places such as Columbus, Portland, Oregon, and Omaha,
no single nationality group, including Jews, ever constituted a majority in
any area as large as a half-mile square. And even the densely Jewish neighborhoods in Milwaukee, Detroit, and Cleveland were ethnically heterogeneous, with significant numbers of individuals circulating, in the larger
American stew pot, outside their particular immigrant enclaves.

Unlike those in east coast cities, Jews in the interior could not live
entirely within the bounds of the ethnic community. But in these places and
in most cities and towns with Jewish residents, there were neighborhoods
that, like the West Colfax section of Denver, the Suffolk Square area of
Malden, Massachusetts, Decatur Street in Atlanta, and Water Street in Milwaukee, had a highly visible Jewish immigrant settlement with a relatively
autonomous life, distinct Jewish trades, and familiar street scenes. The following description in *American Jewish Archives* (November 1979), by a Jewish
former resident of the East Side of Hartford, Connecticut, is nearly inter-
changeable with descriptions of Jewish immigrant neighborhoods in dozens
upon dozens of other small American cities and towns: "Rows of two and
three story tenement houses, packed tightly together, provide homes for the
newly arrived. Many used the front of the first floor as a place of business.
Windsor Street . . . was alive with people coming and going from these businesses in their homes. The street reverberated, too, with the voices of peddlers hawking their wares from pushcarts and wagons."

The newcomers from Eastern Europe, even where they never made up
more than half a block's population in any given section, formed their own
main "drags" in the heartland of America—on Ferry Street in Springfield,
Massachusetts, or on tree-lined William Street in Buffalo, or on the North
Side of Minneapolis, where on Fridays one could literally smell the fish and
the chicken, the preparations for the Sabbath.

In places even more isolated from the mainstream of American Jewish
life, ethnic and religious cohesion was harder to maintain, and sometimes
it disappeared. Jews in such towns as Mora, New Mexico, spoke Spanish,
worshiped as Catholics, and ultimately were completely absorbed into the
native population. But this was rare. More often, Jews, no matter how few
and how distant from the larger centers of Jewish culture, tried, sometimes
against great odds, to maintain Jewish identity even as they Americanized. In
Phoenix, for example, there were no formal Jewish religious institutions until
1910. High Holy Day services had to be held in homes or rented halls. In

1897, Jewish worshipers had to be sure that their Yom Kippur service at Elks Hall ended at 8 P.M. so that the lodge members could hold their regularly scheduled meeting.

Even where formal institutions existed, there were problems. Many Jewish communities emerged between Harrisburg and Pittsburgh, each with its own small synagogue, but none with a qualified spiritual leader. The same situation prevailed southward from Harrisburg to Baltimore, eastward to Philadelphia, and northward to Rochester. Circuit-riding rabbis such as Eliezer Silver, who served in Harrisburg early in his career, traveled often to these communities to provide guidance. Farther west, Benjamin Papermaster of Grand Forks was the only rabbi serving Jews in all of North Dakota and western Minnesota.

Many communities, even some of those not so far from the large cities, had to "import" at least some of their *yiddishkayt*. On Willard Avenue or on Gay Street in Providence, Rhode Island, families read aloud from the Bintl Brief section of the *Forward,* which came in daily from New York along with the *Tageblatt;* and in Sioux City, Iowa, the Chicago edition of the *Forward* was available, as was an occasional Yiddish theater group on tour from New York. But in these same communities, immigrant Jews also managed on their own. They derived their security and identity from a structured system of relationships and values which emerged from the private spaces of Jewish family and from *landsmanshaftn,* synagogues, and self-help and cultural institutions as much as from the physical proximities and densities of the Jewish immigrant communities.

The smaller cities and towns may have had neighborhoods that were less densely Jewish and less culturally diverse than the Jewish communities of the larger cities, but with increasing numbers of East European Jewish immigrants, these smaller places continued to permit and even encourage Jewish ethnic and religious identity. In Springfield, Massachusetts, for example, the German Jews had failed to organize a congregation or any other visible sign of Jewish life. But after 1880 and an influx of new immigrants, there emerged in Springfield a thriving Jewish community, mostly the conscious creation of East Europeans. Sioux City witnessed a similar development. The German Jews there had practically merged with the Unitarians, but the arrival of the East European immigrants, with their Zionist as well as socialist elements, their Orthodox as well as their "free-thinkers," breathed new life into the Jewish community. This sometimes happened even in cities of some size. In Cleveland, for example, a Reform rabbi said of the East European newcomers: "We look with disfavor upon their quaint customs, particularly . . . their religious observances. [But] if immigration has brought with it a Jewish problem, it has also brought much good, and one is the preservation of Jewish ideals."

The East Europeans helped revitalize Judaism in the American interior, but nowhere was the relationship between the German Jews and the East Europeans a one-way street. Most newcomers in need of aid were succored by relatives and friends, but in the early years a good number of immigrants, particularly refugees from pogroms and those arriving under the auspices of the Industrial Removal Office or the Galveston Plan needed the help of German Jewish institutions.

The established, prosperous German Jews everywhere supported their coreligionists by funding relief efforts, providing temporary shelter, and procuring employment. But members of the Jewish elites in the smaller cities and towns, like their large city counterparts, were at first ambivalent about mass immigration, and certainly about encouraging large numbers of East Europeans to settle in their localities. Sometimes resistance was direct, as when a spokesman for the United Jewish Charities of Rochester declaimed that "organized immigration from Russia . . . and other semi-barbarous countries is a mistake." Sometimes resistance took the form of directing immigrants elsewhere. In San Francisco several leading German Jews urged the members of Congregation Emanu-El to purchase Baja California from the Mexican government in order to settle Yiddish speakers there; in Portland, Oregon, the International Society for the Colonization of Russian Jews was organized with the goal of settling refugees on land in northern California; and in Cleveland, some new immigrants were assisted to move on to the short-lived Jewish agricultural colony at Painted Woods, North Dakota.

None of these efforts at diversion and dispersal succeeded, and the East Europeans continued to settle in the cities and towns of the American interior. The Germans initially responded with condescension and by maintaining their social distance. In Milwaukee and Detroit they complained that "the immigrants have been a class that reflects no credit upon their brethren." In Cleveland in 1895, a German Jewish public school teacher contended that her immigrant pupils needed to be removed from the influence of their homes and neighborhoods, which were filled with "bigoted followers of the orthodox rabbinical law [and] uneducated paupers . . . whose minds are stunted [and] whose characters are warped." In San Francisco the leading Reform rabbi and editor of the most influential Jewish periodical in the West described the growing Jewish immigrant neighborhood as a "reeking pesthole." In Columbus the Germans moved about as far away from the Russians as they could get; in Waterbury and Bridgeport, Connecticut, they tried to keep the East Europeans out of their synagogues and schools, and in Hartford, as late as 1901, the Touro Club was established for Germans only.

Despite the arrogance and hostility, however, the German Jews responded munificently. Rabbi Leo Franklin of Temple Beth-El in Detroit, where feelings seem to have been particularly bitter, reminded his congregation that as Jews their first obligation was to help the unfortunate. "How dare we expect the world to look with unprejudiced eyes upon us so long as Jew stands against Jew." German Jews responded positively to this kind of charge by rabbinical and lay leadership. Settlement Houses, Federations of Jewish Charities, and branches of the National Council of Jewish Women were established in Kansas City, Portland, San Francisco, Denver, Los Angeles, Indianapolis, Cincinnati, St. Louis, Omaha, Hartford, Pittsburgh, and Atlanta.

Extraordinary amounts of money, time, and energy were spent in philanthropy and Americanization projects. But condescension continued to taint the benevolence. East European immigrants in Rochester saw German aid as "cold charity and colder philanthropy." And charity applicants in Indianapolis, Columbus, Milwaukee, and Atlanta, like those in New York and Philadelphia, felt demeaned by the impersonal approach of the Germans and by the restrictions and stipulations attached to their benevolence.

The free medical care, the day nurseries, the orphanages, and the settlement houses produced important benefits for the East European Jews, but at least up to the period 1914–20, these failed to assuage entirely the bitterness stemming from German Jewish arrogance. Moreover, East Europeans were feeling the need to exercise their own creativity and leadership. And at the first opportunity, as they did in New York and Boston or Baltimore, the East Europeans created parallel institutions in almost every city or town they inhabited. In Cleveland, for example, where Germans had established the Russian Refugee Society and the Hebrew Temporary Home, in 1897 the new immigrants built their own Hebrew Shelter Home, which they described as "the only institution in town which asks no questions of its clients." Perhaps the most striking cases of duplication occurred in Denver and Los Angeles. In each city both Jewish communities built national institutions dedicated to the treatment of tuberculosis.

The conflict between Germans and East Europeans was occasionally bitter, but sometimes it was softened by the sensitivity and commitment of extraordinary leaders. In Portland, Oregon, Ben Selling, a businessman and philanthropist, and Ida Loewenberg, who helped found Neighborhood House and a branch of the National Council of Jewish Women, were indefatigable in their relief work and in their efforts to promote cooperation and mutual understanding. Rabbi Stephen Wise, the outspoken social reformer and Zionist, who served Portland's Jewish community between 1900 and 1906, also brought his enormous talents to bear on the problem of building bridges between the Germans and the East Europeans. In Kansas City, Jacob Billikopf, a young Eastern European immigrant trained in America as a professional social worker, was himself a bridge between the two communities. Very much reflecting the background, career, and orientation of David Blaustein of New York's Educational Alliance, Billikopf served as secretary of the United Jewish Charities in Kansas City and sponsored the Jewish Educational Institute, one of the most successful settlement houses in the United States.

German Jews of the interior were discomfited by the class and cultural differences of their East European coreligionists, and they feared that visible concentrations of new immigrants would generate or intensify Jew-hatred. They were far from wrong. Anti-Semitism, in the form of serious discrimination and physical abuse as distinct from mental attitude and vulgar rhetoric, may have affected cities more than small towns and may have been more apparent in the East and the older Midwest than in the trans-Mississippi West and the South. But no part of the country escaped entirely the status anxieties, economic discontents, and inner-city ethnic territorial conflicts of the late nineteenth century which promoted anti-Jewish feeling.

In most places the anti-Semitism experienced by East Europeans took the form of verbal abuse. This was particularly true among young children. But Jewish adolescents often found themselves engaged in street battles with non-Jewish immigrants or native-born ethnics, and adult immigrant peddlers were beaten and attacked sporadically in Milwaukee, Detroit, and Rochester, New York, as well as in all the larger cities.

Occasionally there was a chilling reminder of the Old World, as when Irish workers attacked the funeral procession of Rabbi Jacob Joseph in New York in 1902, or when forty young Irishmen in Malden, Massachusetts, armed with iron bars, stones, and broken bottles, converged on the immigrant Jewish neighborhood of Suffolk Square in 1911 with shouts of "death to all the Jews." No one was killed, but the police hesitated to intervene while two dozen Jewish men and women were bloodied, grocery and meat market windows smashed, and an entire community terrorized.

German Jews were more likely to experience anti-Semitism as social

discrimination—exclusion from prestigious clubs and desirable neighborhoods. And they could not help but notice that exclusion intensified as Jewish immigration from Eastern Europe swelled. But in some places anti-
Semitism was more moderate than in others. In parts of the West, particularly
San Francisco, where German Jews settled early relative to most of the population and where they had become relatively prosperous and influential with
non-Jewish elites, they were better able to modify the anti-Semitism directed
against themselves as well as against their East European cousins.

In San Francisco and the West generally, with its Indian, Mexican, and
Asian populations, the drive to maintain white supremacy also helped dilute
anti-Semitism. But more important was the fact that the German Jewish arrival and influence in the West predated the crystallization of the scramble
for social status of the late nineteenth century. In San Francisco there were
Jewish mayors, judges, financiers, and merchants who helped construct the
basic institutions of the city, and acceptance of Jews extended widely to elite
social organizations. This situation remained virtually undisturbed even as
the new East European immigrants gradually pushed San Francisco's Jewish
population to nearly 7 percent.

By contrast, in Minneapolis, where the first German Jewish settlers
arrived only in the late 1860s and never acquired a position of any impor-
tance in civic affairs, the later Russian and Rumanian ghettos faced a much
rockier road to integration into city life. By 1920, German Jews were
excluded from Rotary, Kiwanis, and Lions service clubs, as well as from
social clubs and local realty boards.

Anti-Semitism in the South, while sometimes dramatic and explosive,
is more difficult to measure and characterize. The region was inhabited by
large concentrations of Black population, and like the West, it was marked
by a strenuous devotion to white supremacy, which undoubtedly deflected
some anti-Semitism. Moreover, German Jews arrived in the South relatively
early, and their presence as peddlers, merchants, and innovative businessmen
was seen as useful, partly making up for the lack of a native merchant class.
In the 1860s and 1870s, before the contentious battles for status, German
Jews belonged to fashionable social clubs in several southern cities, and they
were admired by many for their inventiveness and commercial energy. There
is a thin line, however, separating these perceptions from Shylock images of
cunning and avarice; and by the 1890s, when the whole country, including
the South, was undergoing rapid economic change, when status concerns
became paramount, and when Eastern Europeans became more visible be-

low the Mason-Dixon line, a new era appears to have been initiated. It began with the nightriders in Georgia, Louisiana, and Mississippi in the early 1890s (see ch. 3), and reached its zenith with the lynching of the German Jewish Atlanta factory manager Leo Frank in 1915.

The second or third largest Jewish community in the deep South, Atlanta appeared to be hospitable to its enterprising "Israelites" in the nineteenth century. Between 1874 and 1890, German Jews were deeply involved in Atlanta's civic life and achieved considerable political representation. But the beginnings of status rivalries, the psychological insecurities of gentile capitalists, and the arrival in Atlanta of several thousand Russian Jews between 1890 and 1910 all came together to create tension and trouble.

Between 1890 and 1930 only one person of Jewish descent was elected to office in Atlanta, and he had long since given up any attachment to or identification with Judaism. By the early twentieth century, Jews as a group were excluded from Atlanta's most prestigious clubs. Not long afterward they were excluded as well from clubs in Richmond, Virginia, and from elite Mardi gras festivities in New Orleans. Rabbi David Marx, the spiritual leader of the Reform Hebrew Benevolent Congregation (The Temple) in Atlanta, believed that the presence of unassimilated, lower-class East Europeans had negatively affected the image of the Jews within the gentile community. Significant numbers of German Jews in Atlanta appear to have agreed with Marx; in 1905 they formed the exclusive Standard Club, from which they barred Eastern Jews in an attempt to maintain social distance and distinction and to ape gentile society.

The Germans believed that the "contemptible" Russians were the reason for the new anti-Semitism; the Russians in turn thought the "arrogant" Germans were deceiving themselves about their acceptance in the host society and about the positive qualities of rapid assimilation. Tension within each group of Jews as well as between them mounted in 1906, when Atlanta was the scene of a major race riot. Speeches and newspaper articles preceding the riot pointed to Jews as saloon keepers and brothel owners and fed the popular conviction that Jews encouraged Black licentiousness. Jews constituted only a tiny percentage of tavern owners and do not seem to have had any commercial connection to brothels. They did, however, live among Blacks, and their small stores were sometimes near or in the same buildings as brothels. This was enough to produce vicious anti-Semitic diatribes and, in the context of anti-Black violence, substantial damage to Jewish property.

The part of the riot that touched the East European community was seen by them as a rather benign American version of an all too familiar Old World phenomenon. The Germans, on the other hand, were seriously shaken, but not as thoroughly as they would be seven years later, when the arrest of Leo Frank encouraged the pervasive expression of latent anti-Semitism in Atlanta and in the Deep South generally.

Leo Frank, brought from New York by his uncle, a respected citizen of long standing in Atlanta, quickly became a member of the Temple community. He married into an established family and was elected president of the local B'nai B'rith lodge. When in 1913 Mary Phagen, a thirteen-year-old employee of his factory, was found brutally murdered, Frank was arrested, and, on only scanty evidence and contradictory testimony, convicted and sentenced to death.

The Reverend Luther Bricker, the murdered girl's pastor, later wrote that "When the police arrested a Jew, and a Yankee Jew at that, all of the inborn prejudice against the Jews rose up in a feeling of satisfaction that here would be a victim worthy of the crime." The courthouse during the trial was surrounded by throngs of people making anti-Semitic speeches and remarks, and Populist Tom Watson's *Jeffersonian* unleashed a series of vituperative attacks, alleging that Jews were involved in international plots and that they secretly lusted after Christian girls.

Frank's sentence was later commuted to life imprisonment by the state governor. This greatly angered many Georgians, who reacted by calling for the governor's impeachment. Unsuccessful here, they soon took matters in their own hands. In 1915, after one attempt on Frank's life failed, the prisoner was taken by a mob from the Atlanta Penitentiary to Marietta, Georgia, Mary Phagen's hometown, and lynched. While other anti-Semitic incidents and insensitive actions occurred before and after the Frank episode, none equaled it in its impact on the German Jewish community. Whereas in New York anti-Semitic violence mainly took the form of Irish workers rioting against Jewish workers, in the South, Jews were disproportionately socially mobile, and working-class whites had attacked a white middle-class manager. Class antagonism had been added to ethnic and religious anti-Semitism, and the Germans now viewed their acceptance in Atlanta as fragile and tenuous. Some even left the city.

The Frank lynching pales in comparison to the violence done to Blacks in the South and even to Italians—twenty-two Italian immigrants were lynched by southern mobs between 1891 and 1901. Moreover, although a revived Ku Klux Klan emerged in Atlanta and spread throughout the South, the anti-Semitism of Klan members appears to have been discharged more often against the imaginary distant Jew, the Rothschild, than it was against Jewish neighbors and merchants.

Recognizing this, Jews made no mass exodus from the South, nor did they retreat entirely behind closed doors. But the events leading up to the Frank lynching ended the most active period of political involvement by Jews in the South prior to World War II. Southern anti-Semitism may have been less consistent and excessive than that of the Northeast, just as American anti-Semitism in general was less potent and pervasive than that of Europe, but it could have important consequences nonetheless.

American Jewish life in the South, as in all other regions of the country, was not essentially characterized by struggles against anti-Semitism. Much more markedly, the American Jewish experience, as I have noted throughout, was shaped by mobility and the rhythms of the great American balancing act—the need for acculturation on the one side, and the desire to retain something of a Jewish world on the other. This dynamic was a central and defining experience for both German and East Europeans Jews everywhere in the United States.

Beyond New York City and the other large metropolitan centers, adventurous East European immigrants joined and ultimately vastly outnumbered the Germans. In every place the newcomers created problems for the Jewish establishment, but over time they were accommodated and integrated. Indeed, in many areas the new immigrants, with their penchant for residential and business clustering and their strong Jewish identity, resuscitated Jewish community. The confluence of Jewish stores, institutions, workplaces, and residences transformed the public character of the neighborhood streets wherever significant numbers of immigrant Jews settled. Less densely populated than those of New York, Boston, Philadelphia, and Baltimore, and perhaps less culturally diverse than the Lower East Side, which could afford the luxury of innumerable intramural arguments, Jewish communities in the smaller cities and towns remained visibly Jewish.

In these smaller cities and towns, East European Jews, like the Germans who preceded them, were highly mobile. In the American interior, where Jews were more involved with commerce, business enterprise led more frequently and easily to success than in the northeast urban corridor, where the majority of immigrant Jews were laborers.

But in the cities, too, the proletariat also made gains. Some of the improvements in the physical environment of the Jewish ghetto dwellers and laborers were the result of factory and tenement investigations, new legislation, and intensified implementation of older laws. Other material improvements, including better working conditions and increased income, were partly the result of a labor movement that educated and mobilized Jewish workers and became another vital ingredient in the culture of a transforming American Jewry.

7

Jewish Labor,
American Politics

The great mass of gainfully employed Jews in Eastern
Europe had been small businessmen and independent craftsmen for generations. The development of working-class consciousness among them began
in earnest only in the late nineteenth century, when large numbers of petit-
bourgeois Jews suffered precipitous economic displacement and were forced
to work for wages. The making of the Jewish working class continued and
intensified with immigration to the larger American cities, where most Jewish newcomers confronted an even more highly industrialized environment
than they had begun to experience in Eastern Europe. The implications of
Jewish proletarianization were articulated and reinforced by the activities of
a remarkable group of radical intellectuals and organizers—young Jewish
men and women, mostly former students—who provided leadership and a
persuasive and attractive socialist critique of capitalism.

The struggle to mobilize and improve the lot of Jewish workers in the
United States, as in Eastern Europe, occurred within the ideological framework of socialism. It also occurred almost entirely within the Jewish ethnic
economy. Successful Jewish entrepreneurs, German and East European, were
confronted by mainly Jewish laborers, who were led by an energetic group
of radical Jewish organizers. The workers grew increasingly receptive to the
radicals, who learned to explain socialism and class struggle in terms of social
justice, the prophetic tradition, and the concept of *tikn olam,* an injunction,
derived from Judaic religious culture, to repair or improve the world. By invoking a sense of shared Jewish cultural heritage, the radicals demonstrated
that they had not strayed so far, after all, from the traditional culture, and they
facilitated the temporary conversion of many workers to the new creed.

But most Jewish proletarians were not far removed from their petit-bourgeois origins or from the religiously based tradition of *takhles* (purposefulness); while sympathetic and responsive to the message of the socialists and the social idealism of the labor movement, Jewish workers retained their own goal of rising out of the working class rather than with it. These workers, in fact, helped teach the organizers and radical intellectuals that immediate incremental improvements were as important as the longer-term goal of restructuring society.

Participation in socialism and trade unionism pulled Jewish workers and labor leaders deeper into the modern world and farther into the dynamic processes of American life; but the Jewish labor movement never completely cast off its unique ideological baggage. Although the movement lasted little more than one generation, its accomplishments and progressive echoes continue to reverberate in the contemporary world and to inform Jewish American social and political values.

Like the radicals who remained in Russia, at least up to the 1890s, many of the immigrant intellectuals failed to connect in any significant way to the emerging Jewish proletariat in America. They spoke Russian to immigrants whose language was Yiddish, and for a time they focused mainly on the possibilities of revolution in the Old World. But exposure to intolerable working conditions in the garment industry increased the sensitivity of the intellectuals to the needs of the Jewish working class. Abe Cahan, Michael Zametkin, Louis Miller, Zalman Libin, Morris Hillquit, and many other intellectuals worked, at least for a time, in the shops. American conditions, which produced the first solid Jewish proletarian bloc and forced the radical intellectuals into the factories, generated the belief in some that there *was* a Jewish working class and that it could be organized.

In 1885 the intellectuals made their first systematic effort to organize the proletariat by creating the Jewish Workingmen's Association, the first union to carry the label *Jewish*. Keeping the Jewish workers organized, however, proved to be a difficult task well into the first decade of the twentieth century. The intellectuals, having proceeded directly from messianic politics to labor organizing, continued to place more emphasis on abstract radical principles and less on specific conditions of individual trades. This gave, and would continue to give, Jewish unions an idealistic character that distinguished them, as one union executive put it, from the "purely business proposition" of the American Federation of Labor. But in the early years there was repeated failure to keep membership together once strikes ended or during the slack season.

There had been successful strikes by Jewish cap makers, men's coat tailors, and cigar makers in the 1870s in New York and Chicago, but the union locals that emerged in consequence were ephemeral, none lasting more than six years. In 1886 there was a massive cloak makers walkout that led to an enduring Cloakmakers Benevolent Association, but this development was exceptional. In 1888, when the socialists created the United Hebrew Trades, a labor union "federation," only the typesetters and choristers were firmly organized.

Although between 1888 and 1890 nearly forty unions were established and brought together in the United Hebrew Trades, it continued to be difficult to maintain union solidarity in the off season or after a strike. This had to do with the historical fact that Jews, denied purchase of land and proscribed from participating in a variety of occupations and fields in the Old World, had worked in crafts and small businesses for generations and had come to believe that a "melukhe iz a malkhes" (a trade is a kingdom). The ambitions, therefore, of Jewish immigrant workers often lay elsewhere than in the factory or shop. Israel Barsky, who came to the United States with the Odessa group of Am olam, complained that few workers were class conscious; each "wants to become a capitalist." Some of the workers would not have put it quite that way. They wanted to escape the torments of the shops; some thought they could do this more quickly as individuals than as members of a class or a union. Labor activist Rose Cohen's father's dream was "some day to lay down his needle and thread and perhaps open a little candy store or a soda water stand."

The horrors of the sweatshop system which led many workers to think about escaping were made possible by the continued arrival of new immigrants in need of immediate income. They were reinforced by ambitious former workers, now contractors in competition with one another to offer manufacturers lower bids and speedier deliveries, and by the manufacturers, who naturally encouraged the cutthroat competition between the increasing number of contractors. This system and the uneven flow of work caused by the idiosyncracies of the clothing market compelled workers to toil at incredible speed during the busy season, only to find themselves unemployed months later. According to some observers, sweatshop work was so enervating that the productive life of an operator was about twenty years.

Factories, or "inside shops," were not much better, and often the routine was worse. Speed-ups were frequent, and the work was dangerous. Bosses took even greater advantage of "girls," most of whom they assumed were timid and green. Women, for example, were paid less than men for the same work, and they were timed when they left to go to the toilet. And bosses were not the only exploiters. Male workers did "inside contracting" by employing "girl helpers" as "learners" at three of four dollars a week. More than 20 percent of the work force, these women were often kept "learners" long after there was little left to learn. Accidents and shop fires were not uncommon. Clocks could be slowed down during working hours, and workers were charged for needles and the cost of electric power to run machines and irons. Until 1907 most workers had to provide their own "katerinka" (sewing machine) and pay a freight charge for transporting it from place to place. There were charges, too, for lockers and chairs, and fines were imposed for damaging garments, breaking needles, and arriving late. Understandably, Jewish workers wanted better jobs than these. Therefore the fluid, fragmented structure of the garment industry and a relatively steady influx of new immigrants contributed to an outflow of experienced workers into more tolerable, if not always more profitable, forms of employment. Such fluidity hardly lent itself to the maintenance of unions with stable memberships.

Jews, of course, also belonged to other organizations of mutual aid, and union dues were sometimes resented as an additional burden, especially when added to wages forfeited during strikes. One of the most important organizations of mutual aid was the *landsmanshaft,* and it provided benefits that fledgling socialist unions could not afford. The labor movement came to accept the concept of mutual aid associations, and many unions eventually adopted services similar to those offered by the *landsmanshaftn*. But in the beginning it was difficult for unions to compete with the more pervasive and attractive benevolent societies.

There were other barriers to large-scale mobilization. In 1913 there were still more than 16,500 garment shops dispersed throughout the larger cities of the United States, employing between five and twenty workers each. In addition, ethnic divisions between Jews and Poles and Italians, and even between the trained Jewish tailors from Posen and the more recently arrived, less experienced Russian Jewish needleworkers, often stood in the way of class consciousness.

Another barrier to effective union organization of Jewish newcomers was the lack of encouragement and support from the American labor movement. The reluctance of the more conservative union leaders and, indeed, their discrimination against Jewish workers were partly a response to the fact that Jewish unions were led by radicals. It was also partly the result of ethnic prejudice. But the basic cause of discrimination within the labor movement was economic interest. The late-nineteenth-century U.S. labor movement, represented by the American Federation of Labor, was built around skilled workers organized in craft unions. These unions stressed control over the supply of labor, and when the Industrial Revolution reduced the role of skill, thereby radically increasing the supply of labor, the unions turned to exclusion of new workers of all types in order to raise the price of labor. Most immigrants, then, including Jews, faced the paradoxical situation of an American trade union movement that sought *not* to organize workers.

Unions were also discouraged by bosses and managers. A variety of techniques, sometimes repressive, sometimes merely manipulative, were used to prevent unionization. Marsha Farbman, who had fled the Kishinev pogrom in 1903, went to work in a New York factory making false braids. She tried almost immediately to organize her women co-workers. "My Yiddish was not so good, but I spoke Russian. A few girls understood . . . so we were able to get together to plan a strike . . . . The forelady spotted right away that I was a socialist. She met with us and raised the wages to avert the strike and unionization. We got the few cents more on the braids and we went back to work. But we didn't get a union."

Despite all this, and despite the depression of 1893, the immigrant socialists garnered a mass following in New York and Chicago in the 1890s. Twenty-seven unions and socialist organizations from New York, with a membership close to fourteen thousand, were represented at a United Hebrew Trades conference in 1890, and UHT federations were created in Philadelphia in 1891 and in Chicago in 1896. As late as 1906 the majority of Jewish workers, like the majority of American workers generally, remained unorganized. But in fits and starts the combination of unionism and radical propaganda did provide a real connection between the socialists and the masses even in these early years.

Socialism was a vigorous and vital theme in Jewish immigrant life almost from the beginning, and thousands of Jewish workers made their first entry into American political life in association with the radical movement. In 1886 the Jewish Workingmen's Association formally affiliated with the Socialist Labor Party, led by a Sephardic Jew, Daniel DeLeon. In the same year the association joined a coalition of liberals and socialists to support the New York mayoral candidacy of Henry George. In 1887, two Jewish foreign-language federations were formed in the Socialist Labor Party, section 8 for Yiddish-speakers and section 17 for the Russians. Fourteen more Jewish sections were added in the 1890s, and as early as 1889 the party press celebrated the rapid development of socialist influence among Jewish workers.

Later, in 1901, Morris Hillquit, Eugene V. Debs, labor lawyer Meyer London, and Milwaukee's Victor Berger, "evolutionary socialists" who demurred from the "intransigent revolutionary determinism" of DeLeon, became founding fathers of the Socialist Party of America. One of the factors that sparked the withdrawal from the Socialist Labor Party and the creation of the new party was DeLeon's emphasis on "dual unionism." The brilliant but unbending class warrior demanded that several UHT unions detach themselves from the American Federation of Labor in order to join the Knights of Labor, an organization DeLeon hoped to control as a revolutionary base. Dissidents from the Socialist Labor Party who moved into the Socialist Party maintained that socialism was dependent upon the support of *existing* trade unions. They also believed, in contrast to the followers of DeLeon, that working to ameliorate the conditions of the working class through reforms of capitalism was not counterrevolutionary.

Jews came to support the candidates of the new party in increasing and disproportionate numbers. In 1908, Jews made up about 39 percent of the Socialist Party membership in Manhattan and the Bronx. Although many immigrants could not vote, they turned out en masse for rallies and organized enormous campaign meetings on the East Side for Eugene Victor Debs, the Socialist candidate for president. It was possible for the American journalist Ray Stannard Baker to believe in 1909 that "most Jews of the East Side, though not all acknowledged socialists, are strongly inclined toward socialism."

At the same time that the Socialist Party was attracting increasing numbers of Jews, the socialist-led Arbeiter Ring, or Workmen's Circle, was doing the same. A nationwide fraternal order and mutual aid society, the Workmen's Circle, organized in 1892, had only 872 members in 1901. But in 1905, after the organization received a charter from New York State and could offer safer and more attractive medical and insurance benefits, its membership grew to nearly 7,000. The worker members accepted the long-range socialist goals of the radical leaders, as well as the fact that the Workmen's Circle helped finance the socialist movement. In turn, the leadership gave first priority to meeting the immediate needs of workers. By 1908 the Workmen's Circle boasted ten thousand members, most of whom were not socialists but the vast majority of whom were sympathetic to the socialist movement.

As late as 1910 the Dillingham Commission reported that Southern and Eastern Europeans were "unstable" in their industrial relations and tended to "demoralize" labor organizations. These observers were blinded by ethnic prejudice. Isidore Schoenholtz, who came to America at the age of sixteen in

1906, just prior to the decade of mass labor struggle and victory in the American Jewish world, put it well: "Some did not believe that [Jewish workers] could be organized. . . . Time showed just the opposite. These were false prophets."

The true prophets were those who could talk about the discontent of Jewish shop workers in terms meaningful to potential recruits for labor activism. Union organizers, intellectuals, journalists, and political activists, in their efforts to mobilize the Jewish proletariat, tried to synthesize the essential values of Jewish culture with the modern goals and values of the socialist movement. They consistently wove biblical references, Talmudic aphorisms, and prophetic injunctions into their socialist appeals. They wrote and spoke particularly about the concepts of *tsedaka* and *tikn olam*. In all, they emphasized communal responsibility and secular messianism. Even Benjamin Feigenbaum, a writer who had rebelled against Hasidic parents, fiercely attacked the supernatural, and wished for speedy assimilation of the Jews, would frequently make some socialist concept clear and more acceptable by relating it to Jewish ethical precept. This was no mere expedient on Feigenbaum's part. He himself maintained a deep moral commitment organically connected to Jewish commandment.

Jewish labor spokesmen were in revolt against formal Judaism. But they were not yet secular; indeed their religious vitality was clearly visible. Religious values and ethnic attachments, in the richest sense of those terms, operated even upon those who thought they had discarded them as backward, and they certainly were meaningful to the average Jewish worker who read the radical Yiddish newspapers. In 1890, Abe Cahan began a weekly column in the *Arbeiter Tseitung* known as the "Sedre," the portion of the Pentateuch read each week in Sabbath services. Cahan would begin each essay with a formal element in the liturgy, but after a paragraph or two, he connected this to socialist principles and activity. A workman leaving his job on *erev shabos* (the eve of the Sabbath) and looking forward to a day of rest left this response to one of Cahan's columns:

> One Friday going home from work and considering what paper to buy, I noticed a new Yiddish paper. I bought it and began to read it, and remarkably, this was the thing I wanted. It was a Yiddish, socialist newspaper. Although till then I never heard about socialism, still I understood it without any interpretation. I liked it because its ideas were hidden in my heart and in my soul long ago; only I could not express them clearly. . . . The *Arbeiter Tseitung* preached "Happiness for everyone" and changes for the "betterment of the people." . . . This I could sign with both hands!

Abe Cahan's pieces proved so popular that even the anarchists tried to imitate them in the *Freie Arbeiter Shtime* (Free Voice of Labor) with a column called "Haftorah"—the segment from the prophets used to elucidate the weekly portion of Torah read in synagogue on Sabbath mornings.

Even more important to the socialist movement was the *Jewish Daily Forward,* which Abraham Cahan edited at its founding in 1897 and to which he returned permanently in 1903. In Cahan's hands the *Forward* became, along with the UHT and the Workmen's Circle, a critical component of the Jewish labor movement and of Jewish socialism. Cahan quickly changed the somewhat formal language of the paper to the Yiddish of the streets and shops. If "you want the public to read this paper and assimilate Socialism," he told his staff, "you've got to write of things of everyday life, in terms of what they see and feel."

Despite their cosmopolitanism and class war vocabulary, the "liberated" radical leaders and Jewish labor militants did not secede from the ethnic community. They helped Jewish workers in the struggle to create new identities out of traditional materials in a modern context. This struggle was not always conscious, nor was it simple. But it was made a good deal easier between 1905 and 1910 when large numbers of Bundist socialists reached New York after the collapse of the 1905 revolution in Russia.

The Bundists, like the radicals who preceded them to American shores, also celebrated the breakup of religious hegemony, but they strongly resisted further assimilation. They desired to remain Jews—atheists, socialists, but Jews. They brought with them sophisticated ideological defenses for this position, and they articulated them with spirit and dedication. They were effective. By 1906 there were three thousand members in *Bund* branches in America, more even than the enrollment in the Jewish branches of the Socialist Party.

At the same time that Bundists and other socialist labor leaders were invoking the familiar concepts of *tsedakah, tikn olam,* and communal responsibility, they were also appealing to the longstanding value of *takhles,* an orientation to hard work and sacrifice in order to attain an ultimate outcome, a significant individual accomplishment. The immigrant Jews had been raised in Eastern Europe to believe that there could be neither meaning nor satisfaction in simply living one's life; one had to achieve something. And because the socialists were no exception to this general pattern of energy and aspiration, they could serve as role models for the immigrant masses.

The career of David Dubinsky is a good example, and his story was very appealing to Jewish immigrants. Dubinsky came to the United States in 1910 with experience in radical politics and the desire to become a doctor. Full of energy, he went to work to earn money for his education but soon got caught up in socialism and union affairs. "With double pay for overtime, I was making as much as $50 a week," Dubinsky recalled. "But making money and making soapbox speeches at night for the Socialist Party didn't keep me busy enough. I began to get active in the union." He gave up his job as a cutter and took a full-time union position. "I wanted the job because there was so much to be done." Union leadership proved to be the perfect arena for Dubinsky's energy and ambition. He went on to serve more than fifty years in a labor career, holding many important positions, including the presidency of the International Ladies Garment Workers Union (ILGWU) and a vice presidency in the American Federation of Labor.

Socialist trade unionism appears to have offered to Jews something similar to what the Catholic Church offered the Irish Americans: the opportunity for the achievement of both common goals and personal promotion. A significant number of Jewish radicals and organizers, almost all of whom had been shop workers, made careers in the labor movement. Jewish unions, however, were not only agents in the class struggle; they were also social centers, political forums, and training schools. Ambitious young people could, with practice, learn to hold meetings, to speak publicly, and to develop ideas and talents for political leadership. This not only promoted the rise of a professional cadre of Jewish union leaders, but it also enabled others to rise out of the unions and enter the middle class or to follow intellectual callings.

Men and women who moved along these paths were attractive role models for the Jewish masses. When large audiences of Jewish workers listened to the speeches of Morris Hillquit, who had risen in less than two decades from indigent cuff maker to socialist theoretician and prosperous lawyer, many, though committed to socialism, must also have been dreaming of such a meteoric rise for themselves or their children.

Jewish immigrant desire to rise in station was strong and unrelenting, but it was also full of shadings and complexities. Just as Jewish socialism was a creative synthesis of older cultural values and the newer requirements of an industrial order, so participation in socialism for some Jews was an energetic merging of individual ambition with collective idealism.

Visions of proletarian solidarity would dim over time to become overshadowed by the remarkable upward mobility of Jewish immigrants and their children. In the meantime the socialists furnished the Jewish labor movement with important vehicles of worker education and mobilization—the UHT, the Workmen's Circle, and the *Jewish Daily Forward*. With these institutions the East European newcomers built the first consciously Jewish power base in America. Using that base, the socialist movement set out through strikes and union building to solve some of the more practical problems of the workers.

In response to horrendous working conditions in the garment industry, there were arduous but successful strikes in New York and Philadelphia in 1890, and there was a series of minor victories in several cities in 1899 and the early 1900s. Samuel Gompers, president of the American Federation of Labor (1886–95 and 1896–1924), played an important role as a mediator for Jewish labor at this time. In principle, Gompers was against separate ethnic unions and was a conservative craft unionist and vocal antisocialist. But recognizing the potential power of a mobilized Jewish garment proletariat, Gompers volunteered his assistance to the UHT in forming Jewish unions between 1894 and 1896, and later as well.

Union organizing was inhibited by the depression of 1907–8, but with economic recovery the unions were reenergized. On 22 November 1909, twenty thousand shirtwaist makers, mostly Jewish women between the ages of sixteen and twenty-five, went on strike. Only a small minority were members of the ILGWU. Yet in the year following this general "uprising," Local 25 alone counted over ten thousand members. The shirtwaist makers' rebellion, the largest strike by women in the United States up to that time, stimulated more strikes and victories, which led to the emergence of the ILGWU as a major force in labor relations and to the formation of stable and enduring socialist unions. It is important therefore to examine the conditions that led to the 1909 strike.

Conditions in the shirtwaist factories were somewhat better than in other parts of the garment industry. The shops tended to be newer and cleaner. But hours were long and speed-ups were common. The women, moreover, were victimized by sex discrimination in addition to poor working conditions. They were also vulnerable to sexual harassment. Fannie Shapiro had to leave her job because "the boss pinched" her. She "gave him a crack and he fell. He was very embarrassed; so the whole shop went roaring." The workers laughed, but sexual harassment was a serious problem; it is reported in a significant number of memoirs, and once women were organized and union grievance procedures established, charges of sexual abuse abounded.

In 1909 the Triangle Shirtwaist Company, one of the largest manufacturers, had fired a number of workers suspected of organizing activities. Local 25 of the ILGWU called a strike against the firm in September. The

Leiserson shop also went out. Weariness and demoralization set in among the strikers after a month of hunger, beatings by hired thugs, and bullying by police. At a meeting of thousands of workers at Cooper Union on 22 November, Local 25 proposed a general strike. A debate ensued which dragged on for hours.

One of the strikers from Leiserson's, "a wisp of a girl," who in several weeks of picket line scuffles was arrested seventeen times and had six ribs broken, asked for the floor. Clara Lemlich addressed the audience in Yiddish: "I am a working girl; one of those who suffers from, and is on strike against the intolerable conditions portrayed here. I am tired of listening to those who speak in general terms. I am impatient. I move a general strike—now!"

The enthusiasm of the crowd was tumultuous. The chairman, Benjamin Feigenbaum, who later wrote a book on the labor laws of the Talmud, grabbed the young woman's arm, raised it, and called out in Yiddish: "Do you mean faith? Will you take the old Hebrew oath?" With a sea of right arms raised, the crowd recited, "If I turn traitor to the cause I now pledge, may this hand wither from the arm I now raise." The general strike was on.

Clara Lemlich was no stranger to radicalism and strikes. From the time she was ten in the Ukraine, she had been reading Turgenev, Gorky, and revolutionary literature. She arrived in the United States after the Kishinev pogrom of 1903. Within a week the fifteen-year-old was at work in New York's shirtwaist industry. She was a relatively well-paid draper, saving money for medical school, when in 1906, as she put it, "some of us girls who were more class-conscious . . . organized the first local." Lemlich was one of seven young women and six men who founded Local 25 of the ILGWU. She participated thereafter in a number of strikes that led up to the major conflict of 1909, by which time she had become well known in trade union and socialist circles.

Clara Lemlich was part of a growing and important cadre. In many shops there were young, unmarried women like her who influenced significant numbers of others. They did this through persistent discussion, by invoking a sense of sisterhood, and by example. Most Jewish women workers looked to marriage to save them from the shops. But many, whose aspirations had been raised by changes in the old country and by the promise of the New World, were going to school at night, saving some of their wages, and dreaming of self-sufficiency.

Even though a good part of their wages frequently went to supplement family income, to support the education of brothers, or to help bring relatives across the Atlantic, the working women could feel some sense of self-confidence and some hope of eventual independence. Flora Weiss, for example, who came to America at age fourteen, quickly landed a job and almost immediately enrolled in night school. She wanted to learn and she also "wanted to earn a lot of money." "I wanted to support myself. I also wanted to organize the workers . . . to do something for mankind. I thought I would see a better world." It was this characteristic combination of high aspiration and social idealism that led a disproportionate number of young Jewish women to become active in the labor movement.

Some women such as Pauline Newman, Rose Schneiderman, Theresa Malkiel, Fannia Cohn, and Rose Pesotta, despite the sacrifices, the loneliness, the resistance of union men, and the condescension of the Socialist Party, devoted their entire lives to the radical labor movement. Although denied an equitable share of executive positions, these women helped build a number of important union locals. They also pioneered new union programs, which were significant long-term accomplishments, including, for the ILGWU, a successful vacation retreat and an effective workers' education department.

The example of activist Jewish women workers energized the entire Jewish labor movement. The men's Great Cloak Makers' Revolt in 1910 was partly the result of the new sense of combativeness and commitment demonstrated by the women in the great uprising of 1909. In July 1910, after careful preparation by the ILGWU, approximately sixty-five thousand workers, mostly male, left their workbenches in the cloak and suit trade and walked the picket lines.

The strikers, well organized and financed, made the closed shop an important demand. The manufacturers believed that giving in to this demand would turn control of the industry over to the union, and they opposed it with all their resources. The battle was long and bitter and again, unfortunately, marked by violence. Some leaders of the Jewish community, particularly the uptowners, were distressed by the "scandal" of downtown Jews warring against one another before the unsympathetic eyes of the public.

Invoking Jewish tradition, several among the establishment called for mediation to end the dispute. Jacob Schiff got involved; so did social worker Henry Moskowitz, Boston department store magnate A. L. Filene, attorney Julius H. Cohen, and many other prominent German Jews. Samuel Gompers also intervened for a time, but it took the talents of Louis Brandeis, the Boston "people's attorney," and Louis Marshall to break the deadlock.

The agreement that emerged, the Protocol of Peace, abolished the detested charges and fines, prohibited subcontracting and homework, raised wages, and decreased the work week to fifty hours. On the issue of the closed shop, Brandeis came up with the "preferential shop," a new concept temporarily tolerable to both sides which called for showing preference in hiring to union members.

Of even greater consequence were a variety of provisions designed to promote long-term peace in the industry, including the union's giving up the right to strike in return for the manufacturers' surrender of the lockout. A board of arbitration was created to settle major disputes and a board of grievances to resolve minor conflicts and complaints. In addition, a joint board of sanitary control was established to supervise the maintenance of decent working conditions. Despite evasion and ultimate breakdown, the protocol, which represented both an employers' association and unions constituting 60 percent of the industry, pioneered new paths for industrial peace. All subsequent labor conflicts in the apparel field drew upon the protocol experience.

At the end of September 1910, three weeks after the Great Cloak Makers' Revolt had been settled, nearly one thousand workers struck in Chicago to protest pay cuts at Hart, Schaffner and Marx, the city's giant manufacturer of men's clothing. In less than a month there were more than thirty-five thousand mostly Jewish strikers on the picket lines, confronting more than fifty firms.

The more than seven thousand employees of Hart, Schaffner and Marx and thousands of other garment workers, through the intervention of an arbitration committee, eventually emerged victorious, and their victory, like that of the New York cloak makers, had ramifications beyond their shop and even beyond the garment industry. Permanent arbitration machinery was set up which eventually grew into the "impartial chairman" system—agreements, rules, and regulations recognizing the mutual interests of employers and workers and binding upon both. In 1914 these same tailors, joined by others in New York, mostly Jews under the leadership of Sidney Hillman, broke away from the United Garment Workers to form the Amalgamated Clothing Workers of America, which became a massive and powerfully effective labor federation.

Although in several cities the Jewish labor leaders and workers accepted, and perhaps counted on, mediation by the uptown German Jews in settling with the downtown Jewish manufacturers, bitter class conflict continued to mark American Jewish life through the period of World War I. Jewish, and increasingly Russian Jewish, owners of factories and shops were persistent in their attempts to destroy Jewish union organization. They hired spies, fired activists, used a combination of bribery and threat, and finally resorted to brute force against fellow Jews. In Philadelphia in 1906, one of the largest shirtmakers, Tutelman Brothers and Fagen, determined to rid themselves of unions by any means, including anti-Semitic rabble-rousing, which provoked serious street battles between gentile and Jewish workers. And in Baltimore in 1913 police reacted so brutally to striking Jewish clothing workers that leaders of the gentile community were impelled to aid the strikers and even walked the picket lines.

The strikes in the period from 1907 to 1913 were marked by violence on both sides. It is clear that the employers were the aggressors, but in order to protect themselves and their picketers, union leaders also sometimes used goons and gangsters. Israel Cohen, for example, a labor leader in the fur trade, hired tough "boys" to protect strikers who were "bearded and skull-capped Jews or young girls." But tough boys too often turned out to be tar babies who "stuck," and violence never quite disappeared from the labor struggles.

Perhaps no single development galvanized Jewish immigrants for militant unionism and socialism more than the Triangle Shirtwaist fire of 1911. The blaze, which killed more than 140 women, broke out in the nonunion shop on the top floors of the Asch Building off Washington Square in downtown Manhattan. The tragedy made the deepest impression on laborers and nonlaborers alike and touched lives far and wide. Indeed, the news reached into the *shtetlekh* of Lithuania and deep into the Ukraine, where relatives, friends, and neighbors knew one or more of the victims. Rose Pesotta's sister had worked in the Triangle shop until 1910 and wrote to her parents in Derazhnya in 1911 that two young girls from that provincial town had perished on the sidewalks of New York. The Yiddish press repeated the harrowing details of locked doors, inadequate fire escapes, burning bodies.

At protest meetings after a stirring mass funeral for the victims, organizers and activists such as Rose Schneiderman hammered home the message: "I know from . . . experience it is up to working people to save themselves. The only way they can . . . is by a strong working-class movement." Audiences were responsive. In 1912 another general strike rocked the garment industry; this time some ten thousand furriers walked the picket line. Employers' representatives refused to enter the negotiating room with union officials, but Rabbi Judah Magnes's intercession brought a settlement modeled on the Protocol of Peace.

Memories of the Triangle disaster still haunted the community in the early months of 1913, and strikes in the shirtwaist, dress, and other industries that employed mostly women attracted wide sympathy from the public. The strikers were supported or encouraged by some of the city's leading preachers, including the Reverend Charles Parkhurst and Rabbi Stephen Wise, by the middle-class women of the Women's Trade Union League, and by former President Theodore Roosevelt, who called for a state factory investigation. Employers came to terms, and an attempt was made to create a blueprint for future negotiations in the chaotic women's clothing industry.

Still, after years of mutual suspicion and bitter conflict, industrywide peace was hard to achieve. A delicate balance of power and goodwill was required from both sides. But these qualities were strained by the depression of 1913, which reduced union membership and strength and put pressure on employers to cut costs. The Protocol of Peace was unilaterally abrogated by a group of manufacturers in 1915, and in April 1916 in the garment trades, there was a massive fourteen-week strike to win back the benefits of the 1909–14 period.

The years from 1909 to 1914 saw increased activity among working-class people throughout the United States, but the militancy of Jewish workers was particularly intense. In several major cities, as we have seen, tens of thousands of Jewish workers struck for higher wages, better conditions, and union recognition. The UHT experienced a phenomenal growth: in 1910 there were fewer than ninety constituent unions, with approximately 100,000 members; by 1914 there were more than one hundred unions in the federation with a total of 250,000 members.

In the same period, Jewish socialists broadened their influence in several Jewish communities, especially New York. In addition to actively building and strengthening unions, many socialists worked for the Socialist Party, recruiting members and garnering votes for Socialist candidates. Socialists rarely received more than 3 percent of the votes in New York; but between 1910 and 1914, Jewish assembly districts in the city delivered 10–15 percent to Socialist Party office seekers, and after 1914 the figure climbed past 35 percent. Jewish votes in 1917 were responsible for the victories of ten Socialist state assemblymen, seven Socialist aldermen, and a Socialist municipal judge.

Because socialism was also on the rise in America itself and reached a peak of influence between 1912 and 1916, many Jewish socialists felt that they were part of a movement that in the not too distant future could emerge victorious. This was a miscalculation, but understandable, and based on objective realities as much as on wishful thinking. As early as March 1900, the Socialist Party could claim the support of 226 branches in thirty-two states, and in November of that year there were Socialist candidates on the ballot in thirty of those states. Party membership in the United States went from 15,975 in 1903 to 118,045 in 1912, more than a 700 percent increase.

In 1910 the party elected its first congressman, the Wisconsin German-born Victor Berger. It also won control in twelve cities and towns and elected nineteen members to various state legislatures. In 1911 there were seventy-four Socialist mayors and other major municipal officers, and by 1916, twenty-nine Socialist state legislators in eighteen states. This was not simply the foreign-born's "tempest in a teapot." Socialists received significant pro-portions of the vote in several "American" towns. In Hagerstown, Maryland, in 1917, where only 1.5 percent of the population was foreign born, 15 per-cent voted Socialist. In Reading, Pennsylvania, a constituency with 9 percent foreign born gave 33 percent of its vote to Socialist candidates. And the vot-ers of Hamilton, Ohio, where only 6.7 percent were foreign born, gave 44 percent to the Socialist Party.

Native-born Americans made up an important segment of the Socialist Party. In addition, the most militant of revolutionists within the party were generally American—William Haywood, Jack London, and Frank Bohn, for example. The leading "conservatives" in the party, Morris Hillquit, Victor Berger, and John Spargo, were all immigrants. None of this should suggest replacing the older myth of immigrant radicalism with a newer one of native radicalism. Neither native-born Americans nor newcomers were monolithic groups, nor were they ideologically homogeneous. But Jewish immigrant socialists received supportive, encouraging signals from at least some mem-bers of the American host culture. Adolph Held sensed this. "The Americans that came to us," he said, "were always more radical than we were."

There were also some less supportive signals from a culture that was basically antiradical. The death sentence for the Haymarket anarchists in 1886–87 and the popular association of anarchism with foreigners no doubt had a chilling effect on many who contemplated espousing "dangerous" views. There was a growing anti-immigrant sentiment at the turn of the century, reflected in a series of restriction laws, and by 1903, Congress passed a bill that allowed for the deportation of immigrants deemed subversive. Further-more, repression of worker militancy in factory and mill towns such as Home-stead, Pennsylvania, and Lawrence, Massachusetts, was common between 1880 and 1920.

In some of the metropolitan areas, however, particularly New York, Philadelphia, Boston, and Chicago, where the Jewish working population was significant, there was also innovation and reform. In the years from 1906 to 1915, a period known as the golden age of Yiddish socialism, American urban Progressivism was reaching its peak. Native-born Protestant Progres-sives, mainly interested in restoring security, morality, and prosperity to

American life, pointed to the abuses of modern urbanism and capitalism, and they were often vividly descriptive. Many supported tenement and child labor reform and the regulation of working conditions in factories.

The Progressives, unlike the socialists, generally opposed a class analysis of society. Many were interested in controlling what they considered the pathologies of immigrant life, and often they ministered to the lower classes in condescending fashion. Organized labor, including the ILGWU, recognized and resisted the paternalism inherent in Progressivism and was wary of efforts by social Progressives to eliminate workers' problems by extensive legislation, particularly in the area of hours and wages. But some Progressives went beyond noblesse oblige and beyond the framework of legislative reform. Gertrude Barnum, the daughter of a prominent Chicago Democratic family, who moved from genteel middle-class reformism to the rough-and-tumble existence of an organizer for the ILGWU, represented the less numerous but more militant reformers who actively entered the trade union area.

John Dewey, the Progressive philosopher-educator, and Charles Beard, the activist Progressive historian, also had aims that were much broader than philanthropy or legislative reform. They advocated the right of workers to organize in unions to achieve their own formulated goals. This was true, too, for the middle-class membership of New York Women's Trade Union League, which contributed to strike funds for women garment workers. Mary Dreier, one of the league's more socially prominent and influential members, was arrested for picketing in the shirtwaist strike of 1909 and evoked widespread publicity and sympathy for the garment workers. Jane Addams, founder of the Hull House Settlement in Chicago, who looked forward to the elimination of unemployment and gross inequality, was also an advocate of worker organization. Abraham Cahan spoke kindly of Progressive settlement work and settlement people, and even the fiery anarchist Emma Goldman had positive things to say about Lillian Wald, the Progressive nurse who founded the Henry Street Settlement. Clearly, there were supportive links between American Progressivism, the American-led settlement house movement, and the radical Jewish labor movement.

The Jewish labor movement, by accepting allies in the nonradical world, by incorporating the Progressive tendencies of American life, and by learning to use its power day to day, in order to bring immediate benefits to workers, was an important Americanizing agency. But despite their new practical hardheadedness, the radical orientation of the socialist labor leaders continued to cause unease and cleavage between the Jewish needle trade unions and the U.S. labor movement.

The unease turned to serious concern during World War I when the leadership of the American Federation of Labor feared that the socialist pacifism of some Jewish unions would call the loyalty of the entire labor movement into question. Some Jewish unions, including the ILGWU, equally concerned about the distance between themselves and the national labor movement, began to support participation in the war effort, and they confirmed their new position with huge purchases of Liberty Bonds. Several Jewish labor leaders, in another accommodation to American sentiment, continued the process of moving socialist concerns, such as worker control and the restructuring of society, to the periphery of the movement in favor of a Gompers bread-and-butter type of unionism "pure and simple." They still believed that socialism would bring the better world, but in the meantime shorter workdays and higher wages would be sought.

Idealism and class-consciousness continued to mark the Jewish unions and were reflected in the frequency with which Jewish workers often crossed ethnic barriers to forge links with other working-class groups. Italian, German, and Jewish silk workers struck in Patterson, New Jersey, in 1913, and the support they received from New York City came overwhelmingly from Jewish labor. Irish transit workers struck in Harlem in 1916, and crowds of Jews besieged the trollies and tossed out scab conductors. There was a promise that year from other unions, mostly Irish-based, of a sympathy strike, but only the Jewish unions kept the promise. The Great Steel Strike of 1919 received approximately $300,000 in support from other unions; $175,000 came from the Jewish-dominated garment unions, $100,000 of it from the Amalgamated Clothing Workers alone.

Class consciousness remained an important force, but Jewish workers and Jewish labor leaders did not seek to sharpen the class struggle. Instead they pioneered virtually all the mechanisms for labor-management peace that exist today. As Sidney Hillman put it: "Labor unions cannot function in an atmosphere of abstract theory alone. Men, women, and children cannot wait for the millennium. They want to eat, mate, and have a breath of ease *now*. Certainly I believe in collaborating with employers!"

Jewish unions committed to socialism not only pioneered in labor-management cooperation, but they also became laboratories for testing social welfare programs such as the forty-five-hour, five-day week, paid vacations, unemployment and health insurance, pensions, medical care, educational and recreational facilities, credit unions, and low-rent housing cooperatives. These experimental programs reflected the Jewish unionists' vision of the good life—consisting of meaningful work, refreshing leisure, good health, and social commitment—and of the good state—consisting of an activist body politic and a government pledged to equity and social justice. Several of the programs were implemented later by the New Deal, in part because union officials such as Hillman and Dubinsky had a background in the socialist movement which prepared them for and moved them toward participation in the American political process. Here Jewish union leaders contributed significantly to keeping concepts of human interdependence and government responsibility for social welfare in the political dialogue, and they shared responsibility for several decades of reform legislation.

In sum, then, a radical Jewish labor movement combined socialist principles with practical day-to-day experience to build a power base for East European Jews in the United States. The movement, without jettisoning its idealism, used that power to establish an enduring union movement, institutionalize labor-management cooperation, and improve the conditions of life and labor under capitalism. In the process, the radical labor movement served immigrant Jews as a powerful agent of acculturation.

8

Varieties of Jewish Belief and Behavior

To the German Jews who settled in the United States in the nineteenth century, the "spirit of the times," with its egalitarian ethic and its emphasis on individualism, seemed to call for accommodation to the prevailing Protestantism of the new environment. They responded by gradually adapting Jewish religious ideology and form to the Protestant model, ultimately producing from indigenous sources an American Reform, similar in some respects to, but quite distinct from, the Reform Judaism then prevalent in Germany.

Reform emphasized ethical monotheism, rationalism, and the mission of justice as stated by the Prophets; and it moved toward universalism and away from the idea of separate Jewish peoplehood, as well as from the demanding rules of the Mosaic codes. Leaders of the Reform movement in America radically abridged the length and content of religious services, though not without dissent from traditionalists on the inside and from Orthodox resisters on the outside. Reform congregations decreased the use of Hebrew in favor of German and later, English. Many did away with prayer shawls and skullcaps, and some even introduced Sunday services and organ music. These changes were made partly out of concern for gentile approval, but also in the belief that the pervasive secularism of American culture would make strict adherence to religious law difficult, if not impossible.

Reform universalism appeared to be genuine and transcended tradition even to the point of including women. Most Reform temples permitted women to sit together with men in family pews and to sing in the choir. The Reform prayer book excised the male benediction thanking God "that I am not a woman," and women were counted as part of the *minyan* (the ten-person quorum necessary to hold services). Through Reform temple sisterhoods women administered charitable and other social services and tended to temple maintenance and to the religious education of children.

An attractive blend of egalitarianism, American secularism, and the highest principles of the prophetic tradition, Reform Judaism appeared in the 1870s to be at the threshold of making a triumphant sweep through organized Jewish religious life in the United States. Reform leader Isaac Meyer Wise established the Union of American Hebrew Congregations in Cincinnati in 1873 and the Hebrew Union College two years later, confident that these institutions would eventually unite and serve all American Jewry. The Hebrew Union College did not fulfill Wise's initial goal that it would be the only rabbinical seminary in the nation, but it did flourish, and in 1883 it graduated a distinguished first class including David Philipson and Joseph Krauskopf.

Institutional success did not, however, mean the end of religious contentiousness between Reformers and traditionalists, within the Reform movement or without. In the context of American secularism and anti-authoritarianism, the organizational rule in most religions was congregationalism. Final authority rested with devotional groups voluntarily associated with a movement or denomination rather than with the rulings of a central authority. Individual congregants exercised the same freedom to take from the faith what they desired and to ignore the rest. Sometimes the differences generated by voluntarism led to division and sharper denominational definitions. Judaism was no exception. There were many Jews, for example, who continued to be meticulous in their observance of the dietary laws; others accused these traditionalists of practicing an ancient barbaric cult and poked fun at "kitchen Judaism." The conflict came to an open breach at the "*treyfa* [unkosher] banquet" in Cincinnati on 11 July 1883 at the celebration of the tenth anniversary of the Union of American Hebrew Congregations and the first ordination of Hebrew Union College graduates. The first course was shellfish, which propelled a number of shocked observant Jews from the room, and eventually from the Union of American Hebrew Congregations. Visible insult had been added to the decades-old verbal attack on traditional Jewish practice. The provocative episode led to an enduring split within American Jewry.

Several Jewish leaders and groups, particularly in the East, were outraged by the *treyfa* banquet. The *American Hebrew,* for example, denounced the public flouting of ritual law by a rabbinical school supposedly serving all varieties of Judaism. By 1884 there was mounting pressure on congregations to withdraw from the Union of American Hebrew Congregations and to establish a new, more traditional rabbinical seminary in the East.

In this context and in part because of the arrival of new waves of traditional Jews, some Reformers such as Kaufman Kohler expressed the need for an explicit "Declaration of Independence" from "half-civilized orthodoxy." The goal was to distinguish Reform Judaism not only from the more traditional expressions of the Jewish religion, but also from the wholly nonsectarian universalism that was gaining popularity with Reform Jews whose Jewish identity had become marginal.

A major challenge to Reform Judaism had arisen in 1876 with the establishment of Felix Adler's New York Society for Ethical Culture. Adler, a former rabbinical student and the son of the rabbi of the nation's leading Reform synagogue, Temple Emanu-El in New York, saw no need for continued Jewish separation. He aimed to build a more moral "theology" and, in turn, a more moral world that drew from multiple religious traditions. Throughout the 1880s, Felix Adler, a brilliant and effective orator, drew enormous crowds, mostly Jewish, to his weekly Sunday morning lectures.

Threatened from the left by the universalism of Ethical Culture and from the right by Orthodoxy, leaders of the Reform movement held a conference in Pittsburgh in 1885. There they promulgated the Pittsburgh Platform, which emphasized Reform principles that were designed to distinguish people in the Reform movement from the ritualistic traditionalists and the radical universalists. The "Mosaic and Rabbinical laws that regulate diet" were rejected, as was the concept of heaven and hell. But it was maintained that the moral laws of Judaism continued to represent "the highest conception of the God-idea." The Reformers also made it clear that they saw themselves as a modern, progressive religious community and not a people expecting "a return to Palestine."

The radical spirit of the platform in time influenced the entire Reform rabbinate. In 1892, for example, the Central Conference of American Rabbis, representing nearly every rabbi serving congregants of the Union of American Hebrew Congregations, eliminated circumcision as a requirement for conversion to Judaism. It also approved the traditionally prohibited practice of cremation. Five years later, in 1897, the Central Conference of American Rabbis eliminated the traditional *get* (divorce decree) and *ketubah* (marriage contract) and reaffirmed the radical view that all Jewish legal codes were nothing more than "religious literature." In the same year, in response to the nascent but energetic Zionist movement, the Central Conference of American Rabbis rejected once more the goal of establishing a Jewish state. After Kaufman Kohler's assumption of the presidency of Hebrew Union College in 1903, Zionists and suspected Zionists were dismissed from the faculty.

Radical Reform generated efforts by the Orthodox to put their own houses in order and to establish institutional frameworks for recruiting and holding adherents. This competition during the 1880s and 1890s, when a mass influx of East European Jews inundated the German Jewish community, led to the now familiar trifurcation of American Jewry into Reform, Orthodox, and Conservative branches, as well as to significant division within each of these loosely organized denominations.

Some eighteen to twenty major synagogues in the United States were still Orthodox in 1881 when East Europeans began to arrive in large numbers. But for the most part the early newcomers encountered Reform Judaism, and they were clearly repelled by it. Many were already alienated from strict faith and observance when they arrived, but a break with Orthodox tradition did not necessarily mean a break with an ethnic culture rooted in the traditions of religious consciousness. Moreover, an important minority of transplanted Jews continued to envelop their lives in Orthodoxy. Others were what some have labeled "orthoprax," Jews who continued traditional practices but who did not believe in divine revelation. Even larger numbers of immigrants, though less observant, continued to conform to some traditional norms such as dietary regulations and *shul* attendance. Participation in synagogue services was especially noticeable during the Jewish High Holy Days of Rosh Hashonah and Yom Kippur. Indeed, in many cities during the Holy Days, congregations could not accommodate all who wished to attend services. On the Lower East Side of New York, for example, in 1917 it was necessary prior to Rosh Hashonah to create hundreds of temporary synagogues with a seating capacity of 164,000.

In 1881 only a tiny minority of the two hundred major synagogues in the United States were Orthodox. As early as 1890, however, after nearly a decade of mass immigration, the majority of congregations adhered to the traditional service, and by 1910, 90 percent of more than two thousand synagogues called themselves Orthodox. It appeared that the traditional Jewish religious spirit was being rekindled in America. But this was mostly an illusion. The growing number of synagogues reflected more the need for the regional ties and social familiarity of the old country, as well as lingering antagonisms between groups of Polish, Russian, Hungarian, and Sephardic Jews. And most congregations, whether in New York or Chicago, Providence, Cleveland, Milwaukee, or Indianapolis, were small *landslayt* groups without permanent rabbis or buildings.

Jewish piety never fully dissipated, but in individualistic America it did soften, and many Jews, even some only recently observant, gradually drifted into a secular mode of life. Those who remained pious faced great difficulties in America. The renowned rabbi from Slutz David Willowski (the Slutzker Rav) described the United States as "a treyfe land where even the stones are impure." The most poignant figures in the immigrant community were the small number of East European rabbis who came to the United States. Bearded, Yiddish-speaking, dressed in the Old World style, and stubbornly resistant to accommodation, these rabbis were unable to make life bearable for themselves; nor were they able to lead congregants in any meaningful way or to provide appropriate, attractive models for the younger generation. "The average Jewish boy of fifteen," reported the *New York Tribune* in 1905, "lives the life of New York contemporaneous to the minute," while his elders still live in "the existence of Kishinev, Lemberg or Jassy."

Lincoln Steffens, in the course of his newspaper work,

> would pass a synagogue where a score or more of boys were sitting hatless in their old clothes, smoking cigarettes on the steps outside, and their fathers, all dressed in black, with their high hats, uncut beards, and side curls, were going in . . . tearing their hair and rending their garments . . . . Two, three thousand years of devotion, courage, and suffering for a cause [were] lost in a generation.

The sympathetic Steffens was premature in his judgment. Jewish spiritual life in America, including Orthodoxy, would undergo redefinition and revitalization in the coming years and particularly after World War I. But Steffens correctly sensed that in the early years of the twentieth century, there was a sharp drift toward secularization in the Jewish community, as there was in most religious groups.

In those early years traditional Jews struggled to establish and maintain their own network of institutions, including *hederim,* or Jewish schoolrooms. But staffed by poorly trained, poorly paid, impatient, and frustrated teachers and attended by tired and bored boys, the schools lost more than half their pupils each year. Between 1903 and 1907, only 25 percent of Jewish children between 6 and 16 were receiving Jewish instruction, and significant numbers of these were taught at home by itinerant rebbes.

There were some schools of quality, particularly the communally run Talmud Torahs in New York. Originally established for the poor and situated in congested immigrant quarters, the Talmud Torahs on East Broadway and in Harlem, Brooklyn, and the Bronx attracted many pupils. Even in the best circumstances, however, Hebrew schools had to compete for the student's time and interest with the public schools and with the diversions of the American environment such as stickball and other group activities of the street.

A number of modern schools were also established by the Labor Zionists, the Workmen's Circle, the anarcho-communists, and the Yiddishists in an effort to link the generations by teaching the Jewish language and religion from a cultural and historical standpoint. These experiments generally remained on the fringe of the immigrant community. They imparted to some a strong attachment to Yiddish and *yiddishkayt,* but they could not stop the general tide of Americanization and secularization.

If the rabbis mourned on the one side the lack of religious observance among Jews, Christian missionaries despaired on the other about the failure to convert Jews. All through the 1890s and early 1900s, Jews were subjected to a campaign of proselytizing by missionaries who established headquarters in many cities. In Cleveland, for example, the Josephine Mission, a branch of the Euclid Avenue Baptist Church, opened its doors in the midst of the Jewish immigrant district and enticed Jewish children to classes with candy.

In some of the settlement houses attended by Jewish children seeking recreation or a hot lunch, the foundations of Judaism were attacked in less blatant but nonetheless irritating ways. Walls were adorned with crosses and crucifixes, while Jewish students were taught lessons in Christian ethics, or "universal values." The public schools, too, in their attempts to Americanize the immigrants, presented irksome difficulties for Jews, especially at Christmas time. Explicit attempts at conversion elicited rage and even violence from the immigrants; implicit attempts were met with boycotts of public schools and lobbying of school authorities to stop inflicting "repugnant religious convictions on the school children."

Despite the uproar against missionaries, official or unofficial, they posed little danger for the Jews. As the *New York Herald* put it: "The Jew of the second generation does not become a Christian. He is as far from any such conversion as his father." A more significant threat came from activities and diversions in the Jewish community that competed with religious observance and attendance at synagogue, such as the theater, night school, the labor union, the fraternal lodge, and the nonreligious Yiddish press.

The greatest danger, however, lay in the secular American environment and the fact that the business life of the nation ran according to the Christian calendar. The quest for economic mobility and the need to work on the Sabbath made piety difficult. This "economic factor," Rabbi Mordecai Kaplan complained, makes "the distinctive religious expression of Jewish life very difficult." Over time, as Orthodoxy became less necessary as a cultural and psychological anchor, its ritual aspects and social relations grew increasingly difficult to sustain. The *tsitsis,* the fringed cloth worn by males beneath their outer garments, and the *teffilin,* phylacteries wrapped on the arm and head every morning, were discarded. Wigs, prayer shawls, and skullcaps became less obvious. Synagogue attendance and affiliation plummeted.

The consciousness of religious tradition, however, was not lightly abandoned. Many Jews moved toward a compromise between the need for continuity and the need for change and did not discard their entire heritage. Some observant Jews steadfastly refused to give in to the pressures of altered circumstances and continued to try to recreate the religious milieu they had left behind in Eastern Europe. Centered after 1902 in Agudath Harabonim (the Union of Orthodox Rabbis), this constituency, including Jews from New York, New Haven, Connecticut, Providence, Rhode Island, Minneapolis, Minnesota, Omaha, Nebraska, and Louisville, Kentucky sought to reestablish the traditional authority of the European rabbi and frowned on any attempt at Americanization. Typical was the denunciation in 1900 by the Slutzker Rav of the English sermon, a danger so grave, according to him, that if it were allowed to go unchecked, "there is no hope for the continuance of the Jewish religion." The rigorous demand for traditionalism was not unique to the Jews. The Slutzker Rav's late-nineteenth-century denunciation was not so different, after all, from Pope Leo XIII's condemnation in 1899 of what he called Americanism, the attempt by some churchmen to accommodate Roman Catholic practices to the American culture; or from Pius X's critique of "modernism" in 1907, in which he predicted fifty more years of intellectual darkness for the American church.

The orthodox in many religions felt besieged by modern Western culture. A leading rabbi in Eastern Europe went so far as to tell those who had already emigrated to the United States that an "individual who truly fears the Lord . . . must not settle in [America]"; he must "return to his homeland where he can inculcate his children with Torah." Others among the Jews, however, believed that the Jewish religion had no future unless Orthodoxy adapted to an American idiom. This more modern group of traditional Jews, mainly from Western Europe, had its nucleus in the Union of Orthodox Jewish Congregations of America, established in 1898, and was represented by

Rabbis Henry P. Mendes, the spiritual leader of the Spanish and Portuguese (Sephardic) Synagogue of New York, and Bernard Drachman, an English-speaking minister and one of the first American-born, university trained, Orthodox rabbis to serve the needs of an American-born population.

Several Orthodox synagogues designed to serve "modern" young Jewish adults were established in uptown New York, as was the new "American" rabbinical association, the Orthodox Union. Drachman, Mendes, and other antiassimilationists who feared that young Jews were being driven from Judaism by intransigent Old World Orthodoxy hoped to serve as models for downtown Jews and to attract acculturated English-speaking East European Jews who wanted to retain a relatively traditional form of prayer service while eliminating some of the "unattractive" immigrant trappings of worship. But East European Jews most often preferred to remain nonobservant or less observant Orthodox rather than associate with the new American Orthodox religious life style.

There was a minority in the immigrant community, however, responsive to the antiassimilation crusade of the modernizers. East European Rabbi Philip Hillel Klein, a leader of the Union of Orthodox Rabbis and head of a large downtown congregation, broke with his rigidly traditional rabbinical organization and joined the Orthodox Union, which was American Orthodox. Klein also opened rooms in his synagogue for late-Sabbath afternoon services to accommodate those forced to work in the earlier part of the day. By 1910, Klein was joined in his action by at least two other East European rabbis.

A loose coalition of young downtowners, with help from Rabbi Klein and his East European colleagues, as well as from American Sephardic Rabbis Mendes and Henry J. Morais and German American Rabbis Drachman and Henry Schneeberger, established Young People's Synagogues offering "dignified services to recall the indifferent in Jewry back to faith." The English liturgy, the orderly rituals, and the general aesthetic reflected the congregants' growing identity as Americans. And making the late Saturday afternoon service into the major service of the week reflected the realities and rhythms of the American economy. Young People's Synagogue leaders did not approve of Sabbath violation, but neither would they condemn Sabbath breakers. They accepted them and served them. At the same time these leaders tried to make observing the Sabbath easier by lobbying against Sunday closing laws and by fighting for a five-day work week.

The Young People's Synagogues, the Orthodox Union and its unofficial youth division—the Jewish Endeavor Society, established in 1900—and the

modern Talmud Torah movement were all part of the antiassimilation crusade. Its goal was the adoption of American mores without the destruction
of the essence of Jewish faith and tradition. This was also the goal of the men
who founded the Jewish Theological Seminary of America (JTS) in New
York City. In response mostly to the need for an American Orthodoxy but
also to the antinationalistic and antitraditional postures assumed by the Reform movement at Hebrew Union College and in its 1885 Pittsburgh Platform, plans were made for a new rabbinical seminary in 1886.

Although the seminary developed into the central institution of a new
Conservative Judaism, none of the founders believed at the start that they
were promoting a separate denomination or movement. Indeed, many of
those men who later came to be known as the fathers of Conservatism were
difficult to distinguish from many of their colleagues who stayed with American Orthodoxy. Of the rabbis on the original faculty of JTS, four were considered at the border of Reform, but five—Drachman, Abraham Mendes, H.
P. Mendes, Henry J. Morais, and Henry W. Schneeberger—were Orthodox.
Furthermore, the seminary's constitution insisted on remaining "faithful to
Mosaic Law and ancestral traditions."

JTS, then, was first and foremost a rabbinical seminary dominated by
Orthodox Jews committed to combating radical Reform. Many on the faculty and on the advisory board, however, were dedicated to what Morais
called the preservation of "positive historical Judaism," a phrase that suggested discomfort not only with radical Reform but also with unbending Old
World Orthodoxy. And it was no accident that the new institution was called
the Jewish Theological Seminary, the same name as the spiritual center of the
positive-historical school at Breslau.

The positive-historical school, which came into being in Central and
Western Europe in the second half of the nineteenth century, maintained that
Judaism was the totality of Jewish experience—a dynamic and therefore
changing religion. It emphasized the "evolving religious experience of the
Jewish people" in their commitment to God and Torah. And while it spoke
for the authority of tradition, it also allowed for *wissenschaft,* freedom of research and expression.

In an address at the ceremony opening JTS in January 1887, Alexander
Kohut already envisioned an institution where "a different spirit will pre-
vail, . . . that of *Conservative Judaism.*" But the seminary, like the movement
for an American Orthodoxy, lacked a natural constituency. That constituency—acculturated East Europeans, and more so, their grown children—
had not yet emerged. By 1900 only seventeen rabbis had been ordained and

six congregations that had been affiliated with the seminary moved into the Reform camp. There were few new students and almost no funds.

It was this depressed set of circumstances that Cyrus Adler determined to remedy. Adler, an Arkansas-born pupil of Sabato Morais who went on to earn a doctorate in Semitics at Johns Hopkins, brought the seminary's condition to the attention of Jacob Schiff. An uptown philanthropist known for his devotion to Jewish causes, Schiff had long been committed to the Reform movement. But he saw that a revitalized modern seminary might succeed where Reform Judaism had not: in building a bridge to help immigrants cross over to American Judaism and the American mainstream.

Jacob Schiff persuaded his wealthy friends Daniel and Simon Guggenheim, as well as Mayer Sulzberger and Louis Marshall, to help. In a marvelous demonstration of patrician intelligence and commitment to the preservation of a religious-ethnic heritage, the group raised a half-million dollars to begin to refinance and reorganize JTS.

Solomon Schechter, whose reputation as a brilliant reader in rabbinics at Cambridge had preceded him, was recruited to lead the institution, which was to be housed now in an impressive new building in uptown Manhattan. He arrived in 1902 and brought with him a collection of brilliant scholars including Louis Ginzberg, Alexander Marx, and Israel Friedlander. All the men were products of traditional East European schooling who continued their studies in the more modern German and American universities. All were sympathetic to the need for a synthesis of the old and the new, the rational and the spiritual. And all were committed to an evolutionary perspective on Jewish law.

Under Schechter, a leading exponent of the unique blend of tradition and innovation that was at the heart of Conservatism, JTS stressed loyalty to *halakha* (Talmudic law), reverence for the Jewish past, the centrality of Torah and synagogue, and perhaps most of all, the unity of the Jewish people. But Schechter also clearly allowed for change when consecrated by general use and the conscience of the Jewish people, or in his words, by "catholic [universal] Israel." Despite his sincere disclaimer about starting a new Jewish denomination, Schechter, almost from the start and throughout his career, described his views by repeatedly using the term *Conservative Judaism,* and always with a capital *C*.

Leaders of the Reform movement, especially those associated with Hebrew Union College in Cincinnati, were predictably hostile to the new upstart JTS, which challenged Hebrew Union Colleges's hegemony in the field of rabbinic training. Similar sentiments were expressed on the other end of the ideological spectrum. The Union of Orthodox Rabbis in 1904, one year after naming the more traditional Rabbi Isaac Elchonen Theological Seminary in New York as the only legitimate institution for rabbinical training and ordination in America, issued a writ of excommunication against Schechter's seminary. Cut off from the left and right in American Jewish religious life, the leaders of JTS began to delineate more self-consciously the contours of Conservative Judaism.

In 1909 work began to establish a union of sympathetic congregations that could promote Conservatism, and by 1913 the result was the organization of the United Synagogue of America. It was a union of twenty-two congregations located in various Jewish centers ranging from Syracuse, New York, through Chicago to Sioux City, and from Newton, Massachusetts, through Norfolk, Virginia to Birmingham, Alabama. United Synagogue, with its emphasis on "tradition without Orthodoxy," represented perhaps the clearest beginnings of Conservative Judaism in America.

But what precisely the new movement's theology represented remained unclear. Distinct Conservative practices and rituals were only somewhat more discernible than its ideology. Many aspects of the Conservative service, though everywhere traditional in content and dignified in form, varied from congregation to congregation. A significant number of Conservative synagogues, mirroring Reform synagogues, had organs, mixed choirs, family pews, and English translations of prayers; some, however, had none of these. In other instances the Conservative service was not distinguishable from what Jews were doing in the Orthodox Young People's Synagogues, the American Orthodox synagogues, or after 1912, in the Orthodox synagogues associated with the Young Israel movement (see ch. 4).

Conservatives, as distinct from the Orthodox, who believe in a literal, direct verbal revelation from God, felt little pressure to conform to any particular theological doctrine or religious practice. There was instead respect for attempts to harmonize Jewish belief and ritual with modern thought. As a result a broad spectrum of theological positions, sometimes at odds, were held by the JTS faculty, the Conservative rabbinate, and the Conservative congregants. The laity wanted to preserve traditional forms, memories, and even the binding nature of Jewish law. But it wanted to choose for itself which specific aspects of traditional Judaism to maintain. Since all acknowledged that *halakha* was not divinely revealed but a living thing, Conservatism was constantly subject to variation and continued to contain within itself all the quarrels Orthodoxy and Reform Judaism had with each other.

The outstanding difference between the Conservative movement and the other Jewish denominations in the United States developed over the question of Zionism. On the one hand, the original classic Reform position emphasized universalism to the point of anti-Zionism; a negative attitude toward establishing a Jewish state also prevailed for several decades in the Orthodox wing. On the other hand, Conservatism, with its emphasis on Jewish peoplehood, had been the most comfortable home for Jewish nationalism and Zionism in America. Indeed, after Solomon Schechter gave strong support to the kind of redemption Zionism held out for Jews, it came to be seen as a kind of secular equivalent of Conservatism.

Despite its lack of official ideology and its ambiguities about what was unchanging and what was evolutionary in Judaism, the Conservative movement offered the children of East European immigrants an attractive option, one far more traditional than Reform yet significantly more American and modern than the Orthodoxy of their parents. Not surprisingly, a number of Conservative congregations appeared even in ghetto areas, and as early as 1916 many more functioned in areas of second settlement across the United States.

Erosion of strict religious observance and belief in the early decades of the twentieth century led not to assimilation but to Jewishness expressed in a variety of new religious formulations. Jewish identity was also maintained in new secular modes some of which continued to contain important dimensions of spirituality and ritual. One of these was Zionism, the movement to give the Jewish people its own home, preferably in Palestine.

Centuries of enforced isolation in the old countries had promoted a separate Jewish language and literature and a set of distinctive values and traditions. Indeed, in their predominant presence in the Pale, the Jews, though hardly sovereign, might even be considered to have had their own territory as well as their own culture. All of this reinforced a rich and powerful national-cultural heritage, difficult to give up. For American Jews, although Zionism never implied a personal imperative to settle in Palestine, the movement provided a vehicle for steering a course between assimilation and Jewish survival in the United States. More than the Kehillah, Zionism, with its emphasis on common tradition, history, and fate, offered a spiritual communalism that buttressed a sense of Jewish peoplehood.

In the late twentieth century, Zionism, or as some would have it, Israelism, had become one of the most important elements in Jewish American identity. But at the turn of the century, Zionism was poorly organized and without a large constituency. Except among a handful of East European Jews in the sweatshops, tenements, and cafés of New York's Lower East Side,

Zionism had little appeal in the unthreatening environment of America. Its strength lay in Eastern Europe, where emergent non-Jewish nationalisms were accompanied by new, strident forms of anti-Semitism.

The bloody pogroms that began in earnest in 1870 in Odessa and other Russian cities and towns helped produce a countervailing nationalism among Jews. Among the first spokesmen to promote a Jewish national cultural regeneration was the Odessa physician Leon Pinsker. In his book *Auto-Emancipation,* published in 1882 while pogroms raged across the Ukraine, Pinsker, although an acculturated cosmopolitan, rejected the assimilationist solution to the "Jewish problem." He focused instead on the possibility of creating a Jewish nation in its own national home, preferably Palestine.

But Zionism was neither immediately nor widely popular, even among the victims of pogroms. Orthodox Jews, believing they could not press for redemption through physical means, chose to wait for the Messiah to restore Zion, and they rejected the presumptuousness of the secular nationalists. Believing that anti-Semitism, like all oppressions, was rooted in the rotten soil of capitalism, the socialists worked not to foster Jewish nationalism but to abolish the bourgeois system. For these radicals, a just social order, not the "tribal particularism" of Zionism, would liberate all peoples, including the Jews.

The difficulty of pulling up stakes and leaving even an inhospitable environment was reinforced by the unattractiveness of Palestine as either haven or home. Though it had been the site of ancient Jewish territorial sovereignty and continued to shelter a small traditional Jewish population, Palestine did not appear to be the best place to reestablish a Jewish national homeland. Not only was the region ruled by hostile Ottoman Turks, but it was also poor and disease-ridden.

The beleaguered Jews of Eastern Europe who sought a haven emigrated most often to the United States. But a small stream of refugees, encouraged by Lovers of Zion clubs and various Zionist colonization societies, chose Palestine. The East European pioneers in some two dozen agricultural communities faced extreme hardship, and their experience discouraged a major migration. But the émigrés represented at least a beginning for the Zionist movement, which would soon find ideological support in the West.

An upsurge of political and racial anti-Semitism in Austria, Germany, and France throughout the 1880s and 1890s convinced many Jews that emancipation in Western Europe had failed. This conviction led, even among some assimilated Jews, to a reawakening of Jewish national consciousness. Theodore Herzl, an upper-middle-class, Hungarian-born journalist, had witnessed the resurgence of anti-Semitism; and in 1894, while serving as the Paris correspondent of the *Neue Freie Presse*, he was profoundly affected by the infamous treason trial and public degradation of the Jewish French army officer Alfred Dreyfus. "Death to the Jews!" Herzl had heard the French mob howl, "as the decorations were . . . ripped from the captain's coat." He was convinced that the Dreyfus case, with its travesties of justice and ugly race hatred, embodied "the desire of the vast majority of the French to condemn a Jew, and to condemn all Jews in this one Jew." That France, the very first Western state to emancipate its Jews, could continue to manifest such powerful Jew-hatred reinforced Herzl's growing conviction that anti-Semitism was ineradicable and moved him to publish *Der Judenstaat* in 1896, a proposal for the founding of a modern Jewish state.

Theodore Herzl proved to be a charismatic leader who gained financial and political support for Zionism in the West while simultaneously rejuvenating the pioneer Lovers of Zion movement in the East. In 1897, Herzl brought the two groups together at a World Zionist Congress in Basel, Switzerland. Here Jewish leaders dedicated themselves to the promotion of settlement in Palestine, "the organization and binding together of the whole of Jewry," and the strengthening and fostering of "Jewish national sentiment and consciousness."

Jewish nationalist sentiment in the form of the Zionist idea had surfaced in the American Jewish community as early as the colonial period. But substantial support for a Jewish home in Palestine developed only in the late nineteenth century in the context of Russian depredations against Jews. Still Zionism was slow to develop among American Jews. The economic difficulties experienced by immigrants in the United States between 1883 and 1886 and again between 1893 and 1897 drained potential enthusiasm. Zionism, moreover, ran counter to the desire to root oneself in America, which, despite occasional economic difficulties, seemed to Jews more and more like the true promised land.

In some Jewish quarters actual hostility to Zionism was manifest. Reform rabbis led by Emil Hirsch of Chicago, proud of their universalism and their Americanization and fearing the charge of dual or divided loyalty, ridiculed the Zionists' dream of Palestine. At the same time, Orthodox leaders in America viewed the Zionists as "going against God's will." Like their counterparts in the *shtetlekh* of Eastern Europe, New World traditionalists believed that if God "wanted us to have Zion again, He would restore it without the help of the so-called Zionists." In addition to opposition from religious groups, Zionism in America faced opposition, just as it had in Russia, from the Jewish antinationalist radical labor movement.

In such a context it is not hard to understand why American Jewry was represented by only one official delegate at the first World Zionist Congress in Basel in 1897. Although the Congress itself appears to have served as an energizer for the American movement—there were eight thousand American Zionists in 1900 and twenty-five thousand in 1905—these numbers represented a very small percentage of the more than one million Jews in the United States, and only a handful were actually active in the movement. Moreover, important American Jewish leaders associated with Reform and fearful of the charge of divided loyalty, such as Jacob Schiff and Louis Marshall, continued to express disapproval. Established Reform Jews, mainly of German descent, were particularly distressed when several of their own, such as Columbia University Semitics professor Richard Gottheil and Rabbi Stephen S. Wise, openly identified with Zionism.

For different reasons, East European Jews were also unhappy that important Zionist leaders such as Gottheil, president of the Federation of American Zionists, were part of the German Jewish establishment. The tensions between the East Europeans and the Germans promoted divisiveness in the movement; and the fragmentation was reinforced by the emergence of new groups of religious Zionists and socialist Zionists (Poale Zionists). Even earlier, the "territorialists," Jewish nationalists who were concerned more with speedy Jewish resettlement than with any specific locale, had engendered a split in the Zionist movement. Under the leadership of Israel Zangwill, who headed the Jewish Colonization Society, the territorialists looked for any "suitable" space, and when the British offered Uganda in 1905, the Zangwill group, unlike most of the Zionist movement, favored accepting it. In this way the territorialists alienated the more historically conscious Jews, who sought not only a haven but also a regeneration of the Jewish people and who thus insisted that the Jewish nation be rooted in Palestine, Israel's ancient homeland.

Some of the disunity and loss suffered by the Federation of American Zionists was repaired during these years by the administrative ability and energy of Louis Lipsky, an attorney. Zionist momentum was also maintained and aided by the leadership of the JTS. Although several seminary figures such as Judah Magnes and Solomon Schechter never came to support Jewish political independence, they were men of national stature who brought an important vitality to religious and cultural Zionism. Mordecai Kaplan and

Israel Friedlander, too, with their emphasis on Jewish peoplehood, promoted the cause of Jewish cultural nationalism.

Another important element sustaining pre–World War I Zionism was the Jewish women's club movement. Although some women in the movement, such as Hannah Solomon, resisted Jewish nationalism, many others saw in Palestine an opportunity to do good works and "social housekeeping." Rosa Sonneschein, Mary Fels, and Emma Gottheil devoted great energy to the promotion of Palestine as a Jewish refuge and as a center for the revitalization of the Jewish religion. And Henrietta Szold, a teacher and educational administrator who ran a night school for Russian immigrants in Baltimore between 1889 and 1893 and came to be one of Zionism's most prominent and influential figures, made her first pro-Zionist speech in 1896 at a local chapter of the National Council of Jewish Women.

In 1909 at her mother's suggestion, Szold visited Palestine and was shocked by the horrendous quality of health care available to the *yishuv,* the small Jewish settlement there. Her Zionist sympathies were reinforced, and by 1912, in addition to having served two years as secretary of the Jewish Agricultural Experimental Station in Palestine, Szold had generated the American Women's Zionist Organization out of a Zionist study circle. Soon renamed Hadassah, the organization emphasized the need for a public health and nursing system for the *yishuv* and promoted the resettlement of Jewish youth in Palestine. Hadassah grew to become the largest Jewish women's organization in the world and one of the largest women's organizations in the United States.

The Zionist movement, despite its organizational problems and ideological quarrels, had established roots in the Jewish community in the prewar period. In 1913 there were fewer than fifteen thousand members in organizations associated with the Federation of American Zionists, but that made the American federation the second or third largest in the world. In addition there were numerous Zionist organizations detached from or in uneasy relationship with the federation, which bolstered the Zionist movement. Although the primary loyalty of the Poale Zionists, for example, was still socialism, abhorrence of continued anti-Semitism in Europe often outweighed ideology and promoted cooperation.

The idea of a sovereign Jewish commonwealth remained anathema to the vast majority of German Jews; but many, including such important figures as Jacob Schiff and Louis Marshall, came to see Palestine as a potential haven for Jews and as a center for the cultural revitalization of Judaism. Both men favored colonization in Palestine and contributed funds for the economic development of the region. Even Julius Rosenwald, the entrepreneur who ran Sears, Roebuck and Company and an outspoken anti-Zionist, gave millions of dollars to support specifically Jewish projects in Palestine.

Beginning in 1914, certain developments served to strengthen the American Zionist movement in more dramatic ways. First and foremost was the opportunity for the realization of the Zionist dream presented by World War I (see ch. 9). Second was the recruitment of Louis Brandeis to the Zionist cause and his ascendancy to leadership of the movement. Third was the resolution of some of the longstanding operating difficulties of the Federation of American Zionists. In 1915 the Federation—soon to be renamed the Zionist Organization of America—with Brandeis at the helm achieved organizational efficiency and, more important, a cloak of respectability, and a way to deal with the charge of divided loyalty. American born, Harvard educated, a prominent Progressive attorney, and a Woodrow Wilson confidant, Brandeis gave American Zionism a new image.

Louis Brandeis was in his fifties when he began to think about Jewish identity, between 1905 and 1914, and he became totally committed to the Zionist cause. His attraction to Zionism grew out of a combination of positive experiences with East European immigrants and Jewish nationalists and disenchantment with New England Brahmin society. Between 1906 and 1909 it was increasingly apparent to Brandeis that his most valued Progressive ideas, which he associated with the Puritan pioneers and Yankee heritage, were rejected by the New England elite. In 1910, however, while serving as chairman of the arbitration board that produced the Protocol of Peace for the garment industry, Brandeis thought he found in the immigrant Jewish community, particularly its labor leaders, new and true carriers of the Progressive tradition. In his speech accepting the chairmanship of the Provisional Committee of the Zionist Organization of America (ZOA) in 1914 and again in an interview in *Invincible Ideal* in 1915, Brandeis said that his experience at the negotiating table in 1910 taught him that "the Jewish people had something which should be saved for the world." He had sensed there a deep concern for "true democracy" and social justice and "love of liberty and freedom," concerns that Brandeis shared and pursued for most of his adult life.

It was in 1910, too, that Louis Brandeis met Jacob de Haas, who had been Theodore Herzl's secretary. Initial contact led to a series of discussions of Zionism between the two, and a deepening sense of Jewishness for Brandeis. Around the same time, Brandeis had also been impressed by the work and pioneering personality of a Palestinian agronomist, Aaron Aaronson.

World famous for his discoveries of wild wheat in Palestine, Aaronson raised funds in the United States for an agricultural experimental station near Haifa. Brandeis, the Progressive, wedded to ideals based on smallness, efficiency, and pragmatism, was reinforced in his vision of Jewishness as democracy and Zionism as Progressivism.

Brandeis was also profoundly influenced by the ideas of Horace Kallen, a Harvard-educated Progressive, who taught philosophy and psychology at the University of Wisconsin before World War I. Between 1913 and 1914, in letters and conversations, Kallen helped his fellow New Englander perceive more clearly the relationship between Americanism, Hebraism, and Zionism. Hebraism, for Kallen, was not mere Judaism or religion but a construct that described the "total biography of the Jewish soul." Its spirit represented the prophetic legacy of social justice, international righteousness, and peace and was inseparable from the American core tradition with its universalistic and unique democratic mission. Indeed, Kallen believed that the biblical prophets had shaped the Hebraic character traits of the Puritans and, by extension, the American Republic.

The concept of a useable Hebraic past led to Kallen's vision of an America enriched by its distinctive ethnic groups: a rejection of the melting pot and an embrace of what Kallen later called cultural pluralism. Like the older Jewish nationalist Chaim Zhitlowsky, Kallen called upon the United States to shelter the "commonwealth of national cultures." Not only would the individual be blessed by the life-giving cultural sustenance of ethnic attachment, but also the creative unity of a variety of national cultures would lead to mutual enrichment. America would not be a melting pot but a symphony, one, as Judah Magnes put it earlier in a sermon, to be "written by the various nationalities which keep their individual and characteristic note and which sound this note in harmony." In this way the individual nationalities would not only deepen and enrich American culture but would also become channels for the most precious gift America could give, a model for a united states of the world.

Louis Brandeis gradually came to accept Zionism and cultural pluralism and, most importantly, their interdependent relationship. He saw Judaism and Zionism as essential parts of a democratic, ethnically pluralistic society; and he believed that Jews, in pursuing Zionist goals, would revive their great humanistic civilization. Two Jewish centers, America and Palestine, would feed each other, promoting a renaissance vital to American Jewish life as well as to society at large. In his writings and speeches between 1913 and 1915, Brandeis developed the classic syllogism summarizing his position: "To be good Americans, we must be better Jews, and to be better Jews we must be Zionists."

Not only did Brandeis supply an epigrammatic refutation of the charge of divided or dual loyalty so often leveled at Zionists; his formulations, emphasizing Zionism's benefit to America and the world, also allowed Jewish nationalists, both religious and secular, to make the case for cultural pluralism and the congruity of Jewish ethics and American ideals. Zionism or Jewish nationalism, like American nationalism, it was argued, gained at least part of its value in its universal mission, in its emphasis on democracy and self-determination.

The idea of mission, or the idea that Zionism, like American democracy, could serve as a model and a beacon to the world, had appeared in the words and deeds of Stephen Wise, Judah Magnes, Israel Friedlander, and others. But Brandeis made it popular and respectably American, especially after he penetrated the sacred precincts of American political life with his appointment to the Supreme Court of the United States in 1916. Brandeis also recruited notable and talented American Jews to the movement. Felix Frankfurter, Nathan Straus, and Louis Kirstein added stature to American Zionism and credibility to Brandeis's insistence that "there is no inconsistency between loyalty to America and loyalty to Jewry," indeed, that "loyalty to America demands . . . that each Jew become a Zionist."

Zionism as it developed in the second decade of the twentieth century enabled American Jews to support the ideal of Jewish restoration in Palestine without fear of compromising their American patriotism—that is, to remain American—and it also encouraged and helped American Jews to remain Jewish. As early as the 1890s, Richard Gottheil argued that Zionism would keep many Jews in the fold of Judaism who might otherwise depart. Solomon Schechter by 1906 saw Zionism as "the great bulwark against assimilation." The movement "must not be judged by what it has accomplished in Zion and Jerusalem but *for* Zion and Jerusalem, by awakening the national Jewish consciousness. Our [American] synagogues and homes show plainly the effect."

Judah Magnes also believed that Zionism would be a tonic for American Jewry. "The entire people must be organized in different forms, in different countries," he wrote to Chaim Weizmann in 1914. "Palestine should be the connecting link, the summit of organized [Jewish life]. The Jews of the world influence Palestine, Palestine influences the Jews of the world." Israel Friedlander agreed. Indeed, he went so far as to argue that American Jews would disappear unless they retained their vital links to the spiritual center in Palestine and to world Jewry generally.

Cultural pluralists, seeking ethnic harmony and a vital civilization, promoted the value of Jewishness and the idea that Zionism enriched American life; but Jewish nationalists in their advocacy of Zionism also promoted another complementary goal: the group survival of American Jews. Zionist appeals, however they were pitched, attracted increasing numbers of American Jews in the immediate prewar years. Membership in the movement climbed from about 13,000 in 1912 to 150,000 in 1914. By 1919, after the reorganization of the Federation of American Zionists into the more efficient Zionist Organization of America, and after five years of Louis Brandeis at the helm preaching the need for "Men! Money! Discipline!" the Zionist movement had reached a peak of 180,000 members.

Growth promoted optimism, but it hid some important fissures. The Brandeis leadership believed that the political and educational work of the Zionist movement could be ended and that the primary, if not the only, remaining task for Zionists was "the task of reconstruction" in Palestine. Building a potash plant along the Dead Sea appeared to be more important to the Brandeis group than the cultural and ideological programs that emphasized Jewish peoplehood, and this alienated many immigrant Zionists. The narrower focus was reflected at a convention in Pittsburgh in 1918, which issued a program concerned primarily with land, natural resources, public utilities, and cooperative organization in Palestine. A visit to Palestine in 1919 reinforced Brandeis's opinions, and he outlined blueprints for additional projects such as reforestation and the eradication of malaria. His plans, in true Progressive fashion, underscored efficiency, scientific management, and the completion of specific, attainable objectives.

To the East European Jewish immigrants, this American Progressive version of Zionism seemed devoid of *yiddishkayt,* the stuff of Jewish peoplehood. But Brandeis ignored complaints, further antagonizing the pre-1914 leadership and its immigrant constituency. Brandeis also separated himself from the East European rank and file by his refusal to be active in the World Zionist movement and by his attempt to reach reconciliation with the wealthy German Jews.

Everything came to a head at the Cleveland convention of the Zionist Organization of America in 1921 when those leaders who were Brandeis supporters were forced to resign. The majority East European membership, proud of Brandeis and grateful for his contribution, were nonetheless alienated by his patronizing ways and weak ideological commitment. Practical development and philanthropic Zionism were simply not enough for those who emphasized political action and worldwide Jewish cultural renaissance.

The split contributed to a serious decline in membership, to twenty-five thousand by 1920 and to fewer than nineteen thousand by 1921. Zionism, however, even in the face of the "100 percent Americanism" of the 1920s, did not disappear. It stayed alive in movements and organizations such as Conservative Judaism and the American Jewish Congress (see Ch. 9), which was revived after 1921. The growth of these crucial movements in the 1920s and 1930s insured that Zionist sentiment would remain a foremost component of American Jewish identity. Indeed, in 1927 a leading Zionist could declare without fear of contradiction that Conservative Jews viewed Palestine with "an intuitional, unreasoning love" and, like Torah, "as an ultimate, a thing that is good in itself, whose welfare we seek for its own sake."

By the end of the nineteenth century and throughout the early decades of the twentieth, the nucleus of Jewish communal consciousness in the United States was not so much strict adherence to traditional Judaism as a transformed Jewishness that manifested itself in many forms. Not the least of these transformations was Zionism, but there were other ways, too, of formulating a Jewish American identity.

9

Power and Principle: Jewish Participation in American Domestic Politics and Foreign Affairs

Jews at the end of the twentieth century have a well-deserved reputation for active participation in the American electoral process and for demonstrating concern for the welfare of coreligionists abroad. Although "Jewish foreign affairs" were of interest to American Jewry from as early as the late nineteenth century, before 1914, Jewish immigrants usually viewed the general run of domestic party politics with indifference.

The pious had always held secular politics inherently suspect, and free-thinkers and radicals had neither a grounding in routine political processes nor familiarity with the realities of power. Inexperienced, wary of bureaucracy, and still haunted by memories of oppressive old-country governments, the Jewish immigrants were satisfied to be left alone. And the major political parties accommodated them. Rarely in the early years of mass immigration did mainstream politicians address issues vital to the new communities.

Irish domination of urban politics was another factor contributing to the slowness with which East European Jews entered American political life. The Irish had several advantages. Early arrival, familiarity with the English language, and an ethnic unity forged within the Catholic Church readily translated into Irish political power out of proportion to their number. Moreover, many had arrived in the United States fresh from the momentous experience of the Catholic Emancipation, which served the Irish well in mass politics.

At the same time, the Irish carried on here a cultural tradition of viewing formal government as illegitimate. Most were convinced that true sovereignty was reflected only in the informal politics of personal fealty. "All there is in life," said New York City boss Richard Crocker, "is loyalty to family and friends." The mix of cynicism and benevolence made a powerful cement. Through intimate networks built on a combination of graft and services rendered, the Irish came into control of political machines in several large cities.

In New York the Tammany machine interceded with officials to provide jobs, to drop charges and fines, and to help real estate men and contractors gain favors. It also dispensed free coal and food to the needy and helped with medical care, social services, and burial arrangements. Maintaining this system of services took will, talent, and energy, and it brought votes, power, status, and modest affluence to Tammany leaders and operatives. The Irish had no intention of sharing these advantages and risking loss of control to newcomers, least of all to Jews from Russia and Poland.

Jews, moreover, were not exactly breaking down Tammany doors. The self-help traditions and the elaborate networks of social and charitable agencies in the Jewish community made the Tammany leaders' "generosity" less necessary. Tammany operations in many ways anticipated the welfare state and were appreciated in most immigrant communities. But among Jews favors bestowed by the machine appear to have counted for less.

When they did become full participants in the game of American politics, Jews did not until the 1920s fall into any clearly discernible or predictable voting pattern. Personal issues, class and ideology, group interests, and sometimes even simple ethnic loyalty divided Jews among Democrats, Republicans, Socialists, and Progressives.

Jewish voters, though spread across the political spectrum, viewed politics mainly as a vehicle for achieving justice. And everywhere they injected a serious moral dimension into the political dialogue. Their moralism stemmed partly from the influence of Socialism in the Jewish world; and partly, but less directly, from the political concepts embedded in the sacred Hebrew Scriptures, particularly the Prophets, who emphasized social justice, messianism, and government as a system established by consecrated mutual promise and obligation.

Eventually these conceptions and inclinations, in combination with the experience of political freedom in the United States, led Jews to constitutionalism and republicanism. For the same reasons, Jews also came to support an activist state, one that vigorously pursued the protection of vulnerable individuals and promoted public regulation of individual enterprise on behalf of the common good. Although most clearly manifested in the 1930s and 1940s, the liberal dimension of the Jewish political profile was already a constant by 1920.

In nearly every presidential election between 1900 and 1920, more Jews voted for Republicans than for Democrats. But this was a preference that seldom extended to local politics. Jewish voters in the cities, when they were not supporting Socialists, or reformers such as Seth Low and William T. Jerome, tended to vote Democratic. In New York this meant Tammany.

By 1900, Tammany appeared to be paying more attention to Jewish interests, especially the crucial question of immigration restriction, on which they took a liberal position. The Tammany Democrats gained the edge in the ghetto but held no monopoly. Elections in the immigrant community were always hard fought, and sizeable numbers of Jews continued to vote for Socialists and Progressives as well as for Tammany.

Voting was less divided when there was no controversy about where the Jewish interest lay. Immigration was one such issue. When James G. Curley, a jealous guardian of Irish power but a strong supporter of liberal immigration policy, ran for mayor of Boston in 1913, he received 85 percent of the Jewish vote. The national campaign in 1912, however, posed a great quandary for Jewish voters because all four presidential candidates had come out strongly against immigration restriction. The problem was met by ticket splitting, and a substantial proportion of the Jewish vote went to Woodrow Wilson and to Eugene V. Debs, the Socialist Party candidate.

Socialism never captured the entire community, but with its explicit appeals to moralism and justice, it was an important force on the Lower East Side. Indeed, the rise of the Socialist Party vote in the United States from 16,000 in 1903 to more than 118,000 in 1912 was partly the consequence of increasing Jewish support. Socialist candidates were especially attractive to Jews when they represented a combination of ideological and ethnic interests. Socialist Morris Hillquit, though Jewish, had not openly identified with specific Jewish interests and was defeated in the 1908 congressional race. Meyer London, who replaced Hillquit as the Socialist Party's candidate, clearly identified himself as a Jew and a Socialist and allied himself with the vital interests of the Lower East Side. Although it was rare, even from the Lower East Side, for Socialists to be sent to Congress, London was elected three times between 1914 and 1920.

The strength of the Socialist Party in the Jewish community should not be overstated. Socialists certainly received disproportionate support from the Jewish electorate, but most Jews were not Socialists. Moreover, in 1914, of eleven Jews elected to the New York State Senate, two were Republicans and nine were Democrats. In the same year seven Jews sat in the Assembly; only two were Socialists, the rest Republicans. At the presidential level, Woodrow Wilson's earnest intellectualism and moralism in 1912 and again in 1916 attracted Jews toward the national Democratic slate. This included not only former Socialists but also wealthy Jews with a civic conscience, such as Jacob Schiff and Bernard Baruch, both of whom were generous contributors to the campaigns of liberal and moderate candidates.

The gradual shift of Jews from Republican and Socialist to Democratic affiliation on the national level was reinforced by the liberal, progressive role Louis Brandeis played as Wilson's advisor, especially after Brandeis became head of the American Zionist movement in 1914. Later, Wilson's crusade for the League of Nations, as well as his initial support for the Balfour Declaration, which promised the establishment of a Jewish homeland in Palestine, further strengthened Jewish links to the Democratic Party.

If, early in their history, immigrant Jews showed little taste for local politics, their interest in foreign affairs was heightened by concern for the welfare of their *landslayt* overseas. It was this concern that stirred them to political activism in times of crisis and helped produce, during the first two decades of the twentieth century, an extraordinary network of new Jewish institutions. In the face of pogroms and the deteriorating condition of Jewish communities in Eastern Europe, the American Jewish Committee (AJC) was formed in 1906 by an elite group of German Jews. One of its most important goals was aiding fellow Jews abroad by pressing for diplomatic intercession and by resisting legislation at home designed to restrict immigration. In turn, another national organization, the American Jewish Congress, was established to confront and transcend the more oligarchic ways of the AJC and to address the interests and minority rights of Jews in postwar Europe.

World War I exacerbated the needs of European Jewry and tested American Jewish will and ability. In order to bring relief to Jewish communities abroad, it was necessary for American Jews to rise above social and religious divisiveness. The challenge was met with the establishment of yet another major organization, the American Jewish Joint Distribution Committee. The crisis of European Jewry also invigorated Zionism, which itself produced a variety of new organizations and forced American Jews to confront their hyphenate identities.

American Jewish political activity in response to needs of Jews abroad had important precedents in the nineteenth century. The first concerted nationwide action by American Jewry took place in 1840 to protest the torture of nearly one hundred Jews of Damascus who had been accused of murdering Christian children in order to use their blood in Jewish rituals. The Jewish community was roused to action again in 1858 to try to protect Edgar Mortara, an Italian Jew, whose nurse secretly arranged for him to be baptized in infancy and who at age six was seized by papal troops and forcibly converted to Catholicism.

In the late nineteenth century the attention of American Jewry was turned increasingly toward the mistreatment of fellow Jews in czarist Russia. The policy of discrimination against Jews in Russia involved the United States in several ways. Most important, Russian anti-Semitism was responsible for the immigration of millions of Jews to American shores. In addition, the czarist regime, in the latter half of the nineteenth century, began to subject American Jews who returned to Russia on business or visits to the restrictions under which Russian Jews were forced to live.

The leadership of American Jewry disavowed that, while it had the ability to arouse public opinion and elicit real sympathy for the plight of Jews overseas, it lacked the organization and power to gain direct government intercession. By 1904 there was some movement away from pressing for diplomatic intervention and toward economic retaliation. The new emphasis was reinforced by the desperation American Jews felt as over three hundred pogroms took place in the Russian Empire between 1903 and 1906. And economic pressure, such as the threat to abrogate the treaty of 1832 that governed all commercial relations between the United States and Russia and gave Russia access to the U.S. market, became the preferred strategy.

President Taft entered office in 1909 having spoken out forcefully on the treaty issue during the campaign and even at his inauguration. Yet a series of delegations to the White House were unable even to elicit an acknowledgment from the new president that American Jews in Russia were entitled to legal protection. Early in 1911, one group representing the AJC, the Union of American Hebrew Congregations and B'nai B'rith left the oval office in anger. Later, Jacob Schiff recalled, "I told the President: . . . 'We had hoped you would see that justice was done us but you have decided otherwise; we shall go to the American people.'"

Jewish organizations redoubled their agitation on the treaty question and stressed the point that discrimination against U.S. citizens abroad was not a Jewish problem but an American one. Newspapers were supplied with relevant data and magazines with popular articles, and open meetings were sponsored throughout the country. Finally, after a series of well-publicized congressional hearings and the wooing of key members of both chambers, a resolution calling for the immediate termination of the commercial treaty with Russia passed by a vote of three hundred to one in the House and unanimously in the Senate.

In the process of mobilizing their strength between 1903 and 1913, American Jewish leaders learned that some goals could be achieved by effective organization. Galvanized into action by the pogroms in Russia, especially a second one in Kishinev in August 1905, sixty leading American Jews met in New York City in February 1906 and organized a new defense organization called the American Jewish Committee. The AJC was to be a body of the Jewish establishment. Jacob Schiff, Oscar Straus, Cyrus Adler, the Guggenheims, Louis Marshall, and other prominent German Jews would now speak and act in the name of and for the defense and welfare of the Jewish community. The concern of Jews of high station with the protection of general Jewish interests was a familiar element of Jewish tradition. The AJC, as a tightly knit, prudent group working quietly through government authorities in behalf of fellow Jews, had simply institutionalized the customary function of the *shtadlanim,* the Jews at court who mediated with the princes and powers of the past.

The single most important figure behind the AJC was the brilliant, fifty-year-old attorney Louis Marshall. He used his talents to plead the causes of American Jews before various administrations in Washington, and he was indefatigable in his struggle for the abrogation of the commercial treaty with Russia. Marshall felt little of the disdain for the new Jewish immigrant so often noted among his uptown compatriots, and he was able to serve as a bridge between the preexisting German Jewish community and the new arrivals from Eastern Europe. Indeed, Marshall was involved in almost every cause close to the heart of the newcomers, particularly the battle against immigration restriction. Marshall's proposal to broaden the base of the committee to include immigrant leaders won the approval of Jacob Schiff, the aristocrat who came closest to recognizing the obligation of grooming the immigrants for a share of the leadership.

Most East European Jews in the United States had from the beginning applauded the functioning of the AJC, whose stated purpose was to help relieve the suffering of their relatives and *landslayt* in the Old World. Support continued during World War I because of the AJC's leadership in organizing both the American Jewish Relief Committee and the Joint Distribution Committee, whose chief beneficiaries were the Jews in war-ravaged Eastern Europe. In the war zone, Jews not only suffered incidentally on account of their unfortunate location but also were targets of deep-seated anti-Semitism, especially in Russia. Indiscriminate rape and murder of Jews accompanied the movement of the czarist armies, and some three hundred thousand Jews were expelled from their homes as potential spies and traitors.

Several relief agencies, including the American Jewish Relief Committee, mainly the product of the AJC, were formed to aid the devastated communities. The national organizations participating in the unprecedented enterprise of a united community ran the gamut of American Jewish life and included the Orthodox Agudath Harabonim, the Reform Central Conference of American Rabbis, the Conservative United Synagogue of America, and the People's Relief Committee, representing the Jewish labor movement. In the face of crisis abroad, even representatives of the anti-Zionist Workmen's Circle sat with the delegates from the Federation of American Zionists.

Diversity was maintained, but some of the day-to-day contentiousness that marked the life of the American Jewish community was put aside. In November 1914 the different relief committees combined to form the Joint Distribution Committee of American Funds for the Relief of Jewish War Sufferers ("the Joint" as it came to be known affectionately). The confederation thought of itself as a purely administrative organization collecting funds through existing groups and distributing them through established channels of overseas relief work. This posture, carefully avoiding the pitfalls of Jewish community politics, and an efficient executive board with Felix Warburg as its first chairman, helped the Joint raise $1,550,000 in 1915.

At a rally in Carnegie Hall in 1916, Julius Rosenwald of Chicago made the first of his great pledges, $1 million. Over a three-year period he gave more than $3.5 million. There were countless small contributions as well, solicited mainly by the Joint's constituent organizations. All the funds were entrusted to the Joint, which by 1918 had distributed some $20 million for more than 700,000 Jews in the East dependent on its largess.

After the war nine million homeless Jews tried to put their lives back together in a chaotic, hostile Europe. The difficulties faced by Russian Jewry were intensified by the revolution and subsequent civil war and by mass pogroms in the Ukraine. In this postwar crisis, the Joint came through once again. It secured the cooperation of the U.S. government and of private national relief agencies and an additional $27 million for relief of Russian Jewry. Herbert Hoover, who directed the massive postwar relief effort of the U.S. government, singled out the Joint for praise: "There is," he said in 1923, "no brighter chapter in the whole history of philanthropy than that which could be written of the work of the American Jews in the last nine years."

Several events beginning in 1914 had made it essential that the American Jewish community settle promptly or at least put aside issues that divided it. Along with the emergencies created in the Jewish communities of Eastern Europe, the war brought an unexpected opportunity to realize the Zionist goal of establishing a Jewish homeland in Palestine. But the war also posed a dilemma for the World Zionist movement: which side should it support? European Jews, after all, were fighting and dying on both sides. Moreover, early in the conflict between the Allies and the Central Powers, the outcome was unclear. Some European Zionists such as Shmaryahu Levin leaned toward the Germans, especially after the Russian revolution brought to power a regime basically hostile to the Zionist program. Others, best represented by the University of Manchester scientist Chaim Weizmann, sided with the British.

Ultimately the hostility of the Ottoman Empire, associated with the Central Powers, toward the *yishuv* brought Zionists closer to the British and the Allies. The course of the war itself eventually did the same, especially after the entrance of the United States in mid-1917 dramatically changed the odds in favor of the Allies and after it became clear that the disintegration of Turkey promised to leave the Middle Eastern segments of the Ottoman Empire in British hands.

Since the beginning of the war, Chaim Weizmann had been negotiating with British cabinet members for a public endorsement of Zionist territorial aims. Partly out of the desire to woo American and Russian Jewry to the Allied cause, the British seriously considered such a move. They needed assurance, however, that the Wilson administration would back them. Louis Brandeis, Stephen Wise, and Felix Frankfurter, American Zionists who had access to Wilson, used their influence to that end. Despite the anti-Zionism of Secretary of State Robert Lansing and a presidential advisor, Colonel Edward M. House, Wilson promised his support to British recognition of a Jewish national home in Palestine.

Historians have not been able to agree on the extent of Wilson's commitment to the Zionist cause. But it is at least arguable that had it not been for the president, the anti-Zionist posture of the State Department would have triumphed. Reinforced by the influence of Protestant missionaries, who were vexed by the inconvertibility of the Jews in the Holy Land, and by businessmen interested in Arab oil, the State Department was prepared to quash Zionist plans. But to the evangelical Wilson, the role of facilitating the divine design of Jewish restoration to Zion was appealing. The president was also attracted to Brandeis's vision of a Palestine built on the democratic, Progressive ideals that Wilson himself advocated. An endorsement of the Zionist goal also gave concrete proof of the president's concern for national self-determination. And, just as important, a pro-Zionist position was justified in terms of wartime diplomacy, for the Allies knew that Germany, like Britain, was prepared to use Palestine in a bid for Jewish support.

The final product of the British deliberations, the Balfour Declaration, was announced on 2 November 1917 and favored the establishment of a national home for the Jewish people in Palestine. Marked by ambiguities about sovereignty and about the rights of non-Jewish communities in Palestine which would haunt the Zionist movement for decades, the Balfour Declaration was nevertheless hailed by Jewish nationalists all over the world. American Zionists called it the "Jewish Magna Charta." With a stroke of the pen, the early Zionist vision had been transformed from fantasy to reality.

Hope had also been enhanced by the burst of organizational energy in the United States following Louis Brandeis's emergence as the leader of the American Zionist movement in 1914. This hope, combined with the deteriorated Jewish condition in war-torn Eastern Europe and the proposed creation of new nation-states in regions populated with large Jewish minorities, made it critical to have a Jewish delegation at the postwar peace conference. East European Jews in America demanded a part in that enterprise, and American Zionists, buoyed by international developments, took the lead in pressing for the establishment of a new national organization to fulfill this potentially momentous role.

The AJC, still relatively elitist in composition, and anti-Zionist in ideology, would not do. Instead, a democratically elected representative body, "A Congress for and from all Jews," was urged by Bernard Richards, a publicist and communal activist, as well as by Nachman Syrkin and Baruch Zuckerman, both labor Zionists. Many Jewish leaders at first saw the Congress idea as a form of Jewish national autonomy, and therefore as something alien to the American political and social structure. At best, Jewish autonomy had been considered suitable only to the multinational empires of Eastern Europe. But in the United States, Jewish nationhood, embodied in a quasi-parliamentary institution, appeared to deny the American concept of equal citizenship and the American dream of "one nation."

During the emergency of World War I, however, the concept of the Congress was transformed from what looked like a political eccentricity into a pivotal issue in American Jewish life. In 1915 an organizing committee headed by Louis Brandeis and a religious Zionist, Gedaliah Bublick, set out to create a democratically elected body to represent the entire American Jewish community. The new organization would be designed to deal with matters affecting the welfare of Jews everywhere. But highest priority was given to securing civil and political rights for Jewish communities in reconstructed postwar Europe.

The Zionists, a small but articulate and dedicated group, who played a critical role in the Congress movement, hoped it would especially serve their cause: the right and ability of Jews to leave Europe and settle in a new Jewish commonwealth in Palestine. They argued that the Congress should fight for "free immigration for all peoples and automatically for Jews." Even if equal rights were guaranteed, many Zionists, along with Nachman Syrkin, correctly predicted, "social and economic hostility to the Jews will rise," making "mass emigration . . . the only salvation."

When Louis Brandeis was condemned for furthering the fragmentation of the American Jewish community by lending his name to the American Jewish Congress, as the new organization came to be known, he retorted that only an American Jewry united in a body organized on the principle of Jewish peoplehood and dedicated to mass democratic participation would have the power to obtain equal rights for their brethren in Europe. In March 1916 nearly four hundred representatives of a wide variety of organizations met in Philadelphia to formulate more sharply the goals of the American Jewish Congress. What the group wanted was stated most succinctly by Stephen Wise in *Challenging Years:* "not relief, but redress, not palliatives but prevention, not charity but justice." It was eloquent shorthand not only for the basic grievances of Jews abroad but also for the resentments harbored by East European immigrants against the *shtadlanim* of the AJC.

The AJC recognized in the Congress movement a challenge to its hegemony, and Louis Marshall referred to Congress supporters as "noisy, blatant demagogues, principally nationalists and socialists." In its confrontation with pro-Congress forces, AJC leaders even went so far as to make an anti-Zionist alliance with the socialist-oriented National Workmen's Committee on Jewish Rights. Still, the AJC was convinced it could do little to prevent the Congress from coming into existence, and therefore finally it sought only to limit the new organization's function and duration.

The AJC supported the American Jewish Congress on the condition that the new organization refrain from ideological pronouncements and concern itself only with the postwar problems of Jewry to be dealt with at the peace conferences. At the end of its work the Congress was to disband and all other existing Jewish organizations were to remain inviolate. Even this compromise proposal had been resisted by those who saw in the pro-Zionism of the Congress movement the implication of divided loyalty and a threat to the foundations of the American Jewish community. But leaders such as Schiff and Marshall, though hardly reconciled to the idea of a Jewish political commonwealth, were in sympathy with the idea that a cultural and religious center in Palestine would help revitalize world Jewry. They prevailed, and a compromise was reached in July 1916 covering all the previously cited points including a dual approach to the Jewish problem in Europe: The Congress delegation to the treaty conferences was to urge the protection of minorities in the various new states to be created; and for those Jews who wanted to leave Europe, the delegates were to press for a Jewish national home.

In order to select representatives to the peace conference, a convention of the American Jewish Congress had to be scheduled. This produced a stunningly unique event in American history: on 10 June 1917, one of the nation's many ethnic groups conducted an internal election to choose delegates to the American Jewish Congress and in effect to determine an important part of the future course of American Jewry. Over thirty Jewish organizations and more than eighty cities participated. Some 335,000 votes were cast. Almost four years after the idea had first surfaced and barely a month before the nations were to meet at Versailles, the American Jewish Congress officially convened in Philadelphia in December 1918. The nearly four hundred delegates elected Judge Julian W. Mack of Chicago as president. A founding member of the AJC and president of the Zionist Organization of America, Mack could serve as a symbol of the unity of the AJC and the Congress in commitment to their brethren overseas.

The delegation chosen to represent American Jewry at the peace conference also symbolized unity. It was representative of nearly all elements in the American Jewish community. The Zionists included Mack, the chairman, Reform Rabbi Stephen S. Wise, and a former labor leader, Joseph Barondess. Louis Marshall and Harry Cutler spoke for the AJC. A Labor Zionist, Nachman Syrkin, and the proletarian poet and Socialist Morris Winchevsky represented a segment of the labor movement. Also attending was Bernard Levinthal of Philadelphia, an Orthodox rabbi and religious Zionist.

German and Russian Jews, Zionists and non-Zionists, Orthodox and Reform, and leaders of labor were united in common purpose; but discordant voices were heard. From the start the Jewish Socialist Federation and the National Workmen's Committee on Jewish Rights, representing an important body of Socialists, had been unable to decide whether to join or denounce the Congress, which included the participation of Zionists and capitalists. The Socialist organizations made several ill-timed changes of course —including a temporary alliance with the "bourgeois element" in the Congress—made out of a profound dread of Zionist domination of the Jewish community. By early 1919 the Socialists, infuriated by the pro-Zionist resolutions of the Congress and convinced that the system then being implemented in the Soviet Union meant that the solution to the "Jewish question" was already at hand, withdrew from the American Jewish Congress. The AJC, also not entirely comfortable in the Congress delegation, sent its own as well. In addition, conflicting views as to the order of priorities vis-à-vis Zionist goals and minority rights continued to surface. It took all the energy and skill of Louis Marshall, who replaced Judge Mack as head of the delegation, to maintain unity and discipline.

At home, too, unity was threatened. On 5 March 1919, three days after the American Jewish Congress presented President Wilson with a memorial urging him to support the Balfour Declaration at the peace conference, an anti-Zionist memorial appeared in the *New York Times*. Signed by Adolph Ochs, the publisher of the *Times,* and by dozens of other members of the stridently anti-Zionist faction of the AJC, the memorial warned against the "reorganization of the Jews as a national unit to whom territorial sovereignty in Palestine shall be committed." This dissenting voice would not be stilled until the rise of the Nazis in the 1930s made tragically clear the prescient logic of the Zionist aspiration for territorial sovereignty to serve as a haven for European Jewry.

In addition to the conflicts within the Jewish community, opposition from other quarters posed difficulties for the Zionists. The Arabs, of course, were adamantly opposed to naming Britain the mandatory power in Palestine. France, Britain's traditional rival in the Middle East, joined the dissent, as did the Vatican and Protestant missionary groups. Despite these obstacles, negotiations brought some nominally positive results. Civil rights were guaranteed to Jews and other minority groups within the domain of the newly formed or reshaped nations of Poland, Czechoslovakia, Yugoslavia, Rumania,

Hungary, and Austria. The guarantees, as several Zionist spokesmen had foreseen, failed in practice to provide protection for the Jews of Eastern Europe. But the right of free immigration for all peoples had been asserted. In addition, the mandate over Palestine was granted to Great Britain, which had issued the Balfour Declaration, and the declaration itself would soon be incorporated in the peace treaty with Turkey. Its work completed at Versailles, the Congress delegation returned to Philadelphia to make its report. At the end of the session on 30 May 1920, the American Jewish Congress, true to its word, disbanded. But already there were plans afoot to bring it back to life.

10

Mobility, Politics, and the Construction of a Jewish American Identity

$\mathbf{I}$n the span of only one or two generations, East European Jews rose from a mainly working-class population to a middle-class group in business, white-collar jobs, and the professions. This new social status was achieved by the Jews a full generation before other groups of the so-called new immigration, including Greeks, Slavs, Italians, and other Southern and Eastern Europeans.

One of the explanations for the remarkable social mobility of the Jews is that they invested more, and earlier, in their own human capital than other groups, partly by staying in school longer. Jews had something of a running start, having arrived in the United States with a literacy rate of approximately 74 percent, compared to 34 percent for Italians, for example. Jews were also more receptive to educational possibilities and opportunities and were familiar with the drill, recitation, and rote learning that had characterized their Old World *hederim* as well as the American public school system in the interwar period.

Scholarship had great standing in a traditional Jewish culture that revered learning, and the utilitarian nature of education in the United States reinforced that prestige. For Jewish immigrants school was an important arena where hopes could be fulfilled and where children, who had internalized the drive to achieve, could prove themselves. One East Side mother of five wrote to the Bintl Brief section of the Yiddish-language *Daily Forward:*

> I am a widow . . . [with] a store and barely get along. . . . I employ a sales-man. If I were to withdraw my [15-year-old] son from high school, I could dispense with the salesman, but my motherly love and duty . . . do not per-mit me. . . . So what shall I do when the struggle for existence is so acute? . . . I cannot definitely decide to take him out of school, for he has inclina-tions to study and goes to school dancing. I lay great hopes in my child.

This relatively widespread attitude should be compared with the atti-tudes of those groups for whom education was generally a matter of indif-ference or even hostility. The most studied people, and those who present the sharpest contrast, are the *contadini* (roughly, peasants and farm laborers) from the *mezzogiorno* in southern Italy. There was nothing irrational about the active disparagement of education found among them. The *contadini* lived in the old country in a state of significant material deprivation. They resided in towns with castelike social structures rather than in homogeneous peasant villages, and their condition was made even more painful by the close prox-imity of more fortunate neighbors.

Education in these circumstances was correctly perceived as having no relevance to upward mobility. Moreover, parents believed that schools would deprive them of their children's incomes and would likely teach values at vari-ance with those of the home. This dimension of resistance to acculturation is not dissimilar to Jewish reaction to state schools in Galicia and Russia in the early nineteenth century and particularly to the "crown schools" under Czar Nicholas I in the 1840s and 1850s; but Jewish parents did not withhold their children, primarily boys, from education. They enrolled them in their own communal *hederim* and *yeshivot.*

Indifference to education among Italian immigrants in the United States was at least partly reinforced by their high repatriation rate. Between 1892 and 1896, 43% of the Italians who emigrated to the United States returned to Italy. For the period 1907–11, the percentage of repatriates increased to 73. In the same era only 7 percent of Jews from the Russian Empire returned to their countries of origin. The pursuit of education, however, remained a low priority even among those Italians who stayed into the second and even third generations. Italian children by the 1920s were more often allowed to finish elementary school, but not without considerable grumbling by their parents. "The schools made of our children persons of leisure—little gentlemen," complained one mother. "They lost the dignity of good children to think first of their parents, to help them whether they need it *or not*."

This parent's statement implies that the choice in the Italian community was as much between education and family as between education and work. Children who could not obtain jobs also stayed away from school or withdrew at the earliest legal age. For Jews, in contrast, achievement measured by academic performance reflected a deeply treasured cultural value, supported not only by the tradition of study but also by the promise of reward.

In any event, formal education as an instrument of mobility developed fully during the 1920s, and Jewish students were attending high school longer than other groups and were more likely to graduate. In Pittsburgh and several other large cities, Jews completed high school at double the rate of non-Jews, and in New York City 80 percent of Regents Scholarship winners in 1921 were Jewish. But education was not the main ingredient for the upward mobility of second-generation Jews. Trade was the more important route out of the working class for Jews in the first half of the twentieth century. And their relative success at trade was facilitated by a combination of things: their greater urban orientation; their well-honed and longstanding commercial skills and experience; their mutual aid societies; and their credit unions and free-loan associations. Access to relatively easy credit within the Jewish community, as in other ethnic communities such as the Greek and Scandinavian, was extremely useful. Before 1925 only one bank in all of the Northeast extended credit to Jews. Moreover, 85 percent of the Jewish population was too poor to supply the collateral necessary to qualify for bank loans.

At the beginning of the twentieth century, 60 percent of the Jewish employed were in manufacturing, and 25 percent in trade or clerical work. Three decades later 57 percent were in trade and clerical work, and nearly 40 percent owned commercial enterprises, approximately three times the figure for the general population. The children of the immigrants had become proprietors of stores and factories. In fact, by 1937 Jews owned two-thirds of the 34,000 factories and 104,000 wholesale and retail establishments in New York City. A similar pattern was evident in other large cities. Jews in the twenties and thirties were also, increasingly, salespeople, white-collar workers, and providers of commercial services such as dry cleaning, car washes, and private transportation. John Hertz, a Jewish immigrant from Czechoslovakia, founded both the Yellow Cab Company and Hertz Rent-a-Car.

So successful were the Jews at commerce that by 1930 in Boston and other large cities on the east coast, those of East European Jewish descent were sufficiently well established to give their children, primarily their sons, as large a head start as the German Jews had given their offspring in the late nineteenth century. Indeed, in 1930, 71 percent of Russian Jewish sons held first jobs that were classified as middle class. This Jewish social mobility took place in the general prosperity of the twenties. New, less expensive sources of power and continuing mechanization of the workplace meant more than a 40 percent increase in productivity; and from 1920 to 1929 real income rose 11 percent, even as the workday shortened. During the same period, advertising and the increasingly widespread practice of installment plan payments for purchases extended and reinforced consumerism. There was a tenuousness to the prosperity which was testified to by more than five thousand bank failures nationwide and a persistent depression in the agrarian sector of the economy. But the children of the immigrants demonstrated an enterprising spirit that was very much in line with the business ethos of the decade.

Although Jews earned 16–20 percent more than other groups because of their longer schooling and academic performance, they followed the business route to moderate prosperity more often than they finished school. The myth of education as a magic carpet of upward mobility is undermined by the history of the Jews, the Greeks, and later the Japanese, who first rose by their labor, self-exploitation, and business acumen and only later could afford to send their children to college. And indeed, although second-generation Jews reached the ivy-covered halls of academe well before other groups of the post-1890 immigration, it was not until the 1930s that Jews finished high school and entered college in great numbers. By the 1940s, when public high schools had become much more numerous and students were legally compelled to stay in school longer, nearly 80 percent of Jewish students in New York completed high school, compared to less than 35 percent of the general population, 20 percent of the sons and daughters of manual laborers, and only 10 percent of Black youth. In New York the Jewish rate for completing college was almost three times greater than the rate for non-Jews.

By the mid-1930s, 50 percent of the applicants to medical school and an almost equally disproportionate number of applicants to law school were Jewish. A massive alteration of the American Jewish occupational structure had begun in the 1920s, and by 1934, 13–17 percent of the Jewish employed were professionals, up from 3 percent in 1900. In 1937 in New York City, Jews, who constituted 25 percent of the population, made up 65 percent of the lawyers and judges, 64 percent of the dentists, and 55 percent of the doctors. In Cleveland in 1938, Jews, less than 8 percent of the population, were 23 percent of the lawyers, 21 percent of the doctors, and 18 percent of the dentists.

Other professions, less lucrative but very attractive to second-generation Jews, were pharmacy and, increasingly for Jewish women, teaching and
social work. Many college-educated second-generation Jews were culturally
predisposed in their career choices toward the helping professions. Large
numbers had been raised in politically progressive communities and had been
surrounded by institutions for mutual aid. They were virtually primed to be
attracted to social work and teaching, careers that in the 1940s emphasized
a connection to social action and change. Although those who entered such
fields were now at least lower middle class, they were as disproportionately
involved with unions as were their proletarian parents. Jews were significantly
overrepresented in the teachers' unions and in the pharmacists' and social
workers' unions, which were established largely through Jewish effort.

A growing number of young Jews also embarked on careers in jour-
nalism, and several chose the national press to develop their talent. Before
1920 some major newspapers such as the *Washington Post* and the *New York
Times* were owned by Jews, and there was also Jewish representation among
reporters, editors, columnists, and feature writers. But no Jews were among
the owners of the powerful newspaper chains that had developed during the
twenties. Despite this and despite the fact that Jewish journalists had no
"Jewish agenda" but generally wrote for the American reader, the notion of
Jewish conspiratorial control of the flow of information became a mainstay
of the anti-Semitic propagandists by the early 1920s.

That conspiratorial notion was fed by the fact that the first nationwide
radio networks, NBC, organized by RCA in 1924, and CBS in 1927, were in
large part products of Jewish entrepreneurship. But there were few Jewish
names to be found among the sources of capital to build these networks and
in the ownership of local stations, of which there were 562 by 1924. Moreover, the founders of the major networks only marginally identified as Jews.

This was true, too, for the men who "invented Hollywood," several of
whom changed their names, all of whom distanced themselves from Judaism, and all of whom eventually married gentile women. Several, especially
Harry Cohn and Louis B. Mayer, flirted with conversion to Catholicism, and
Jack Warner and Jesse Lasky practiced Christian Science. Their moving pictures were produced (approximately 1 per week by 1930) with general audiences in mind, the very key to their success. And in this most powerfully influential medium of the arts, they demonstrated a powerful devotion to and
celebration of America and Americanness.

Yet these filmmakers did make some fifty films in the twenties and
thirties overtly focusing on Jewish characters, such as *The Jazz Singer* (1927).

This first talkie was an archetypical Jewish American story about a second-generation Jew experiencing the tensions between Jewish group identity and American acculturation. There were also dozens of movies dealing with inter-ethnic relations, and even intermarriage, such as the popular *Abie's Irish Rose* (1928). These films generally projected positive images of Jews, but mostly by "dejudaizing" them, that is, by removing any hint of difference between them and gentiles other than privately held religious convictions. In fact, non-Jews were increasingly cast as Jews.

Also, as with the broadcasting networks, the further development of the film industry compelled Jewish moviemakers to turn to sources outside the Jewish community for financing. Although at the start of the thirties, all but one of the major movie companies were owned by Jews, by 1936 only three of the "big eight" studios were still fully in Jewish hands. Jews remained prominent in all phases of the Hollywood world, including directing, acting, and especially writing, but actual ownership and control had already become diverse before 1940.

Jewish success was also visible in the world of publishing. The seven small but prestigious houses founded by German Jews, including Knopf, Simon and Shuster, and Viking, were thriving in the 1920s. But here too, these were not Jewish publishers in the sense that they favored Jewish authors or subjects. Their distinction and the basis of their prosperity, as in so many Jewish-led businesses since the 1830s, lay in innovation. These firms had introduced, for example, the Little Leather Library, the Modern Library, the Book-of-the-Month Club, and the Literary Guild, among other means of increasing readership and sales.

In addition to the Jewish publishers, journalists, filmmakers, and radio magnates, individual Jewish writers of fiction—screenwriters, playwrights, novelists, and songwriters and composers—were making their mark on the American and Jewish public in the years between the world wars. It is difficult to know for certain why Jews were once again disproportionately represented in these enterprises, and in law and science, in the professorate, and in so many other fields having to do with mental acuity and verbal skill. But the answer is probably not unrelated to centuries of Talmudic study and disputation, to an inheritance from a traditional culture preoccupied with inquiry, argument, and systematic thought. In any case, the secularized values Jewish immigrants transmitted to subsequent generations included literacy, achievement, professionalization, and respect for ideas.

Some of the writers, such as playwrights Lillian Hellman and George S. Kaufman, and composers, such as George Gershwin and Irving Berlin, betrayed little in their work that was Jewish. Indeed, these writers of Jewish descent could easily be seen as interpreters and shapers of American culture. Others, such as novelists Anzia Yezierska, Edna Ferber, and Fannie Hurst, retained and reflected more of their ethnic identity in their art. But they, too, were very much part of the larger culture.

In her semi-autobiographical novel, *Bread Givers* (1925), Yezierska tells of her struggle to separate from her authoritarian Orthodox father and to get a secular education. She succeeds but ultimately there is a reconciliation. Ferber's autobiographical novel, *Fanny Herself* (1917), features a Wisconsin Jewish family headed by a widow. The daughter, Fanny, despite the isolation of the Midwest, learned to love Judaism and never abandoned it. Later, in 1939, Ferber wrote a two-volume autobiography in which she clearly demonstrated her continuing commitment to Judaism. She was known more, however, for her American work, and when she won the Pulitzer Prize in 1924 for her novel *So Big*, the citation read that her writing "best reflects the wholesome atmosphere of *American* life and highest standards of *American* manners" (my emphasis). Fannie Hurst, whose sympathies were with the immigrant generation, wrote a short story, "The Gold in the Fish" (1927), that satirized the eager Americanization of Jewish children. But, like Ferber's, Hurst's most successful fiction dealt with nonethnic Americans.

There were those such as Meyer Levin and Henry Roth who were more thoroughly Jewish in the content of their work and in their literary and cultural reference points. Roth's psychological novel *Call it Sleep* (1934) depicted through the eyes of a young boy, David Shearl, the second generation's precarious balance between the traditional values of mother, home, and *heder* and those of the outside world. Mike Gold, Edward Dahlberg, Samuel Ornitz, and Nathanael West also wrote "Jewish stories," but unlike Roth, they were not sympathetic to Jewish American life, where they perceived only crassness and greed. Gold ended his now classic *Jews without Money* with a paean to the worker's revolution: "You are the true Messiah. You will destroy the East Side when you come, and build there a garden for the human spirit." Jerome Weidman's *I Can Get It for You Wholesale* and Budd Schulberg's *What Makes Sammy Run?* were similar in their disdain for the Jewish entrepreneurial impulse, and their portrayals of Jewish life bordered on self-flagellation.

This public washing of dirty laundry, however, was not necessarily the self-hatred sometimes associated with marginal groups. America's major writers from the nineteenth century on, including Hawthorne, Melville, Whitman, and Twain, had often been ferocious in their attacks on the unauthentic, materialistic aspects of American culture as contrasted with the

American ideals of equality and freedom. In the twentieth century this kind of exposure of the underbelly of American life appeared often in Dreiser, Hemingway, Dos Passos, and Fitzgerald, to name only a few. And it was in this tradition that American Jewish writers came of age. The "exposés" of Ornitz and Schulberg and the others which so distressed the Jews of the 1930s were actually part of a literary mode refined and reintroduced by Sinclair Lewis, who was equally frank about general American life in his popular novels *Main Street* (1920) and *Babbit* (1922).

The increasing visibility of Jewish writers, journalists, filmmakers, and publishers veiled the fact that Jews were not exempt from the devastations of the Great Depression (1929–41). They were hit hard materially, especially those in the professions and those who were purveyors of luxury goods, two categories in which Jews were overrepresented. It was not until after Roosevelt's 1941 executive order establishing the Commission on Fair Labor Employment Practices and after World War II had generated economic recovery that job discrimination against Jews declined. Psychologically, too, the disappointment of losing hold of the American Dream, even if only temporarily, may have been more painful for Jews than for less achievement-oriented groups. But only 12 percent of Jewish heads of household were unemployed, which was less than other groups, and only 12 percent of Jewish youth needed welfare support compared with 21 percent for young Italian Americans, for example. It appears also that Jews recovered faster from the fall than other ethnic groups.

Jews in the interwar period, the Depression notwithstanding, were not only moving up but also moving out to better neighborhoods. As more than one student of demography has suggested, "In America it is 'normal' for parents, relatives, and friends to convince the younger generation that their success in life will be demonstrated to others by their ability to move out (and presumably upward) via residential mobility." Second-generation Jews were no exception to this American rule.

Within the city of New York, some Jewish communities rose and fell during the 1920s and 1930s. Of almost 180,000 Jews living in Harlem in 1923, for example, fewer than 5,000 remained in 1930. But Harlem, where vast physical deterioration drove upwardly mobile Jews out, was exceptional. In New York neighborhoods that had significant Jewish population before World War I, that population generally increased through World War II. Most of the old neighborhoods during this era remained distinctively Jewish, but Jews carried their culture with them to the areas of second settlement as well. In many of the new neighborhoods, the Jews were just as concentrated as in the ghettos they had left behind. Bias and restrictive housing practices explain these "concentrated dispersions" in part, but just as important was the manifest desire to remain in a Jewish milieu. In places such as the East Bronx and Brownsville in New York City, Greater Lawndale in Chicago, Brookline in Boston, and in West Philadelphia, the Jews transplanted and transformed their cultural traditions and behaviors.

Residential clustering by Jews also meant continued endogamy, or marrying within the group. Marriages were usually between people who lived within a twenty-block radius of each other. Despite the popularity of the stage play and film *Abie's Irish Rose,* in which the daughter of the Irish policeman, after much hand wringing on both sides, marries the son of the Jewish merchant, mixed marriages for second-generation Jews, as for their immigrant parents, were quite rare. In 1908 the intermarriage rate for Jews was less than 2 percent, and it remained around 3 percent until the 1940s.

The new Jewish neighborhoods looked and sounded less foreign, less Orthodox, and less working class radical. But they were still demonstrably Jewish. It is true that the Yiddish theater on the Lower East Side in New York or on Arch Street in Philadelphia was left behind by the migrants as they made their way to new areas, and by 1940 the decline of Yiddish theater in the old places was obvious. It is also true that by that time, although more than one-third of the American Jewish population declared Yiddish to be its native tongue and at least ten Yiddish dailies were still published in the Northeast, knowledge of Yiddish among the native born had declined precipitously. In addition, in New York City second-generation Jewish parents failed to fight for the proposal to make Yiddish an acceptable language of study in the public schools. It should not be assumed, however, that all of this was a rejection of Jewishness. The same parents, for example, who did not fight for Yiddish, which they associated with Orthodoxy, radicalism, and being foreign, instead mounted, along with Jewish parents in Chelsea, Massachusetts, a successful campaign for Hebrew, which they saw as neither fully religious nor fully secular. There is other evidence, too, that the children of immigrants were not so much abandoning the world of their fathers and mothers as constructing alternative ways of being both Jewish and American.

Nevertheless, the hypothesis that second-generation Jews departed radically in norms and values from their immigrant parents, becoming significantly less Jewish in the process, was common coin in the historical and sociological literature until the 1970s. John Higham, a historian of immigration and ethnicity, wrote the following in his introduction to the 1960 Harper edition of Abraham Cahan's great immigrant novel, *The Rise of David Levinsky:*

"Since 1950 the problems that weighed so heavily on the second generation have ceased to be oppressive. Discrimination has vastly diminished. The strains of extreme mobility have let up. A third generation, more self-assured, has come on the scene, and it is willing to recall what its fathers tried to forget." And Will Herberg, in his classic *Protestant, Catholic, and Jew* (1955), said more concisely: "The grandchildren of the immigrants are trying to remember what the children tried to forget."

While suggesting a "return" by the third generation, each scholar implies a significant and sharp discontinuity between first and second generations. But the course of acculturation for Jews was neither simple decline—the immigrant grandparent believing, the parent doubting, and the grandchild denying—nor the variation that has the grandchild returning. Third-generation sons and daughters may have returned, but the second-generation parents never fully left. Instead, these children of Jewish immigrants, as historian Deborah Dash Moore has shown, "constructed a moral community with supports borrowed from American culture . . . as well as from their Jewish heritage."

One of the ways some members of the second generation promoted Jewish continuity was to send their children to the Jewish schools maintained by their congregations for part of the day or week. Reform congregations generally ran a Sunday school, and the Conservative congregations an afternoon school two to four times a week. Only the Orthodox community supported day schools. The congregational schools faced a formidable task, seeing the children for only a few hours a week and having to teach them Jewish history and the difficult Hebrew language. But by the 1920s, six nondenominational Hebrew teachers' colleges had been established, as well as Dropsie College, a graduate school of Judaic studies, in Philadelphia.

Only about one-fourth of second-generation Jewish parents sent their children to Jewish schools. They appeared to be satisfied with the public schools in pursuit not only of achievement and reward but also of citizenship and acceptance. In those same schools, however, they fought for Hebrew language study. They also, like their parents before them, very much resisted the schools' assimilationist propensities, including the routine of daily prayers and the annual Christmas shows and celebrations. At the same time they called for recognition of Jewish "historical" holidays such as Hanukkah. In so doing, they were once again being both Jewish and American. They were protecting their Jewish religious and ethnic heritage using both the newly minted American concept of cultural pluralism, which they themselves were helping fashion, and the venerated American constitutional principle of separation of church and state, a principle they continued to defend as staunchly as if it were an item of a new faith.

The second-generation Jews, even as they Americanized, wanted to remain Jewish and to live among Jews in a Jewish environment. This may help explain why, although, like other Americans seeking comfort and status, they changed their neighborhoods, they clustered together there and rarely changed their cities. The five cities that accounted for almost 65 percent of the Jewish population in 1918 were the same, and in the same rank order, in 1939. One noticeable harbinger of future change, however, was that Los Angeles entered the list of the top ten Jewish cities in America in the 1930s in seventh place.

In their cities and neighborhoods, Jews associated with one another in a variety of spaces, especially in community centers, synagogues, and political clubs. In nearly every Jewish neighborhood one could find a community center, affiliated with a synagogue or even physically attached to one, and a Young Men's Hebrew Association. The centers and the Y's, supported by Jewish federations and managed by professionals, though nonsectarian in theory, were in reality Jewish havens from social discrimination encountered by Jews outside their neighborhoods. Simultaneously the centers provided American recreational, social, and educational functions and a familiar context of continuity and tradition.

In the 1920s more than one thousand synagogues were established in new neighborhoods in cities and suburbs, and many Conservative and Reform synagogues and even a small number of Modern Orthodox synagogues gradually became "center synagogues." Indeed, by 1930 there were three hundred center synagogues with four hundred thousand members. There were Jewish leaders and spokesmen who saw this accommodation to American culture as evidence of assimilation and decline, who believed that the organization of new congregations and the building of new synagogues simply concealed the waning of piety and learning, which were the traditional sources of Jewish vitality. There were others, however, particularly Mordecai Kaplan and his "reconstructionist" followers, who believed Jews should not only pray as Jews but, perhaps even more importantly, should also work and play together and fulfill their social needs together.

The Reconstructionist movement, not until 1963 denominationally or institutionally separate from Conservative Judaism, recognized that a mostly unmodified Orthodox Judaism was in crisis and would never retain the adherence of more than a very small minority. Aiming to preserve and revitalize Judaism for larger numbers, Kaplan stressed a commitment to both Jewish and American civilizations, which he saw as having much in consonance, each generally democratic, this-worldly, and covenantal, each believing in the separation of church and state. Although Kaplan himself was a rigorously observant Jew, he called for a new perspective on the rituals of Judaism, which he said were not commandments, not binding laws of the Torah, but folkways retained for the social and anthropological needs they fulfilled. This was a logical corollary of his celebration of Jewish peoplehood as distinct from the religion of Judaism and was also a confirmation of Kaplan's notion that one's vision of, or even belief in, God is less important than being part of the Jewish community.

Kaplan's Reconstructionism in the 1930s was probably a reflection of where most Jewish Americans were heading, even though they retained an *institutional* affiliation to the theology of the major denominations of American Judaism. In any case, Kaplan certainly appeared to be right about Orthodoxy, which suffered its highest attrition rate during the 1920s despite a movement to Americanize through the establishment of Yeshiva College in 1928, through English-speaking rabbis, decorous services and "relevant" sermons, and, in the South and West, through mixed seating. And although in the late 1930s there was a reenergizing of Orthodoxy brought about by the transplantation of European Jewish academies in the face of the Nazi threat, Orthodoxy was also rent by schisms, and by 1940 few could say with certainty who spoke for traditional Judaism.

Reform Judaism, which had virtually abandoned *halakha* and until the 1930s even the concept of Jewish peoplehood, was also having its problems. Despite the production of an indigenous Reform rabbinate by the Hebrew Union College in Cincinnati and Stephen Wise's Jewish Institute for Religion, established in New York City in 1922, the laity in the 1920s and 1930s was shrinking in numbers and commitment. Conservative Judaism, conversely, experienced growth. The movement, adopting some of the changes of Reform Judaism, instituted family pews, eliminated references in the prayer book to resurrection and the renewal of the sacrificial system, and in 1935 through its Rabbinical Assembly, voted to allow driving on the Sabbath to get to synagogue. It, too, stressed an evolving revelation through experience and the "scientific study of Judaism," but unlike Reform, it did not dispense with *halakha*. This combination of Jewish tradition and modern American ways attracted new members, making Conservatism the largest branch of Judaism by 1945.

Conservatism was particularly attractive to women, because while remaining traditional, the movement was responsive to their expressed need to be a more active, more direct part of the synagogue world. Jewish women had always been active in that world through organizations associated with synagogues such as the Hebrew Ladies Benevolent Society. And by the 1890s they, like their talented and intelligent gentile sisters, had become part of the women's club movement, associations outside synagogue and church for self-education, social activity, and improvement of their communities. The National Council of Jewish Women was founded in 1893, Hadassah (Zionist) in 1912, the National Federation of Temple Sisterhoods (Reform) in 1913, and the National Women's League of the United Synagogue of America (Conservative) in 1918. Their sense of accomplishment in these organizations encouraged women to participate also in the larger society: in schools, in the professions, and in public affairs generally. Their expanded role raised women's expectations even further, and in the 1920s those expectations were intensified by and reflected in a combination of social and economic factors.

For one thing, Jewish women were having fewer children as they moved into the middle class in the 1920s and 1930s. Between 1900 and 1920 the size of Italian and Jewish families was similar. But by 1925 the Jews of New York had a birth rate lower than any other ethnic group, and lower than the rest of the indigenous white population, whose birth rate was also in decline. Indeed, between 1920 and 1940 the decline in Jewish fertility was double that of the native-born white population.

In addition, the separation between the sexes, for Jews as for most Americans, had begun to erode. Small apartments, women in the workplace (a growing number of second-generation women had some work experience outside the home), social dancing, and increasingly unsupervised contact between boys and girls in the streets meant men and women were living in the same world. This generally produced a further elevation in the status of women and in their aspirations. Jewish women responded by challenging and ultimately changing the parameters of appropriate behavior for themselves in and out of the synagogue circle. Women in the Reform and Conservative movements founded synagogue libraries, taught Sunday schools, and led summer services. Both movements developed educational programs for women, slowly introduced the bat mitzvah in the 1930s (Mordecai Kaplan had already had his daughter become a bat mitzvah as early as 1922), and allowed women to say *kaddish,* the traditional prayer for the dead. There was even a call for the ordination of women. This did not happen until later, but in 1931 the Jewish Theological Seminary, the Conservative movement's rabbinical training school, did set up the Women's Institute of Jewish Studies.

The women's "movement" in Judaism was and continues to be a salient example not only of the possibility of revitalizing Judaism but also of a synthesis of Americanism and Jewishness. Since the nineteenth century some Jewish women demonstrated that what was American about the history of Jews and Judaism in the United States was that here, for the first time anywhere in the world, the synagogue became a place in which women could express themselves as Jews. And these same Jewish women expressed themselves outside the synagogue as American citizens. Some of this expression seemed to take the apparently superficial form of imitating men—wearing masculine clothing and short hair, and smoking—but many Jewish women were also active politically, especially in the suffrage movement, which culminated with the granting of voting rights to women in 1920. The movement for more equitable divorce laws and laws to protect working women and children also had its strongest support among second-generation Jews.

Most Jewish women were still focused on family life and were not radical feminists, but they were certainly aware of their abilities and needs, and in the 1930s and 1940s, their broadened horizons meant energetic participation in lobbying for welfare state legislation and in the movement for public health measures and racial tolerance. Clearly they helped fuel the extraordinary activism of Jewish political culture in the interwar years.

And an extraordinary political culture it was. One of its more remarkable dimensions was that many Jews from 1917 to about 1924 were very attracted to the Soviet revolution. The regime in Moscow seemed eager to recruit Jewish talent, and the hope of progress and modernity inherent in communist ideology found resonance in Jewish political life in America. It was estimated that in the 1920s, Jews in the United States gave 4–5 percent of their votes to Communist candidates at the same time as they were giving approximately 10 percent to Socialists, both figures substantially higher than the national average.

About 15 percent of the members of the Communist Party in the United States in the 1920s were Jewish (Finnish Americans were at that time about 50%). And in 1924 a small but determined communist group, with the help of numerous sympathizers, had gained control of three locals of the heavily Jewish International Ladies Garment Workers Union. Communists were also strong in shirtwaistmakers' Local 25, which had a predominantly Jewish membership and a long history of radicalism. During the last half of the twenties, the party's general secretaries, Benjamin Gitlow and Jay Lovestone (born Jacob Liebstein), were both Jewish. And during the 1930s the radical student movement, with its communists and socialists of varying stripes, was strongest on campuses with large numbers of Jewish students—

City College of New York, Columbia University, New York University—and a significant percentage of the leaders were Jewish.

The Communist Party had adopted a "united front" policy of making alliance with other left-leaning and liberal groups (which in New York were also disproportionately Jewish), and a strategy of infiltrating Jewish organizations. Partly as a result, Jewish membership in the party climbed to an estimated 35–40 percent during the Depression. Also, five thousand of the thirteen thousand members of the Young Communists League were Jewish. Jews were clearly overrepresented in the communist movement, but only a very small percentage of Jews were communists. This, however, did not stop anti-Semites from speaking of "Judeo-bolshevism," which became a buzzword of the Right in the interwar period.

By the mid-1920s much of the enthusiasm of the Jews for communism was already dissipating. Lenin had earlier ordered an end to anti-Semitic movements in Russia and the Ukraine which had left seventy-five thousand Jews dead between 1918 and 1920. But this did not exempt the Jewish bourgeoisie from being considered "class enemies" of the revolution, and the general antibourgeois, antireligious policies of the Soviets under Stalin continued to create desperate conditions for Russian Jewry, including the wanton destruction of Jewish cultural and religious institutions and the imprisonment of thousands of Jewish leaders.

By 1928, Jewish leaders of liberal or socialist persuasion in the United States, such as Lillian Wald, Horace Kallen, and David Dubinsky, realized there were anti-Semites among the Stalinist heirs of Lenin's mantle. Socialists like Baruch Vladek, managing editor of the *Forward,* and Morris Hillquit, head of the National Committee of the Socialist Party, became so disaffected that they refused even to support extending diplomatic recognition to the Soviet Union.

The ravages against Jews in the Soviet Union, coupled with the drive of communists in the United States to coopt Jewish unions and cultural institutions, continued to diminish communism's mystique. Many Jewish union members supported the communist factions in their organizations because elements of the established leadership were often corrupt and the communists promised "democratization." But communist behavior diluted good will. In a general strike in the cloak trade in 1926, for example, the workers had elicited a favorable offer from management. The Communist Party, however, forced a continuation of the strike which ended in a disaster. After twenty-six weeks of unemployment and an expenditure of $3.5 million, the union was compelled to settle for virtually the original terms. The International Ladies Garment Workers Union was temporarily broken, but so was the communist faction.

The Jewish unions distanced themselves from the more radical left wingers. So did the vast majority of ordinary Jews. The purge trials of the 1930s in Moscow and the Non-Aggression Pact between Nazi Germany and the Soviet Union in 1939 also cut into Jewish support of the communists. Membership in the Communist party of the United States dropped by more than one-third in 1939, and most of those who departed were Jews, virtually all of whom had been attracted to the party in the thirties because they believed it to be the only effective enemy of fascism. Of an estimated eight hundred thousand Jewish votes cast in New York State in the 1930s, only fifty thousand went to Communist candidates. This was meager considering that the Jewish population had been intensely targeted by the party.

With the communist group out of the way, the needle trades unions after 1928 could get on with ameliorating conditions for workers rather than fighting for the remote possibility of a classless society. The unions also paid more attention in the 1930s to progressive issues that were also particularly Jewish. For example, The Jewish Labor Committee was formed in 1933 to counteract anti-Semitism in the United States and the Nazi threat in Europe. There was a small irony in this new "Jewish orientation"; Jewish membership in the garment industry unions in the 1930s had dropped below 50 percent. But the leaders were Jewish and still considered themselves part of the progressive non-Communist left.

Many Jewish writers also had leftist leanings in this era. Yiddish-speaking secularists such as Chaim Zhitlovsky, a champion of Jewish cultural nationalism, Nachman Syrkin, the foremost spokesman for Labor Zionism, Shmuel Niger, a literary critic, and Hayim Greenberg, essayist and editor, constituted a small cadre of Yiddish intellectuals who manifested a strong interest in Jewish national resurgence. But most expected that resurgence to come associated or through a synthesis with socialism. Sidney Hook, Horace Kallen, Harry Wolfson, Lewis Mumford, and others under Elliot Cohen's editorship of the *Menorah Journal* were also inclined to support a "humanistic social order." And a third group of Jewish writers on the Left, the New York intellectuals, included Philip Rahv, Lionel and Diana Trilling, Meyer Shapiro, and Harold Rosenberg. They expressed themselves mainly through the *Partisan Review* and were held together by their utter revulsion against the Soviet experiment under Stalin, with which they had initially flirted; but they clearly maintained their socialist sensibilities, especially in the face of the strident anti-Semitism of the Right in the 1930s. If these cosmopolitan intellectuals were on their way to losing varying degrees of their Jewish identity, there was still something familiarly Jewish in their penchant for a kind of Talmudic argumentation, in their assumption of the inherent worth of intellectual pursuits, and in their left-leaning proclivities.

A good number of Jewish writers of fiction were also on the left in the 1930s, several radicalized by the Depression and its attack on the American Dream. Henry Roth joined the Communist Party in 1933; Mike Gold, who had joined some ten years earlier, became even more enthusiastic in the 1930s, especially about enlisting writers and artists in the revolutionary struggle; and Daniel Fuchs, Samuel Ornitz, and Edward Dahlberg, under the influence of the socialist realism school, were harshly judgmental of the low level of class consciousness and the high level of materialism and exploitation they perceived in American and Jewish society.

Jews generally remained overrepresented in left-leaning cultural, political, and social movements right to the end of the twentieth century, but the vast majority ended up in the left wing of the Democratic Party. Starting as early as 1912, there was a gradual shift of Jewish votes at the presidential level from Republican and Socialist to the Democratic Party. The shift was reinforced by the liberal, progressive role played by Louis Brandeis as President Woodrow Wilson's advisor, especially after Brandeis became head of the American Zionist Movement in 1914. Wilson was also advised by Rabbi Stephen A. Wise and Henry Morgenthau Sr., the real estate tycoon, who served the president in a variety of positions including ambassador to Turkey. Later, Wilson's crusade for the League of Nations appealed to the universalism and internationalism in modern Jewish political culture, and his initial support for the Balfour Declaration, promising a Jewish homeland in Palestine, further strengthened Jewish links to the Democratic Party.

In 1924, Jews voted 51 percent for John Davis, the Democratic candidate, and 22 percent for Robert LaFollette, the much more Progressive candidate; and in 1928 they gave 72 percent of their vote to Democrat Al Smith. Smith had recognized what he called "Jewish brains," he spoke a little Yiddish, he was one of the few Democratic leaders with courage to advocate an anti–Ku Klux Klan plank in the campaign of 1924, and he had helped engineer the appointment of Benjamin Cardozo, a Jew, as chief justice of the New York State Court of Appeals. Above all, he was an intelligent legislator and a reformer. Not surprisingly, during the election of 1924, Smith, who clearly had won the affection of the Jewish voters, ran ahead of Calvin Coolidge and John Davis in several Jewish election districts.

The Jewish community was proud of the growing number of high government officials who were Jewish, such as Eugene Meyer, a member of the Federal Farm and Loan Board, on whom Coolidge depended for advice, and the Jewish advisors around Al Smith such as Belle Moskowitz. But the parochial aspect of ethnicity, the narrow group interest or group pride dimension, was more often blunted by the strong universalist strain in Jewish political culture. The Jewish community had an uncommonly broad interpretation of its group interest, and Jews repeatedly crossed ethnic lines and even party lines to support candidates they felt best upheld the liberal values they cherished. Fiorello LaGuardia in 1920 and Franklin Delano Roosevelt in 1928 both defeated more conservative, Jewish opponents with the help of a sizeable Jewish vote.

Consistent loyalty to the Democratic Party manifested itself most powerfully in the 1930s during the Depression and New Deal (sometimes called by its enemies the Jew Deal). The Socialist Party lost virtually its entire Jewish mass base in 1936 when socialist union leaders such as David Dubinsky and Sidney Hillman took the lead in forming the American Labor Party in New York and gave their backing to Franklin Delano Roosevelt. Continued support for Roosevelt's programs led many one-time Jewish socialists to become liberal Democrats. And Jews, whether former socialists or not, gave Roosevelt an extraordinary proportion of their votes, always hovering around 90 percent; and they were the only ethnic group in the United States to increase its support for him over the four elections through 1944.

The political vision of second-generation Jews, with its focus on urban and labor welfare, civil rights, civil liberties, and internationalism reflected a distinctive American faith that was equated with the liberal wing of the Democratic party. But it was a faith held so tenaciously by Jews—Americanized but still deeply connected to the traditions of communal responsibility, mutual aid, *tzedakah,* and *tikn olam*—that liberalism could be seen as the political ideology of Jewish American ethnicity. By the mid-1930s many Jewish voters were beginning to think of themselves as liberals because they were Jews and as Jews partly because they were liberals.

By the 1930s, too, in addition to their attachment to the Democratic Party, the 4.5 million Jews of the United States were represented by more than 17,000 registered organizations that supported their political, social, economic welfare, and defense needs. There were some fifty different types of organization ranging from the Hebrew Immigrant Aid Society to the Joint Distribution Committee, most of which, including the federations, were philanthropic in nature. Giving money to Jewish causes—helping fellow Jews overseas, sustaining the Zionist movement, aiding the Jewish poor at home,

battling anti-Semitism everywhere—was seen as a *mitzvah,* a sacred obligation, even when the cause itself was defined as secular more than religious.

For Jews in the larger cities of the United States, residing in a Jewish
neighborhood, working in the Jewish ethnic economy, reading Jewish writers, socializing mainly with Jewish friends, defending Jewish interests, voting Democratic, and performing *tzedakah* (giving and acting to correct injus-
tices) meant Jews could live in a world of Jewish "unselfconsciouness," in a
place where no "membership card" was required to be Jewish. Some believed,
however, that this lack of self-consciousness was portentous, an ominous signal of an attenuated Jewish future. Ritual observance was down. The consumption of kosher meat, for example, declined 30 percent between 1914
and 1924. And by 1930, despite the rash of synagogue building, only about
33 percent of American Jewry was affiliated with a synagogue, and only 25
percent of Jewish children attended any kind of religious school. In the suburbs synagogue membership was relatively high mainly because the rival
forms of Jewish identity, especially Jewish neighborhood and political
activism had not yet been transplanted there. In a Los Angeles suburb, for
example, fewer than 2 percent of its members reported that they joined the
local synagogue for religious reasons.

A debate ensued in the 1920s and 1930s between the transformationists, who insisted that Judaism could be accommodated to the American
environment, and the survivalists, who predicted that tampering with religious principles and ignoring ritual observance would lead to assimilation
and decline, that is, lack of survival as a Jewish group. The debate has continued into the final decades of the twentieth century. Both the transformationists, who thought, perhaps overoptimistically, that they had found a
haven and a home as Jewish Americans, and the survivalists, who thought,
perhaps overpessimistically, that they would see the total absorption of the
Jews into an undifferentiated American culture, were given pause by the intensification of anti-Semitism in the 1920s and 1930s.

II

Almost at Home
in America, 1920–1945

Jewish immigrants and their children demonstrated a profound appreciation of America and an unwavering loyalty to their newly adopted country and its norms and obligations. They were now Jewish Americans as much as, or more than, they were American Jews. At the same time they retained their Jewishness—through reformulated religious identities and social activism, through mutual aid, community responsibility, and Zionism—behaving in ways that made the ideal of cultural pluralism increasingly real. The host society, however, often had other ideas and sometimes sent "signals of unwelcome." For many Americans, including some among the nation's intellectual and political elite, cultural pluralism remained suspect, a complex and unwieldy concept. Much more popular was the idea of the melting pot, an idea with clear implications as to who would melt whom.

Ellwood Cubberly, a leading educator, could say without apology in 1909 that Southern and Eastern European immigrants "tend to settle in groups . . . and to set up here their national manners, customs and observances. Our task is to break up these groups . . . to assimilate and amalgamate these people as part of our American race." Even President Woodrow Wilson said, as late as 1915, the same year in which Horace Kallen's classic essay on cultural pluralism and democracy was published, that "America does not consist of groups. A man who thinks of himself as belonging to a particular national group has not yet become an American."

Yet Jews continued to perceive of themselves as a people and not merely as Americans of a particular religious persuasion. This unfortunately increased the possibility that under certain historical conditions, American

Jews would be subject to a variety of exclusions. An especially intense anti-Semitism made itself felt simultaneously in the United States and Western Europe in the 1880s and 1890s and again during and immediately after World War I. Both periods of anti-Semitic agitation were marked by such rapid structural change and by economic crises so severe as to suggest to people the collapse of social systems. And both periods witnessed, as a result, powerful displays of narrowly conceived nationalism and xenophobia. Jews, the universal and centuries-old scapegoats, were prominently targeted.

The last two decades of the nineteenth century saw the rise of racial anti-Semites Adolf Stocker and Karl Lueger in Germany and Austria, the Dreyfus case in France, and massive pogroms and the discriminatory May Laws in Russia. In the same period the United States was marked by agrarian and small-town Jew-hatred, widespread social discrimination against Jews, intense patrician anti-Semitism, and rising sentiment against open immigration. The second period, from about 1914 to the 1920s, saw the circulation in many countries of the notorious anti-Semitic forgery, the *Protocols of the Elders of Zion,* the resurfacing of violent anti-Semitism in the Ukraine, and the rise of the Nazis in Germany. In the United States the period began with the lynching of Leo Frank, and by the 1920s, following the artificial temporary harmony generated by the war, there was a crystallization of anti-Semitic trends in American culture. This was evident in the Jew-baiting crusade of Henry Ford, in college and university quotas, and in the virtual locking of America's golden door against Southern and Eastern Europeans through restrictive immigration legislation.

In America the decade after the war was marred by the resumption of conflicts generated by industrialization and urbanization, and the twenties became known for the extreme nativism that attended these conflicts. There were widespread economic hardship and bitter confrontations between labor and management, including actual pitched battles, as in the Great Steel Strike of 1919. In the same year racial animosities led to riots in twenty-six cities, the worst of which was in Chicago, where Blacks and whites terrorized one another for months, leaving many dead and injured and more than one thousand Black families homeless. In the West and Southwest, American Indians and persons of Asian and Latino descent were resented and persecuted. And in 1920 marauders invaded the Italian community of West Frankfurt, Illinois, and burned the neighborhood to the ground.

Also in 1919 and 1920 a climate of fear, created by the ongoing Bolshevik revolution in Russia, allowed the attorney general of the United States to launch a campaign against radical foreigners. Known as the Red Scare, the crusade led to the deportation of thousands of aliens alleged to be subversives, a sizeable number of whom were Jews; it also led to the removal of socialists and their "alien" ideologies from duly elected positions in the New York State legislature. The *New York World* believed that "no more lawless act was ever enacted in a lawmaking body." Extreme nativism was reflected, too, in the growth of the Ku Klux Klan, which expanded its hate list to include Catholics and Jews as well as Blacks.

The essential driving force behind these repressive activities was anti-modernism, a fear held by many that alien forces were corrupting their country. It is striking to note how frequently in the literature of the era, in popular parlance, in the media, and in political rhetoric, Jews in particular among "aliens" were blamed for the "ills" brought by modernization.

Anti-Semitism in heterogeneous America was milder than in Europe because it had to compete here with other forms of antipathy, especially anti-Catholicism and racism. It is also true that anti-Semitism in the United States, in contrast to Germany or Poland, has been a distinctly minor feature of historical development associated with no political party of consequence, no powerful social movement, and no periodic mass violence. But from as early as the 1840s, it is relatively easy to document hostile attitudes and discriminatory acts toward Jews in the United States. And in the xenophobic 1920s anti-Semitism was plainly and openly expressed by a variety of important people, institutions, and legislative acts.

The powerful, rustic folk hero Henry Ford was responsible through his newspaper the *Dearborn Independent* for spreading the message that Jews menaced the United States. The paper not only published the fraudulent *Protocols of the Elders of Zion*; it was also filled in the first half of the twenties with pieces on "unproductive middlemen," "currency manipulation by distant banks," and "urban conspiracies," all of which fitted with classic stereotypes of Jews, and were tied to other pieces on the "international Jew as the world's foremost problem" and "aspects of Jewish power in the United States." The following excerpt is typical of the content and tone:

> The Jewish problem in the United States is essentially a city problem.
> . . . As a population, the Jews exert more power in New York than they
> have ever exerted during the Christian era in any place, with the exception
> of present Russia. The Jewish revolution in Russia was manned from New
> York . . . . Politically, while the rest of the country is entertained with the
> fiction that Tammany Hall rules the politics of New York, the fact is rarely
> published that the Jews rule Tammany.

In all of the writings there was expressed this deep distrust of the city which was always identified with Jews. There was also consistent attribution to Jews of traits that Henry Ford refused to recognize in himself. He assigned to them extraordinary power to revolutionize society, for example, while he himself was radically enhancing physical mobility and permanently changing the American landscape, life style, and quality of life through the mass production of automobiles. Ford was also capable of accusing Jews of exploitation while he himself was cheating his car dealers.

Ford's vision of Jews as capitalists and communists was a classic anti-Semitic fantasy even in its seeming contradictions: Jews have enormous power, which they yield for evil, or at least destabilizing, purposes—international financial chicanery or international bolshevism. Moreover, there was a myth that Jews were powerful enough to defend and manipulate the capitalist establishment at the same time that they undermined the Christian establishment with their inferior religion; this double-edged sword made Jews the top and bottom of society all at once—a perfect target, a useful all-purpose scapegoat for social discontent.

Many people were apparently willing to overlook Ford's improprieties and his anti-Semitism. After all, here was the living embodiment of the American Dream: a poor, humble farm boy who rose to heights of wealth and power, and not by stealth or cunning but by putting the automobile within the reach of the average American. In 1923 more than one-third of 260,000 voters polled supported Henry Ford for president. The American Jewish Committee, however, asked for a congressional hearing on Ford's Jew-baiting, and the B'nai B'rith lobbied for stronger laws against libel. In 1927 several Jewish organizations organized an effective boycott of Ford Company products, and in 1929 the famous car maker issued a tepid apology.

Oddly enough, by the late 1930s, Ford seemed to have made a complete turnaround. Although, like the American aviation hero Charles Lindbergh, Ford had accepted a medal from the Nazis, in 1939 he praised his Jewish workers extravagantly, and in 1941 he offered his rubber plantations in Brazil for the resettlement of Jewish refugees. It is impossible to know whether Ford's antipathy to Jews had dissipated or if he had simply learned to keep it hidden.

As dangerous as Ford's power was, his blatant Jew-hatred probably did less material damage than the job and housing discrimination of the 1920s and the more subtle anti-Semitism practiced at American institutions of higher education. Barriers that German Jews had faced since the 1870s had widened to restrain the more modest ambitions of upwardly mobile Russian

Jews. Restrictive "covenants" in housing, where owners pledged not to sell their homes and property to Jews and other "undesirables" proliferated, and economic discrimination was widespread and increasing, particularly in banking, public utilities, and insurance. Some insurance companies went beyond job discrimination. The Connecticut Mutual Life Insurance and the New Jersey Fire Insurance Company urged their agents not to insure Jewish clients because they were "an extraordinary hazardous class."

The Katherine Gibbs School for secretarial training informed a Jewish applicant in 1928 that it adhered to a longstanding policy "not to accept students of Jewish nationality." It was difficult for some Jews, then, to get training and credentials. But qualified or not, Jews had no end of trouble finding positions, as several employment agencies reported. One large firm in New York City, for example, wrote to Cyrus Sulzberger, president of United Hebrew Charities, in 1928: "We are finding great difficulty in placing our Jewish boys and girls, an increasing number of employers absolutely refusing to take them." Newspaper advertisements, especially between 1920 and 1926, and then again with a sharp rise in the 1930s, explicitly discouraged Jews from applying for jobs, especially in large corporations and chain stores. Jews had never been welcome in those enterprises, or in iron and steel manufacture, machine tool production, or the petroleum and automobile industries. They were also systematically denied teaching positions in most colleges and universities. It was not until 1932 that Columbia University's English Department appointed Lionel Trilling, its first Jewish faculty member.

Social discrimination reached new heights in the quota systems adopted by colleges and universities in the interwar years. Some schools set specific limits on Jewish admissions. Others used various subterfuges such as giving preference to students outside the East. Despite these barriers, Jewish students had been admitted to colleges in relatively large numbers; but they experienced social discrimination from the outset, and the practice increased significantly after Russian Jews became more visible on campuses.

Samuel Eliot Morison, the American historian who chronicled three hundred years of Harvard life, wrote: "The first German Jews who came were easily absorbed into the social pattern, but at the turn of the century the bright Russian Jewish lads from the Boston public schools began to arrive. There were enough of them in 1906 to form the Menorah Society and in another fifteen years Harvard had her Jewish problem." Unlike their German Jewish predecessors, the newcomers did not seek to adapt themselves to the "genteel tradition," and it was commonly charged that the Russians studied too hard. One resentful Harvard alumnus recalled that "Jews worked far into each night . . . they took obvious pride in their academic success and talked about it."

Harvard housed its Jewish students in a segregated dormitory, which was soon dubbed "little Jerusalem," and the following little ditty was already making the rounds of the fraternities by 1910:

> Oh, Harvard's run by millionaires
> And Yale is run by booze.
> Cornell is run by farmer's sons
> Columbia's run by Jews.
> So give a cheer for Baxter Street,
> Another one for Pell
> And when the little sheenies die,
> Their souls will go to hell.

The ambitious Jewish students who viewed college as a place for serious intellectual endeavor and not merely for achieving social poise were kept out of the eating clubs at Yale and Princeton. And in 1913 a national fraternity suspended its affiliate at the City College of New York because the "Hebraic element is greatly in excess." All of this led to the rise of Jewish fraternities, from four in 1908 to twenty-five in 1926, and to thirty-seven by 1936.

The social discrimination and insults were usually borne in silence; but when leading educational institutions tried to restrict Jewish admission in the twenties, Jews felt threatened. Between 1920 and 1922, New York University and Columbia University, whose Jewish enrollments had reached nearly 40 percent, instituted quotas. When other universities, including Harvard, the most prestigious institution of higher learning in the United States, followed suit, a cry of outrage arose in the Jewish community.

It was of little comfort that Harvard, according to President Lowell, had instituted quotas not only to protect "the traditional character of Harvard" (upper-middle class, white, native-born, Protestant) but also the better to "absorb" Jews and to decrease the discrimination that allegedly emerged wherever Jews gathered in large numbers. In 1922, Lowell, blaming the Jews for their own victimization, wrote, "There is a rapidly growing antisemitic feeling in this country caused by . . . a strong race feeling on the part of the Jews."

The quotas were repudiated in 1923, but a variety of hidden restrictions, including the "need to correct geographical and social imbalances," were substituted at Harvard and other elite schools. The most pervasive device for excluding Jews was the "character test." Academic achievement had been the most important criterion used by admissions officers, but in the 1920s committees in many colleges began looking more for characteristics such as "fair play" and "interest in fellows," traits not usually associated with Jews in the popular mind. In those ways, between 1920 and 1945, the number of Jews was kept within "reasonable" proportions at most eastern private liberal arts colleges and elite universities and in the major state universities in the South and Midwest, as well as across the country in many professional schools. In medical schools in New York, for example, in 1920 there were 214 Jewish students enrolled, in 1940, only 108.

Restriction in the 1920s was not limited to college and university admissions. An even more significant anti-Semitic discrimination, which would ultimately determine the life and death of many European Jews, was inherent in the immigration laws of 1921 and 1924. The attempt to limit immigration was almost as old as immigration itself, but in the twenties the restriction movement added a more overt racist dimension with its quota system based on national origins. There had been racial motives in earlier legislation too, such as the Chinese Exclusion Act of 1882 and the so-called gentlemen's agreement of 1908 aimed at limiting Japanese immigration. And in 1922 in the Ozawa ruling, the U.S. Supreme Court affirmed earlier decisions that naturalization laws did not apply to Asians. But the restrictive legislation passed by Congress in 1921 and 1924 for the first time made dangerously invidious distinctions between Caucasians, between the old immigration from Northern and Western Europe, from which rural Americans largely stemmed, and the new immigration from Southern and Eastern Europe, which included Jews and flowed mainly to the cities.

Through a complicated legislative formula, Congress ultimately limited immigration to 2 percent of the number of foreign-born residents of each national group who lived in the United States in 1890. Since the vast majority of the new immigrants, "filthy, un-American and often dangerous in their habits," came after 1890, the legislation clearly discriminated against them. Jews were not singled out or attacked directly in the new laws, but in the fiscal year 1920–21, a record number of 119,000 East European Jews had entered America, and during hearings on immigration between 1920 and 1924, many proponents of restriction, including Professor Henry Pratt Fairchild and a journalist, Burton J. Hendrick, cited Jewish criminality, greed, and laziness as reasons why the laws were needed.

General immigration decreased from over 800,000 in 1924 to fewer than 300,000 in 1925. At the same time, the number of Jewish newcomers declined from 120,000 to 10,000. The concept of Northern European

supremacy embodied in the law and its failure to distinguish between ordinary immigrants and refugees, hurt Jews already in America far less, of
course, than it hurt those who were stranded abroad and later murdered in
Nazi-dominated Europe in the name of a similar concept of Nordic or Aryan
superiority. But the declining faith in the power of Americanization implied
in the new restriction laws meant intensified suspicion and hostility toward
"unmeltable" ethnics at home, including Jews.

Still, as Jonathan Sarna has persuasively argued, if America "has not
been utter heaven for Jews, it has been as far from hell as Jews in the Diaspora have ever known." Even in the twenties the picture was mixed. Despite
restrictions, the number of Jews on college campuses, in government service, and in the professions increased significantly, as did their affluence.
Anti-Semitism was mostly private, never becoming part of the national political agenda and never strong enough to deny Jews access to the opportunities offered by American society.

Distress in the Jewish community over discrimination was offset to
some degree by the personal and collective achievements of Jews in the
1920s. But the situation deteriorated markedly in the 1930s. The rise of
Adolph Hitler to power in Germany, the blatant anti-Jewish ideology of the
Nazis, and their outspoken expansionism coincided with intensified anti-
Semitism at home to challenge Jewish confidence. Moreover, the debilitating
effects of the Depression, including economic distress and interethnic competition and hostility, not only provided a fertile field for demagogues but
also made it more difficult for Jewish groups, with reduced financial resources, to counteract anti-Semitism.

There were direct connections between Nazi Germany and rising domestic anti-Semitism. After 1933 there was a steady infusion of economic
and ideological support and even organizational leadership from Berlin and
Rome to anti-Semitic organizations in the United States. More worrisome,
however, was the influence of the home-grown hate-mongers such as Charles
Coughlin, a Roman Catholic priest, who, beginning in 1936, argued in his
journal *Social Justice* and on his nationwide radio broadcasts to some twenty-
five million listeners that European fascism was a legitimate reaction to the
more serious threat of communism. And his anti-communist crusade relied
heavily on the old contradictory but compelling stereotypes of Jews as communist revolutionaries and conspiratorial international bankers.

Father Coughlin's rantings attracted an immense following and continued until he was taken off the air in 1942. Anti-Semitism was kept very much
alive, however, by Fritz Kuhn's German American Bund, the Silver Shirts, the

Friends of Democracy, Gerald L. K. Smith, Dudley Pelley, and other pro-Nazi, anti-Jewish individuals and groups. In fact, more than one hundred new anti-Semitic organizations were formed in the United States in the 1930s.

Even the relatively liberal magazine *Christian Century,* while attacking rising American anti-Semitism, assailed Jews and Judaism: "The simple and naked fact is that Judaism rests upon an impossible basis," the editors argued in 1936. "It is trying to pluck the fruits of democracy without yielding itself to the processes of democracy." And they continued to warn, in classic melting pot rhetoric, that "in a dynamic society a national culture cannot help seeking the unity of its component elements." Jews, therefore, "must be brought to repentance—with all the tenderness, in view of their age-long affliction, but with austere realism in view of their sinful share in their own tragedy."

With friends like these, the Jewish community might ask, to whom could one turn? And the situation became even more acute between 1939 and 1941, when the United States entered the war. Several isolationists including Charles Lindbergh had earlier attacked the Jews, warning President Roosevelt that they were conspiring to bring the nation into a war with Germany and that such a war would prove catastrophic for the United States. This sentiment was echoed in Congress by Senators Burton K. Wheeler and Gerald Nye and reflected in wartime public opinion polls indicating a substantial rise of hostility toward Jews.

That hostility made it difficult for Jewish Americans to mount a successful effort to rescue their fellow Jews trapped in Nazi-occupied Europe. Jewish individuals and groups tried from the very start to warn the American public about the crisis in Germany. Stephen Wise, recognizing the inherent threat of the nascent Nazi Party, sounded the first alarm as early as 1922. By the 1930s, Jewish agencies were in the forefront of those warning their fellow Americans and government leaders against appeasement of the Germans and of the dangers of U.S. isolationism. And after the outbreak of war in 1939, Jews were outspoken in favor of U.S. intervention. In 1940, even before the United States entered the war, the American Jewish Congress had established the National Committee on Jewish Aid to Great Britain, which was already embattled.

The direct interventionist posture of the Jews distinguished them from other hyphenate groups such as German, Italian, and Irish Americans in the ethnic coalition of the Democratic Party, and it led to a significant hue and cry among some about "special pleading," "Jewish war," and "Jewish power." Yet the most revealing sign of Jewish weakness in American society—and therefore the most irrefutable response to anti-Semitic rhetoric and accusa-tions about Jewish power—was the failure of the Jewish community's efforts to change the discriminatory immigration and refugee policy of the United States from the 1920s through the Holocaust.

Despite the Nuremberg Laws of 1935, American attention to a poten-tial refugee problem began only in 1938 after the "Aryanization" of German business, that is, the confiscation of most Jewish businesses by the Nazis. The United States coordinated a conference of thirty-two nations at Evian, France, in July. No country involved, including the United States, was will-ing to change existing immigration laws to permit the entrance of Jewish refugees. And this was prior to the war, with the heads of state or their rep-resentatives discussing only seekers of asylum from Germany, a country whose Jewish population was less than 370,000, or about 0.75 percent of the German population. Once the Nazis occupied much of Europe and much of the territory inhabited by the world's 14 million Jews, the need for Jewish havens would become much more pressing, but there was the same lack of substantive response.

The Evian Conference did not even produce a resolution condemning Nazi anti-Jewish persecutions—an unintentional signal to Hitler and his min-ions that they were free to find any solution at all to what anti-Semites called "the Jewish Problem." Soon after, on 9 November 1938, came *Krystallnacht,* a massive government-sponsored pogrom that smashed and burned Jewish storefronts and synagogues throughout Germany and which some historians see as the first explicit action of the Holocaust.

In the United States all efforts to get the government to ease restric-tions on immigrants and refugees failed, including proposals to allow en-trance, above and beyond the quota, to twenty thousand German Jewish children (all of whom ended up in the Nazi death camps); or to borrow on future quotas; or to open Alaska to Jewish resettlement. Instead the State Department introduced even more complicated procedures for obtaining visas. In mid-1940, when precious unused visas would have saved many lives, Breckinridge Long, the American official in charge of issuing them, recom-mended that his staff put "every obstacle in the way" and suggested various methods by which to "postpone and postpone and postpone the granting of visas."

Administrative strategies designed during the Depression to limit im-migration for economic reasons, the risk that someone was "likely to become a public charge," for example, were deliberately applied to restrict the en-trance of Jewish refugees. This was particularly ironic given the performance in the United States of the nearly 120,000 Jewish refugees who did manage to penetrate the bureaucratic "paper walls" between 1935 and 1941. About half settled on Manhattan's West Side and in Washington Heights, which together became known as the "Fourth Reich." Many also settled in Chicago and San Francisco. Most were middle-aged and middle class; nearly 20 percent were professionals including scientists, artists, writers, scholars, and psychoanalysts—figures no less notable than Albert Einstein, Ernst Cassirer, Edward Teller, Erwin Panofsky, Erich Fromm, Hannah Arendt, Erik Erikson, and Herbert Marcuse. Another 60 percent were in commerce and, although their adjustment to their new situation was often painful, the charge that they would become a burden to the economy was roundly refuted by a report in 1941 which showed that in 82 cities the Jewish refugees had established 239 businesses and had created countless jobs for others. Visas were also refused or "postponed" on the unfounded grounds that "spies had infiltrated the refugee stream." By June 1941 it was more difficult to enter the United States, which was still at peace, than it was to enter Britain, which was very much at war.

The State Department continued to be obstinate, and worse. In mid-1942 it knowingly suppressed for months the first credible and authoritative underground reports on the "final solution," the deliberate, systematic extermination by the Nazis of the Jews of Europe. In December 1942 a delegation representing a number of Jewish agencies visited the White House, where the president informed them that he was already aware that the Jews in Nazi-occupied territory were being "resettled" in the east for the express purpose of genocide and that the mass murder of a whole people was well underway. Roosevelt was sympathetic and promised that the Nazis would be held to "strict accountability," but it was another year before he took any action.

At the start of 1944 a report titled "The Acquiescence of This Government in the Murder of the Jews" by three apparently naïve assistants at the State Department charged that the department was "guilty not only of gross procrastination and wilful failure to act, but even of wilful attempts to prevent action . . . to rescue Jews from Hitler." The report was given a new, innocuous title and buried in the bureaucratic morass, but not before it was read by Henry Morgenthau Jr., Secretary of the Treasury, and the Jew closest to Roosevelt. It was through Morgenthau's efforts that the War Refugee Board was established in January 1944 for the "rescue, transportation, maintenance and relief of the victims of enemy oppression." For political reasons any mention of Jews was carefully omitted, but the board, financed primarily with Joint Distribution Committee funds, initiated an effort to save the

Jews of Hungary, the only sizeable Jewish community still surviving in Europe. Money was ferried to the anti-Nazi underground, and Hungary was threatened with retribution, including bombing, if it continued the deportations and killings of Jews.

By June 1944 the immigration laws, thought by rescue advocates to be impermeable, were also skirted. Nearly one thousand refugees, mostly Jewish, were admitted to the United States and temporarily sheltered in an Army Relocation Authority camp in Oswego, New York, until they could be returned to Europe after the war. Non-Jewish refugees were deliberately included, once again so that the Roosevelt administration would not be seen as favoring the Jews. It was hoped that the Oswego case would be an example for other countries to follow, but few did. A senior Canadian official, when asked in 1945 how many Jews would be allowed into Canada after the war, said, "None is too many."

Many of the thousands of Hungarian Jews who survived the Holocaust owe their lives to the War Refugee Board, but U.S. initiative, six years in coming, was too late to save the millions. Approximately five hundred thousand refugees, a mere fraction of Europe's Jewish population, found haven, about one hundred thousand in the United States. That tiny number continues to haunt American Jewry.

What went wrong? There are some who argue that the American-Jewish community shares the blame. It is true that American Jewry was not well prepared for the crisis. The traditional sources of unity, religion and a common culture and language, had grown somewhat weaker. It was not so much that acculturating, secularizing Jews felt less Jewish as that they no longer felt exclusively so. The community was rent by various strategies and ideologies and degrees and kinds of religious persuasion, as well as by duplication and competition. The American Jewish Committee, one of four central agencies fighting anti-Semitism and discrimination, generally continued in its rescue efforts to avoid public action, and in the 1930s it clashed with the American Jewish Congress, which under Stephen Wise's leadership was far more aggressive. The relatively conservative Anti-Defamation League tangled with the socialist Jewish Labor Committee when attempts were made to coordinate activities.

Raising funds for relief was the main collaborative effort of the Jewish agencies. Sixty-three local federations and welfare funds joined to establish the Council of Jewish Federations and Welfare Funds. Between 1939 and 1945 the Joint Distribution Committee sent $80 million to Europe for relief and escape through the underground, and the United Jewish Appeal, reconstituted in 1939 by the confederation of several fund-raising organizations, raised $124 million. But even in these successful examples of Jewish American unity during the Holocaust, Zionists and non-Zionists clashed. And the Zionist leadership itself was old, tired, and divided into factions. Some argued for investing their limited energy in the development of the *yishuv,* the Jewish settlement in Palestine; others pushed rescue, though most were unwilling to expend precious resources in settling European Jews outside Palestine. There was enough unity to get one Zionist resolution in 1942 calling for a Jewish commonwealth in Palestine and another condemning Britain's white paper virtually closing that land to Jewish refugees after 1939, but these had little effect on the Roosevelt administration and still less on the British.

In 1943 an American Jewish Conference attempted to establish a representative body to coordinate political activities and rescue efforts. It achieved substantial agreement on a program, but a resolution supporting the establishment of a Jewish commonwealth led to the withdrawal from the conference of two important groups, the Jewish Labor Committee, which, in its continuing commitment to socialist universalism, was critical of "nationalism," and the American Jewish Committee, which feared the reemergence of the divided loyalty issue. Once again, at a critical time, the leaders could not speak with a single voice.

Even if they had been consistently unified, however, it would not have made much difference in the rescue effort. U.S. policy makers either were unable to fathom the meaning of the Holocaust, or they shared the anti-Semitism with which the State Department was riddled in the 1920s and 1930s. Most likely, for many, both were true. The Jews were seen as an unpopular minority, their plight an "incident" in the war. The administration persisted in the argument that winning the war against the Nazis was the way to save the Jews, and all other rescue efforts, including the proposed bombing of Auschwitz or the rail lines leading to that factory of death, were dismissed as diversions that would delay victory over the Germans.

Moreover, many in the Roosevelt administration worried about a backlash if the war, so costly in blood and treasure, were perceived, because of the alteration of wartime policies, as merely a war to save the Jews. They were already stuck with the epithet *Jew Deal,* because of the visibility of Jews around Roosevelt, such as Samuel Rosenman, his political manager, Benjamin Cohen, his legislative craftsman, and Felix Frankfurter, a trusted advisor. Jews were also concentrated in those regulatory agencies, especially in the Labor and Agriculture departments and in the Securities and Exchange Commission, that dealt directly with the public as representatives of government. But Jews were no more present in the Roosevelt administration than they had been in three previous Republican administrations, and most of them were products of several generations of acculturation; they rarely advocated a Jewish cause or interest even when they could recognize it. Jews were visible, however, and in politics, appearances are everything.

On the other hand, Roosevelt had little need to worry about losing the backing of the Jews, the most loyal Democratic group in the history of the party. Despite his feeble rescue policy, his failure to support a Jewish commonwealth in Palestine, and his failure to oppose the British white paper, Roosevelt was perceived as the great leader who pursued in war the Nazis, the archenemy of the Jews. Jews voted for Roosevelt in unprecedented proportions and increased their support with each of three subsequent elections. Therefore, even if they had been unified, the leaders of the Jewish community would still have had trouble putting pressure on Roosevelt because they would have had difficulty detaching the ordinary Jewish American voter from loyalty to the president.

To criticize American Jewry for lack of unity, moreover, is to apply a postwar reality to the Holocaust period. Indeed, it was the Holocaust that taught the lesson of the need for unity, and Jewish Americans learned it relatively well. It would also be wrong to accuse, as some have done, an American Jewry that was faithful to Roosevelt of indifference to the fate of Jews in Nazi-occupied Europe. Jewish Americans throughout their history were and still are largely defined by their protection and nurture of Jewish communities abroad. And World War II was no exception. Many Jews and Jewish organizations did indeed go public in their efforts to rescue their trapped brethren, aggressively organizing demonstrations, rallies, marches, mass meetings, and boycotts, as well as putting pressure on figures in U.S. government behind the scenes. Jews in America were convinced that Hitler posed a threat not only to Jews but to civilized world order, and many urged military intervention early, even at the risk of criticism by isolationists and American popular heroes such as Lindbergh and Ford. By 1941, Jewish Americans were virtually unanimous in their support of the entry of the United States into what they saw as a just war. And in the end, the nation's entry into that war to defeat Nazism actually helped restore Jewish confidence and a sense of solidarity with America.

The administration's position that an allied victory was the most effective way to save the Jews was not entirely or directly disputed by American Jews. Not only were they patriotic, but they also feared the charge that they were lobbying for a particularistic ethnic interest rather than a national one.

Therefore for most Jewish Americans, winning the war, not rescue, was the priority. But it is important to see, as Henry Feingold, the foremost scholar of the politics of rescue, reminds us, that "the two objectives did not seem in conflict because few understood until 1944 that by the time victory came European Jewry would be in ashes."

General Dwight David Eisenhower, standing over a pit containing the remains of uncountable death camp victims, ordered his troops to look closely at the consequences of genocide directly around them and at their very feet. The evident "starvation, cruelty, and bestiality were so overpowering," as to leave many of the soldiers sick. But Eisenhower insisted on seeing everything, and he urged his government to dispatch congressmen and reporters because he wanted to "leave no room for cynical doubt." The pictures and reports that filtered back to the United States made a deep impression on the Jewish American psyche and eventually on American and Jewish American life and culture as well.

12

American Jewry Regroups, 1945–1970

As a result of the destruction of European Jewry, the United States became the most important Jewish community in the world —in numbers, in wealth, and in intellectual resources. Moreover, postwar American Jewry, largely native born of Russian Jewish parentage, compared equally or favorably with white Protestant society in education, income, and life style. But in 1945 these children of Jewish immigrants in America faced an extraordinary challenge: they had to nurture the remnants of European Jewry, aid the *yishuv* (settlement) in Palestine, and, in the United States, maintain a vibrant Jewish life attractive enough to sustain the affiliation of the younger generation. The last of these challenges was actually met in part by the first two. For eventually it was the trauma of the Holocaust and the memory and needs of the survivors, combined with the struggle for independence in Palestine, which reinforced Jewish religion or provided a secular ethnic replacement for it. In both cases, American Jewry was revitalized.

The impact of the Holocaust, except insofar as it drove support for a Jewish homeland, was not immediately registered on American Jewish consciousness. Shortly after her arrival in the United States, one survivor, for example, had the experience of being told by her American-born Jewish neighbor in Brooklyn that she should write stories. "You have a terrific imagination," the neighbor told her after hearing the survivor's vivid recollection of the gas chambers. In New Orleans a truck driver who had served in World War II had given up talking about the sights he had seen in the extermination camps to anyone but people who had been there. He told a survivor: "Don't try to tell people here what happened in Europe: forget about it. I was in the

American Army. I walked into those camps and I saw all the things the Germans did and people here don't believe it when you tell them."

In some respects these attitudes were the beginning of a conspiracy of silence between Holocaust survivors and American society which would last for almost a quarter of a century. For many Americans the survivors were refugees who had arrived in the United States with incredible tales to relate but who relatively soon stopped talking and interacting with the American community. It would not be until the 1970s that the Holocaust—the consciousness of its enormity and the struggle with its meaning—took its place as one of the pillars supporting Jewish American identity.

In the meantime the Jewish community in Palestine was a major concern of American Jews, and their support was critical to the establishment of the independent state of Israel. It was necessary to get the U.S. government to support the United Nations resolution that would partition Palestine in preparation for the establishment of a Jewish state alongside a new Arab state. This meant persuading President Harry Truman to override resistance to partition in the State Department, whose members feared alienating the oil-rich Arab countries in the region. Jewish lobbying was successful mainly because the president was already moving in the direction of supporting partition. Truman's primary concerns were containing Soviet ambitions in the Middle East and upholding and strengthening the United Nations. Once he was persuaded that partition would not be defied by the non-Arab member states of the United Nations, that the Soviet Union would go along out of eagerness to displace the British, and that no U.S. troops would have to be used to keep the peace, Truman was satisfied with the two-state solution.

Ethnic politics, then, was only one determinant of U.S. support for partition. But Jewish Americans could feel that they had had something to do with the vote of the General Assembly of the United Nations on 29 November 1947 to set up both a Jewish state and an Arab state in the land of Palestine. The Jews in the region accepted statehood, even if some were disappointed with the established borders. The Arabs not only rejected it but at once attacked Jewish settlements in every part of Palestine. A fierce civil war went on for months, with death and injury on all sides. Despite U.S. pressure to wait, Israel proclaimed its independence at the very earliest opportunity: 14 May 1948, the day the British mandate ended. Truman immediately extended de facto recognition to the new state, but on the very next day, six Arab armies from neighboring countries invaded Israel and threatened to obliterate it. After ten days of resistance the Israelis were able to counterattack, and a truce was agreed to on 11 June. Israel and Egypt, however, resumed fighting intermittently, and their particular war did not end until January 1949.

It was obvious from the start that the beleaguered state required more than political support from the American Jewish community. The continuing needs of the new nation—in resettling the remnant of European Jewry and later in absorbing the refugees from Muslim-dominated countries in the Middle East and North Africa, all in the face of the persistent threat of attack from neighboring Arab countries—produced an outpouring of financial aid from Jews and Jewish organizations in America. In 1940 the United Jewish Appeal had raised only $14 million, but after the murder of six million European Jews, nearly half the world's Jewish population, it raised $131 million dollars in 1946 and even larger amounts between 1947 and 1948.

It was during these immediate postwar years that the United Jewish Appeal became the preeminent American Jewish organization, and philanthropy, particularly for support of Israel but also for Jewish social welfare agencies and communities everywhere, became one of the most popular and important expressions of Jewish American identity. The heavy emphasis on raising money had "redemptive" features. Giving was a central Jewish value and had been for centuries, and in America it was still seen, even by those no longer religiously observant, as a sacred task, reflecting a profound spiritual commitment to Jewish survival.

Israel benefited greatly from the flow of aid from the United States, and the relationship was reciprocal. The philanthropic activity in response to Israel's needs allowed American Jewry to regroup, perhaps even to atone, after their frustrating inability to rescue their relatives and friends and *landslayt* from the murderous hands of the Nazis. Philanthropy, largely but not only for Israel, became a touchstone, a standard or pattern, for Jewish survival and a permanent part of the American Jewish community structure and of Jewish American identity.

Once again Jewish Americans displayed their commitment to building and reshaping a religiously authenticated ethnic identity by using supports from two cultures. The Holocaust had promoted a greater sense of group identity and a more powerful sense of connection to world Jewry. At the same time middle-class American Jews were hopeful that the new Jewish state would become a liberal democracy like the United States, as well as a center of Hebrew culture which would reenergize the global Jewish community. They also hoped, as they always had, that Israel would be a haven for Jews who needed it. But Jewish Americans did not count themselves needy in that way. They were feeling ever more comfortably integrated at home in the post-

war United States. This was true partly as a result of the further Americanization some 550,000 Jewish Americans experienced serving in the armed
forces; partly because the United States had, after all, fought a successful war
against the common Nazi enemy; and partly because after 1944 anti-Semitism was beginning a steep decline.

Decreased anti-Semitism meant among other things that Jews in the
postwar period were less restricted in their geographic mobility. As in the
past, they changed neighborhoods, but now in the new areas they were somewhat less concentrated. They also changed their cities: Miami and Los Angeles began to rise in the ranks of Jewish communities; Chicago, Cleveland, and
Detroit began to fall. Some prewar Jewish working-class neighborhoods with
strong communal institutions persisted, especially in New York City's bor-
oughs of Brooklyn and the Bronx. Others were sustained by filling the communal needs of the Orthodox, and some were even bolstered by the postwar
immigration of traditional Jews from Europe. But by the late 1950s many of
the urban Jewish neighborhoods of the interwar years were being abandoned,
except for enclaves of mostly older and poorer Jews, and surrounded by
mainly Black and Puerto Rican newcomers.

The Brooklyn neighborhood of Brownsville is a case in point. In the
ten years from 1950 to 1960, the white population of Brooklyn declined by
almost 20 percent while the Black population increased by 150 percent and
the Puerto Rican population went from less than 2 percent to 7 percent of
Brooklyn's general population. A similar dynamic was experienced in heavily Jewish Brownsville. Blacks in the neighborhood were younger, poorer,
more recently uprooted, and more recent victims of historic oppression
and deprivation than the whites they were displacing. Understandably, then,
Blacks, were also disproportionately the perpetrators and victims of vandal-
ism and violence in Brownsville; and "race fear" was part of the reason some
whites, including Jews, decided to leave.

There had been a history of Jewish criminality in Brownsville. Indeed,
the neighborhood had been the home of "Murder, Inc.," and adult crime as
late as the 1940s was still part of the Jewish ethnic milieu of Brownsville and
other neighborhoods in cities such as Chicago, Philadelphia, and Detroit. But
after the war, Jewish criminals were fewer and much less tied to a Jewish
environment. Now, as one former Brownsville resident said: "There was an
influx of a new breed of people, muggers, burglars, murderers and drug ad-
dicts. The decent citizen had to move away. The synagogues were closing.
Older Jewish people retired to Florida. Children fled." One Jewish woman,
a veteran of liberal political activity and still infused with the social concern

she had absorbed from the *Jewish Daily Forward* and from her socialist brothers, stayed on as her Brownsville housing project turned Blacker, poorer, and tougher. She tried to understand, reminding herself of her brothers' aphorism, "Blacks are the last hired and first fired." But one day in the laundry room of her building, she was beaten by a Black girl. She gave in and joined the exodus.

Race fear was not necessarily the primary reason for leaving Brownsville; but when added to a variety of other important factors, it made leaving easier. Brownsville, since the 1920s, before any appreciable nonwhite population had arrived there, was stigmatized as a slum and a place to get away from. For Jewish immigrants, mainly from the Lower East Side of Manhattan, moving to working-class Brownsville had been a first step up. And their children, aspiring second-generation Jews, like others in quest of material comfort and convenience, moved to "better" neighborhoods including Flatbush and Boro Park even before significant Black and Puerto Rican migration into Brownsville. In short, race fear intensified a steady flight of the upwardly mobile that was already in progress.

In addition to moving to new neighborhoods within their cities, second- and third-generation Jews, along with the white middle class, flocked to the suburbs in the 1950s and 1960s. The relatively easy availability of automobiles, the new highways, and the continuing postwar prosperity contributed to an explosion of suburbanization. The process was intensified by the extraordinary demand for housing and space created by the Depression and war-generated shortages. Suburbanization was enhanced too by the cult of domesticity that took hold in the late 1940s and 1950s when postwar Americans craved peace and "normality." And during the baby boom of the 1940s and 1950s, even the drastic drop in the Jewish birth rate was arrested, though only temporarily.

The process of suburbanization was made possible, too, by the historic developments in real estate initiated by William Levitt. Levitt, a child of Jewish immigrants, virtually single-handedly transformed the social landscape of American home ownership. He borrowed funds during the period of acute housing shortage and bought four thousand acres of land near the town of Hempstead, Long Island, approximately fifty miles from New York City. Using efficient mass production techniques learned in World War II, Levitt built seventeen thousand single-family homes on former potato-farming land. He sold these homes, initially to veterans only, at a price he thought younger families could manage. In addition to the dwellings, Levitt laid out six "village greens," twenty-four playing fields, and nine community swimming pools, as well as several large sites for schools and religious institutions. Levittown eventually grew into a community of eighty-two thousand people.

Levitt went on to develop other towns in various parts of the United States and Europe. His pilot model made history not only as a prototype for towns but also for reasonably priced neighborhood developments in cities. This, for the first time, put affordable housing within the reach of middle-income and working-class Americans, and the opportunity lasted for several decades.

The new neighborhoods and suburbs witnessed an extraordinary burst of synagogue construction in the 1950s, even as many older synagogues also experienced a growth in membership. In all, synagogue membership increased from approximately 20 percent of the Jewish population in 1930 to just under 60 percent by 1960. Growing synagogue membership, however, did not necessarily mean a growing religiosity; there was little evidence of an intensification of faith or increased ritual observance among Jews. But building synagogues may have been a way for Jews to participate in the larger revival of institutional religion that characterized the United States at mid-century. This was a time when America, emphasizing what was described in the 1950s as its Judeo-Christian roots, confronted "Godless" communism in the Soviet Union. Seeking domestic consensus, a binding of Americans more tightly together, rabbis and ministers exchanged pulpits and promoted interfaith movements, and Christian theologians focused on the Jewish roots of Christianity.

By building synagogues and participating in seemingly religious activities therein, second- and third-generation Jews may have been acting more like quintessential postwar Americans than "reborn" Jews. But, one may infer, even in the writings of astute observers such as Will Herberg (*Protestant, Catholic, Jew*), that this did not mean Jews were assimilating. Herberg and others questioned the depth of the religiosity of those who were eager to affiliate with synagogues (or churches for that matter) and characterized Jewish involvement with synagogues as "religiousness without religion . . . a way of sociability or 'belonging' rather than a way of orienting life to God." But the "belonging" was still as much to the Jewish people as to America. The synagogue was a means to interact with other Jews and to pass on a sense of Jewishness. It may have been a public façade, as some have charged, but it was a genuine arena for promoting the essentially communal content of Jewish identification.

There were good reasons for third-generation Jewish Americans who had experienced no religious revival to define themselves nonetheless as pri-

marily a religious community. In the postwar United States before the late
1960s, Americans were notably tolerant regarding religious differences, but
they still looked with some suspicion at the persistence of national or ethnic
identities and hyphenate loyalties. Third-generation Jews therefore turned to
the synagogue in a way that would define and sustain their Americanness and
yet confirm ties to their forebears.

The synagogue, with the exception of a small number of viable Orthodox congregations, did become more important as a vehicle for ethnic identity and continuity than as a house of worship. Even when 50 percent of a
Jewish community belonged to a synagogue, only 15 percent attended religious services at all regularly. Moreover, except for a minority in the right
wing of the Conservative movement, few members of the Reform or Conservative laity took seriously the ritual demands of their denominations. They
were as casual about religious observance as their gentile compatriots, perhaps even more so. In surveys of the major American religious groups in the
late 1960s and 1970s, Jewish lay persons generally placed last in religious
attendance and belief. This applied to some clergy as well; only 10 percent
of Reform rabbis reported that they believed in a "personal God."

But Jews did belong to synagogues, and they did associate and interact
there as Mordecai Kaplan had encouraged, even if not very often in communal prayer or ritual. By 1960 they were sending five hundred thousand of their
children to congregational schools for at least part of the day or week. And
many of these children stayed in the schools beyond the age of bat and bar
mitzvah. In 1970, 84 percent of young men and 72 percent of young women
aged 15 to 19, were receiving some form of Jewish education. Adults, especially women, were attending classes too, in Hebrew, Bible, and Talmud. In
addition, by the late 1960s several hundred colleges and universities were
offering well-enrolled courses and even majors in Jewish studies. The academic analysis of Jewish history and culture was not related to faith in the
strict sense; in fact, it broke the traditional connection between piety and
learning, but it also largely attested to a heightened sense of Jewish identity
and commitment.

Between 1945 and 1970 there was also a vast increase in the number
of Jewish theological seminaries and rabbinical associations that supported
Judaic research and training. One of the new theological seminaries was
the Reconstructionist Rabbinical College, which opened near Philadelphia
in 1968. The emergence of Reconstructionism as a distinctive movement
rather than as the left wing of Conservatism began when Mordecai Kaplan
retired from Jewish Theological Seminary in 1963 at the age of 82. Kaplan

had hoped to reconstruct Judaism from within an already established denomination, but in the early 1960s a number of his disciples, including his son-in-law, Ira Eisenstein, convinced him of the need to establish an independent movement.

Almost immediately the Reconstructionists approved patrilineal descent as a way of identifying who was a Jew, though this would have little effect until the Reform movement did the same in 1983. And in 1974, no more than six years after it opened its doors, the Reconstructionist Rabbinical College ordained a woman as a rabbi. Reconstructionism became an important feature in Jewish American life; but it was the 103 men and women ordained as rabbis during the first two decades of the Reconstructionist Rabbinical College who provided Reconstructionism with a presence within the Jewish community far more visible than the relatively few congregations officially confederated in the Reconstructionist movement.

Once again, as in the prewar period, it was Conservative Judaism, with its continuing combination of innovation and traditional liturgy, that appealed most to the children and the grandchildren of the East European immigrants. In 1955 the Rabbinical Assembly of the Conservative movement, in addition to changes it had already instituted such as mixed (male and female) pews and mixed choirs, approved a controversial resolution allowing women to be called up to the platform of the synagogue to bless and read from the Torah. Conservative Judaism also sponsored social and recreational programs more readily than its Reform or Orthodox counterparts, and in the 1950s and 1960s it grew more quickly than the other denominations. Some caution is in order here, however; the increase in the number of Conservative congregations may have been a result, in part, of a kind of default system rather than of studied choice. One organizer admitted, "We figured that the Conservative [synagogue] was 'middle of the road,' and would not offend any group in the community. So we called it a Conservative congregation." Default or not, in 1948 there were 217 Conservative congregations in the United States, and by 1970, 832. The Conservative movement also ran sixty-five day schools, six summer camps, and a seminary in Israel.

The Reform branch of Judaism also grew in the same period. Part of its attractiveness was that since the 1930s the movement had been increasingly sympathetic to Zionism and the concept of worldwide Jewish peoplehood. In 1935, Felix Levy, an outspoken Zionist, was elected president of Reform's Central Conference of American Rabbis; in 1937 a Reform platform adopted in Columbus, Ohio, radically altered the Pittsburgh Platform of 1885, which had eschewed Jewish nationalism; and in 1963, Hebrew Union

College, the training school for Reform rabbis, opened a branch in Jerusalem, where it required its students to live and learn for at least a year.

In the late 1940s the Reform movement also launched an intensive drive to win the unaffiliated, and it moved its headquarters to New York from Cincinnati. A branch of Hebrew Union College was opened in Los Angeles as well in 1954. Reform, recognizing its earlier overemphasis on universalism, also had reintroduced Jewish "national" holidays such as Purim and Hanukkah, increased the use of Hebrew in services, and even begun to encourage some ritual observance including Friday night candle lighting and the wearing of skullcaps. Not everyone in the movement found these changes palatable. Typical of the view of the classical Reform rabbis were these remarks made by Jacob R. Marcus of the Hebrew Union College in 1959:

> There are today too many Reform Jews who have ceased to be liberals. Their Reform, crystallized into a new Orthodoxy, is no longer dynamic. Shocked by the Hitlerian catastrophe, many have turned their backs on the future to seek comfort in the nostalgia of a romanticized Jewish past which never existed. We cannot lead our people forward by stumbling backward.

At the same time that Jews were being described by some observers as having a religious identity but no religion, some classical Reformers were accusing Jews of being too religious. In any case, the changes emphasizing tradition instituted by Reform Judaism continued into the 1970s and 1980s. A new prayer book focusing on Sabbath observance and religious commandment was published in 1979, and Reform Judaism instituted a day school movement in 1985, thereby moving from its classic universalism to a somewhat more particularistic position. The changes partly eroded that denomination's reputation as cold and overly rational, and the number of Reform congregations increased from 360 in the late 1940s to 698 by 1970.

Orthodoxy was also reenergized by an infusion of traditional leaders, institutions, and the thousands of committed believers who left war-torn Europe for the United States between 1939 and the early 1950s. The refugees came from diverse Jewish environments ranging from Lithuania to the Balkans and from the more acculturated Orthodox communities of Germany to the more insular, self-segregated communities of Hungary. The new immigrants missed the nearly all-encompassing Jewish lives they led in Europe and tried to transplant as much of it as possible to American soil. Some lived in the voluntary ghettos of Boro Park and Crown Heights in Brooklyn, or in Monroe and New Square in Rockland County. Some continued to wear Old

World clothing and communicated mainly in Yiddish. Most saw themselves as representing authentic, authoritative Judaism and regarded innovations in religious life with contempt.

The new immigrants eventually assumed important roles in many sectors of the Orthodox world in America, serving as rabbinic authorities, teachers, ritual functionaries, and charismatic holy men. Their presence and activities helped stimulate growth in the Orthodox movement. Programs were launched to help other Jews "return" to Judaism, that is, become Orthodox Jews. In the 1970s, Lubavitcher Hasidim dispatched their "*mitzvah mobiles*" into neighborhoods and college communities where they pressed "lapsed" Jews to perform *mitzvot* such as putting on phylacteries and lighting candles. In the short run the phenomenon of nonobservant Jews turning to Orthodoxy raised the movement's self-esteem and increased its prestige within the broader Jewish American community.

Orthodox day schools also increased from about thirty prior to World War II to more than three hundred by the 1960s. By 1975, there were 425, including 138 high schools, with a total enrollment of eighty-five thousand. But there were also signs of weakness. Several hundred Orthodox congregations closed or changed affiliation to Conservatism after the war. And the Orthodox movement, with its multiplicity of rabbinical associations, rabbinical training organizations, and diverse congregations, was institutionally fragmented in a way not duplicated in the other denominations.

By 1945 it was already possible to discern at least four distinct types of Orthodoxy. The right-wing ultratraditionalists were represented by the transplanted Hasidic communities, mainly in Brooklyn, totaling some one hundred thousand people, and by Agudath Israel, the American branch of a world movement to preserve "Torah-true" Judaism. Founded in Lakewood, New Jersey, by Rabbi Aaron Kotler, who arrived here in 1941, Agudath Israel of America by the 1970s had branches in dozens of cities in the United States. Like Kotler himself, many of the residents of Hasidic and Agudath Israel communities in America were survivors or children of survivors of the Holocaust. Even if they had not been devout in the old countries, many of those who had witnessed events in Nazi-dominated Europe attached themselves to Orthodoxy here, seeing it as the culture that Hitler tried to destroy.

There were others who called themselves Orthodox, maintained traditional customs, dress, and style, but were somewhat more flexible in their adherence to Jewish law, and for want of a better term, they have come to be known as Traditionalists. There were also the Modern Orthodox (see ch. 7), more American in style than the Traditionalists and less rigorous in halakhic observance than the right-wingers. They had been dominant in American Orthodoxy between the world wars, but the influx and influence of the ultra-traditional refugees during and after World War II eventually challenged the hegemony of the Modern Orthodox. Lastly, and least in numbers, there were the nonobservant or casually observant Orthodox—Jews who were in fact much more secular than religious but who recognized Orthodoxy as the only authentic, authoritative branch of Judaism.

By 1970 approximately 40 percent of the Jewish American community identified as Conservative, 30 percent as Reform, and 10 percent as Orthodox. That last number may appear small, but its persistence has confounded those who predicted that modernization and the temptations of the open secular society would lead to the total collapse of traditional religion including Orthodox Judaism. Orthodoxy was not the only identity slated for demise according to many historians and sociologists. It was confidently assumed that Jewish identity in general, and indeed all hyphenate identities, would melt in the heat of American mobility and the pressures and temptations to assimilate. But even the third- and fourth-generation descendants of immigrants, Jewish and non-Jewish, have remained tied to selective ethnic symbols, institutions, and values; and they have transformed these in dynamic and creative interaction with their American environments.

Within the realm of the explicitly spiritual, a number of transformations took place which had some durability into the 1990s. The most widespread of these was the *havurah* movement, which began in the 1960s. Viewing the established synagogues they knew from their youth as large and impersonal, small groups of Jews, mostly college students, created *havurot*—literally, "committees," but really intimate fellowships for study, prayer and friendship. The *havurah* allowed for individual participation and spontaneity, but already by the 1970s there was impatience on the part of some members with the casual approach to Jewish tradition. The search for a more systematic alternative led to a reengagement with the synagogue. By the mid-1970s the *havurot,* which once represented a break with establishment Judaism, now served as a bridge linking former members of the student movement with the larger Jewish community.

Also in the sixties, a Reform Rabbi, Sherwin Wine, formed a "secular humanistic" congregation in Farmington Hills, Michigan, to provide a setting for Jews who rejected a belief in God but who wanted a communal structure for meeting with fellow Jews. Eventually the new congregation attracted five hundred families. The congregants did not pray, make blessings, or read from the Torah. Instead they celebrated life cycle events with nontheistic symbols connected to the larger tapestry of Jewish history. Twenty-five additional congregations were formed in the United States and elsewhere, and they affiliated with the Society for Humanistic Judaism, which by 1990 had an international membership of thirty thousand.

An even larger movement that has sought since the 1960s to merge Eastern religion, the self-actualization movement, and the counterculture outlook with Jewish religious traditions, particularly Jewish mysticism, is Zalman Schachter-Shalomi's P'nai Or Religious Fellowship. The fellowship emphasizes "Jewish renewal," and members not only dance and sing to stimulate spirituality, but, unlike the secular humanists, they also pray.

The new movements were attractive to Jews who wanted to remain Jews but who felt discomfort for one reason or another with the established synagogue or were alienated by parts of the tradition. This was probably most true for homosexual Jews, and in 1972 the first homosexual congregation, Beth Chayim Chadasim, was organized in Los Angeles. There have been more than twenty since then, including the largest, Beth Simchat Torah in New York City, which claims four hundred members and one thousand worshippers on High Holy Days. Most of these congregations use the traditional liturgy but with new prayers emphasizing gender neutrality.

Since the 1960s, Jewish women have also sought to establish gender-neutral language in religious services and, further, to develop a distinctly Jewish feminism. Much of their work concentrated on modifying ritual and writings to eliminate sexism and to introduce women's perspectives and values. The results have ranged from revised feminist *haggadahs* to *Lilith* (1976), a magazine focused on the concerns of Jewish women, as well as the establishment of religiously oriented feminist organizations. And as has already been observed, women achieved more participation and equality in services and more religious study and training. Women were ordained as rabbis at Hebrew Union College in 1972, the Reconstructionist Rabbinical College in 1974, and Jewish Theological Seminary in 1985. By the end of the 1980s, more than 150 women were presidents of Reform and Conservative congregations. Also, although progress was slow, women gained greater access to executive positions in Jewish organizations such as the Council for Jewish Federations and its member associations.

Even Orthodox women mounted challenges from within. Members of Modern Orthodox synagogues, these women were forced to meet to pray and organize in private homes, since with only a few exceptions, rabbis responded negatively to their calls for reform. The women accepted separation and men's prayers and agreed not to call themselves a *minyan*. But in running their own religious services, they represented the coming of age of Orthodox women who had acquired a high level of literacy in Hebraica and Judaica in day schools, and they continued throughout the 1970s and 1980s to try to reconcile their commitment to Jewish tradition with the new American feminist consciousness.

Some Jewish Americans, as we have seen throughout, remained Jewish by translating the injunctions of *tsedakah,* the obligation to perform charitable acts and to promote social justice and righteousness, and *tikn olam,* the injunction to repair and improve the world, into political liberalism and even radicalism. In the postwar period this tendency continued, and Jews steadfastly remained liberal Democrats even as they rose in class status, which they did with remarkable rapidity.

Prosperity and the decline of anti-Semitism, especially in education, opened great opportunities for Jews of the postwar generation. Standing on the shoulders of their parents, many of whom were independent business people, third-generation Jews en route to economic success continued to be innovative in the areas of consumer goods and services. This was evident in the areas of jewelry, automobile parts, electronic supplies, and especially cosmetics, where Estée Lauder, Helena Rubinstein, Clairol, Fabergé, Max Factor, Revlon, and other Jewish firms literally became household names. Real estate entrepreneurship, as in the example of William Levitt, was even more impressive, allowing some East European Jews to surpass the great German Jewish fortunes by the third quarter of the twentieth century.

Additional evidence of upward mobility is provided by the fact that by the late 1960s almost 40 percent of Jewish Americans were employed as managers or administrators, a rate three times higher than for the general population. Furthermore, an astounding proportion were professionals—29 percent of the men and 24 percent of the women. The figure rose to 42 percent for Jews younger than thirty-five. In the 1970s, 80 percent of college-aged Jews were in college, more than double the general population, and 71 percent of all Jews between the ages of twenty-five and twenty-nine already had college degrees. Equally impressive were the proportions of postgraduate degrees earned by Jews in many fields including law, medicine, and accounting. Jews were also very much overrepresented in the academic world: while they were only 2.8 percent of the population in 1970, they held 10 percent of the professorial positions in the United States and more than 30 percent at the most prestigious institutions including Harvard and Yale.

It was presumed that the education, occupations, and income of Jewish

Americans would dislodge them from the Democratic Party and move them to vote Republican. But postwar Jews confounded the experts and stuck with the Democrats even in the landslide Eisenhower elections of the 1950s. Eisenhower was a popular hero who rose to distinction in the war against Nazism, and thereby, at least indirectly, he was seen as a benefactor of the Jews. Moreover, Israel no longer appeared to be a partisan issue; and Eisenhower was as passionate as his opponent Adlai E. Stevenson in his opposition to Stalinism, which was oppressing and even murdering the Jews of the Soviet Union. In addition, Eisenhower accepted the New Deal. He said he would not dismantle the liberal welfare state but would merely run it more efficiently. Despite all this, only 25 percent of Jewish voters cast ballots for the Republican Eisenhower; the remainder voted heavily instead for his liberal Democratic opponent, the badly defeated Stevenson. In 1956, Eisenhower was reelected by an even larger margin, but Jews again voted overwhelmingly—67 percent—for Stevenson. Jews as a group had become more affluent and were assumed to have a vested interest in the success of the Republicans, who tended to support less government spending and lower taxes. But except for Blacks, no group voted as consistently for liberal Democrats as did Jews.

Jewish liberalism was also apparent in the opposition to Joseph McCarthy, the senator from Wisconsin who in the early fifties made repeated demagogic charges of political disloyalty with little or no regard for evidence. Though his attack on "communists" never included overt anti-Semitism, Jews mobilized against McCarthy around the principles pronounced in the Bill of Rights, especially freedom of speech. No group has shown itself more committed to that principle; and this despite the fact that the First Amendment protects not only minorities such as Jewish worshippers or Jewish leftists but also Ku Klux Klansmen and fascists.

In the hotly disputed Rosenberg case, however, Jewish liberalism appears to have yielded to Jewish insecurity in the 1950s over widespread public identification of Jews with communism and the "spy network." Trial evidence demonstrated that Julius Rosenberg was guilty of espionage for the Soviet Union and that his wife Ethel was indirectly involved as an accomplice in conspiracy. However, as Justice Felix Frankfurter put it, the Rosenbergs were tried for conspiracy but sentenced to death for treason, a crime of which they were not guilty. At the time of their espionage activities, the Soviet Union was an ally of the United States. Moreover, even those guilty of the far more serious crime of treason during World War II, including Tokyo Rose and Axis Sally, had been sentenced to no more than fifteen years in prison.

Not only did major Jewish organizations fail to condemn the conspicuously unjust sentencing; they also went out of their way to attack the Rosenberg defense committee publicly as a communist-inspired group. The National Community Relations Advisory Council, an umbrella organization
including the American Jewish Committee, the American Jewish Congress,
the Anti-Defamation League, and other Jewish communal organizations,
joined the chorus. Lucy Dawidowicz, a leading Jewish historian and perhaps
representative of Jewish worry over the smear of "communism," argued that
Jews must not support the clemency campaign, even out of purely humanitarian concern, and the American Jewish Committee actually became an advocate of the death penalty, endorsing every aspect of the government's
treatment of the controversial case.

Apart from this remarkable exception, however, Jews for the most part
consistently adhered to liberalism. Organizations actively worked to expose
and diminish anti-Semitism, but from as early as the 1880s through the
post–World War II period, Jewish voting and political action were more
often consistent with general adherence to liberal principles such as freedom
of speech than to particular short-term, narrow self-interests such as gagging
anti-Semites. A survey of Jews in Chicago in the 1950s indicated that 67 percent of the respondents answered the question "What is a good Jew?" with
definitions such as someone who "supports all humanitarian causes" or someone who is "liberal on political and economic issues." Jews proved to be a
unique force in American politics, exhibiting the capacity to vote and act
beyond both their class interest and the narrow interests of their group.
Their consistent liberalism was simply unmatched by other groups. One
highly reputable study on religion and politics in Detroit, for example,
showed Black Protestants to be liberal on questions of the welfare state and
civil rights, but not so much in regard to international affairs and civil liberties. White Protestants were relatively hostile to racial integration and to
government intervention in the economy. Catholics also opposed civil rights
and were moderate, not liberal, on questions of freedom of speech, foreign
aid, and government regulation of the economy. Only the Jews could be classified as liberal in all categories, especially when civil rights for Blacks were
at stake.

For most of the twentieth century, there had been in the United States
an affinity, even a sense of kinship, between Blacks and Jews. Both groups had
had rich histories as peoples apart. Both had suffered, to varying degrees of
intensity, discrimination from the majority white Christian society. Although

the anti-Semitism Jews faced in the 1920s and 1930s did impose significant social and economic barriers, Blacks faced a racism more endemic, more virulent, more deeply institutionalized, and more disabling. But Jewish history in Europe, Jewish experience in 1930s America, and the racist foundation of the Holocaust made Jews especially sensitive to the Black plight. Both groups also had a highly developed sense of ethnic consciousness. Both had supported movements for intensified ethnic self-definition, and important minorities within each group had even supported their own nationalist movements, such as Zionism, and Black nationalism.

Blacks, representing 10 percent of American society in the immediate postwar period, or about 15 million people, and Jews, representing 3.2 percent, or about 4.9 million people, often lived in the same regions, the urban Northeast and the industrialized Midwest, for example; and often, for significant periods of time, they lived in the same neighborhoods. Although Blacks and Jews lived cheek by jowl in the cities, most often they did not meet as equals. They would meet as Jewish landlord, Black tenant; Jewish merchant, Black customer; Jewish employer, Black worker; Jewish housewife, Black domestic; and later, Jewish teacher, Black student; Jewish social worker, Black client; Jewish union leader, Black rank and filer; Jewish club owner, Black entertainer.

The interactions between Jews and Blacks were not simply exploitative; they were also often positive. But since Jews were virtually the only whites whom Blacks saw in any significant numbers, and since Jews were the classic intermediaries between the urban elites and the Black poor, it was relatively easy for Blacks to see Jews as surrogates for the white establishment. And Blacks did come to hold negative economic stereotypes about Jews. Yet in all of the survey research studies we have, beginning with those from the 1930s, at least 75 percent of the Black respondents in each city studied did not feel that they personally had ever been unfairly treated by a Jewish businessman. In addition, the majority in every sample believed Jews were more liberal than other whites in extending credit and more flexible in dealing with those who were lax in making payments. The complexity of the Black perspective here is partially captured in the remark by a Black entertainer in the 1940s who believed that the Jews made "a gold mine out of us," but that "if Jews didn't give us bookings or parts we wouldn't work."

In addition to the interactions of the Black and Jewish masses, certain spiritual elites in both communities, at least since the earliest decades of the twentieth century, had found it mutually advantageous to join forces to fight specific obstacles that did indeed affect both groups as well as other minorities, particularly nonwhite minorities. There was much work to be done. Lynchings of Blacks were still common before World War II, and during that war against racism in Europe, race riots broke out against Blacks and Mexican Americans in many American cities, the worst occurring in Detroit and Los Angeles in 1943. And for the duration of the war, more than one hundred thousand Japanese Americans were relocated and interned in camps. Moreover, it continued to be perfectly legal until well after World War II to deny "undesirables" equal access to jobs, homes, and education. Color barriers limited the rights of Asian, Hispanic, and African immigrants. And Italians, Mexicans, Chinese, Japanese, and Blacks continued to face occasional violent assault.

Black and Jewish clergy, union leaders, activists, and journalists paid attention to all of this. And they especially attacked restrictive housing covenants, segregation in schools, corporate expressions of racism that targeted Jews and Blacks, and lynchings. During the best of times, the masses of each group were influenced by the moral leadership of these elites. A formal alliance of Blacks and Jews, however, had arisen only after World War II. And ironically it was forged only after the specific economic interests of the two groups—one upwardly mobile, the other in a constant struggle to survive—were more clearly diverging. It is true that Jews and Blacks continued to share an agenda that included open housing and an open job market. But by the 1950s, Jews were battling restrictive covenants in suburbia or posh urban neighborhoods, while Blacks continued to be trapped in inadequate housing in crowded ghettos. Jews faced discrimination in the executive suites, especially in banking and insurance, but most Blacks were still fighting to leave the most menial jobs in America.

These divergences were not publicly discussed much, prior to the early 1960s. But as early as 1943 the Committee for Justice and Peace of the Central Conference of American Rabbis issued a statement on race relations which implied that the Black-Jewish relationship was being seen less as a "comradeship of excluded peoples," and more as a relationship in which Jews, a relatively accepted people, following their traditions and the injunctions of their faith, demanded justice for an oppressed people. The rabbis pointed out the unconscionable conditions under which Blacks lived, and the committee indicted those Jews who accepted this situation as violators of the Jewish way of life: "It is we, their fellowmen, who have acquiesced in or been apathetic about their maltreatment, who have suffered spiritual hurt, for no soul that tolerates oppression remains unspoiled or unsullied."

Here at the very least is the hint that Jews, despite their very different social condition, continued to see a role for themselves in the movement for Black rights and opportunities. Black Americans were desperate for financial, legal, and moral support in the fight against racism, lynchings, and exclusion from important institutions of American life. American Jews were sincere idealists who could be responsive to the call to stay true to their prophetic tradition, and they wanted a meaningful role, perhaps even high status, in American society. One way to fulfill their moral commitment, as well as to develop a meaningful and important American identity, they believed, was to make an assault on prejudice in general through sponsored research and educational campaigns and to serve as intermediaries between Blacks and whites.

There was self-interest here, but this was self-interest in the best and broadest sense of the term. For Jewish liberals, it was a self-interest that had more to do with personal satisfaction through commitment to ethical principle than with concern for narrow personal gain. More generally, it was a self-interest that recognized that the creation of the kind of society that will protect minorities from oppression will also protect Jews. And it was also a self-interest that asserted that everyone in the long run has a vested interest in everyone else's well-being. A narrower, meaner self-interest might logically have compelled the Jews to make themselves more acceptable to the right by joining the white majority against the movement for social justice for Blacks. Some did, but most did not.

In the late 1950s a persuasive poll showed that one in five Jews thought being a good Jew meant it was essential to support Israel; two in five thought it meant support for the "Negro struggle." This was not mere lip service: one-third of the funding for the National Association for the Advancement of Colored People and for the Urban League in the 1950s came from Jewish contributors; and major Jewish organizations filed supportive friends of the court briefs in the cases brought by the two organizations to eliminate poll taxes in the South and to end segregation in education. About two-thirds of the freedom riders of the early 1960s were Jewish, as were half the white civil rights attorneys in the South. And although most southern Jews remained neutral, or at best ambivalent, on desegregation after 1954 and resented the arrival in Birmingham in 1963 of a contingent of nineteen northern rabbis desiring to hold a vigil with Dr. Martin Luther King, they did not cut themselves off from the national Jewish organizations.

One of the most powerful events of the period was the murder of three civil rights workers during the Mississippi Summer voter registration campaign in 1964. Two of the martyrs, Michael Schwerner and Andrew Goodman, were Jews, and one, James Chaney, was Black. Perhaps the most powerful positive images of that era in terms of Jews and Blacks were the pictures of Rabbi Abraham Joshua Heschel and the Reverend Martin Luther King Jr. walking hand in hand in Selma, Alabama, in 1965 and Blacks and Jews together at the head of the March on Washington in 1963. But even in that year, not all was well with the alliance, especially in regard to how the struggle for equality would be waged. Even the presumed moderate Dr. King, at the opening of his Washington address, said: "There will be neither rest nor tranquillity in America until the Negro is granted his citizenship rights. The whirlwinds of revolt will continue to shake the foundations of our nation until the bright day of justice emerges." Black leaders were increasingly impatient not only with the gradualism inherent in traditional liberal politics but also with those Jews who continued to discriminate against Blacks in employment and housing and who, while contributing to civil rights organizations, continued to send their children to lily-white or only slightly integrated schools.

By the 1960s, Blacks were also showing signs of rejecting the paternalism of many Jews involved in the civil rights struggle. Indeed, as early as 1960, the Student Nonviolent Coordinating Committee declared that Blacks alone would lead their movement, and by the end of 1966, in the name of "Black Power," whites were excluded altogether. But Jews, and Jewish youth in particular, continued to affirm their commitment to the prophetic tradition and continued to participate in the Black struggle in disproportionate numbers. Jews continued, too, for the next few years to furnish 25–30 percent of the financial support of important Black organizations, even of the Student Nonviolent Coordinating Committee; and visible, influential Jews such as I. F. Stone, Theodore Bikel, and Rabbi Harold Saperstein continued public support, at least until 1967. Rabbis went by the planeload to Selma in 1965; Albert Shanker, the head of the powerful American Federation of Teachers, joined them in the march. And as late as May 1967, the Anti-Defamation League published five volumes of findings disputing the idea that there was more anti-Semitism among Blacks than among other groups.

But while the Jewish elites, college students, and suburbanites continued to talk the language of social conscience, many less prosperous Jews— aging working people, small businessmen, and white-collar civil servants— who still lived in the cities, faced riots by Blacks and were in direct battle with them over busing, housing, and affirmative action.

Polarization between Blacks and Jews in the 1960s and 1970s was partly the product, but also partly the shaper, of the new politics of ethnicity. The ethnic revival, or "the rise of the unmeltable ethnics" as Michael Novak called it, which included Italians, Poles, Greeks, and Slavs, among others, was partly white backlash against Black militancy, partly pride in cultural heritage and the search for group self-esteem, and partly ethnic mobilization for a larger share of the pie. Many of the people and organizations that promoted the renewed pluralism, including the American Jewish Committee, did help to make diversity acceptable and tried to build bridges from group to group and even coalitions between them. But their initial emphasis on "differences" did not reassure a nation already confused and divided in the 1960s and early 1970s over runaway inflation, over the war in Vietnam, over urban violence in Black, Puerto Rican, and Mexican American communities, and over the excesses of student radicals and police repression.

The tensions between Blacks and Jews became much more apparent in the summer of 1967 after Israel's victory in the Six Day War against the Egyptian, Jordanian, and Syrian armies. Although Martin Luther King and labor and civil rights leader A. Philip Randolph were sympathetic to Israel, the Student Nonviolent Coordinating Committee, which had even before the war denounced Zionism, now openly opposed Israel and adopted the Arabs, especially displaced Palestinians, as fellow third-world allies of color. Some Blacks had already been looking to and identifying with Africa, and in the process they learned that the dominant organized religion in Africa, as among the Palestinians, was Islam; in their attempt to form an international brotherhood with people of color, they unleashed even more anti-Zionist anti-Semitism. Blacks looking at Africa also saw racist white regimes in Rhodesia and South Africa, and given Israel's economic involvement with South Africa, it was predictable that some Black Americans would link the Palestinian struggle against Israel with the struggle by Black South Africans against apartheid. And many Blacks simply turned inward, away from the politics of coalition, and devoted more energy to issues of Black unity and ethnic identity.

For American Jews, on the other hand, the Israeli victory in 1967 was a reassertion of the nationhood of the Jewish people, especially since the very real threat of extinction was suddenly turned into a miracle of triumph. Significant numbers of Jews became more Jewish now insofar as they identified with Israel; and many turned communally inward, devoting somewhat less energy to larger issues of social justice and more to Jewish survival and Jewish unity.

13

Israel, the Holocaust, and Echoes of Anti-Semitism in Jewish American Consciousness, 1960–1995

After 1967 support for Israel became the common denominator of American Jewish life—so much so that no Jew who was not a staunch advocate for the Jewish state could expect to occupy a responsible position in any major Jewish organization. Many Jews had been militant in their support of Israel in the 1940s and 1950s. But some in those early years felt uncomfortable about the state because its very creation raised expectations in some circles that all "good Jews" would make *aliyah,* or emigrate to Israel. And other Jewish Americans in the postwar period were generally unconcerned about Israel because they thought that the new state was protected by the Great Powers. In 1967, however, when Israel, outnumbered three to one by the mobilized armies of her Arab neighbors, appeared fated to undergo a second Holocaust, any lingering discomfort or complacency was eliminated.

That Jewish American commitment was reawakened and intensified was indicated by the spontaneous and enthusiastic giving of money for Israel in the summer of 1967. Five men at a luncheon in New York pledged one million dollars each. In fact fifteen million dollars were raised there in fifteen minutes. The Jews of Boston, Cleveland, and St. Louis raised nearly seven million dollars overnight, and throughout the country, Jewish children went out with jars and cans to collect coins and bills for the emergency. Between 23 May, when Egypt closed the Gulf of Aqaba, and 10 June, when the war ended, over one hundred million dollars were raised for the Israel Emergency Fund of the United Jewish Appeal. This was unprecedented not only in Jewish experience but also in the history of private philanthropy in the United States.

Giving continued for years and was reinforced in the early 1970s with the increased emigration to Israel of Jews from the Soviet Union. For more than fifty years this, the second largest Jewish community in the world after the United States, had been cut off from world Jewry. Now the possibility of a wave of Soviet Jewish refugees to Israel moved American Jewry to action. They pressed the U.S. government to use its influence to liberalize the emigration policy of the U.S.S.R., and they raised large sums to help with resettlement. They continued to help in the late 1970s, when the gates out of the Soviet Union opened a bit wider for Jews, and again after 1989, when it began the restructuring that would end in its dismantling—and an emigration of more than three hundred thousand Jews.

More money even than was raised in the historic 1967 outpouring during and after the Six Day War was raised in October 1973 after Arab armies attacked Israel once again from the west and north, this time on the Jewish holy day of Yom Kippur. Jewish Americans pawned jewelry and begged and borrowed in order to help in the new emergency. Students on college campuses raised more than seven hundred thousand dollars. Polls indicated that 80 percent of American Jews would consider the destruction of Israel as the "greatest personal tragedy in their lives." And by the 1980s the community supported more than seventy political action committees throughout the country to help fund the campaigns of politicians sympathetic to Israel. The Jewish community also financed the American-Israel Public Affairs Committee, an effective pro-Israel lobby in the nation's capital.

Jewish organizations did not always get what they wanted from Washington. Important figures in the Departments of State and Defense saw a "Jewish policy" as a strategic liability. They thought it would be an obstacle to U.S. patronage of Arab governments whose cooperation was deemed necessary for access to oil and containment of the Soviet Union. Jewish agencies could not push their special interests at the expense of vital security objectives. This had been true from the start. Despite persistent lobbying by Jewish groups in the 1950s, for example, the United States cut off economic aid to Israel until the new state halted work on a hydroelectric plant on the Jordan River. The U.S. government also refused to move its embassy to the contested city of Jerusalem after Israel located its foreign ministry there. Nor did it have any effective response to the economic boycott of Israel by the Arabs or to Egypt's blockade of the Suez Canal. Indeed, when in 1956 Israel, along with Britain and France, tried by force to break that blockade and the blockade of its own port of Eilat, all three nations were condemned by the United States in the United Nations.

In 1957, after forcing Israel to withdraw from territory in Egypt which it had occupied during the Suez episode, Secretary of State John Foster Dulles said, "I am aware of how almost impossible it is in this country to carry out a foreign policy not approved by the Jews." Despite the fantastic power ascribed to Jews in the imaginings of anti-Semites, it remained true that no matter how strongly the Jewish American community pressed any of its cases, it was able to influence U.S. foreign policy only to the extent that it did not make any substantial difference to what was otherwise considered the national interest. But Jewish organizations and agencies almost always made the argument that what was good for Israel and for Jews abroad was indeed also good for America, as in the lobbying to rescue Jews during the 1930s and 1940s, to break the Arab economic boycott imposed in the 1950s, to pass the Jackson-Vanick amendment to the Trade Reform Bill with the Soviet Union, to end Soviet harrassment of applicants for emigration in the 1970s, and to gain loan guarantees in the 1980s. Except for Jackson-Vanick, lobbying failed, but Jews continued to try to wield constructive influence even if that influence never went beyond what political scientist Earl Raab calls the "rule of marginal effect" described above.

Even after the establishment of the more powerful lobbying apparatus in the 1970s and 1980s, Jewish Americans could not always persuade the U.S. government to take the pro-Israel position. In 1975, for example, President Gerald Ford froze military aid to Israel in an attempt to compel its withdrawal from the Egyptian Sinai, and in 1991, during the administration of George Bush, the American-Israel Public Affairs Committee failed to get the U.S. government to guarantee a ten-billion-dollar housing loan for Israel.

Jewish Americans in the 1960s and 1970s still cared about social and racial justice in the United States, and they still wanted to end the war in Vietnam, but they cared most about Israel. This remained true into the 1990s. There were mumbled misgivings and even some vociferous arguments and noticeable splits in the Jewish American community over Israeli policies from time to time, especially over the invasion of Lebanon in 1982, and during the Intifada (the Palestinian uprising in the occupied territories), which began at the end of 1987. But the commitment to Israel remained fairly steady throughout. Even Breira and Peace Now, Jewish organizations devoted to a speedier peace and more concessions to Palestinians, were dissenters only in terms of particular Israeli policy and not over the existence of a viable and secure Israel. The election of Benjamin Netanyahu of the right-wing Likud Party as Israeli Prime Minister in 1996 and the emergence of a governing coalition dependent on support from the religious parties may contribute to the erosion of the powerful bonds between American Jews and Israeli Jews. But "Israelism," after taking its place in the 1960s and 1970s alongside political liberalism, philanthropy, and the battle against residual anti-Semitism, has remained one of the foundation stones of Jewish American ethnic identity.

Haunting memories of the Holocaust and the failure to rescue strengthened the passion of Jewish Americans for Israel and informed the newly organized Student Struggle for Soviet Jewry; at the same time, the perilous situation of the twenty-year-old Jewish state in the 1960s encouraged Jews finally to bring into the open the pain they carried because of the Holocaust. During the 1950s concern about the Nazi era had apparently reached an all-time low. Survivors themselves wanted "normalcy" and were momentarily still. The fifties did produce two important scholarly works, Leon Poliakov's *Harvest of Hate* and Gerald Reitlinger's *Final Solution,* but neither received much attention at the time. However, Anne Frank's *Diary,* a powerful and moving account of a Jewish thirteen-year-old in hiding from the Nazis, was widely popular. But the diary focused on ideals and hopes and the preservation of faith in humankind and thereby, ironically, promoted a kind of historical amnesia.

Beginning in the 1960s, however, with the capture and 1961 trial in Israel of the Nazi war criminal Adolf Eichmann and with the publication of Raul Hilberg's *Destruction of European Jewry* (1961) and of Hannah Arendt's *Eichmann in Jerusalem* (1963), the amnesia was challenged. But it was the Six Day War in 1967 and the fear it engendered for Israel's continued existence which ended the silence. It took ten more years for the Holocaust survivors themselves to reemerge, but when they did, they found receptive audiences. By 1978 there was even a television movie on the Holocaust which shattered the taboo, psychological and commercial, against airing the subject in the wider world. Although nothing can "represent" the Holocaust, the program did stimulate other films and memoirs and finally the creation of resource centers and museums. What effect all this had on public consciousness is difficult to measure, but for Jewish Americans, identification with the Holocaust was added to Israelism, political liberalism, philanthropy, and anti-anti-Semitism as an important ingredient of their ethnic identity.

Anti-Semitism by the 1970s had dwindled to the point of insignificance. But Jews, having lived through the 1930s, the worst decade of anti-Semitism in American history, and living still in the shadow of the Holocaust, found this difficult to admit; and Jewish defense agencies such as the Anti-Defamation League and the American Jewish Committee remained devoted largely to exposing and fighting discrimination against Jews. Jewish Americans, influenced by painful memories and by sporadic instances of anti-Semitism, persisted in the notion that it is better to overestimate than underestimate Jew-hatred. After all, even as late as 1945, when Jews were celebrating Hank Greenberg's ninth-inning home run to win the American League pennant for the Detroit Tigers baseball team and when Bess Myerson was crowned as the first Jewish Miss America, both events representing the extent of Jewish acceptability in America, a significant number of job listings in the Jewish-owned *New York Times* used coded language implying that Jews need not apply.

Between 1940 and 1962, however, polls revealed sharp decreases in anti-Semitic attitudes. There were fewer and fewer gentiles who believed that Jews wielded too much influence in America, or who believed that Jews were unscrupulous or had other objectionable traits. In 1948 only 20 percent of respondents said they objected to Jews as neighbors, but even that number had dropped to a mere 2 percent in 1959. And in 1956 most Americans believed that Jewish support of Israel did not mean less loyalty to the United States. These responses are indicative of increasing acceptability for Jews, especially since they were made in an era that witnessed the execution of Julius and Ethel Rosenberg as atomic spies for the Soviet Union in 1953 and the 1956 Suez crisis, in which the United States voted against Israel at the United Nations.

In 1959 slightly more Americans were ready to vote for a Jewish presidential candidate than for a Roman Catholic, and a far higher percentage was willing to vote for a Jewish man than for a Christian woman for president. By 1962, three-quarters of Americans said they would vote against an anti-Semitic candidate on that ground alone. By 1969 pollsters could find no serious trace of political anti-Semitism in the nation.

Between 1964 and 1981 the percentage of gentiles who said they would accept the marriage of a child to a Jew increased from 55 to 66. Attitudes clearly changed over a forty-year period, but so did behavior. In 1960 less than 7 percent of Jews found marriage partners among the gentiles, but between 1962 and 1972 the intermarriage rate averaged 32 percent. That the increasing mixed marriage rate stemmed from diminishing anti-Semitism and the rapid social and economic mobility of Jewish Americans was obvious to all. Moreover, discernible discriminatory acts against Jews, by the 1970s, were few and far between. This remained true even during the 1974 oil shortage created by the Arab-Israeli struggles in the Middle East and right through the "Wall Street crisis" of the 1980s, when Jews such as Ivan Boesky and Michael Milken were highly visible among the financial wrongdoers.

In the 1980s, Jews were also increasingly visible in positions of power in the United States. The highly respected and often quoted chairman of the Federal Reserve System, Alan Greenspan, was Jewish, as was Kenneth Duberstein, chief of staff to the president from 1988 to 1989. The heads of the president's Council of Economic Advisors, Murray Weidenbaum (1981–82) and Martin Feldstein (1982–84) were Jews, as were Eliot Abrams, Richard Perle, and Kenneth Adelman, all of whom held important national positions. The venerable Henry Kissinger, who continued well into the 1990s to be sought out for his advice on foreign policy, had been the first Jewish secretary of state (under Nixon), and there had been two Jews, Abraham Ribicoff and Arthur Goldberg, in Kennedy's cabinet in the 1960s.

Jewish political figures from states with sizeable Jewish populations were well known nationally. These included Emanuel Celler, Jacob Javits, Edward Koch, and Bella Abzug of New York, Arlen Specter of Pennsylvania, and Diane Feinstein and Barbara Boxer of California. And by the 1980s, Jewish Americans had been elected to the United States Senate even from states with very few Jewish voters such as Minnesota, Nebraska, Nevada, New Hampshire and Wisconsin. Jews had also been elected to the House of Representatives from districts with minuscule Jewish populations in Alabama, Georgia, Colorado, and Kansas. In the 1980s, New York City, with its large Jewish community, had a Jewish mayor, but so did Atlanta, Kansas City, Omaha, San Francisco, and Portland, Oregon.

Politics had clearly become more open to Jews, and the walls of academia were also breached, beginning with a Jewish president for the University of Chicago in 1968, followed in the 1980s by Jewish presidents at several other universities including Columbia and Princeton. Jews in the 1970s and 1980s were finally also employed at the highest echelons of major corporations, including several that had had few if any Jewish employees only a short time before, such as Bank of America, Chrysler, Disney, and DuPont.

Unquestionably there was a retreat from earlier, higher levels of anti-Semitic attitudes and overt bias.

It was readily apparent that Jews contributed mightily to American life: in business, the labor movement, and the university; and in intellectual and aesthetic achievement, too, as scientists, writers, artists, scholars, and musicians. Though still distinctive in their political behavior and liberal values, Jews had achieved a virtually complete identification with the American middle class. They had proven to be solid citizens. Perhaps even more importantly in terms of acceptance, Jews were prominent and admired as reflectors and shapers of American popular culture. From among those of Jewish immigrant origin came the Hollywood giants such as Samuel Goldwyn and Louis Mayer and later, producer-directors Steven Spielberg and Woody Allen. The Jewish community also produced musical luminaries such as George and Ira Gershwin, Leonard Bernstein, Isaac Stern, Beverly Sills, Bob Dylan, Benny Goodman, Barry Manilow, and Barbra Streisand; entertainment stars such as the Marx brothers, George Burns, Gertrude Berg ("Molly Goldberg"), Jerry Lewis, Richard Dreyfuss, Dustin Hoffman, Mel Brooks, and Neil Simon; writers such as Saul Bellow, Bernard Malamud, Clifford Odets, Cynthia Ozick, Ayn Rand, Philip Roth, Isaac Bashevis Singer, and Herman Wouk. Many of these Jewish men and women had become household words in America, a fact that undoubtedly contributed to the increasing acceptance of Jews by non-Jews.

As late as 1989, however, most Jews continued to feel that anti-Semitism was a serious problem in the United States, and a surprising three-quarters of Jewish respondents disagreed with the statement that "virtually all positions of influence in America are open to Jews." Memories of earlier anti-Semitism and the historical image of the "suffering Jew" lingered. But even more important, their self-definition as Jews was so inextricably bound to battling anti-Semitism that it was extremely difficult for Jewish Americans to believe what the pollsters and sociologists were saying. Some observers in the 1980s and 1990s suggested that Jews clung to the notion of a persisting anti-Semitism because their Jewishness had been hollowed out, that it was based on nothing more solid than paranoia. After all, it was argued, even their Israelism and their identification with the Holocaust were connected with defensiveness.

If the idea that Jews had to stick together to battle their enemies were to evaporate, so too, it was thought, would the Jewish American community. This was a proposition difficult to test, however, since echoes of anti-Semitism continued to reinforce the perceived need for Jewish bonding.

Mainstream, middle-class Jews thought they heard some of those echoes even within the Jewish American milieu itself, particularly within its literary realm.

Major figures in American literature in the nineteenth and early twentieth centuries, such as Henry James, had seen Jews as aliens and as inferiors who would ruin the English language; by the 1960s, however, Jewish writers were a dominant force in the American literary world. Saul Bellow's Chicago, Philip Roth's Newark, and Bernard Malamud's New York were taking their place as legitimate regions of American experience alongside William Faulkner's Yoknapatawpha County in Mississippi and John Cheever's Yankee Connecticut.

But as many in the Jewish community asked themselves, and as the saying went, Was this really good for the Jews? Gentile readers were, after all, being introduced to a highly subjective, often negative image of the Jewish American subculture. Many Jews found Alexander Portnoy's complaints absurd and his behavior embarrassing; and they did not like Philip Roth's depiction of Portnoy's overbearing Jewish mother either. The *schlemiels* (anti-heroic victims), the *schnorrers* (manipulative spongers or dependents), the lechers, the quack psychiatrists, and the crass materialists in the novels and stories of Bernard Malamud, Joseph Heller, and Saul Bellow were not endearing to Jewish readers, who knew that non-Jews were reading them too.

Jewish American writers were indeed writing for a general public, not so much to shame the Jews before the *goyim* as much as to address universal themes. They scorned the shallowness of their Jewish elders, but they were also critical of the vacuousness of American society. Their works were filled with Jewish characters and situations, but like Samuel Ornitz, Nathanael West, and Budd Shulberg before them, Roth, Bellow, Malamud, and Heller were expressing or portraying the alienation and universal discontent shared by gentile writers and intellectuals including Faulkner, who wrote about gentile drunks and perverts, and J. P. Marquand, who told stories about disintegrating Yankee aristocrats.

The Jewish writers sometimes made the general middle-class Jewish community uncomfortable. They did not, however, threaten its peace and sense of security as did the more ominous anti-Semitic noises emanating from other sources, especially the New Left—the student radical movements of the 1960s and early 1970s and the militant Black movements of the 1960s through the 1990s.

There were two main constituents of the New Left in the 1960s: the Students for a Democratic Society (SDS), who, beginning in the early 1960s, protested against the Vietnam War, the hugeness and bureaucratic nature of the university, and what they saw as the general hypocrisy of the American social system; and the Black militant Stokely Carmichael's Student Non-violent Coordinating Committee, which was articulating a radical new program demanding equality of result as distinct from equality of opportunity. The New Left had risen partly out of the ashes of the old left; indeed, some of the leaders of the New Left, including Columbia's radical student leader Mark Rudd and Berkeley's Bettina Aptheker, had been "red diaper" babies, that is, children raised in left wing households of the 1930s and 1940s. Many of the others were radical children disappointed or angry with their parents for failing to bring the older generation's espoused liberal ideals of freedom and equality to full fruition.

By the mid-1960s a significant minority of the leadership of the New Left was Jewish. Political inspiration and radical materials were supplied on campuses by a disproportionate number of Jewish professors including Gabriel Kolko, Noam Chomsky, and Howard Zinn. Their off-campus counterparts were Jewish journalists and social critics such as Paul Goodman and I. F. Stone. And even from the pulpit some rabbis railed against the American military-industrial complex. In 1969 the Central Conference of American Rabbis was forced to drop its draft of chaplains for the armed forces when a majority of Reform rabbis refused to serve in Vietnam. The charismatic spiritual leader Arthur Waskow, who searched for ways to couch his tirades against American values and behavior in specifically Jewish terms, reflected on the reasons for the overrepresentation of young Jews in the New Left.

> Brought up on memories of the Holocaust and genocide, [they] were horrified to discover that the United States government . . . was behaving in Vietnam like Hitler. . . . "Holocaust" began to ring with new meaning around these young Jews. . . . They whose parents had proudly embraced the American Promise, the quasi-Methodist suburban synagogue, and the quasi-Rotarian B'nai B'rith lodge, fiercely rejected being American at all.

Since no more than 6 percent of Jewish college and university students were even peripherally involved in campus radicalism, and since many of those who were left the movements with the end of the Vietnam War, Waskow's statement, although representative of an important segment of Jewish analysis, appears overstated as well as overwrought. But many young Jews *were* angry that issues of Jewish unity seemed to have won out over progressive causes as the primary focus of Jewish American attention. And Jews were indeed a disproportionate presence in the new movements. One of the many pins that antiwar protestors wore in the 1960s reflected a popular impression: "You don't have to be Jewish to be against the War in Vietnam." And statistical evidence supported the popular impression that Jews were disproportionately involved in the antiwar movement. In its 1967 study of student activism, the American Council of Education concluded that a Jewish background was the single most important "predictor of participation" in antiwar or antiadministration protests. Moreover, among SDS's thirty thousand members, the percentage of Jews ranged from 30 to 50 throughout the late 1960s and early 1970s. It is also worth mentioning here that six of the Chicago Seven, who mounted an antiwar agitation in Chicago and attempted to disrupt the Democratic National Convention held there in the summer of 1968, were Jewish, including Jerry Rubin, Abbie Hoffman, and Lee Weiner, as was their attorney, William Kunstler.

Up to a point, Jewish overrepresentation in New Left movements looked like Jewish overrepresentation in old left movements. But by late 1967 serious strains were showing between the New Left and the mainstream Jewish community. The National Conference for New Politics, held in Chicago during the 1967 Labor Day weekend, adopted a resolution drafted by a Black caucus denouncing Israel for making an "imperialist Zionist war." At the same time, the SDS officially denounced Zionism as "imperialist racism" and condemned Israel's Jewish American supporters as members of the "imperialist establishment."

Only three months earlier in the period from mid-May to mid-June 1967, Jewish New Leftists had shared with Jews everywhere and with Jews of almost every ideological description the trauma of a potential second Holocaust in the Middle East, followed by the euphoria of Israel's military deliverance in the Six Day War. Now, of course, since few if any in the New Left raised a voice against the anti-Semitic rhetoric of some Black nationalists or even tried to find a rationale for such demagogy, it became much more difficult to be both an active member of the New Left and a supporter of Israel or, for that matter, a Jew. Some Jewish New Leftists actually joined the chorus of anti-Israel condemnation; others established radical peace groups such as the short-lived Committee on New Alternatives in the Middle East; but the great disillusioned majority of Jewish SDS members simply drifted away. Many, openly or otherwise, sympathized with the feelings expressed in the *Village Voice* in February 1969 by a former SDS member, Jay Rosenberg. "From this point on I shall join no movement that does not accept and support my people's struggle. If I must choose between the Jewish cause and a 'progressive' anti-Israel SDS, I shall choose the Jewish cause. If barricades are erected, I will fight as a Jew."

Jewish women in feminist organizations were also angered and frustrated over the years by anti-Semitism and by controversies regarding Israel and international politics. In the 1940s internal dissension over the establishment of the state of Israel drove some Jewish women from a number of international feminist organizations, including the International Alliance for Women. Since the 1960s, as with SDS, disagreements over Israel continued to surface, especially in international settings, such as the United Nations conferences on women and the Mexico City feminist conference of the mid-1980s. Israeli women as well as Jewish American women were sometimes simply locked out of these meetings. This despite the remarkable number of feminist theorists and leaders in mainstream organizations who have been Jewish, including Gloria Steinem, a cofounder of *Ms.* magazine, and Betty Friedan, whose book *The Feminine Mystique* (1963) was arguably the most important founding document of the American feminist movement.

The anti-Semitism associated with SDS and the New Left, the excesses of the movement, including its ideological authoritarianism, and worse, the bombing of buildings related to military recruitment and research—all these not only made some Jewish women and men think twice about this 1960s breed of radicalism but also made other Jews rethink their longstanding commitment to liberalism generally. *Commentary* magazine, for example, an important and influential Jewish journal of opinion, while anti-Communist from its founding in 1945, had become, under the editorship of Norman Podhoretz beginning in 1960, a liberal periodical. But after the 1967 war in Israel and the anti-Semitism evident in the student and Black liberation movements, the magazine by 1976 increasingly took what came to be described as a neoconservative position: anti-Communism abroad; racial equality, but not affirmative action, at home; and in general, the safety net of the welfare state, but not group rights at the expense of governmental interference with individual freedom and enterprise. Many of the writers and editors, including Podhoretz, Irving Kristol, Nathan Glazer, and several others who had been part of the second-generation New York intellectual scene, had gone from socialism of one stripe or another to liberalism and finally to centrism or neoconservatism. Several were Democrats trying to rescue their party from the "new leftist liberalism" they believed had infected it since the 1972 presidential campaign of George McGovern.

Interestingly, however, neoconservatism, so heavily represented by Jews, was still not like the old conservatism espoused by gentiles such as William Buckley or Russell Kirk. These old conservatives favored a wholly unregulated economic system and rejected "environmentalist" explanations for personal failure or antisocial behavior, insisting instead on the full responsibility of the individual actor. On the other hand, Irving Kristol, a Jew, a registered Republican, a columnist for the *Wall Street Journal*, and a fellow at the American Enterprise Institute, explained that in contrast to old conservatism "Neoconservatism is not at all hostile to the idea of the welfare state. . . . In general, it approves of those social reforms that, while providing needed security and comfort to the individual in our dynamic, urbanized society, do so with a minimum of bureaucratic intrusion in the individual's affairs." Those reforms included social security, unemployment insurance, national health insurance, some kind of family assistance plan, and more. And although Kristol was a Republican, most neoconservatives in the 1980s still considered themselves Democrats.

Even among conservatives, then, neoconservative Jews appeared to be on the left edge. Certainly they were seen that way by much of the Right. The Christian New Right, represented by Pat Robertson, and the staunch Republican old right, represented by Pat Buchanan, continued into the 1990s to view the neoconservatives as "alien intellectuals" opposed to the basic ideals of authentic conservatism. More importantly, most Jewish socialists and liberals did not become centrists. Many even of that group of New York intellectuals that included Kristol and Podhoretz, people such as Susan Sontag, Leslie Fiedler, Theodore Solotaroff, Alfred Kazin, and Irving Howe, were hardly classifiable as neoconservative. Indeed, Howe, a prolific literary and social critic and editor of *Dissent,* remained very much an anti-Stalinist democratic socialist, even as he expressed his disdain and revulsion for the infantile leftism of the 1960s student movements.

The student movements included some Black caucuses, as well as some separate Black organizations, which added intimidation and volume to the anti-Semitic echoes of the 1960s. Black nationalist groups often took anti-Zionist, anti-Semitic positions, especially during this era of newly emerging African states, and particularly after the 1967 Six Day War, which, from the Black radical's perspective, pitted a "white, Western, racist, imperialist, Zionist entity" against victimized "people of color" in the Middle East. To the existing differences in social conditions between Blacks and Jews, to the already troubling Black accusations of Jewish paternalism and Jewish accusations of

Black anti-Semitism, and to the intensifying struggle between Blacks and Jews for jobs and turf in the cities were now added broader issues of politics and ethnic identity dramatized in larger global conflicts.

To get a sense of the complex domestic context within which Blacks and Jews were relating to one another in the 1960s, one need only mention the assassination of the Black civil rights leader Medgar Evers, the civil rights March on Washington, and the Birmingham, Alabama, bombings of Black churches by whites in 1963; the murders of civil rights workers James Chaney (Black), Andrew Goodman, and Michael Schwerner (both Jews) in 1964; the assassination of Malcolm X and the Selma-to-Montgomery Freedom March in 1965; the Voting Rights Act and the race riots in the Watts section of Los Angeles in that same year; the enunciation of Black Power, the Chicago race riots, and the founding of the Black Panthers in 1966; race riots is Boston, Cincinnati, Newark, Brooklyn, Detroit, and New Haven in 1967; and the Kerner Commission Report detailing the existence of two nations, one black, one white, separate and unequal, the assassination of the Reverend Martin Luther King, the Civil Rights Act, and the founding of the Jewish Defense League by Meir Kahane, all in 1968. All of this in a period of five years.

In 1968, too, came the New York City teachers' strike in response to the dismissal of nineteen teachers and administrators by the Ocean Hill-Brownsville experimental district in its quest for local control. Since a significantly disproportionate number of schoolteachers, administrators, and teachers' union leaders in New York City were Jewish and a disproportionate number on the district's governing board were Black, the events surrounding the strike escalated into the most vicious and visible Black-Jewish confrontation in the history of the United States. The conflict was exacerbated by the union and by the Black militants, but tension had been building for years. Even before 1968 some Black militants, especially in the Northeast, spoke and acted as if *emerging ethnicity* meant "nationalism" or even "racialism." They preferred separatism and rejected authentic intimate engagement with whites. Many demanded that Black students have only Black teachers. A year before the strike, one Black schoolteacher, John Hatchett, had written: "We are witnessing today in New York City a phenomenon that spells death for the minds and souls of our black children. It is the systematic coming of age of the Jews who dominate the educational bureaucracy of the New York Public School system and their power starved imitators, the Black Anglo-Saxons."

To Blacks like Hatchett the liberal Jews who staffed many of the public institutions of New York, and especially the schools, were the worst racists of all. They were, as Jim Sleeper has written, the most accessible "beneficiaries of an oppressive system, the closest of strangers, the easiest targets." It did not seem to matter much that Jews had led most of the racial justice efforts or that so many non-Jewish institutions, including unions, remained closed to Blacks. By the mid-to-late 1960s, the politics of ethnic pride in the Black community had turned for many to the politics of spite seasoned with anti-Semitism.

In the teachers' strike, Blacks saw the Jews as materialistic and greedy, as abandoning the civil rights movement, even as racist, while they failed to see that Jews were merely defending their own self-interest, as was their right. The Jews saw the Blacks as ungrateful and undemocratic and as abandoning the liberal ideal of equality of opportunity in favor of a demand for equality of results, and even as anti-Semitic. The Jewish teachers, many of whom were left liberals, also defended their action more in terms of the best interests of the Black schoolchildren and even of Black teachers who might become victims of an overpowerful, arbitrary local board, than they did in terms of their own protection. They failed to see that Blacks were merely responding to the fact that the ostensibly "fair" system was not working for them. Although the school strike finally ended on 18 November 1968, with places found elsewhere in the system for fired white, mostly Jewish teachers, its negative repercussions lasted for years.

The community control movement, because it was perceived as a vehicle for Black nationalism and racial separatism, was ultimately a political failure. But after the fiery rhetoric on both sides cooled, the movement also had a positive legacy. Increasing numbers of people and activists, Black and white, were convinced that Blacks must be seen not as an inferior or peripheral group to be pitied but as a legitimate ethnic group asserting its demands and interests as others in a pluralistic society did.

In the face of all of this, the Jewish establishment admitted more explicitly that the relationship with Blacks could no longer be defined as a comradeship of excluded peoples, as it had been in the 1940s and early 1950s, or as the paternalistic concern of Jews for the less fortunate, as in the late 1950s. Jews would have to learn how to deal with Blacks who could not be patronized, even by their friends. Blacks and Jews would have to inhabit the kind of America James Madison envisioned: an untidy collection of conflicting interest groups with no deference to elites.

In the meantime, several other incidents in New York City in 1968–69 exacerbated Black-Jewish tension and received national attention. A Black radio host, Julius Lester, allowed a Black school teacher to read one of his

student's poems on the air: "Hey Jew boy, with that yarmulke on your head /
You pale faced Jew boy—I wish you were dead." The radio station had a limited audience, but when the *New York Times* published the story, it created an
outcry of anger in the Jewish community and a demand for revocation of the
station's broadcasting license.

A short time later the following excerpt from an essay by a sixteen-
year-old Black girl was included in a Metropolitan Museum catalog for the
exhibit *Harlem on My Mind:* "Behind every hurdle that the Afro-American has
yet to jump stands the Jew who had already cleared it. Jewish shopkeepers
are the only remaining survivors in the expanding black ghettos. The lack of
competition allows the already exploited black to be further exploited by
Jews." Without fully considering the context of these remarks or the limita-
tions of adolescent perspective, knowledge, or sense of the appropriate, Jewish critics, frightened now by any overt manifestation of bigotry, zeroed in.
Radio station WBAI's license was not revoked, but the offending passage was
excised from the museum catalog.

In the 1970s leading Black and Jewish organizations wanted to heal existing ruptures and to some extent did so, but one overriding issue, affirmative action, prevented a complete rapprochement. Jews supported an affirmative action program that promoted equal opportunity in school admission
and in job competition, but for understandable historical reasons, and because
Jews had been successful enough to be overrepresented in many desirable
positions and professions, they feared quotas. But even here, in terms of racial
justice and progressivism, Jews were well ahead of other white groups, most
of which opposed any kind of affirmative action or preferential treatment to
right past racial wrongs. In the landmark 1974 Supreme Court case *DeFunis
v. the University of Washington,* the National Council of Jewish Women and the
Union of American Hebrew Congregations stood with the National Urban
League, a leading civil rights and Black opportunity agency, in contending
that test scores alone were an inadequate university admissions criterion and
that race could be taken into account.

In a 1978 case some thought that Jewish organizations had switched
sides when the American Jewish Committee, among others, supported Allan
Bakke against the University of California, which had maintained a 16 percent minority quota for admission to its medical school. But the position of
the Jewish organizations had not really changed. They said yes to an affirmative action that encouraged the use of race as a criterion in admissions, but
no to numerical quotas. Jews were still supportive of enhanced equality of
opportunity for all, but according to a Harris poll in the late 1970s, a heavy

majority of Blacks, 74 percent, felt that "unless quotas are used, blacks and other minorities just won't get a fair shake." New strain was added to Black-Jewish relations.

Anti-Semitism might not have been caused or aggravated by any of this had there not already been latent hostility. The same could be said of another incident, the 1979 resignation of Andrew Young, the U.S. ambassador to the United Nations. Young had had, contrary to U.S. diplomatic policy, secret meetings with the Palestine Liberation Organization. And more importantly, he had apparently covered up his illegal action by lying to Washington. This was reason enough for his dismissal, according to Secretary of State Cyrus Vance, but some Blacks assumed that American Jews, who had put pressure on the Carter administration, were alone responsible. Black anti-Semitism was reinforced enough by the Bakke case and the Young affair to give Nation of Islam Minister Louis Farrakhan a responsive audience among some Blacks in the United States when he referred in the 1980s to Judaism as a "dirty religion" and Hitler as a "great man" and contended that Israel and its "friends" were "engaged in a criminal conspiracy."

Few Blacks spoke out against Farrakhan, for all kinds of complicated reasons, but one of those reasons must have been that some Blacks agreed with him. When Vernon Jordan of the National Urban League praised Jews in 1985 for their support in the civil rights movement and stated that "Black Jewish relations should not be endangered by ill-considered flirtations with terrorist groups devoted to the extermination of Israel," he found a coalition of so-called grassroots leaders camped in front of his offices denouncing him for his blasphemy. And other Black leaders, including the Reverend Jesse Jackson, clearly favored Palestinians over Israelis, Jackson going so far as to proclaim that supporting the Palestine Liberation Organization marked "Black America's finest hour."

Despite the evidence of increasing Black anti-Semitism in some circles and greater support for the enemies of Israel within the Black community, Jewish organizations, even if with diminished fervor, stayed in the struggle for Black equality into the 1970s and 1980s. Indeed, Jewish contributions continued to provide between 30 and 50 percent of the financing of the Urban League and the National Association for the Advancement of Colored People (NAACP), and Jewish youth continued to be disproportionately represented in racial justice movements. In Congress, as well, Jewish members were consistent and nearly unanimous in voting for social programs. Likewise, the Black Caucus was equally consistent and almost equally unanimous in voting for aid packages to Israel. In 1984, and again in 1988, Jesse Jackson expressed some public distemper toward Jews and embraced the Palestinians, but he pulled back from questioning the compact that Jews and Blacks had made in Congress.

Outside Congress and outside the major Jewish organizations, Jewish liberalism on questions of racial and economic justice was still viable as far as voting behavior was concerned through the 1980s and into the 1990s. For example, in 1982, Jews voted 77 percent for Democratic candidates in congressional elections, a substantially higher proportion than among any other group of whites. Blacks voted 84 percent for Democrats.

In that same year, 1982, Tom Bradley, the Black mayor of Los Angeles, was defeated for governor of California by Republican George Deukmejiian by less than 1 percent of the vote. Bradley won 42 percent of the total white vote, but 75 percent of the Jewish vote—more support from Jews than he got from Mexican Americans. In 1983 the Black mayoral candidate in Philadelphia, Wilson Goode, received 23 percent of the white vote in the Democratic primary against Frank Rizzo, but 50 percent of the Jewish vote. And in Chicago the Black leader, Harold Washington, competing against a Jewish Republican, received 35 percent of the Jewish vote, twice the overall white vote for Washington.

In the 1984 presidential election, only 41 percent of the nation voted for the Democratic candidates Walter Mondale and Geraldine Ferraro, but Jews voted for the Democratic ticket more than two to one, and this despite the failure of the Democratic party to make a forthright, explicit denunciation of the anti-Semitism associated with Democrat Jesse Jackson which emerged during the primary campaigns. Only Blacks and the unemployed outdid Jews in the percentage of votes that they gave to the Democratic presidential ticket.

Similar results were to be seen in the 1988 and 1992 elections. Among those in the general electorate who earned more than thirty thousand dollars a year, two-thirds voted for George Bush in 1988, whereas more than two-thirds of Jewish voters in that income category voted for the liberal Democrat Michael Dukakis; and almost four-fifths of all Jews voted for Bill Clinton in 1992. Affluent Jews voted for the men most likely to raise taxes to help the disadvantaged and to foster racial equality. Moreover, the 1990 General Social Survey of the National Opinion Research Center at the University of Chicago, using thirty different comparisons, found "no evidence of [a] Jewish backlash against the goal of racial equality or against blacks as a group, either as part of a general movement away from liberalism, or as a specific result of racial conflicts with blacks." Jews were still consistently more

supportive of racial integration than whites of every other religious preference, and they were consistently more favorable toward Black civil rights
leaders. Only toward racial extremists who targeted them were Jews, understandably, less favorably disposed than other non-Jewish white groups.

By many measures, then, Jewish Americans continued into the 1990s
to define themselves not merely by their anti-anti-Semitism but also by their
liberal political activity. Indeed, political liberalism, for an important segment of American Jewry, remained something of a religious principle, or at
least a principle with spiritual dimension, and an important way of reformu-
lating or transforming part of an authentic Jewish American identity. This
had been true from Socialist Abraham Cahan, who had labored mightily to
transform Jewish immigrants into a great new American public worthy of
their ancient tradition, through Judah Magnes, who combined radical reform
politics and pacifism with Jewish ministry. And from Stephen Wise, the energetic rabbi, steeped in American social gospel and secular Jewish messianism, to Albert Vorspan, the head of the Reform movement's Social Action
Commission, who said late in the twentieth century that "a commitment to
social justice is inherent in Judaism," many American Jews remained vitally
and intensely Jewish by their liberal political activism.

Into the 1990s, Jews remained disproportionately liberal universalists
at the same time when they felt secure enough in America to pursue their
particular group interests aggressively. By the 1970s, whenever and wherever anti-Semitism resurfaced, it distressed Jews and promoted a degree of
insecurity among them, as it always had, but it did not deter them either
from publicly identifying as Jews or from militantly espousing Jewish interests. In the case of Jonathan Pollard, for example, a Jewish American convicted, along with his wife, of spying for Israel in the 1980s, a number of Jewish leaders and spokespersons, fearful of the old charge of dual or conflicting
loyalties, rushed to castigate and condemn the couple and their illegal deeds,
and several other leaders remained silent in the face of one of the harshest
sentences, life imprisonment, ever imposed for passing classified information. The American government had allowed non-Jewish spies such as the
Walker family, unmasked in the U.S. navy in the 1980s, to serve lighter sentences, even though the Walkers had given vital information to the Soviet
Union, an "unfriendly power," thereby endangering U.S. security far more
than the Pollards had in helping Israel, a "major non-NATO ally." Still, the
head of the Conference of Presidents of Major American Jewish Organizations went so far as to support the life sentence for the Pollards publicly, dis-
playing what Israeli Shlomo Avineri called, at the time, classic "diaspora in-

security." But the days of Jewish insecurity, displayed in the Rosenberg case of the 1950s, were virtually over by the 1980s. Many Jewish Americans, including activist Rabbi Avi Weiss, historian David Biale, the members of the executive committee of the Central Conference of American Rabbis, and thousands of ordinary Jewish men and women, were openly critical of the U.S. government. Most did not deny the guilt of the Pollards, who had after all confessed, and who had done damage to the United States, but Jewish Americans vehemently decried in print and in public meetings the double standard of the Justice Department and of the White House.

The vast majority of Jews continued to prove throughout the 1980s and 1990s that they were neither nervous nor cringing. Many wore skullcaps openly in the last quarter of the twentieth century, thousands of Jewish students were deeply involved in the struggle for Soviet Jewry, and tens of thousands of Jews turned up for Israel Day parades. But American Jewry's sense of security was perhaps most strikingly displayed at the White House in 1985. President Reagan announced late in 1984 that he had scheduled a visit to Germany and that he planned to lay a wreath at a military cemetery in Bitburg as a gesture of American goodwill. It was soon discovered, however, that forty-seven members of the Waffen SS, a military unit that had participated in Nazi atrocities, were buried there. The president was caught between the public outcry of Jews, World War II veterans, and other angry Americans, on the one hand, and Helmut Kohl's insistence that the Bitburg visit proceed as scheduled, on the other.

Just before Reagan's trip, Elie Wiesel, perhaps the most famous of Auschwitz survivors—and certainly, through his prolific writings and public appearances, one of the Holocaust's most eloquent witnesses—was scheduled to receive the Congressional Gold Medal of Achievement, the U.S. government's highest civilian honor. In a dramatic televised confrontation, Wiesel, instead of politely accepting the honor, politely chided Reagan, saying the president of "the freest nation in the world, the moral nation," had no business at Bitburg. "That place, Mr. President, is not your place. Your place is with the victims of the SS." Though he spent as little time as possible at the cemetery, the president did lay the wreath at Bitburg. The important thing, however, was that the public rebuke of the president in the White House by a Holocaust survivor manifested a sense of security unprecedented in American Jewish history. Wiesel's words were a powerful signal that the Jewish worry over "what the gentiles might think" was finished. It had died years before, but Wiesel at the White House wrote its epitaph.

In 1937, Alvin Johnson, who created an academic home for German Jewish refugee scholars at the New School for Social Research, had offered the following well-intentioned advice to Jews on how to deflate anti-Semitism: Jews should not espouse Zionism; they should avoid supporting the causes of other oppressed minority groups such as American Blacks; they should not be conspicuous or notorious. Yet doing precisely the opposite in each instance, Jews prevailed and thrived in a more open social environment than anyone could have imagined.

14

The Ever-Disappearing People

In the 1990s, as peace between Israelis and Arabs became a real possibility for the first time in more than a century of conflict, there were several isolated but worrisome attacks on Jewish institutions by Arab rejectionists in a number of countries including the United States. Jews and Jewish organizations were also targeted in the disintegrating Soviet Union, where vulgar right-wing nationalism was unleashed in several of the newly emerging states, including Russia, whose Jewish population was still more than one million.

These actions were troubling in their own right, and they made Jewish Americans even more worried about continued anti-Semitism in their own country among militant Black separatists and marginal neo-Nazi hate groups. In the late 1980s and early 1990s, there were still about one thousand anti-Semitic incidents annually, including cemetery desecrations, threats, and arson, the most serious of which were perpetrated by neo-Nazi "skinhead" youth in Chicago, Los Angeles, Miami, and other U.S. cities. There had also been an increase in anti-Semitic incidents on college campuses between 1988 and 1989, including the drawing of swastikas, and highly publicized expressions of Jew-hatred and Jew-baiting by invited speakers of Louis Farrakhan's Nation of Islam. Other speakers on campuses and elsewhere in the early 1990s minimized and even denied the reality of the Holocaust. These deniers were part of a movement calling itself historical revisionism. Beginning with the publication of Arthur Butz's *Hoax of the Twentieth Century* (1976), the deniers gained a degree of legitimacy on the fringes of academia by the 1980s, the lunacy of their unsubstantiated theories notwithstanding. Despite the animus and negative activities of their enemies, however, and despite Jewish responses in polls demonstrating continued Jewish suspicion and wariness about anti-Semitism, most Jews indicated in those same polls and by their overall behavior that they felt generally free and secure in an America to which they had contributed mightily and which had widely accepted them.

An old question, nonetheless, continued to haunt: Would the Jewish people and their distinctive culture, which had survived several centuries of global oppression, be able to survive several decades of American freedom? That question had been asked virtually from the very beginning of the American Jewish experience and had often been answered, by implication at least, in the negative. In 1905 the *New York Tribune* was certain that:

> from the very start . . . [the Jewish] child unconsciously acquires a contempt for the un-American habits and characteristics of his father. The American public school and associations with business do the rest. . . . The laissez-faire spirit of our national life seems in many cases to accomplish what the persecution of ages has failed to bring about—namely, the alienating of the Jewish child from the strict observance of his racial religious rites.

And nearly one hundred years later, in the mid-1990s, the survivalists—those still fearful of assimilation—pointed to the "perilous erosion of any distinguishing boundaries that define 'Jewishness'" in America. Is the fact that the obituary for the Jewish people had to be rewritten every ten or fifteen years over the past century cause for complacency or even optimism about the future, or has the distinctive Jewish tradition, transformed or otherwise, reached a true dead end in the United States on the threshold of the new century? The unpredictability of American history and of Jewish history makes any definitive answer appear naïve or arrogant. But it is useful to ponder the contours of the Jewish American present with that question in mind.

If residential concentration is necessary, even if not sufficient, for Jewish continuity, then it may be important that Jewish Americans in the 1990s were more widely distributed than ever in the various regions of the United States. In the late 1940s more than 67 percent of America's Jews (4.5 million) still lived in the Middle Atlantic and New England states. But by the 1990s only 40 percent lived in the Northeast. More Jews lived in San Francisco than in Baltimore, for example, and more lived in Phoenix than in Pittsburgh. As many—or more—Jews lived in new locations in the Southwest such as San Diego as lived in the older cities of the Midwest such as Detroit.

And Los Angeles and Miami were among the cities showing the fastest growth in Jewish population in the postwar period. In 1970, Los Angeles had 440,000 Jews, and by 1980 more than 500,000. Miami's Jewish population grew from 230,000 in 1970 to 290,000 in 1975, and, with nearby Fort Lauderdale, to 363,000 by 1985. Greater Los Angeles and greater Miami in the late 1980s represented more than 15 percent of American Jewry. By the 1990s, California had nearly one million Jewish inhabitants, and Florida was not far behind New York and New Jersey in Jewish percentage of population (see table 3, ch. 5).

Some demographers have argued that these shifts may give the growing Jewish communities the population density needed to maintain the institutions essential for group survival and enrichment. The evidence, however, is mixed. In Atlanta, for example, membership in Reform and Conservative synagogues increased 50 percent from 1970 to 1984; but Denver, over the same period and into the 1990s, revealed very low levels of affiliation with Jewish institutions and very high rates of intermarriage. In Denver 75 percent of Jews who married had a non-Jewish spouse, compared with an overall Jewish intermarriage rate in America of approximately 52 percent since 1985.

Studies of the "new," postwar Jewish cities of choice, and especially Los Angeles and Miami, allow us a window on some of the concerns about a Jewish future. In the 1940s, Jewish GIs stationed in Los Angeles and Miami were absolutely amazed that these places, with palm trees, large juicy oranges, and consistently warm weather, were actually part of the United States. Most dreamed of returning to what seemed paradise after the war, and many did. Energized to some extent by their confidence-bolstering experiences in World War II and spurred by the image of the independent Jew emerging in the young state of Israel, Jews began, in the late 1940s and early 1950s, to move in relatively large numbers from the familiar milieu of the Jewish cities of the Northeast to Miami, and from the comfortable Jewish homogeneity of their communities in the Midwest to Los Angeles.

Jewish migrants were enchanted by the spacious, clean, eternally balmy cities, especially when they compared them with the grimy environs of New York City, Newark, Chicago, and Detroit. They were attracted not only by the climate, however, but also by the opportunities to establish new economic enclaves, especially in the hotel and real estate businesses. And if we may derive motivation from consequence, they may also have been motivated by the desire, conscious or otherwise, to leave some religious and ethnic baggage behind, to reconstruct on the open frontiers of California and

Florida a more individualistic faith, a more voluntary Jewishness, one less tied to established traditions, institutions, and communities.

Rabbis Isaiah Zeldin of Los Angeles and Leon Kronish and Joseph Narot of Miami, for example, were willing to experiment with new forms of Judaism and to mold religious practices in response to the desires of individuals, most of whom were uprooted newcomers like themselves. The Judaism that developed in Los Angeles and Miami, according to Deborah Dash Moore, the leading historian of Jewish life in the "golden cities," proved to be "a bland, positive, upbeat, and affirming Judaism that placed few demands upon its adherents." Several other observers also noted "blandness," but beginning in the 1970s with Moses Rischin, who described Jewish life in Los Angeles as "problematic" and unsustained by either traditional religion or vigorous secular ethnicity, they were not as enthusiastic about that blandness as Moore. They pointed out that in Los Angeles, for example, in the 1980s, only 25 percent of Jews belonged to a synagogue compared with a national average of approximately 40 percent, and fewer than 7 percent contributed to the local Jewish federation. Many analysts viewed the low level of synagogue affiliation, the absence of public or private ritual, and the high rates of intermarriage, all of which characterized both Los Angeles and Miami, as precursors of doom.

These descriptions of Los Angeles and Miami, however, seemed by the 1990s to apply more generally to most American Jews. The Jews of the golden cities may simply have arrived at the future sooner than their less mobile relatives up north or back east. Significantly, however, Jewish life in Los Angeles and Miami in the late 1990s, more than a quarter-century after the first forecasts of total assimilation, had not disappeared; it persisted and even flourished. There were West Coast branches of Conservative Judaism's Jewish Theological Seminary and Reform Judaism's Hebrew Union College, and even a Los Angeles branch of Orthodoxy's Yeshiva University. In addition to Rabbi Zeldin's monumental Stephen S. Wise Temple and Shlomo Bardin's innovative Brandeis Camp in Los Angeles, there was a network of Orthodox day schools and a number of quite viable Orthodox congregations in the city. And in Miami, too, Orthodox day schools and congregations complemented the classical Reform teachings at Temple Israel and the "liberal Judaism" at Beth Sholom.

Jewish newcomers to Miami and Los Angeles may have encountered the increased openness of postwar America more readily and sooner than many other Jews in the United States, but Jewish life in the golden cities was nonetheless the offspring of Jewish New York and Chicago and of the more modest Jewish communities in such cities as Omaha, Cleveland, and Detroit. Los Angeles and Miami Jews in the 1990s, like the Jews of the Northeast and Midwest, continued to choose to live in urban areas primarily, to have few children (usually two), to complete college (90 percent), to obtain graduate degrees (35 percent), and to enter the professions and managerial levels of business. Israel continued to be central to their politics and to their religious identity, and political liberalism and civic-mindedness continued to define their mainly secular humanist faith. And even as they intermarried, Jews of Los Angeles and Miami, like most of their fellows elsewhere, continued to think of themselves as Jews.

Those still fearful of assimilation in the 1990s downplayed the evidence of continuity and persistence of Jewish identity which they said experienced not only a blandness but also a "hollowing out," and not only on the California and Florida frontiers but in the older regions too. In 1970 nearly 86 percent of Jewish Americans had identified with either Conservative, Reform, Orthodox, or Reconstructionist Judaism. But by 1990, according to an impressive, wide-ranging survey done at the City University of New York's Graduate Center, only 65 percent of Jewish Americans identified with a particular branch of Judaism, while 90 percent of non-Jewish Americans continued to identify with myriad religions and their denominations.

It was also apparent that relations between the various Jewish religious groups had deteriorated. All the movements, in varying degree, faced the same challenges: the decline in both affiliation and involvement by the third and fourth generations; the rising level of intermarriage and the related problem of raising children with Jewish values and Jewish community; feminism and the transformation of basic tradition. Yet each movement responded to the challenges unilaterally with virtually no consultation with the other denominations.

The Orthodox remained steadfast in their adherence to tradition, and indeed many in the movement turned rightward in terms of strict ritual observance and insistence on rigid interpretation of *halakha*. This resulted in defections from among the Modern Orthodox, but traditional Orthodoxy continued to claim the loyalty of about 9 percent of American Jewry. Approximately 20–25 percent of the Orthodox community in the late 1990s consisted of *baalei teshuvah*—that is, people who had returned to rigorous observance and faith after having lapsed. Another 15 percent came to Orthodoxy through the Yeshiva world. Yet another large proportion had had a solid religious education outside the Yeshiva, and many were the children of immigrants from postwar Europe. The vast majority of the Orthodox were not seekers flitting capriciously from one spiritual home to another; they had arrived at their religious positions as a result of a powerful socialization within their tightly knit communities and families or through careful study and analysis.

There continued in the 1990s to be more women than men in the Orthodox movement. Despite the Orthodox exclusion of women from anything like an equal role in synagogue life and despite the growing assertiveness of women inside and outside Judaism, Orthodoxy with its apparent family stability, moral coherence, and psychological security remained attractive to an important segment of women faced with the confusions and brutalities inherent in modern American life. There is evidence, too, that some teenagers, male and female, particularly those raised by excessively intellectual or ambivalent Jewish parents, are finding Orthodoxy appealing. They are apparently alienated by "pure reason" and are drawn by a belief system that recognizes the mysterious in life and purports to have something to say about it.

Recognizing the undiminished appeal of tradition and spirituality to important portions of the Jewish community, few in America in the 1990s believe any more that Orthodox Judaism is so out of tune with currents in modern life that it will disappear. But informed observers understand, as many overconfident Orthodox Jews failed to do in the 1970s and 1980s, that acculturation and the general problems of modern life which had impact on the non-Orthodox Jewish communities affect the Orthodox as well. Though the divorce rate among Orthodox Jews remained lower than for other Jewish groups, it did increase dramatically from 1980 to 1990. Moreover, by the 1990s homes for abused wives and children became a more visible feature of the Orthodox community, and infidelity and several other problems related to gender roles and expectations were no longer rare.

Unlike Orthodoxy, with its strict adherence to Jewish law and its ideological and moral coherence, the Reform movement at the end of the twentieth century appears to be marked by two apparently contradictory impulses. On the one hand, there has been among Reform Jews, since 1945 and especially since the late 1970s, a renewed emphasis on tradition. Skullcaps, prayer shawls, Hebrew usage, and kosher meals have reappeared, and religious circumcision, bar and bat mitzvah, and the marriage canopy have grown increasingly popular. On the other hand, there have been a number of radical breaks with tradition: the Reform movement was the first Jewish denomination to ordain women as rabbis and cantors; the Central Conference of American

Rabbis has refused to discipline rabbis who officiate at mixed marriages; and the movement has unilaterally redefined Jewish identity by accepting as a Jew a child raised as such by a Jewish father, regardless of the mother's religion.

Reform Judaism's patrilineal definition of Jewishness, some have warned, will be increasingly divisive within Judaism, especially when added to the fact that Orthodox Jews do not recognize conversions carried out by Reform or Conservative rabbis. By the end of the twentieth century, it has been predicted, as many as a half-million children, born to mothers converted by non-Orthodox rabbis or accepted as Jewish under the patrilineal definition, will not be accepted as Jews by other Jews. Moreover, within approximately thirty years there will be rabbis of patrilineal descent who will not be recognized as Jewish by either Orthodox or Conservative rabbis. Nonetheless, with the notable exception of the Orthodox, and of the Conservative rabbinate and synagogue presidents, the overwhelming majority of American Jewry agrees with the Reform position: The child of a Jewish man, if raised a Jew, is a Jew.

In addition to approving patrilineal descent in 1983, the Reform movement in 1994 announced that it would not only reach out to non-Jews in mixed marriages but would also seek converts among non-Jews generally. Many Orthodox and some Conservative leaders described this attempt at proselytizing among Christians as analogous to trying to save a crumbling empire by invading new territory, and they insisted that the plan will do "violence to the integrity of Judaism and produce an historic hodgepodge." Reform leader Rabbi Alexander Schindler, however, predicted that the greatest benefit of the new plan would come to those already Jewish who will have to explore their own relationship to Judaism in order to pass it on to others.

While the great majority of the Jewish community seems to have responded positively to the call for outreach, the Reform laity itself in the 1990s appears to be only mildly interested in encouraging the conversion of their gentile sons- or daughters-in-law. Yet they were ready to accept their non-Jewish in-laws into membership and even leadership positions in Jewish organizations including Reform synagogues. Some Jews, even in the Conservative movement, have wondered whether such extraordinary openness will not erode the distinguishing boundaries that define Jewishness in America, especially since Reform Judaism is the fastest growing Jewish denomination in the 1990s.

Whatever the future may bring in this area, it is clearly necessary for Jewish leadership in the 1990s to respond to the phenomenon of increasing intermarriage and its attendant problems as they relate to Jewish identity. Marriage between Jew and non-Jew was not a serious concern for Jewish

Americans until the 1960s, when the intermarriage rate changed from approximately 6 percent to more than 17 percent. By 1972 the proportion of Jews choosing non-Jewish spouses climbed to 32 percent, and between 1985 and 1995 it reached 52 percent. In the 1980s and 1990s, 20 percent of gentile marriage partners did convert to Judaism. And the children of these "conversionary" marriages were three times more likely to identify as Jews than children of "mixed" marriages, in which the gentile partner did not convert. But even in those mixed marriages, 25 percent of the children were being raised as Jews. This meant that though the erosion was not massive, there was a net decrease in the number of Jewish Americans. Intermarried couples have fewer children in any case, and Jews, intermarried or not, were among the college-educated, upwardly mobile, affluent urban residents who produced fewer children. By the late 1980s, Jewish Americans had the lowest birth rate of any major ethnic or religious group in America. In 1992 the Jewish population of the United States was approximately 5.8 million, or 2.3 percent, down from the numerical high of 5.9 million in 1980, and from the proportional high of 3.65 percent of the population in 1940.

It should also be pointed out that although the intermarriage rate continues to grow in the 1990s, Jews, as in every period of American history, have not converted to Christianity in any but negligible numbers. Still, in addition to the problem of decreasing numbers, there is the continuing struggle to keep Judaism central to a Jewish American ethnic identity in the late 1990s. The numerical strength of Orthodoxy in New York City, the largest community of Jews in the country, gives traditional Judaism a visibility that belies its actual size. Orthodoxy is still strong, especially among the young and the very old; but some observers have measured a 10 percent decline in the movement since 1985. Conservatism is also losing members, especially younger Jews, and Reform is a label often chosen by Jews who have told pollsters that they have no strong religious allegiance or commitment to the movement.

Moreover, whenever confronted with the tension between individual freedom and more rigorous guidelines for belief and practice, Reform Judaism has most often opted for the former. The pluralism resulting from free choice within Reform has obvious attraction, but it fails to address the issues of intellectual coherence and of boundaries. Even Conservative Judaism appeared to embrace the idea of nearly complete individual freedom. The Conservative movement did issue a Statement of Principles in 1988, but it agreed that the guidelines therein need not be accepted "as a whole or in detail . . . [as] obligatory upon every Conservative Jew, lay or rabbinic."

It is possible to argue, as some transformationists have done, that Judaism is and has always been what Jews do and value together and therefore that Judaism has been changed but not necessarily attenuated. Gersom Scholem, the distinguished historian, made much the same point in the mid-twentieth century.

> There is no way of telling *a priori* what beliefs are possible or impossible within the framework of Judaism. . . . The "Jewishness" in the religiosity of any particular period is not measured by dogmatic criteria that are unrelated to actual historical circumstances, but solely by what sincere Jews do, in fact believe, or—at least—consider to be legitimate possibilities.

But in his use of terms such as *sincere* and *legitimate,* Scholem certainly implies that there is something authentic about traditional belief systems and ritual observance. And it is not merely the pessimistic survivalists who argue that without some substantive connection to *halakha,* without some boundaries around what Jews must not do, and without a prophetic vision at the core of Jewish identity, the triumph of ethnicity alone may yet prove shallow and perhaps even expendable.

Some take heart from the fact that 20 percent or more of Jewish Americans (just less than half of them Orthodox) remain religiously observant. It is difficult to know for certain, but that elite of believing Jews, obedient to *halakha* and consistent in their attendance at synagogue, may be large enough to sustain Judaism and Jewishness for a very long time to come. Continuity appears more likely, too, since in the 1990s the vast majority, not just the elite, persists in a number of important ritual observances: 70 percent fast on Yom Kippur and place *mezzuzot* on their doorposts; more than 80 percent light Hanukkah candles, and more than 90 percent attend Passover seders. In these things the behavior of Conservative and Reform Jews approximates that of the Orthodox. In addition, the Jewish renewal movements such as P'nai Or continued to attract the formerly disaffected and have achieved a degree of institutional stability.

Just as important, the religion of Jewish Americans is found not only in the realm of the synagogue and in denominational affiliation but, as we have seen throughout, also in the ideologies and activities of a wide spectrum of Jewish organizations and individuals usually described as secular. American Jews practiced a civil religion virtually from the start, through institutions devoted to philanthropy and social work and to the welfare of the Jewish people abroad. The early steps in this direction were not always consciously ideological, but the eventual development of the Jewish American civil

sphere, distinct from, though not necessarily antagonistic to, religious institutions, helped American Jewry achieve unity, purpose, and identity as a
moral community.

Over several decades of Jewish life in the United States, religion and
ethnicity were combined in a number of important new syntheses and placed
firmly within the embrace of the American liberal tradition. Giving—performing *tsedakah*—is a good example of the combination of religious and
secular impulses that helped form a Jewish American civil religion and ethnic identity. The root of the word *tsedakah*—*tsedek* in Hebrew—is related to
the concept of justice, as distinct from the root of the word *charity*—*caritas*
in Latin—which is related to love. Better-off Jews, whether they "loved" or
not, were obligated by *halakha* to be generous in their giving in order to
correct social injustice, especially economic inequity, and recipients of aid
were in no way beholden to donors: *tsedakah* was their right. Giving was
always part of Jewish law and continued to be seen as an obligation by Jewish Americans, even those no longer directly influenced by *halakha*. Indeed,
Jewish American philanthropy was so pervasive, so universal, and so regular,
that even non-Jews identified Jewish giving to secular causes as part of Jewish religion. Bernard Cardinal Law of Boston, at a meeting of the Combined
Jewish Philanthropies in 1984, approvingly cited Maimonides on the many
ways of helping the poor, and said that he too "believed" in *tsedakah*.

In addition, and very much related to those many Jews who maintained
their Jewish identity in part by giving, an important segment of American
Jewry in the 1990s remained vitally and intensely Jewish by its liberal political activism. Despite rising class status and despite friction in their relations
with Black Americans, nearly 70 percent of Jewish Americans said in 1990
that it was important for Jews to continue to support "politically weaker
groups"; only 14 percent thought it was a mistake. Another national survey
disclosed that 50 percent of Jewish Americans thought that the most important quality of their Jewish identity was "a commitment to social equality."
The remaining 50 percent were divided between support for Israel, religious
observance, and "other" responses, in that order.

Support for Israel, especially after 1967, was so powerful that it too,
like philanthropy and political liberalism, took on a spiritual quality and a
ritual dimension. There were increased tensions in the relationship between
Israelis and Jewish Americans in the late 1980s and 1990s, especially as Israel appeared to be on the verge of making peace with her Arab neighbors
and the Palestine Liberation Organization and as the Israeli economy experienced, for several years running, a robust growth, making the Jewish state

increasingly independent of the financial support of American Jewry. But Israelism remains an important focus for Jewish American identity at the end of the twentieth century. Indeed, in 1988, nearly 85 percent of American Jews said that Israel was more important to them than receiving the Torah on Mount Sinai. There are important differences between Israelis and Jewish Americans, especially around ritual, and particularism, some of which were intensified after the right-wing victories in the 1996 Israeli elections. But the two peoples continued to share one Judaism.

Jews in both Israel and the United States share a belief in their common peoplehood as well as a set of religious forms and ritual symbols. Each community invariably perceives that an attack on one is the same as an attack on the other. In addition, more than one-third of each community has family members in the other. There is also a continuing exchange of visitors, leaders, and Judaic scholars. All of this exerts an incremental but inexorable mutual influence and enrichment; and it reinforces the perspective shared by American and Israeli Jews alike that they are an extended family with common antecedents, destinies, and obligations.

Also, by the 1970s there were some three hundred thousand Israeli immigrants living in the United States, and by 1990 that number had increased to more than half a million. Jewish Americans, like the Israelis still in Israel, are ambivalent about these *yordim* (those who have descended), whom they see as having abandoned the Israel and Israelism that are at the foundation of Jewish American ethnic identity. But Israeli residents in the United States have not only contributed to Jewish cultural life here, especially as teachers and community activists; they have maintained very close ties to their homeland as well, visiting frequently, and occasionally returning to fight in its defense.

Israeli immigrants are not the only group to have provided a cultural and numerical infusion for the Jewish American community. Between 1947 and 1956, Jewish immigrants from all over the world, and especially from war-torn Europe, provided 60 percent of the growth of American Jewry. Later, from the 1970s to the 1990s, more than one hundred thousand Jews from the Soviet Union emigrated to some two-dozen communities in the United States including New York, Atlanta, Baltimore, San Francisco, and Youngstown, Ohio. Unlike the Israelis, the Russian Jews bring little if any Jewish background with them. But the challenge of integrating them into a Jewish American community has provided a degree of revitalization for American Jewry.

In 1990 the Board of Jewish Education of Greater New York reported that fifty-five hundred Soviet Jewish children were enrolled in day schools and *yeshivot* and that five Jewish schools, of all denominations, had been established exclusively for the Russian immigrants. Boys who only recently were scarcely aware they were Jewish were now wearing skullcaps and ritual fringes. Parents, in response to their children, were studying Hebrew, keeping the Sabbath, and observing the dietary laws. Some men were even asking for circumcision operations for themselves and their sons.

As the number of Jews emigrating from the former Soviet Union dropped in the early 1990s, Jewish Americans began helping to resuscitate Jewish life in Russia, the Ukraine, and Belarus. Jewish institutions and individuals from America helped refurbish synagogues and establish schools to teach the Hebrew language and Jewish history and culture. They also helped small groups of Jews all over the former Soviet Union make contact with one another as well as with Jewish organizations abroad. As with the Reform movement's program of outreach to non-Jews in mixed marriages, so with the attempt to teach former Soviet Jews, both in the United States and in the former Soviet Union, how to be Jewish, Jewish Americans in the 1990s are reeducating and reenergizing their own Jewish identities.

As I have shown, the content of Judaism for Jewish Americans is partly dependent on recurring reaffirmations that are promoted by events external to the Jewish American community itself. Helping Russian Jews become Jewish is one example in a long list of these rejuvenating events. Others include the relief and rescue of European Jews during World War I, Zionist activism in the early twentieth century, the politics of rescue during the Holocaust, the post–World War II immigration of Jewish survivors, the Six Day War in 1967, the plight of Soviet Jewry in the 1970s, and the resurgence of Islamic fundamentalism with its murder and terrorism and its inherent threat to Israel's survival in the 1980s. All contributed to the galvanization of Jewish Americans and to the redefinition and reintensification of Jewish American identity. But many of these things, including the attention to Israel, though seemingly external, are basic and virtually ingrained in the Jewish American psyche. Jewish Americans continue to see themselves as part of a common peoplehood, a nationality shared with Jews in Israel, in the former Soviet Union, and everywhere else across the world.

Devotion to the welfare of the Jewish people abroad was part of the civil Judaism that helped the community to preserve Jewish group life. Simultaneously, however, civil Judaism promoted maximal involvement in American society and polity. It inspired Jewish particularism in the form of support for other Jews at the same time that it encouraged universalism through the pursuit of social justice for all. Inspired by America's commitment to democracy and pluralism, Jews, albeit through a variety of redefinitions of their original identities, retained their Jewishness but acculturated gladly and became Americans.

Despite the diversity of cultures marking the United States, there was an American civilization to acculturate to, to integrate into, even at the very start of the Jewish experience here. Alexis De Tocqueville, writing back to his much more homogeneous native France in the early 1830s, mistakenly described the more pluralistic United States as having no core culture:

> Imagine . . . if you can, a society formed of all the nations of the world . . . people having different languages, beliefs, opinions: in a word a society without roots, without memories, without prejudices, without routines, without common ideas, without a national character, yet a hundred times happier than our own.

The question of happiness aside, Tocqueville's contention, shared in the last decades of the twentieth century by some multiculturalists, that there has never been (nor ought there to be) a recognizable, accessible shared culture was illogical, bad history, and simply wrong. The culture of America is fluid and permeable, as Tocqueville implies, but the broad majority of Americans, across class lines, have been encompassed in a context of shared values and behavior patterns. The Americanized English language shaped and reflected a pervasive public culture, official and unofficial. National institutions, including the mass press, magazines, radio, television, public schools, and the armed forces, brought a variety of peoples under their influence and into contact with one another; and they were powerful instruments for Americanization. Without melting—that is, without losing many of the characteristics that made them Irish, Greek, Italian, Japanese, Korean, or Vietnamese—the immigrants and their children acculturated and generally accepted Americanization, especially the political ideology of democracy and liberal capitalism and the concept of cultural pluralism which served as the cement of national unity.

With the ending of the prohibition against Asian immigration in 1952 (McCarran-Walter Act) and of quotas based on national origins in 1965 (Immigration and Nationality Act), immigration to the United States not only increased but also changed in ethnic composition. As late as 1940, 70 percent of immigrants came from Europe, but by the 1990s only 15 percent of the newcomers were European, nearly 40 percent were Asian, and, despite a cap of 120,000 on immigration from the Western Hemisphere, 45 percent were from Latin America (mostly Mexico) and the Caribbean. With more than 250 million people, the United States in the early 1990s accepted each year more than half of all the people in the world who migrated permanently across international borders—thousands of Southeast Asians, many of them overseas Chinese driven from their homes by the Vietnam War; large numbers of Koreans, Filipinos, and Indians responding to faster and cheaper transportation and rising aspirations; Jews liberated from a disintegrating Soviet Union; tens of thousands of young Africans, Arabs, Iranians, and Afghans escaping poverty and political turbulence in their countries; and even larger numbers of Latinos, legal and illegal, attracted by perceived opportunities just "next door."

In the late 1980s and early 1990s, when economic problems in the United States intensified, the increasing flow of immigrants engendered a new nativism similar to that provoked in the early twentieth century when masses of Southern and Eastern Europeans, including hundreds of thousands of Jews, arrived. This time it did not lead to the kind of action taken by Congress in the 1920s, when quotas for admission and citizenship were established on the basis of race and ethnicity. But there were continued expressions of fear about labor competition from "too many immigrants" and about the negative impact of masses of newcomers on poor African-American and white natives. And there was much talk about the need for immigration restriction in order to prevent a third world erosion of American culture. In 1986 the Immigration Reform and Control Act outlawed the hiring of illegal aliens and strengthened controls to prevent illegal entry into the United States. But this had little effect either on the number of unlawful border crossings or on resentments against Asian and Hispanic newcomers, legal or illegal, especially those who received some form of government assistance. The resentments were felt by both Blacks and whites, many of whom were descendants of early-twentieth-century immigrants.

Where the question of jobs, welfare benefits and burdens, and an expanding government role in the management of group rights all intertwined, as in preferential employment or college admission policies based on race and ethnicity, tensions spilled over into racial and ethnic antagonism. In the 1980s and 1990s, from Philadelphia to Los Angeles, there was a growing number of assaults on Asians and Hispanics. Korean grocers suffered in New York, as did Cambodians in Massachusetts, Laotian refugees in Wisconsin, and Chicano students in California. To achieve protection, equity, and power in this climate of ethnic change and conflict, the new immigrant minorities were drawn to the relatively recent group rights strategy of the most historic ethnic minority, African Americans, even as they competed with them for empowerment programs.

The new groups promoted the concept of official group identity and pressured government to establish even more mechanisms for managing ethnic relations. Some of these demands were incorporated in new affirmative action and multicultural policies for people of color, including Asians and Latinos, in jobs, education, and voting. There were even echoes of the critique of capitalism and liberal democracy from the 1960s and 1970s and talk of a revolution of third world peoples. No significant third world constituency developed, however. The majority of Japanese Americans and Chinese Americans in San Francisco and Los Angeles, Cuban Americans in Miami, Mexican Americans in San Antonio, and West Indian Americans in New York were enjoying middle-class prosperity or were aspiring to it, as were tens of thousands of their counterparts across the United States. And increasing numbers were pursuing political goals and even political careers through traditional channels, in coalition with whites as well as with other people of color, who had rejected a narrow politics of identity.

These hyphenate Americans were following in the footsteps of the descendants of even the most impoverished and powerless immigrants such as the Jews, Armenians, Italians, Poles, and Irish who had come earlier in the twentieth century and who had obtained better jobs and, later, more education and higher status than their immigrant parents and grandparents. Since the 1890s each succeeding generation from a variety of geographical origins had usually gained in social and economic position over its predecessor, mostly by extending its contacts with the wider society.

For some groups among the new post-1965 immigrants, progress had been made in only small increments. Public education was the classic vehicle for Americanization and, in the second half of the twentieth century, for economic mobility; but the Hispanic high school dropout rate was 45 percent in the early 1990s nationwide, triple the rate for whites and double the rate for Blacks. Hispanic potential for integration was also partly eroded by the ease with which Mexican Americans, living mostly in California and Texas, could visit their homeland and the ease with which they could maintain the Spanish language at the expense of English.

Low levels of education and slow acculturation meant that Latinos remained disproportionately in the lower classes. Discrimination certainly played a role here, but so did the fact that Mexicans and many other Hispanics emigrated from a Latin America with a history of slow economic growth, vast social inequality, and very limited opportunity for political participation. There was also, until the 1960s and 1970s, some evidence of a historically ingrained Latino bias against bureaucracy, which hindered Mexican American efforts to create self-help organizations beyond the family and to build political coalitions to fight poverty. Moreover, by the 1980s government was cutting back substantially on social welfare programs, leaving the community further in need. The problems of Mexican Americans as a group (nearly 15 million in 1995) were intensified, in addition, by the flow of illegal Mexican immigrants vulnerable to exploitation.

For the Puerto Ricans, who remain in the 1990s among the very poorest of the ethnic groups, conditions are similar to those of the Mexicans. There is a general lack of commercial experience, and until the 1960s and 1970s, a low level of political organization, with a strong emphasis on family over community and nation. Family was also a central focus in other immigrant cultures, including Jewish and Asian, but with these non-Hispanic groups, the emphasis on family carried over to community and nation, as evidenced in Asian cooperatives and Jewish self-help societies. There was no Puerto Rican equivalent of the Hebrew free loan society, the Chinese *hui kuan*, the Japanese *kenjikai*, or, for that matter, the Finnish cooperative or the Polish building and loan society.

By the 1960s Puerto Ricans, Mexicans, and other Latinos had become more organized and vocal in their demand for access to a fair share of the American dream. Several organizations battled discrimination and promoted education, including the Puerto Rican Forum's Aspira, which helped youngsters go to college by providing loans, tutoring, information, and general inspiration. Other Hispanic organizations encouraged entrepreneurship and helped some Puerto Ricans and Mexicans get started in their own small businesses. Still others pushed voter registration.

The major political parties, with their eyes on the growing Latino vote, began to reach out to moderate Puerto Rican and Mexican leaders. Herman Badillo's successful career in the Democratic Party was launched in this context. By the 1970s there were several Latino congressmen, and in 1974 Democrats Jerry Apodaca and Raul Castro were elected governors of New Mexico and Arizona, respectively. Henry Cisneros was elected mayor of San Antonio and Federico Peña became the mayor of Denver in 1981; both were made members of President Clinton's cabinet in 1993. By that time, Latinos had been elected mayors in more than seventy cities.

By the 1990s the majority of Hispanics had not achieved social or economic equality. But there were some gains. The number of Latino households earning fifty thousand dollars or more nearly tripled between the early 1970s and mid-1980s. And the percentage living below the poverty line decreased from 66 in 1975 to 28 in the 1990s, still more than double the white rate, but a hopeful trend.

Unlike the Hispanics, Asian immigrants and their descendants by the late 1980s had come to be known as the model minority in the United States. This label, in addition to indicating a degree of condescension, was also something of an exaggeration. While many native-born Chinese and nearly all Japanese and Korean Americans had achieved middle-class prosperity by the 1990s, some of the new immigrant Chinese in San Francisco and New York and the Filipino farm laborers, among others, were not well off materially. And for those who were "making it," a glass ceiling often prevented access to the very highest levels of administration and corporate bureaucracy. There have also been, in the last decades of the twentieth century, continued expressions of anti-Asian sentiment and violence in Philadelphia, Denver, San Francisco, Galveston, Jersey City, and Detroit.

Yet, in spite of earlier, crueler discrimination against the Chinese and Japanese, including denial of citizenship and land ownership, and in spite of the family disruptions and enormous financial loss sustained by Japanese Americans through their forced internment during World War II, many Asians have prospered in the United States. The impressive economic and social development of Taiwan and South Korea since World War II and of Japan since the Meijii Restoration of 1868 no doubt provided the Chinese, Korean, and Japanese émigrés with a cultural base for mobility and success in the their new homeland.

Census data for 1980 indicated that, among native-born Chinese American males between the ages of twenty-five and sixty-four, the average number of years of schooling was 14.9, compared with 12.9 for non-Hispanic American whites. By 1989, Japanese Americans aged twenty-five to forty-four had 17.7 years of education, compared to 16.8 for whites. And as early as 1970 more than 25 percent of Chinese Americans had completed four or more years of college, more than double the percentage of American whites. Moreover, Chinese Americans, along with the Japanese and other Asian Americans, were disproportionately represented in first-rank universities. In the early 1980s, Asian Americans amounted to less than 2 percent of the nation's population and about 5 percent of California's residents, but they made up 20 percent of the University of California at Berkeley's student body. They were 9 percent of the freshman class at Harvard in 1985, and 19.7 by 1991. The numbers were similar at Columbia, Yale, and Princeton. In addition, 33 percent of the students at New York's Juilliard School of Music were

Asians. More education, along with more family members working, contributed to higher average family incomes for Asians than for whites in the
1980s. Indeed, by 1990 Japanese Americans were the second highest ethnic
group in terms of family income, just behind Jewish Americans.

Many among the new immigrants from Asia and their descendants recognized that the politics of identity, although perhaps temporarily necessary
for security and self-esteem, led to further division and mistrust between
groups and to antipathy toward American society and culture. Separation and
the refusal to diversify social contacts and form alliances with others handi-
capped them in terms of economic and political opportunity. They discovered, too, that to become American was not necessarily to become "European" or "white." Jim Sleeper, a journalist who taught briefly in a New York
City high school, recounted in *The Closest of Strangers* that the hard-working
Chinese American students in his class, who diligently studied chemistry,
English, and political science (even during Sleeper's class on Chinese immigration and labor history) were not so much "interested in adopting 'white'
culture as much as they were interested in becoming part of the larger 'universal' culture of constitutional democracy and technological development."

Some minority advocates in the 1990s, especially after the multiethnic
riots in 1992 in Los Angeles, also began to recognize the need to build more
integrated and inclusive political coalitions, educational curricula, and personal identities. Their constituencies were sometimes ahead of them. In the
Latino community, for example, bilingualism in the schools, one of several
educational strategies meant to help Spanish-speaking youngsters learn English, had been turned by some of the "ethnicity entrepreneurs" into a program that virtually neglected English in a single-minded attempt to maintain
Spanish language and culture. Parents were beginning to suspect that this had
hindered students rather than enhanced their educational and occupational
mobility. Many questioned the ways bilingualism had been implemented and
particularly the anti-integrationist rhetoric within which the program had
sometimes been packaged. The rhetoric had encouraged many to believe
that Hispanics did not want to be Americans, a perception that was patently
untrue for the vast majority.

Such an image was also untrue for the newest immigrants—the Pak-
istanis, the Haitians, the Dominicans, and the Koreans—who were changing
the cultural context as much as the context was changing them. Once again
the potential for acculturation of these newcomers grew as the similarities
between them and the America they influenced also grew. The values and
goals of these newcomers, of the Latino parents who wanted their children

to learn English well, and of the Chinese students who wanted to be part of a universal civic and professional culture were representative of a growing perspective that rejected both the homogeneity demanded by the Anglo-conformists and the concept of eternally fixed identities suggested by proponents of a society of separate, autonomous racial and ethnic communities. The newer perspective invoked the image of an American stew, within which the various ingredients, all in the same pot, affected one another's taste and contributed to the overall flavor of the dish even as they remained distinctly recognizable. This perspective revived the more familiar, more flexible concept of cultural pluralism. It rejected the rigid, limiting view of ethnicity, which insisted that people are nothing more than their national origins or their race. It valued openness and cultural fluidity over strict group loyalties, and it recognized that there was a relentless, positive tension not only between the ethnic group and the larger society but also between the ethnic group and the self.

The resistance to inflexible definitions of ethnic group identity suggested that an authentic acculturation, in which group and culture influenced each other, could produce a more universal, nationalizing experience built on less orthodox, more voluntary identities for immigrants and ethnics. And despite the seemingly still raw, intractable nature of racism, it appeared that in the long haul even African Americans could be included in that experience. A new univeralism would revolve around the various ethnic groups' shared vision of American democracy as the best possible vehicle for cultural pluralism, the need to construct interdependent relationships with neighboring ethnic and racial groups, and the common pursuit of truly equal opportunity and citizenship under U.S. law.

The Jewish American experience was the best example of the success of cultural pluralism—the ability to maintain a distinctive ethnic identity and, at the same time, to become American and middle class. When Isaiah Berlin was asked some years ago what it was, if anything, that all Jews had in common, he answered, "a sense of social unease. Nowhere do . . . all Jews feel entirely at home." Perhaps. But diaspora Jews have never felt more at home than in America. In any case, the Jewish immigrants were in the United States to stay and they early sought acculturation. Some, like the department store magnate E. A. Filene and the journalist Walter Lippman, went further and chose assimilation, giving up traditional cultural traits and Jewish identity completely. And significant numbers of second-generation Jews who were college students in the 1920s and 1930s changed their names and otherwise attempted to hide their Jewishness. But as one memoirist put it: "The idea that all immigrants should wipe out their past and become simple imitations of the dominant type is neither possible nor desirable. We cannot wipe out the past and we make ourselves ridiculous in the effort to do so."

There were certainly important changes in the immigrants' traditions, tastes, and habits, but as we have seen throughout this book, these amounted most often to adaptation and acculturation rather than to unreflective imitation or total abandonment of former customs. For example, immigrant Jews as early as 1904 became American Jews by joining in the celebration of the Fourth of July, Thanksgiving, and Labor Day while continuing to honor the Jewish High Holy Days and festivals such as Passover and Hanukkah. Other groups have done something similar with Steuben Day, Pulaski Day, the Chinese New Year, and the Japanese Chrysanthemum Festival. And African Americans readily partake of both Thanksgiving and Kwanza. In addition, many of these holidays were adapted to the new American environment. Hanukkah, for example, became a much more important festival in the United States than it had ever been in the Old World, and it also became infused with the spirit of shopping and gift-giving that marked Christmas. This was not so much an imitation on the way to assimilation as it was a way of keeping children attached to Jewish tradition by incorporating a pervasive American tradition.

Milton Gordon, in *Assimilation in American Life,* distinguished between assimilation—virtual disappearance of ethnic distinctiveness—and acculturation—accommodation to the larger society without total loss of traditional cultural traits. Jews acculturated and became proud, loyal, and contributing Americans, but they did not assimilate, they did not "melt." Jews understood, as Louis Levin, the Baltimore journalist, social worker, and educator, said in a review of Israel Zangwill's play *The Melting Pot* in 1908, that "Mr. Zangwill makes a fatal mistake." The making of a "new type of man does not require that he . . . throw upon the scrap heap all that he has stood for in the past. On the contrary, . . . maintaining intact [the best of his past is] the real contribution that he can make to the betterment of the New American."

In America, where until recently the temptation to abandon a dual allegiance was great, Jews did not throw the past upon the scrap heap. Instead, through the creative transformation of their ancient and more recent past, they constructed a religiously authenticated Jewish American ethnic identity around philanthropy, Israelism, political liberalism, and the search for social justice, as well as around anti-anti-Semitism. The choices Jews made—to be educated, civic-minded secular humanists, to be universalists, even as they

defended their particular culture and values, to be metropolitan and egalitarian—were far more important as the source of Jewish American cultural
distinctiveness than the facts of birth and inheritance. Yet Jews stayed true to
Leon Wieseltier's aphorism "What is made should be celebrated as much as
what is given, not least because it is made out of what is given." Jewish Americans maintained a powerful ethnicity at least unto the fourth generation
without either undermining individual identity or becoming overly particularistic and socially divisive. On the contrary, Jewish American individuals
were conspicuous even as they were sustained by their ethnic attachment,
and they promoted that ethnic attachment as part of a universal, mutually
enriching commonwealth of ethnic cultures, in the larger shared national
culture of American civilization. This was a result of conscious, deliberate
choice. Jewish thinkers had reflected long and hard on questions of ethnic
identity in a heterogeneous society. It was, after all, Jews such as Zangwill
and Horace Kallen who coined the terms *melting pot* and *cultural pluralism.*
And it is no accident that a disproportionate number of America's leading
historians and sociologists specializing in immigration and ethnicity have
been Jews, including Oscar Handlin, Lawrence Fuchs, Arnold Rose, Nathan
Glazer, and Milton Gordon, just to name a few.

American Jews, most of whom are at least two generations removed
and many of whom are three, four, and even five generations removed from
their immigrant origins, have become overwhelmingly American in a period
of nearly two hundred years. Yet Jewish Americans also distinguished themselves significantly from the American norm. The observation of the demographer Barry Kosmin remains apt: "The Jews are . . . too well-educated, too
liberal, too secular, too metropolitan, too wealthy, too egalitarian, too civic-
minded to be normal Americans when compared to the overall U.S. population."

Jewish Americans, using values and behavior patterns borrowed from
two different cultures constructed a religiously infused ethnic identity and
a community marked generally by liberalism and civic mindedness. The process of transforming tradition was not always smooth or completely successful, and Jewish Americans as individuals and as a group face future challenges
from within and without. But into the 1990s Jewish identity and affiliation
have continued to help satisfy the need for authentic social connection, and
continue to address and at least partially fulfill the need for meaning and
continuity.

Bibliographical Essay

PREFACE AND CHAPTER 1   PERSPECTIVES AND PROSPECTS

Most, if not all, of the major themes of the book are introduced in these opening sections; therefore I have included here some published bibliographies, as well as a sampling of works that attempt to survey the general Jewish experience in America. A good annotated guide to articles in the scholarly journals is *The Jewish Experience in America: A Historical Bibliography* (Santa Barbara, Calif.: ABC-Clio, 1983). Sharad Karkhanis, ed., *Jewish Heritage in America: An Annotated Bibliography* (New York: Garland Publishing, 1988) contains references to books as well as articles but is somewhat idiosyncratic in its selections. The best work of this kind is Jeffrey Gurock, *American Jewish History: A Bibliographical Guide* (New York: Anti-Defamation League, 1983). All, however, need to be supplemented by the indexes of journals in the field, including *American Jewish Archives*, *Jewish Social Studies*, *YIVO Annual*, *Modern Judaism*, *Studies in Contemporary Jewry*, the *Journal of American Ethnic History*, and especially the journal published by the American Jewish Historical Society: volumes 1–50 (1893–1961) are entitled *Publications of the American Jewish Historical Society;* volumes 51–67 (1961–78) are called *American Jewish Historical Quarterly;* and issues since 1978 are published under the title *American Jewish History*.

The best one-volume general history is Howard Sachar, *A History of the Jews in America* (New York: Knopf, 1992), but it lacks an overarching thesis and is flawed by a number of factual errors. Undoubtedly the most comprehensive account of the Jewish people in the United States written by a single author are the four volumes by Jacob Rader Marcus, *United States Jewry*,

1776–1985 (Detroit: Wayne State University Press, 1989–93). These books help explain and illustrate several significant Jewish themes: the dominance of the laity over the clergy; the emphasis on this-worldliness and rationalism over mysticism and emotion; the modifications in religious belief and observance; the disappearance of the synagogue-centered community; and the general secularization of institutions. Encyclopedic in scope, the four volumes, constituting more than 2,500 pages, 82 chapters, and uncountable subheadings in chapters, are not quite designed for reading from cover to cover. But the texts, together with their 270 pages of bibliography and notes, are very valuable reference tools. Much more readable is the five-volume *Jewish People in America,* ed. Henry Feingold (Baltimore: Johns Hopkins University Press, 1992).

The *American Jewish Year Book,* published by the American Jewish Committee from early in the twentieth century to the present, is critical for demographic data, catalogs of communal and religious organizations, and statistics on Jewish participation in national and local politics.

CHAPTER 2   THE THRESHOLD OF LIBERATION, 1654–1820

Published primary sources for the study of the Jewish experience in America during the seventeenth and eighteenth centuries can be found in Morris U. Schappes, *A Documentary History of the Jews of the United States, 1654–1875,* 3d ed. (New York: Schocken, 1971); and Jacob Rader Marcus, *American Jewry: Documents—Eighteenth Century* (Cincinnati: Hebrew Union College Press, 1959). For the late eighteenth and early nineteenth centuries, see Jacob Rader Marcus, "The Jew and the American Revolution: A Bicentennial Documentary," *American Jewish Archives* 27 (1975): 103–257; and Marcus, *Memoirs of American Jews, 1775–1865,* vol. 1 (Philadelphia: Jewish Publication Society of America, 1955). See also the collection of documents assembled by Joseph L. Blau and Salo W. Baron, *The Jews of the United States, 1790–1840: A Documentary History,* 3 vols. (New York: Columbia University Press, 1963), which is enhanced by substantive introductory notes and annotations.

No student of early American Jewish history can neglect Jacob R. Marcus's three-volume *Colonial American Jew* (Detroit: Wayne State University Press, 1970), or his two-volume *Early American Jewry* (Philadelphia: Jewish Publication Society of America, 1951–55). A concise history of the Jewish people in America from 1654 to 1820, with an excellent bibliography, is Eli Faber, *A Time for Planting: The First Migration* (Baltimore: Johns Hopkins University Press, 1992), which is volume 1 of the five-volume *Jewish People in*

America, ed. Henry Feingold. There are a number of good studies of local communities including: Edwin Wolf and Maxwell Whiteman, *The History of the Jews of Philadelphia from Colonial Times to the Age of Jackson* (Philadelphia: Jewish Publication Society of America, 1957); Ira Rosenwaike, "The Jews of Baltimore to 1810," *American Jewish Historical Quarterly* 64 (1974–75): 291–320; and Rosenwaike, "The Jews of Baltimore: 1810–1820," *American Jewish Historical Quarterly* 67 (1977–78): 101–24; Hyman Grinstein, *The Rise of the Jewish Community of New York, 1654–1860* (Philadelphia: Jewish Publication Society of America, 1945); and David De Sola Pool, *An Old Faith in the New World: Portrait of Shearith Israel, 1654–1954* (New York: Columbia University Press, 1955); Joshua Trachtenberg, *Consider the Years:The Story of the Jewish Community of Easton, 1752–1942* (Easton, Pa.: Centennial Committee of Temple Beth Sholom, 1944).

Other useful secondary sources are Stanley F. Chyet, *Lopez of Newport: Colonial American Merchant Prince* (Detroit: Wayne State University Press, 1970); and David Brion Davis, *Slavery and Human Progress* (New York: Oxford University Press, 1984), both of which include material on Jews and the slave trade; Jonathan Sarna, *Jacksonian Jew: The Two Worlds of Mordecai Noah* (New York: Holmes and Meier, 1981); Thomas Kessner, "Gershom Mendes Seixas: His Religious 'Calling,' Outlook and Competence," *American Jewish Historical Quarterly* 58 (1968–69): 445–71; Leo Hershkowitz, "Some Aspects of the New York Jewish Merchant and Community, 1654–1820," *American Jewish Historical Quarterly* 66 (1976–77): 10–34; Samuel Rezneck, *Unrecognized Patriots: The Jews in the American Revolution* (Westport, Conn.: Greenwood Press, 1975).

For developments after the Revolution, see Jonathan Sarna, "The Impact of the American Revolution on American Jews," in his *American Jewish Experience* (New York: Holmes and Meier, 1986), 20–28; and Stanley Chyet, "The Political Rights of the Jews in the United States: 1776–1840," in Abraham Karp, ed., *Critical Studies in American Jewish History: Selected Articles from American Jewish Archives* (Cincinnati: American Jewish Archives and KTAV, 1971), 2:27–88.

CHAPTER 3   THE AGE OF REFORM, 1820–1880

Although somewhat dated, the scholarship of Rudolf Glanz remains indispensable for the German Jewish experience in America. His important works include *Jews in Relation to the Cultural Milieu of Germans in America* (New York: Marstin Press, 1947); *The German Jews in America* (Cincinnati: Hebrew Union

College Press, 1969); *Studies in Judaica Americana* (New York: KTAV, 1970); *The Jewish Woman in America*, 2 vols. (New York: KTAV, 1976); "The German-Jewish Mass Emigration, 1820–1880," *American Jewish Archives* 22 (April 1970): 49–66; and "The Spread of Jewish Communities through America before the Civil War," *YIVO Annual* 15 (1974): 7–45.

The most comprehensive works on the German Jews in America are Avraham Barkai, *German-Jewish Immigration to the United States, 1820–1914* (New York: Holmes and Meier, 1991); and Naomi Cohen, *Encounter with Emancipation: German Jews in the United States, 1830–1914* (Philadelphia: Jewish Publication Society of America, 1984). For a more recent and somewhat different perspective see Hasia Diner, *A Time for Gathering: The Second Migration* (Baltimore: Johns Hopkins University Press, 1992), volume 2 of *The Jewish People in America,* ed. Henry Feingold, which argues that the German Jewish and East European Jewish experiences of uprooting and transplanting were more similar than different.

The general consensus, however, is that the Germans experienced an exceptional economic and social mobility via merchandising and finance. See Henry Feingold, "The Success Story of German Jews in America," in his *Midrash on American Jewish History* (Albany: State University of New York Press, 1982), 28; Lawrence Bachmann, "Julius Rosenwald," *American Jewish Historical Quarterly* 66:1 (September 1976): 89–105; Vincent Carosso, "A Financial Elite: New York's German-Jewish Investment Bankers," *American Jewish Historical Quarterly* 66:1 (September 1976): 67–88; Don Coerver and Linda Hall, "Neiman-Marcus: Innovators in Fashion and Merchandising," *American Jewish Historical Quarterly* 66:1 (September 1976): 123–36; Saul Engelbourg, "Edward A. Filene: Merchant, Civic Leader, and Jew," *American Jewish Historical Quarterly* 66:1 (September 1976): 106–22; Robert A. Burlison, "Samuel Fox, Merchant and Civic Leader in San Diego, 1886–1939," *Journal of San Diego History* 26:1 (Winter 1980): 1–10; Tom Mahoney, *The Great Merchants: The Stories of Twenty Famous Retail Operations and the People Who Made Them Great* (New York: Harper, 1955); Stephen G. Mostov, "A 'Jerusalem' on the Ohio: The Social and Economic History of Cincinnati's Jewish Community, 1840–1875" (Ph.D. diss., Brandeis University, 1981); Clyde Griffen, "Making It in America: Social Mobility in Nineteenth-Century Poughkeepsie," *New York History* 51:4 (October 1970): 479–99.

For the general economic context within which the German Jews operated, see Douglass North, *The Economic Growth of the United States, 1790–1860* (New York: Norton, 1966); and George Rogers Taylor, *The Transportation Revolution, 1815–1860* (New York: Holt, Rinehart, and Winston, 1964). Also useful as case studies of relative rates of mobility for different groups are Stephen Thernstrom, "Religion and Occupational Mobility in Boston, 1880–1963," in W. O. Ayedelotte et al., eds., *The Dimensions of Quantitative Research* (Princeton: Princeton University Press, 1972); and Howard Chudacoff, *Mobile Americans: Residential and Social Mobility in Omaha, 1880–1920* (New York: Oxford University Press, 1972).

Mobility for Jews was very real but, nonetheless, hard won, as the following works demonstrate: David Gerber, "Cutting Out Shylock: Elite Anti-Semitism and the Quest for Moral Order in the Mid-Nineteenth Century American Market Place," *Journal of American History* 69 (December 1982): 615–37; as well as his "Anti-Semitism and Jewish-Gentile Relations," in Gerber, ed., *Anti-Semitism in American History* (Urbana: University of Illinois Press, 1986), 3–30; Stephen G. Mostov, "Dun and Bradstreet Reports as a Source of Jewish Economic History: Cincinnati, 1840–1875," *American Jewish History* 72 (March 1983): 333–53. John Higham's *Strangers in the Land: Patterns of American Nativism, 1865–1925*, 2d ed. (New York: Atheneum, 1966), remains a very useful classic in the field; as does "Social Discrimination against Jews, 1830–1930," in his *Send These to Me: Jews and Other Immigrants in Urban America* (New York: Atheneum, 1975), 138–73.

For Jewish life and enterprise in the South and West, there are a number of excellent studies including Steven Hertzberg, *Strangers within the Gate City: The Jews of Atlanta, 1845–1915* (Philadelphia: Jewish Publication Society of America, 1978); Nathan Kaganoff and Melvin Urofsky, eds., *Turn to the South: Essays on Southern Jewry* (Charlottesville: University Press of Virginia, 1979); Marc Raphael, *Jews and Judaism in a Midwestern Community: Columbus, Ohio, 1840–1975* (Columbus: Ohio Historical Society, 1979); Mitchell Gelfand, "Progress and Prosperity: Jewish Social Mobility in Los Angeles in the Booming Eighties," *American Jewish History* 68:4 (June 1979): 408–33; Peter Decker, "Jewish Merchants in San Francisco: Social Mobility on the Urban Frontier," *American Jewish History* 68:4 (June 1979): 396–407.

For important developments in Jewish religious life in the nineteenth century, see Michael A. Meyer, *Response to Modernity: A History of the Reform Movement in Judaism* (New York: Oxford University Press, 1988), which contains good materials and insights on the American as well as the European scene. On early "reforms" within Judaism generally, as well as for Reform Judaism, the following are well worth reading: Alan Silverstein, *Alternatives to Assimilation: The Response of Reform Judaism to American Culture, 1840–1930* (Waltham, Mass.: Brandeis University Press, 1994); Robert Liberles, "Conflict over Reforms: The Case of the Congregation Beth Elohim, Charleston,

South Carolina," in Jack Wertheimer, ed., *The American Synagogue: A Sanctuary Transformed* (New York: Cambridge University Press, 1987), 274–96; Leon Jick, *The Americanization of the Synagogue* (Hanover, N.H.: University Press of New England, 1976); and Sefton D. Temkin, *Isaac Mayer Wise: Shaping American Judaism* (Albany: State University of New York Press, 1992), for the best biography of the most important rabbinical figure in early American history. See also Wise's own works, *Reminiscences*, ed. and trans. David Philipson (New York: Central Synagogue of New York, 1945); and Wise, *Selected Writings*, ed. David Philipson and Louis Grossman (New York: Arno Press, 1969).

CHAPTER 4   THE EASTERN EUROPEAN CULTURAL HERITAGE AND MASS MIGRATION TO THE UNITED STATES, 1880–1920

There are several well-edited anthologies of contemporary writings on Jewish life in nineteenth-century Eastern Europe including Lucy Davidowicz, ed., *The Golden Tradition: Jewish Life and Thought in Eastern Europe* (Boston: Beacon Press, 1967); Jack Kugelmass and Jonathan Boyarin, eds., *From a Ruined Garden* (New York: Schocken Books, 1983); and David Roskies and Diane Roskies, eds., *The Shtetl Book* (New York: KTAV, 1975). Works of history especially relevant to the period in which the future émigrés to the United States were growing up include: Robert J. Brym, *The Jews of Moscow, Kiev, and Minsk: Identity, Antisemitism, Emigration* (New York: New York University Press, 1994); Simon Dubnow, *History of the Jews in Russia and Poland*, vol. 2, trans. I. Friedlander (Philadelphia: Jewish Publication Society of America, 1916–20); Jonathan Frankel, *Prophecy and Politics: Socialism, Nationalism, and the Russian Jew, 1862–1917* (Cambridge: Cambridge University Press, 1981); Ezra Mendelsohn, *Class Struggle in the Pale* (Cambridge: Cambridge University Press, 1970); Elias Tcherikower, *The Early Jewish Labor Movement in the United States*, trans. A. Antonovsky (New York: YIVO, 1961); Joshua Rothenberg, "Demythologizing the Shtetl," *Midstream* 27 (March 1981): 25–31; and Michael Stanislawski, *Tsar Nicholas I and the Jews: The Transformation of Jewish Society in Russia, 1825–1855* (Philadelphia: Jewish Publication Society of America, 1983).

For an overview of general immigration, Philip Taylor, *The Distant Magnet: European Emigration to the United States* (New York: Harper and Row, 1971); and Maldwyn Jones, *American Immigration* (Chicago: University of Chicago Press, 1960), are best. Oscar Handlin's classic, *The Uprooted* (Boston: Little, Brown, 1951), is still worth reading for immigrant motivation and the social and psychological consequences of dislocation; but John Bodnar's more recent *The Transplanted* (Bloomington: Indiana University Press, 1985), is more persuasive, particularly on who came to America and why, and on the resilience of family, tradition, and culture. On these themes see also Milton Gordon, *Assimilation in American Life* (New York: Oxford University Press, 1964); and Victor R. Greene, *American Immigrant Leaders, 1800–1910: Marginality and Identity* (Baltimore: Johns Hopkins University Press, 1987).

For detailed analysis and interpretation of Jewish immigration, the following are indispensable: Liebmann Hersch, "International Migration of the Jews," in Imre Ferencezi and Walter F. Wilcox, eds., *International Migrations* (New York: National Bureau of Economic Research, 1931), 2: 471–520; Samuel Joseph, *Jewish Immigration to the United States from 1881 to 1910* (New York: Arno Press, 1969); Simon Kuznets, "Immigration of Russian Jews to the United States: Background and Structure," *Perspectives in American History* 9 (1975): 35–124. Also useful are Stephen M. Berk, *Year of Crisis, Year of Hope: Russian Jewry and the Pogroms of 1881–1882* (Westport, Conn.: Greenwood Press, 1985); Jonathan Frankel, "The Crisis of 1881–1882 as a Turning Point in Modern Jewish History," in David Berger, ed., *The Legacy of Jewish Migration* (New York: Brooklyn College Press, 1983), 9–22.

Early reactions of German Jews in America to the influx of Eastern European Jews are dealt with in Gary Dean Best, *To Free a People: American Jewish Leaders and the Jewish Problem in Eastern Europe, 1880–1914* (Westport, Conn.: Greenwood Press, 1982); and in his excellent analysis "Jacob Schiff's Galveston Movement: An Experiment in Immigrant Deflection, 1907–1914," *American Jewish Archives* 30:1 (April 1978): 43–78; also useful is Bernard Marinbach, *Galveston: Ellis Island of the West* (Albany: State University of New York Press, 1983).

For Jewish immigrants "diverted" to agriculture, as well as for the very small number who consciously chose farming, see Joseph Brandes, *Immigrants to Freedom: Jewish Communities in Rural New Jersey since 1882* (Philadelphia: University of Pennsylvania Press, 1971), an extensive study of rural immigrant Jewish colonies in New Jersey, of which Alliance was the first in 1882, followed by several others including the more famous Woodbine. The book focuses on the appeal and general "failure" of Jewish agrarianism. Kenneth Kann, *Comrades and Chicken Farmers* (Ithaca, N.Y.: Cornell University Press, 1992); and Uri Herscher, *Jewish Agricultural Utopias in America, 1880–1910* (Detroit: Wayne State University Press, 1981) deal more explicitly with Jewish farming that was based in social ideology. Other useful works include Abraham Lavender, *Jewish Farmers in the Catskills* (Gainesville: University of

Florida Press, 1995); Gabriel Davidson, "The Jew in Agriculture in the United States," *American Jewish Year Book* (1935): 99–134; David Gold, "Jewish Agriculture in the Catskills, 1900–1920," *Agricultural History* 55 (January 1981): 31–49; Helene Gerard, "Yankees in Yarmulkes: Small-Town Jewish Life in Eastern Long Island," *American Jewish Archives* 38 (April 1986): 23–56.

Other dimensions of the Jewish immigration experience are intelligently explored in Eli Lederhandler, "Jewish Immigration to America and Revisionist Historiography: A Decade of New Perspectives," *YIVO Annual* 18 (1983): 391–410; John Higham, *Send These to Me: Jews and Other Immigrants in Urban America* (New York: Atheneum, 1975); Aryeh Goren and Yosef Wenkert, eds., *The Jewish Mass Immigration to the United States and the Growth of American Jewry: A Reader* (Jerusalem: Hebrew University Press, 1976); Joseph Kissman, "The Immigration of Rumanian Jews up to 1914," *YIVO Annual of Jewish Social Science* 2–3 (1947–48): 160–179; Pamela Nadell, "The Journey to America by Steam: The Jews of Eastern Europe in Transition," *American Jewish History* 71 (December 1981): 269–84; August C. Bolino, *The Ellis Island Source Book* (Washington, D.C.: Kensington Historical Press, 1985); Alan Kraut, "Silent Strangers: Germs, Genes, and Nativism," *American Jewish History* 76 (December 1986): 142–58; Jonathan Sarna, "The Myth of No Return: Jewish Return Migration to Eastern Europe, 1881–1914," *American Jewish History* 71 (December 1981): 265–67; and Zosa Szajkowski, "Sufferings of Jewish Emigrants to America in Transit through Germany," *Jewish Social Studies* 39 (Winter–Spring 1977): 105–16.

CHAPTER 5   TRANSPLANTED IN AMERICA: THE URBAN EXPERIENCE

For an overview of late-nineteenth- and early-twentieth-century American history, see Nell Irvin Painter, *Standing at Armageddon: The United States, 1877–1919* (New York: Norton, 1987); and the older but still useful Robert Wiebe, *The Search for Order, 1877–1920* (New York: Hill and Wang, 1967). For the reform context Robert M. Crunden, *Ministers of Reform: The Progressive's Achievement in American Civilization, 1889–1920* (New York: Basic Books, 1982), is best but should be supplemented with Allen F. Davis, *Spearheads for Reform: Social Settlements and the Progressive Movement* (New York: Oxford University Press, 1967).

The most important repository of primary materials for this chapter (and others) was the American Jewish Historical Society Library on the campus of Brandeis University in Waltham, Massachusetts. Particularly useful were the papers of leading figures and witnesses such as Louis Marshall,

Stephen Wise, and Alexander Harkavy. In addition, the Baron De Hirsch Fund papers and the letters and documents in the Galveston Immigration Plan collection proved to be a rich mine of both institutional and social history.

The archives at YIVO (the Max Weinreich Center for the Study of Judaism) in New York City were indispensable. The collections of letters, clippings, and autobiographical essays housed there are of paramount value. The New York Public Library, Jewish Division, the Columbia University Oral History Collection, and the William E. Weiner Oral History Library at the American Jewish Committee also hold important letters, notes, diaries, and interviews, including materials for Lillian Wald, Adolph Held, Isaac Berkson, and Samuel Gompers. The libraries of the Hebrew Union College–Jewish Institute of Religion were likewise useful, particularly for papers and letters of Judah Magnes and a small number for Henrietta Szold.

The most important newspaper for the East European immigrant experience and its expression is Abraham Cahan's *Forverts* or *Jewish Daily Forward*, an incomparable reservoir of contemporary opinion, reportage, and social history; the *Tageblatt* and the *Morgen Journal* are also useful, especially for the more traditional religious perspective. English-language papers containing important material and editorial commentary, particularly for the turn of the century and particularly for the more established Jewish community, are the *American Hebrew* and the *American Israelite*.

U.S. Government documents that were most useful and which are most accessible to readers include the *Report of the Industrial Commission* done between 1900 and 1902, and the *Report of the Immigration Commission*, 1907–11. The United States Census, especially the eleventh through thirteenth (1890, 1900, 1910), also proved valuable.

Among the best-written and most useful memoirs for students of the American Jewish experience in the years from 1880 to 1920 are Mary Antin, *From Plotsk to Boston* (Boston: W. B. Clarke, 1899); and Antin, *The Promised Land* (Boston: Houghton Mifflin Co., 1912), proud expressions of Americanization combined with moments of lucid sensitivity in regard to Jewish immigrants. Miriam Blaustein, ed., *Memoirs of David Blaustein* (New York: McBride, Nast, 1913), is especially good for the reform impulse of the 1890s and for the Educational Alliance. Louis Borgenicht, *The Happiest Man* (New York: G. P. Putnam, 1942), is insightful on economic mobility and the entrepreneurial mentality and valuable for information on garment manufacturers. Abraham Cahan, *Bleter fun mayn leben,* 5 vols. (New York: Forward Association, 1926–31), like the *Forverts* is a gold mine of social and political detail. And for readers without facility in Yiddish, *The Education of Abraham Cahan*

(Philadelphia: Jewish Publication Society of America, 1969), trans. Leon Stein et al. from *Bleter,* vols. 1 and 2, is at least a beginning.

One of the most evocative memoirs of East Side life is Samuel Chotzinoff, *A Lost Paradise: Early Reminiscences* (New York: Knopf, 1955), but many others ought to be read as well. These include Morris R. Cohen, *A Dreamer's Journey* (Boston: Beacon Press, 1949), for the 1890s as well as for life at the City College of New York; Rose Cohen, *Out of the Shadow* (New York: G. H. Doran, 1918); and Theresa Malkiel, *Diary of a Shirtwaist Striker* (New York: Cooperative Press, 1910), for women and for trade union militancy; Morris Hillquit, *Loose Leaves from a Busy Life* (New York: Da Capo Press, 1971), for the socialist milieu; Marcus Ravage, *An American in the Making: The Life Story of an Immigrant* (New York: Harper, 1917); and Alfred Kazin, *A Walker in the City* (New York: Harcourt, Brace and Co., 1951), for serious, often moving reflections on the struggles of acculturation. Harry Roskolenko, *The Time That Was Then* (New York: Dial Press, 1971), is both informative and entertaining; Lillian Wald, *The House on Henry Street* (New York: H. Holt, 1915), is useful for Progressivism and relations between German Jews and East European Jews; Moses Weinberger, *People Walk on Their Heads: Jews and Judaism in New York,* trans. and ed. Jonathan Sarna (New York: Holmes and Meier, 1982), was written in the 1880s and remains a valuable source for early Orthodox reaction to religious life in secular New York. Anzia Yezierska, *Red Ribbon on a White Horse* (New York: Persea Books, 1978), is a poignant portrait of an immigrant woman's search for identity and artistic expression.

Among the astute gentile observers of the immigrant scene is Hutchins Hapgood, whose sensitive writings for the *New York Tribune* about the Jewish East Side are anthologized in *The Spirit of the Ghetto* (New York: Schocken Books, 1966). Portions of Lincoln Steffens, *The Autobiography* (New York: Harcourt Brace and Co., 1931), are insightful about Jewish life; and the same is true for Jacob Riis, *How the Other Half Lives* (New York: Dover, 1971), though Riis is less sympathetic.

Novels that can be read for literary pleasure as well as for their historical and "sociological" value include Abraham Cahan, *The Rise of David Levinsky,* and *Yekl: A Tale of the New York Ghetto;* Mike Gold, *Jews without Money;* Samuel Ornitz, *Haunch, Paunch, and Jowl;* and Anzia Yezierska's *Bread Givers* and *Hungry Hearts* (New York: Arno, 1975).

The dynamics of adjustment, acculturation, and mobility in the immigrant generation are dealt with in Gerald Sorin, *A Time for Building: The Third Migration, 1880–1920* (Baltimore: Johns Hopkins University Press, 1992), volume 3 of *The Jewish People in America,* ed. Henry Feingold; Thomas Kessner, *The Golden Door: Italian and Jewish Immigrant Mobility in New York City, 1880–1915* (New York: Oxford University Press, 1977); Jenna W. Joselit, *Our Gang: Jewish Crime and the New York Jewish Community, 1900–1940* (Bloomington: Indiana University Press, 1983); Albert Fried, *The Rise of the Jewish Gangster in America,* rev. ed. (New York: Columbia University Press, 1995); Hannah Kliger, "Traditions of Grass-Roots Organization and Leadership: The Continuity of Landsmanshaftn in New York," *American Jewish History* 76:1 (September 1986): 25–39; Daniel Soyer, "Between Two Worlds: The Jewish Landsmanshaftn and Immigrant Identity," *American Jewish History* 76:1 (September 1986) 5–24; Deborah Dwork, "Health Conditions of Immigrant Jews on the Lower East Side of New York, 1880–1914," *Medical History* 25:1 (January 1981): 1–40; Jenna Weissman Joselit, *The Wonders of America: Reinventing Jewish Culture, 1880–1950* (New York: Hill and Wang, 1994); and Andrew Heinze, *Adapting to Abundance: Jewish Immigrants, Mass Consumption, and the Search for American Identity* (New York: Columbia University Press, 1990).

Valuable studies on the effects of dislocation and transplantation which focus primarily on women include Charlotte Baum et al., *The Jewish Woman in America* (New York: Dial Press, 1976); Sydney Stahl Weinberg, *World of Our Mothers* (Chapel Hill: University of North Carolina Press, 1988); Ari Lloyd Fridkis, "Desertion in the American Jewish Immigrant Family," *American Jewish History* 71 (December 1981): 285–99; and Reena Friedman, "'Send Me My Husband Who Is in New York City': Husband Desertion in the American Jewish Immigrant Community, 1900–1926," *Jewish Social Studies* 44 (Winter 1982): 1–18.

For studies of New York, Moses Rischin, *The Promised City: New York's Jews, 1870–1914* (New York: Corinth Books, 1964), is a comprehensive, detailed work of meticulous scholarship and remains the place to begin. For a recent reappraisal by scholars, see *American Jewish History* 73 (December 1985). Irving Howe's *World of Our Fathers* (New York: Harcourt Brace Jovanovich, 1976), is a beautifully written, evocative portrayal, particularly good on socialism and the Yiddishists. Other works important for understanding the New York Jewish experience include Arthur Goren, *New York Jews and the Quest for Community: The Kehillah Experiment, 1908–1922* (New York: Columbia University Press, 1970), an extraordinarily thorough book and one of the best on American Jewish history; Jeffery Gurock, *When Harlem Was Jewish, 1870–1930* (New York: Columbia University Press, 1979); and Deborah Dash Moore, *At Home in America: Second Generation Jews in New York* (New York: Columbia University Press, 1981).

The other major Jewish cities in this era, Chicago, Philadelphia, Boston, and Baltimore, are still without satisfactory analytical histories. In the meantime, the following are helpful: Irving Cutler, *The Jews of Chicago: From Shtetl to Suburb* (Urbana: University of Illinois Press, 1995); Edward Mazur, "Jewish Chicago: From Diversity to Community," in Melvin G. Holli and Peter d'A. Jones, eds., *The Ethnic Frontier: Essays in the History of Group Survival in Chicago and the Midwest* (Grand Rapids, Mich.: William B. Eerdmans, 1977), 272–74; Rivka Lissak, "Myth and Reality: The Pattern of Relationships between the Hull House Circle and the 'New Immigrants' in Chicago's West Side, 1890–1919," *Journal of American Ethnic History* 2 (Spring 1983): 25–30; John D. Buenker, "Dynamics of Chicago Ethnic Politics, 1900–1930," *Journal of the Illinois State Historical Society* 67 (April 1974): 175–99.

Many essays in Murray Friedman, ed., *Jewish Life in Philadelphia, 1830–1940* (Philadelphia: Jewish Publication Society of America, 1983), are good for the City of Brotherly Love, especially E. Digby Baltzell, Allen Glickman, and Jacquelyn Litt, "The Jewish Communities of Philadelphia and Boston: A Tale of Two Cities," 290–313; Edwin Wolf, "The German-Jewish Influence in Philadelphia's Jewish Charities," 125–42; Evelyn Bodek, "'Making Do': Jewish Women and Philanthropy," 143–62; Philip Rosen, "German Jews vs. Russian Jews in Philadelphia Philanthropy," 198–212; Maxwell Whiteman, "'The Philadelphia Group,'" 163–78; Robert Tabak, "Orthodox Judaism in Transition," 48–63; Maxwell Whiteman, "The Fiddlers Rejected: Jewish Immigrant Expression in Philadelphia," 80–98. Also see Maxwell Whiteman, "Philadelphia's Jewish Neighborhoods," in Allen F. Davis and Mark Haller, eds., *The Peoples of Philadelphia* (Philadelphia: Temple University Press, 1973), 231–54; Caroline Golab, "The Immigrant and the City: Poles, Italians, and Jews in Philadelphia, 1870–1920," in Davis and Haller, *Peoples of Philadelphia*, pp. 203–30; Maxwell Whiteman, "Western Impact on East European Jews: A Philadelphia Fragment," in Randall Miller and Thomas Marzik, eds., *Immigrants and Religion in Urban America* (Philadelphia: Temple University Press, 1977), 117–37.

For Boston see Isaac M. Fein, *Boston—Where It All Began: An Historical Perspective of the Boston Jewish Community* (Boston: Boston Jewish Bicentennial Commission, 1976); Arnold Wieder, *The Early Jewish Community of Boston's North End* (Waltham, Mass.: Brandeis University Press, 1962); Jacob Neusner, "The Impact of Immigration and Philanthropy upon the Boston Jewish Community, 1880–1914," *Publications of the American Jewish Historical Society* 42:2 (December 1956): 71–85. And for Baltimore, as for Boston, there is little in the modern period, but see the works of Ira Rosenwaike cited for chapter 3; and Isaac Fein, *The Making of an American Jewish Community: The History of Baltimore Jewry from 1773 to 1920* (Philadelphia: Jewish Publication Society of America, 1971).

For Yiddish theater and literary expression generally, see Howe, *World of Our Fathers*; and Ronald Sanders, *Reflections in a Teapot* (New York: Harper, 1972), which are very strong in the area of culture; Faina Burko, "The American Yiddish Theater and Its Audience before World War I," in David Berger, ed., *The Legacy of Jewish Migration* (New York: Brooklyn College Press, 1983), 85–96; Henry Feingold, "The Yiddish Theater and the Genesis of Cultural Consumerism," in his *Midrash on American Jewish History* (Albany: State University of New York Press, 1982), 83–93; Fred Somkin, "Zion's Harp by the East River: Jewish-American Popular Songs in Columbus's Golden Land, 1890–1914," *Perspectives in American History* 2 (1985): 183–220; Ruth R. Wisse, "Di Yunge: Immigrants or Exiles?" *Prooftexts: A Journal of Jewish Literary History* 1:1 (January 1981): 43–61; Mordechai Soltes, *The Yiddish Press: An Americanizing Agency* (New York: Arno Press, 1969); Milton Doroshkin, *Yiddish in America* (Madison, N.J.: Fairleigh Dickinson University Press, 1969).

Chapter 6   Transplanted in America: Smaller Cities and Towns

Three important articles that forecast new research directions are Ewa Morawska, "A Replica of the 'Old Country' Relationship in the Ethnic Niche: East European Jews and Gentiles in Small Town Western Pennsylvania, 1880s–1930s," *American Jewish History* 77 (September 1987): 27–86; Lee Shai Weissbach, "The Jewish Communities of the United States on the Eve of Mass Migration: Some Comments on Geography and Bibliography," *American Jewish History* 78:1 (September 1988): 79–108; and Joel Perlmann, "Beyond New York: The Occupations of Russian Jewish Immigrants in Providence, Rhode Island, and in Other Small Jewish Communities, 1900–1915," *American Jewish History* 72:3 (March 1983): 369–94.

For concise and balanced views of the relationship between German Jews and Eastern European Jews, see Zosa Szajkowski, "The *Yahudi* and the Immigrant: A Reappraisal," *American Jewish Historical Quarterly* 63 (September 1973): 13–44; and Gerald Sorin, "Mutual Contempt, Mutual Benefit: The Strained Encounter between German and Eastern European Jews in the United States," *American Jewish History* 81 (Autumn 1993): 34–59. See also S. P. Rudens, "A Half Century of Community Service: The Story of the New York Educational Alliance," *American Jewish Year Book* (1944–45): 73–86; and June Sochen, *Consecrate Every Day: The Public Lives of Jewish American Women, 1880–1980* (Albany: State University of New York Press, 1981).

Among the most useful analytical community and regional studies are William Toll, *The Making of an Ethnic Middle-Class: Portland Jewry over Four Generations* (Albany: State University of New York Press, 1982); Marc Raphael, *Jews and Judaism in a Midwestern Community: Columbus, Ohio, 1840–1975* (Columbus: Ohio Historical Society, 1979); Steven Hertzberg, *Strangers within the Gate City: The Jews of Atlanta, 1845–1915* (Philadelphia: Jewish Publication Society of America, 1978); Stuart Rosenberg, *The Jews of Rochester, 1843–1925* (New York: Columbia University Press, 1954); Selig Adler and Thomas E. Connolly, *From Aarat to Suburbia: The History of the Jewish Community of Buffalo* (Philadelphia: Jewish Publication Society of America, 1960); Robert Rockaway, *The Jews of Detroit: From the Beginning, 1762–1914* (Detroit: Wayne State University Press, 1986); Judith Endelman, *The Jewish Community of Indianapolis, 1849 to the Present* (Bloomington: Indiana University Press, 1984); Nathan Kaganoff and Melvin Urofsky, eds., *Turn to the South: Essays on Southern Jewry* (Charlottesville: University Press of Virginia, 1979); Leonard Dinnerstein and Mary Dale Palsson, eds., *Jews in the South* (Baton Rouge: Louisiana State University Press, 1973); James A. Gelin, *Starting Over: The Formation of the Jewish Community of Springfield, Massachusetts, 1840–1905* (Lanham, Md.: University Press of America, 1984); Moses Rischin, "Introduction: The Jews of the West," *American Jewish History* 68 (June 1979): 389–95, as well as several other articles in that issue; Stephen J. Whitfield, "Commercial Passions: The Southern Jew as Businessman," *American Jewish History* 71 (March 1982): 342–57; and Sandra Hartwell Becker and Ralph L. Pearson, "The Jewish Community of Hartford, Connecticut, 1880–1929," *American Jewish Archives* 31 (November 1979): 184–214. See also Peter I. Rose, *Strangers in Their Midst: A Sociological Study of Small-Town Jews and Their Neighbors* (Ithaca, N.Y.: Cornell University Press, 1959).

Other works that are chronicles more than they are histories but which can be used with profit are Lloyd Gartner, *History of the Jews of Cleveland* (Cleveland: Western Reserve Historical Society, 1987); Lloyd Gartner and Louis Swichow, *History of the Jews of Milwaukee* (Philadelphia: Jewish Publication Society of America, 1963); Max Vorspan and Lloyd Gartner, *History of the Jews of Los Angeles* (San Marino, Calif.: Huntington Library, 1970); Steven Lowenstein, *The Jews of Oregon, 1850–1950* (Portland: Jewish Historical Society of Oregon, 1987); Bernard Shuman, *A History of the Sioux City Jewish Community, 1869 to 1969* (Sioux City, Iowa: Bostein Creative Printing, 1969); Floyd S. Fierman, *Guts and Ruts: The Jewish Pioneer on the Trail in the American Southwest* (New York: KTAV, 1985); Allen duPont Breck, *The Centennial History of the Jews of Colorado, 1859–1959* (Denver: Hirschfield Press, 1961);

Joseph D. Schultz, ed., *Mid-America's Promise: A Profile of Kansas City Jewry* (Kansas City: Jewish Community Foundation of Greater Kansas City, 1982).

On Hollywood see Lary May and Elaine Tyler May, "Why Jewish Movie Moguls: An Exploration in American Culture," *American Jewish History* 72:1 (September 1982): 6–25; Neal Gabler, *An Empire of Their Own: How the Jews Invented Hollywood* (New York: Crown Publishers, 1988). The Jewish Catskills still awaits a good social history; in the meantime see Stefan Kanfer, *A Summer World* (New York: Farrar, Straus and Giroux, 1989); Betsy Blackman, "Going to the Mountains: A Social History," in Alf Evers et al., eds., *Resorts of the Catskills* (New York: St. Martin's Press, 1979).

CHAPTER 7   JEWISH LABOR, AMERICAN POLITICS

The archives at YIVO (the Max Weinreich Center for the Study of Judaism) in New York City hold collections of letters, clippings, and autobiographical essays, and an invaluable set of interviews with labor activists in the 1960s, most in Yiddish. The Tamiment Institute Library at New York University has an outstanding labor collection, including the papers, letters, notebooks, and typescripts of several important figures in the trade union and socialist movements. Here also is the Oral History of the American Left, interviews with radicals, some in Yiddish, conducted in the 1960s through the 1980s. For Yiddish readers, Abraham Cahan's *Bleter fun mayn leben,* 5 vols. (New York: Forward Association, 1926–31), is a treasure chest, as is the socialist *Jewish Daily Forward.* The views of the communists can be found in the *Morgen Freiheit* and those of the anarchists in the *Freie Arbeiter Shtime.*

Elias Tcherikower, *The Early Jewish Labor Movement in the United States,* trans. A. Antonovsky (New York: YIVO, 1961), is essential. Also useful are several articles in *YIVO Annual* 16 (1976); Irwin Yellowitz, *Labor and the Progressive Movement in New York State, 1897–1916* (Ithaca, N.Y.: Cornell University Press, 1965); and Gerald Sorin, *The Prophetic Minority: American Jewish Immigrant Radicals, 1880–1920* (Bloomington: Indiana University Press, 1985), which makes an argument connecting Jewishness and labor radicalism. The best concise essay remains Will Herberg, "The American Jewish Labor Movement," *American Jewish Year Book* (1952): 3–74.

On socialism see Howard H. Quint, *The Forging of American Socialism* (Indianapolis: Bobbs-Merrill, 1953); David Shannon, *The Socialist Party of America* (Chicago: University of Chicago Press, 1955); Charles Leinenweber, "The Class and Ethnic Bases of New York City Socialism, 1904–1915," *Labor History* 22:1 (Winter 1981): 43; Mary Jo Buhle, *Women and American Social-*

ism, 1870–1920 (Urbana: University of Illinois Press, 1981); Hubert Perrier, "The Socialists and the Working Class in New York: 1890–1896," *Labor History* 22:4 (Fall 1981): 501; Melvyn Dubofsky, "Success and Failure of Socialism in New York City, 1900–1918: A Case Study," *Labor History* 9:3 (Fall 1968): 370–71; James Weinstein, "The Socialist Party: Its Roots and Strengths, 1912–1919," *Studies on the Left* 1 (Winter 1960): 5–27; Richard W. Fox, "The Paradox of Progressive Socialism: The Case of Morris Hillquit, 1901–1914," *American Quarterly* 26:1 (March 1974): 127–40; Arthur Gorenstein, "A Portrait of Ethnic Politics: The Socialists and the 1908 and 1910 Congressional Election on the East Side," *Publications of the American Jewish Historical Society* 50 (March 1961): 202–28.

Also useful for Jewish labor are Melvyn Dubofsky, *When Workers Organize* (Amherst: University of Massachusetts Press, 1968); Irwin Yellowitz, "Jewish Immigrants and the American Labor Movement, 1900–1920," *American Jewish History* 71 (December 1981): 188–217; Moses Rischin, "The Jewish Labor Movement in America: A Social Interpretation," *Labor History* 4 (Fall 1963): 235; Melech Epstein, *Jewish Labor in the United States of America,* vols. 1, 2 (New York: KTAV, 1950); Alice Kessler-Harris, "The Lower Class as a Factor in Reform: New York, the Jews, and the 1890s" (Ph.D. diss., Rutgers University, 1968); Paula Scheier, "Clara Lemlich Shavelson: 50 Years in Labor's Front Line," in Jacob R. Marcus, ed., *The American Jewish Woman: A Documentary History* (New York: KTAV, 1981); Ezra Mendelsohn, "The Russian Roots of the American Jewish Labor Movement," *YIVO Annual* 16 (1976): 173; Israel Knox and Irving Howe, *The Jewish Labor Movement in America: Two Views* (New York: Jewish Labor Committee, Workmen's Circle, 1958); Daniel Soyer, "Landsmanshaftn and the Jewish Labor Movement: Cooperation, Conflict, and the Building of Community," *Journal of American Ethnic History* 7:2 (Spring 1988): 26–27; Maxwell Whiteman, "Out of the Sweatshop," in Murray Friedman, ed., *Jewish Life in Philadelphia, 1830–1940* (Philadelphia: Jewish Publication Society of America, 1983), 64–79; and Leon Stein, *The Triangle Fire* (Philadelphia: J. B. Lippincott, 1962).

Memoirs of activists which can be mined for information and perspective are Marie Ganz, *Rebels into Anarchy and Out* (New York: Dodd and Mead, 1920); Morris Hillquit, *Loose Leaves from a Busy Life* (New York: Da Capo Press, 1971); David Dubinsky and A. H. Raskin, *David Dubinsky: A Life with Labor* (New York: Simon and Schuster, 1977); Elizabeth Hasanovitz, *One of Them* (Boston: Houghton Mifflin, 1918); Rose Cohen, *Out of the Shadow* (New York: G. H. Doran, 1918); Theresa Malkiel, *Diary of a Shirtwaist Striker* (New York: Cooperative Press, 1910); Louis Waldman, *Labor Lawyer* (New York: E.

P. Dutton, 1944); Rose Schneiderman, *All for One* (New York: Paul Erikson, 1967).

The best introduction to the Jewish religion in the United States is Marc Lee Raphael, *Profiles in American Judaism: The Reform, Conservative, Orthodox, and Reconstructionist Traditions in Historical Perspective* (San Francisco: Harper and Row, 1984). Other excellent studies are Arnold M. Eisen, *The Chosen People in America: A Study of Jewish Religious Ideology* (Bloomington: Indiana University Press, 1983); and Jonathan Woocher, *Sacred Survival: The Civil Religion of American Jews* (Bloomington: Indiana University Press, 1987). Useful collections of essays include Jacob Neusner, ed., *Understanding American Judaism: Toward the Description of a Modern Religion*, vol. 1, *The Rabbi and the Synagogue*, and vol. 2, *Sectors of American Judaism* (New York: KTAV, 1975); Jacob Marcus and Abraham Peck, eds., *The American Rabbinate: A Century of Continuity and Change, 1883–1983* (Hoboken, N.J.: KTAV, 1985); Jack Wertheimer, ed., *The American Synagogue: A Sanctuary Transformed* (New York: Cambridge University Press, 1987).

A recent masterful survey of the Reform movement is Michael A. Meyer, *Response to Modernity: A History of the Reform Movement in Judaism* (New York: Oxford University Press, 1988). See also Jonathan Sarna, "New Light on the Pittsburgh Platform of 1885," *American Jewish History* 76:3 (March 1987): 358–68. For Orthodoxy see Charles S. Liebman, "Orthodoxy in American Jewish Life," *American Jewish Year Book* (1965): 21–97; Aaron Rothkoff, *Bernard Revel: Builder of American Jewish Orthodoxy* (Philadelphia: Jewish Publication Society of America, 1972); Aaron Rothkoff, *The Silver Era in American Jewish Orthodoxy: Rabbi Eliezer Silver and His Generation* (New York: Yeshiva University Press, 1981); Abraham J. Karp, "New York Chooses a Chief Rabbi," *Publications of the American Jewish Historical Society* 44:3 (March 1955): 129–98; and the entire issue of *American Jewish History* 69 (December 1979), which is devoted to Orthodoxy.

Jeffrey S. Gurock makes a strong case that change toward an American decorum and more modern style in Judaism came *within* Orthodoxy as well as from the other, "reform" branches. See his "Resisters and Accommodators: Varieties of Orthodox Rabbis in America, 1886–1983," *American Jewish Archives* 35 (November 1983): 100–187; Gurock, and "From Exception to Role Model: Bernard Drachman and the Evolution of Jewish Religious Life in America, 1880–1920," *American Jewish History* 76:4 (June 1987): 481; and

Gurock, *The Men and Women of Yeshiva: Higher Education, Orthodoxy, and American Judaism* (New York: Columbia University Press, 1988). This should be supplemented with William Helmreich, *The World of the Yeshiva: An Intimate Portrait of Orthodox Jewry* (New York: Free Press, 1982).

A useful source book on Conservative Judaism is Pamela S. Nadell, ed., *Conservative Judaism in America* (Westport, Conn.: Greenwood Press, 1988) The bulk of the volume consists of 135 biographical sketches of Conservative leaders. The vital statistics and basic facts are here, but so are sophisticated evaluations of each subject's most important role in and contribution to the development of Conservative Judaism, its institutions, belief systems, central policies, and literature. Marshall Sklare, *Conservative Judaism: An American Religious Movement* (New York: Schocken Books, 1972), is still very useful. Also see Baila Shargel, *Practical Dreamer: Israel Friedlander and the Shaping of American Judaism* (New York: Jewish Theological Seminary, 1985); and Abraham Karp, *The History of the United Synagogue of America, 1913–1961* (New York: Bloch, 1964).

For Reconstructionism see Charles Liebman, "Reconstructionism in American Jewish Life," *American Jewish Year Book* (1970): 189–285; and the key statement of its founder, Mordecai Kaplan, *Judaism as a Civilization: Towards a Reconstruction of American Jewish Life* (New York: Macmillan, 1934).

A valuable general overview of the subject of Zionism is the introductory essay in Arthur Hertzberg's anthology *The Zionist Idea* (New York: Atheneum, 1972). For the American Zionist movement, see Melvin Urofsky's readable and comprehensive *American Zionism from Herzl to the Holocaust* (Garden City, N.Y.: Anchor Press, 1975); and Naomi Cohen's concise analysis *American Jews and the Zionist Idea* (New York: KTAV, 1975). Also worth consulting are Samuel Halperin, *The Political World of American Zionism* (Detroit: Wayne State University Press, 1961); Yonathan Shapiro, *The Leadership of the American Zionist Organization, 1897–1930* (Urbana: University of Illinois Press, 1971); Joan Dash, *Summoned to Jerusalem: The Life of Henrietta Szold* (New York: Harper and Row, 1979); Phillipa Strum, *Louis D. Brandeis: Justice for the People* (Cambridge: Harvard University Press, 1984); Allon Gal, *Brandeis of Boston* (Cambridge: Harvard University Press, 1980); Evayatar Friesel, "Jacob H. Schiff Becomes a Zionist: A Chapter in American-Jewish Self-Definition, 1907–1917," *Studies in Zionism* 5 (Spring 1982): 55–92; Gary P. Zola, "Reform Judaism's Pioneer Zionist: Maximillian Heller," *American Jewish History* 73:4 (June 1984): 375–97; and Melvin Urofsky, *A Voice That Spoke for Justice: The Life and Times of Stephen S. Wise* (Albany: State University of New York Press, 1982).

On the concept of cultural pluralism during this period, see Horace Kallen, "Democracy vs. the Melting Pot," *Nation,* February 18 and 25, 1915; and his *Culture and Democracy* (New York: Arno Press, 1970), 124–25; Moses Rischin, "The Jews and Pluralism: Toward an American Freedom Symphony," in Gladys Rosen, ed., *Jewish Life in America* (New York: KTAV, 1978), is a good overview.

CHAPTER 9   POWER AND PRINCIPLE: JEWISH PARTICIPATION IN AMERICAN DOMESTIC POLITICS AND FOREIGN AFFAIRS

Daniel Elazar, "American Political Theory and the Political Notions of American Jews: Convergence and Contradiction," in Peter I. Rose, ed., *The Ghetto and Beyond: Essays on Jewish Life in America* (New York: Random House, 1969), 203–27, is a good place to start on the subject of Jewish politics in the second decade of the twentieth century. Also see Lawrence Fuchs, "American Jews and the Presidential Vote," in Fuchs, ed., *American Ethnic Politics* (New York: Harper and Row, 1968), 32–53; and his *Political Behavior of American Jews* (Glencoe, Ill.: Free Press, 1956), but these should be used with care, for while there is a distinct tendency for relatively secularized Jews to be significantly overrepresented in liberal or left-leaning political cultures, as Fuchs argues, he overstates the connection between Judaism per se and liberalism. See also Nathaniel Weyl, *The Jew in American Politics* (New Rochelle, N.Y.: Arlington House, 1976); and Jeffery Gurock, "The 1913 New York State Civil Rights Act," *Association for Jewish Studies Review* 1 (1976): 93–120.

Cyrus Adler and Aaron Margalith, *With Firmness in the Right: American Diplomatic Action Affecting Jews, 1840–1945* (New York: Arno Press, 1977), though hardly neutral, is very good for foreign affairs, as are Cyrus Adler, *The Voice of America on Kishineff* (Philadelphia: Jewish Publication Society of America, 1904); and Oscar S. Straus, *Under Four Administrations: From Cleveland to Taft* (Boston: Houghton and Mifflin, 1922). A variety of useful articles include Philip E. Schoenberg, "The American Reaction to the Kishinev Pogrom of 1903," *American Jewish Historical Quarterly* 63 (March 1974): 262–83; Stuart E. Knee, "The Diplomacy of Neutrality: Theodore Roosevelt and the Russian Pogroms of 1903–1906," *Presidential Studies Quarterly* 19 (Winter 1989): 71–78; Judith Goldstein, "Ethnic Politics: The American Jewish Committee as Lobbyist, 1915–1917," *American Jewish Historical Quarterly* 65 (September 1975): 36–58; Zosa Szajkowski, "Private and Organized American Jewish Overseas Relief and Immigration (1914–1938)," *American Jewish Historical Quarterly* 57 (December 1967): 191–253. Joseph C. Hyman, "Twenty-five

Years of American Aid to Jews Overseas: A Record of the Joint Distribution Committee," *American Jewish Year Book* (1939): 141–79, is still useful for the early years, but the best source for the Joint is Yehuda Bauer, *My Brother's Keeper: A History of the American Jewish Joint Distribution Committee, 1929–1939* (Philadelphia: Jewish Publication Society, 1974). Domestic politics and foreign affairs are also discussed in two very good studies: Naomi Cohen, *Not Free to Desist: The American Jewish Committee, 1906–1966* (Philadelphia: Jewish Publication Society of America, 1972); and Daniel Elazar, *Community and Polity: The Organizational Dynamics of American Jewry* (Philadelphia: Jewish Publication Society of America, 1976).

For the American Jewish Congress, see the works on Brandeis and Wise cited above; and Jonathan Frankel, "The Jewish Socialists and the American Jewish Congress Movement," *YIVO Annual* 16 (1976): 202–342; and Isaac Neustadt, "The Unending Task: Efforts to Unite American Jewry from the American Jewish Congress to the American Jewish Conference" (Ph.D. diss., Brandeis University, 1976).

CHAPTER 10   MOBILITY, POLITICS, AND THE CONSTRUCTION OF A JEWISH AMERICAN IDENTITY

A great many works cited as relevant for earlier chapters are also relevant here for Jewish social, occupational, and geographic mobility. In addition, for education see Jeremiah J. Berman, "Jewish Education in New York City, 1860–1900," *YIVO Annual* 9 (1954): 247–75; Stephan F. Brumberg, "Going to America, Going to School: The Immigrant–Public School Encounter in Turn-of-the-Century New York City," *American Jewish Archives* 36 (November 1984): 86–135. For a different perspective look at Selma Berrol, "Education and Economic Mobility: The Jewish Experience in New York City, 1880–1920," *American Jewish Historical Quarterly* 65 (March 1976): 257–71. Worthwhile works on Jews and higher education include: Marcia Synnott, *The Half-Opened Door: Discrimination and Admissions at Harvard, Yale, and Princeton, 1900–1970* (Westport, Conn.: Greenwood Press, 1979); Dan A. Oren, *Joining the Club: A History of Jews and Yale* (New Haven: Yale University Press, 1985); Henry Feingold, "Investing in Themselves: The Harvard Case and the Origins of the Third American-Jewish Commercial Elite," *American Jewish History* 77 (June 1988): 530–53; Susanne Klingenstein, *Jews in the American Academy, 1900–1940: The Dynamics of Intellectual Assimilation* (New Haven: Yale University Press, 1991); Paul Ritterband and Harold Wechsler, *Jewish Learning in American Universities* (Bloomington: Indiana University Press, 1994). Older but still useful is Willis Rudy, *The City College of New York: A History, 1847–1947* (New York: City College Press, 1949); and a sensitive and insightful memoir by Morris R. Cohen, *A Dreamer's Journey* (Boston: Beacon Press, 1949).

Success in business continued, in the second generation, to be an even more important route to upward mobility than education. See Moses Kligsberg, "Jewish Immigrants in Business: A Sociological Study," in Abraham Karp, ed., *Jewish Experience in America* (New York: KTAV, 1969), 5:249–84; Shelly Tenenbaum, "Immigrants and Capital: Jewish Loan Societies in the United States, 1880–1945," *American Jewish Historical Quarterly* 76 (September 1986): 67–77; Abraham Korman, *The Outsiders: Jews and Corporate America* (Lexington, Mass.: Lexington Books, 1988). Nonetheless, there was a remarkable increase in the number of Jews in the educated professions. See Barton J. Bledstein, *The Culture of Professionalism: The Middle Class and the Development of Higher Education in America* (New York: Norton, 1976); Jerold S. Auerbach, "From Rags to Robes: The Legal Profession, Social Mobility, and the American Jewish Experience," *American Jewish Historical Quarterly* 66:2 (December 1976): 249–84; Roy Lubove, *The Professional Altruist: The Emergence of Social Work as a Career, 1880–1930* (Cambridge: Harvard University Press, 1965).

Although physical mobility accompanied social mobility, Jews continued to concentrate in their dispersions, according to Deborah Dash Moore, "The Construction of Community: Jewish Migration and Ethnicity in the United States," in Moses Rischin, ed., *The Jews of North America* (Detroit: Wayne State University Press, 1987), 105–20; and Sidney Goldstein, "Population Movement and Redistribution among American Jews," *Jewish Journal of Sociology* 24 (June 1982): 5–23.

Jewish giving is analyzed best by Jonathan Woocher's *Sacred Survival: The Civil Religion of American Jews* (Bloomington: Indiana University Press, 1987) but see also Harry Lurie, *A Heritage Affirmed: The Jewish Federation Movement in America* (Philadelphia: Jewish Publication Society, 1961); Philip Bernstein, *To Dwell in Unity: The Jewish Federation Movement in America since 1960* (Philadelphia: Jewish Publication Society, 1983); Deborah Dash Moore, *B'nai B'rith and the Challenge of Ethnic Leadership* (Albany: State University of New York Press, 1981).

Jewish politics and political culture are best viewed in the larger context of American politics, as in Warren Moscow, *Politics in the Empire State* (New York: Knopf, 1948); John Shover, *Politics in the Nineteen-Twenties* (Waltham, Mass.: Ginn Press, 1970); William Preston, *Aliens and Dissenters: Federal Suppression of Radicals, 1903–1933* (Cambridge: Harvard University Press,

1963); and Robert K. Murray, *Red Scare: A Study in National Hysteria, 1919–1920* (Minneapolis: University of Minneapolis Press, 1955). Excellent monographs directly relevant to Jewish political values and behavior include: Ronald Bayor, *Neighbors in Conflict: The Irish, Germans, Jews, and Italians of New York City* (Baltimore: Johns Hopkins University Press, 1978); Elizabeth Perry, *Belle Moskowitz: Feminine Politics and the Exercise of Power in the Age of Alfred E. Smith* (New York: Oxford University Press, 1987); Deborah Dash Moore, *At Home in America: Second Generation Jews in New York* (New York: Columbia University Press, 1981). Also see Nathan Glazer, *The Social Bases of American Communism* (New York: Harcourt Brace, 1961); and Arthur Liebman, *Jews and the Left* (New York: John Wiley, 1971), which contain important information about Jewish political behavior but are ideologically skewed and must be used with care.

On the debate between transformationists and assimilationists, which is relevant to almost every section of this book, see especially Steven M. Cohen, *American Assimilation or Jewish Revival?* (Bloomington: University of Indiana Press, 1988), for an optimistic assessment; and Charles Liebman, "The Quality of American Jewish Life: A Grim Outlook," in Steven Bayme, ed., *Facing the Future: Essays on Contemporary Jewish Life* (New York: KTAV, 1989), 50–71, and the limited but useful study by Samuel Heilman, *Portrait of American Jews: The Last Half of the 20th Century* (Seattle: University of Washington Press, 1996), for more pessimistic perspectives.

Other important works for this period include: Jenna W. Joselit, *New York's Jewish Jews: The Orthodox Community in the Interwar Years* (Bloomington: Indiana University Press, 1990); Susan L. Braunstein and Jenna W. Joselit, eds., *Getting Comfortable in New York: The American Jewish Home, 1880–1950* (Bloomington: Indiana University Press, 1991); Stanley Chyet, "Three Generations: An Account of American Jewish Fiction (1896–1969)," *Jewish Social Studies* 34:1 (January 1972): 31–41; Irving Howe, "The New York Intellectuals: A Chronicle and a Critique," *Commentary* 46 (October 1968): 29–51; Patricia Erens, *The Jew in American Cinema* (Bloomington: Indiana University Press, 1985); and Peter Levine, *From Ellis Island to Ebbets Field: Sports and the American Jewish Experience* (New York: Oxford University Press, 1992).

CHAPTER 11   ALMOST AT HOME IN AMERICA, 1920–1945

Leonard Dinnerstein, *Anti-Semitism in America* (New York: Oxford University Press, 1994), is the best single volume on this subject available, and his collection of essays *Uneasy at Home: Antisemitism and the American Jewish Experience*

(New York: Columbia University Press, 1987), is reflective and provocative; David Gerber's anthology of articles by scholars from several disciplines, *Anti-Semitism in American History* (Urbana: University of Illinois Press, 1986), is valuable generally, and particularly for Gerber's introductory historiographical essay. Other important essays include John J. Appel, "Jews in American Caricature: 1820–1914," *American Jewish History* 71:1 (September 1981): 103–33; Leo P. Ribuffo, "Henry Ford and the *International Jew*," *American Jewish History* 69:4 (June 1980): 437–77; Henry Feingold, "Anti-Semitism and the Anti-Semitic Imagination in America: A Case Study—The Twenties," in his *Midrash on American Jewish History* (Albany: State University of New York Press, 1982), 185; John Higham, "Social Discrimination against Jews, 1830–1930," in his *Send These to Me: Jews and Other Immigrants in Urban America* (New York: Atheneum, 1975), 138–73; Naomi W. Cohen, "Anti-semitism in the Gilded Age: The Jewish View," *Jewish Social Studies* 41:3–4 (Summer/Fall 1979): 187–210; and Jonathan Sarna, "Anti-Semitism and American History," *Commentary* 71 (March 1981): 42–47. For the general xenophobic context of America in the era of mass immigration, see John Higham's classic *Strangers in the Land: Patterns of American Nativism, 1865–1925,* 2d ed. (New York: Atheneum, 1966); and a series of recent reappraisals of Higham's work in *American Jewish History* 76:2 (December 1986). These should be supplemented with David H. Bennett, *The Party of Fear: From Nativist Movement to the New Right in American History* (Chapel Hill: University of North Carolina Press, 1988). Restriction in the universities is examined in Stephen Steinberg, *The Academic Melting Pot: Catholics and Jews in American Higher Education* (New York: McGraw-Hill, 1974), as well as in books on education cited for chapter 10.

The best collection of survey research on anti-Semitism for this period is found in Charles S. Stember, ed., *Jews in the Mind of America* (New York: Basic Books, 1966). Good studies include Louise A. Mayo, *The Ambivalent Image* (Rutherford, N.J.: Fairleigh Dickinson University Press, 1988), an insightful monograph on anti-Semitism in the nineteenth century; Leonard Dinnerstein, *The Leo Frank Case* (New York: Columbia University Press, 1968); Naomi Cohen, *Jews in Christian America: The Pursuit of Relgious Equality* (Oxford: Oxford University Press, 1992); Donald S. Strong, *Organized Anti-Semitism in America: The Rise of Group Prejudice during the Decade 1930–1940* (Washington, D.C.: American Council of Public Affairs, 1941); Sander E. Diamond, *The Nazi Movement in the United States, 1924–1941* (Ithaca, N.Y.: Cornell University Press, 1974); Glen Jeansonne, *Gerald L. K. Smith, Minister of Hate* (New Haven: Yale University Press, 1988); Alan Brinkley, *Voices of*

Protest: Huey Long, Father Coughlin, and the Great Depression (New York: Vintage, 1983).

Michael Marrus, *The Unwanted: European Refugees in the Twentieth Century* (New York: Oxford University Press, 1985), is the best overview of the refugee crisis. The motivation of the immigration restrictionists is discernible in the congressional hearings, especially in House Committee on Immigration and Naturalization, *A Bill to Provide for the Protection of the Citizens of the U.S.* (H.R. 14461), 67th Cong., 3d sess., 5 January 1921; and *Restriction of Immigration* (H.R. 5, 101, 561), 68th Cong., 1st sess., 3 January 1924.

For somewhat contrasting views of the relationship of the Roosevelt administration to the Holocaust, see David S. Wyman, *The Abandonment of the Jews: America and the Holocaust, 1941–1945* (New York: Pantheon, 1984), and Henry Feingold, *The Politics of Rescue: The Roosevelt Administration and the Holocaust, 1938–1945* (New York: Holocaust Library, 1980); Henry Feingold, *Bearing Witness: How America and Its Jews Responded to the Holocaust* (Syracuse, N.Y.: Syracuse University Press, 1995). See also Aaron Berman, *Nazism, the Jews, and American Zionism, 1933–1948* (Detroit: Wayne State University Press, 1990); and Richard Breitman and Alan M. Kraut, *American Refugee Policy and European Jewry, 1933–1945* (Bloomington: Indiana University Press, 1988), which places the refugee problem in a broad historical context.

Shlomo Shafir, "American Diplomats in Berlin (1933–39) and Their Attitudes toward the Nazi Persecution of Jews," *Yad Vashem Studies* 9 (1973): 71–104, is a balanced analysis of a complex issue; as are Deborah Lipstadt, "Pious Sympathies and Sincere Regrets: The American News Media and the Holocaust from Krystallnacht to Bermuda, 1938–1943," *Modern Judaism* 2 (February 1982): 53–72; and her *Beyond Belief: The American Press and the Coming of the Holocaust, 1933–1945* (New York: Free Press, 1986). See also Yehuda Bauer, *My Brother's Keeper: A History of the American Jewish Joint Distribution Committee, 1939–1945* (Detroit: Wayne State University Press, 1981); Sharon Lowenstein, *Token Refuge: The Story of the Jewish Refugee Shelter at Oswego, 1944–1946* (Bloomington: Indiana University Press, 1986); and Robert Abzug, *Inside the Vicious Heart: America and the Liberation of the Nazi Concentration Camps* (New York: Oxford University Press, 1987).

CHAPTER 12   AMERICAN JEWRY REGROUPS, 1945–1970

Jonathan Woocher, *Sacred Survival: The Civil Religion of American Jews* (Bloomington: Indiana University Press, 1987), remains the single best analysis of the Jewish philanthropic impulse. See also Marc L. Raphael, *Understanding*

American Jewish Philanthropy (New York: KTAV, 1979); Milton Goldin, *Why They Give: American Jews and Their Philanthropies* (New York: KTAV, 1979); Abraham J. Karp, *To Give Life:The UJA in the Shaping of the American Jewish Community* (New York: Schocken Books, 1981); Michael Dobkowski, ed., *Jewish-American Volunteer Organizations* (Westport, Conn.: Greenwood Press, 1986).

The best books on the postwar Jewish movement to the suburbs include Albert Gordon, *Jews in Suburbia* (Boston: Beacon Press, 1959); Judith Kramer and Seymour Leventman, *Children of the Gilded Ghetto: Conflict Resolutions of Three Generations of American Jews* (New Haven: Yale University Press, 1961); Marshall Sklare and Joseph Greenblum, *Jewish Identity on the Suburban Frontier* (New York: Basic Books, 1979); and Benjamin Ringer, *The Edge of Friendliness:A Study of Jewish-Gentile Relations* (New York: Basic Books, 1967). Several chapters of Gerald Sorin, *The Nurturing Neighborhood:The Brownsville Boys Club and Jewish Community in Urban America, 1940–1990,* (New York: New York University Press, 1990), are also relevant.

On postwar immigration and acculturation, see Haim Genizi, "New York Is Big—America Is Bigger: The Resettlement of Refugees from Nazism, 1936–1945," *Jewish Social Studies* 46 (Winter 1984): 61–72; Herbert A. Strauss, "The Immigration and Acculturation of the German Jew in the U.S. of A.," *Leo BaeckYearbook* 16 (1971): 12–53; and Steven Lowenstein, *Frankfurt on the Hudson:The German Jewish Community of Washington Heights, 1933–1983* (Detroit: Wayne State University Press, 1988).

Will Herberg, *Protestant-Catholic-Jew:An Essay in Religious Sociology,* rev. ed. (New York: Doubleday, 1960), puts the history of American Jewry within the context of the general religious revival of the 1950s. Jacob Neusner's two-volume anthology, *Understanding American Judaism:Toward the Description of a Modern Religion* (New York: KTAV, 1975), contains many important articles on contemporary Jewish belief, practice, and institutional arrangement; and Nathan Glazer's *American Judaism* (Chicago: University of Chicago Press, 1972), is a pessimistic assessment of the adaption of Judaism to American conditions. See also the December 1987 issue of *American Jewish History,* which discusses Glazer's book from a variety of perspectives.

In addition to the books on religion cited for chapter 8, see Solomon Poll, *The Hasidic Community of Williamsburg:A Study in the Sociology of Religion* (New York: Schocken Books, 1962); Jerome R. Mintz, *Hasidic People:A Place in the NewWorld* (Cambridge: Harvard University Press, 1992); M. Herbert Danzinger, *Returning to Tradition:The Contemporary Revival of Orthodox Judaism* (New Haven: Yale University Press, 1989); Deborah Renee Kaufman, *Rachel's Daughters: Newly Orthodox JewishWomen* (Newark, N.J.: Rutgers University Press, 1991); Lynn Davidman, *Tradition in a Rootless World: Women Turn to Orthodox Judaism* (Berkeley and Los Angeles: University of California Press, 1991); Samuel C. Heilman and Steven M. Cohen, *Cosmopolitans and Parochials: Modern Orthodox Jews in America* (Chicago: University of Chicago Press, 1976).

Gerald Showstack, *Suburban Communities: The Jewishness of American Reform Jews* (Ithaca, N.Y.: Cornell University Press, 1988), contains interesting insights on the status of contemporary American Reform; as does Leonard Fein, ed., *Reform Is a Verb: Notes on Reform and Reforming Judaism* (New York: Union of American Hebrew Congregations, 1972). For post-Kaplan Reconstructionism see Rebecca Alpert and Jacob J. Staub, *Exploring Judaism: A Reconstructionist Approach* (New York: Reconstructionist Press, 1985). The *havurah* movement is discussed in James A. Sleeper and Alan Mintz, eds., *The New Jews* (New York: Random House, 1971); and Riv-Ellen Prell, *Prayer and Community: The Havurah Movement in American Judaism* (Detroit: Wayne State University Press, 1989).

The best assessment of changes in Judaism and Jewish life wrought by women is Sylvia Barach Fishman, "The Impact of Feminism on American Jewish Life," *American Jewish Year Book* (1989): 3–62. See also Susannah Heschel, ed. *On Being a Jewish Feminist: A Reader* (New York: Schocken Books, 1990); Paula Hyman, "The Introduction of Bat Mitzvah in Conservative Judaism in Postwar America," *YIVO Annual* 19 (1990): 133–46; T. M. Rudavsky, ed., *Gender and Judaism: The Transformation of Tradition* (New York: New York University Press, 1995); and for a reaction to those changes, National Commission on American Jewish Women, *Voices for Change: Future Directions for American Jewish Women* (Waltham, Mass.: National Commission of American Jewish Women, 1995).

The upward social and economic mobility of Jews after 1945 is described in several excellent essays in Marshall Sklare, ed., *The Jews: Social Patterns of an American Group* (New York: Free Press, 1958); Lawrence Bloomgarden, "Our Changing Elite Colleges," *Commentary* 29 (February 1960): 150–54; Charles Kadushin, *The American Intellectual Elite* (Boston: Little, Brown, 1974); Harriet Zuckerman, *Scientific Elite: Nobel Laureates in the United States* (New York: Free Press, 1977); Richard D. Alba and Gwen Moore, "Ethnicity in the American Elite," *American Sociological Review* 47 (June 1982): 373–83; and Edward S. Shapiro, "Jews with Money," *Judaism* 67 (Winter 1987): 7–16. One should also look at Naomi Levine and Martin Hochbaum, eds., *Poor Jews: An American Awakening* (New Brunswick, N.J.:

Transaction, 1974), for the lingering presence of poverty, particularly among older Jews.

For the resilience of Jewish liberalism, see Arthur Liebman, "The Ties That Bind: The Jewish Support of the Left in the U.S.," *American Jewish Historical Quarterly* 74 (September 1984): 45–65; and Steven M. Cohen, *The Dimensions of American Jewish Liberalism* (New York: American Jewish Committee, 1989). Robert Weisbord and Arthur Stein, *Bittersweet Encounter: The Afro-American and the American Jew* (Westport, Conn.: Negro University Press, 1970), is still useful; but Gary T. Marx, *Protest and Prejudice: A Study of Belief in the Black Community* (New York: Harper and Row, 1969) seriously underestimates the extent of Black anti-Semitism. See Murray Friedman, *What Went Wrong? The Creation and Collapse of the Black-Jewish Alliance* (New York: Free Press, 1995); and Paul Berman, ed., *Blacks and Jews: Thirty Years of Alliance and Argument* (New York: Delacorte Press, 1994).

CHAPTER 13   ISRAEL, THE HOLOCAUST, AND ECHOES OF ANTI-SEMITISM IN JEWISH AMERICAN CONSCIOUSNESS, 1960–1995

For U.S.-Israeli relations see Michael J. Cohen, *Truman and Israel* (Berkeley and Los Angeles: University of California Press, 1990); William B. Quandt, *Peace Process: American Diplomacy and the Arab-Israeli Conflict since 1967* (Washington, D.C.: Brookings Institution, 1993); and Abraham Ben-Zvi, *The United States and Israel: The Limits of the Special Relationship* (New York: Columbia University Press, 1993). Charles Liebman and Steven Cohen, *Two Worlds of Judaism: The Israeli and American Experiences* (New Haven: Yale University Press, 1989), is an insightful, relatively optimistic exercise in comparison and contrast and a commentary on the interaction of Israelis and Jewish Americans. More on the interactions can be found in Moshe Shokeid, *Children of Circumstances: Israeli Emigrants in New York* (Ithaca, N.Y.: Cornell University Press, 1988); and Chaim Waxman, *American Aliyah: Portrait of an Innovative Migration Movement* (Detroit: Wayne State University Press, 1989). See also Ernest Stock, *Partners and Pursestrings: History of the United States Israel Appeal* (Lanham, Md.: University Press of America, 1987); and Drora Kass and Seymour Martin Lipset, "Jewish Immigration to the United States from 1967 to the Present: Israelis and Others," in Marshall Sklare, ed., *Understanding American Jewry* (New Brunswick, N.J.: Transaction, 1982).

On the rescue of Soviet Jewry, see William W. Orbach, *The American Movement to Aid Soviet Jewry* (Amherst: University of Massachusetts Press, 1979); Lewis Weinstein, "Soviet Jewry and the American Jewish Community, 1963–1987," *American Jewish History* 77 (June 1988): 600–613; and Sylvia Rothschild, *A Special Legacy:An Oral History of Soviet Jewish Emigres in the United States* (New York: Simon and Schuster, 1985).

Michael Berenbaum's *After Tragedy andTriumph: Modern JewishThought and the American Experience* (Cambridge: Cambridge University Press, 1991); and his "Nativization of the Holocaust," *Judaism* 35 (Fall 1986): 447–57, are excellent studies of the use and "misuse" of the Holocaust. The last chapter of Judith Miller's *One, by One, by One: Facing the Holocaust* (New York: Simon and Schuster, 1990), also examines the influence of the Holocaust on American Jewish identity. See also Alan L. Berger, *Crisis and Covenant: The Holocaust in American Jewish Fiction* (Albany: State University of New York Press, 1985). For the survivors themselves see Leonard Dinnerstein, *America and the Survivors of the Holocaust* (New York: Columbia University Press, 1982); and William B. Helmreich, *Against All Odds: Holocaust Survivors and the Successful Lives They Made in America* (New Brunswick, N.J.: Transaction, 1992).

Other sources relevant for this chapter are Marshall Sklare, *Observing America's Jews* (Hanover, N.H.: Brandeis University Press, 1993); U. O. Schmelz and Sergio Dellapergola, *Basic Trends in Jewish Demography* (New York: American Jewish Committee, 1988); Lewis Coser and Irving Howe, eds., *The New Conservatives:A Critique from the Left* (New York: New American Library, 1977); Allen Guttmann, *The Jewish Writer in America:Assimilation and the Crisis of Identity* (New York: Oxford University Press, 1971); and Gary Tobin and Sharon Sassler, *Jewish Perceptions of Anti-Semitism* (New York: Plenum, 1988), which, unlike the work of Dinnerstein and others, argues— perhaps too pessimistically—that American anti-Semitism continues to be dangerous. On this see Jerome Chanes, ed., *Antisemitism in America Today: Outspoken Experts Explode the Myths* (New York: Birch Lane Press, 1995). On Jews and Blacks see citations for chapter 12.

CHAPTER 14   THE EVER DISAPPEARING PEOPLE

Nearly all of the citations for chapters 12 and 13 are relevant here as well. In addition, see Gershom Scholem, *On Jews and Judaism in Crisis* (New York: Schocken Books, 1980); Barry A. Kosmin et al., *Highlights of the National Jewish Population Survey* (New York: Council of Jewish Federations, 1991); Chaim Waxman, *America's Jews in Transition* (Philadelphia: Temple University, 1983); Charles Silberman, *A Certain People: American Jews and Their Lives Today* (New York: Summit Books, 1985); Leonard Fein, *Where Are We?* (New York: Harper and Row, 1988); and Stephen J. Whitfield's astute essays on contemporary

Jewish life in his *Voices of Jacob, Hands of Esau: Jews in American Life and Thought* (Hamden, Conn.: Archon, 1984); and his *American Space, Jewish Time* (Hamden, Conn.: Archon, 1988). Also see Seymour Martin Lipset, *Jews and the New American Scene* (Cambridge: Harvard University Press, 1995). Other valuable collections of essays on contemporary American Jewish culture include Peter I. Rose, ed., *The Ghetto and Beyond: Essays on Jewish Life in America* (New York: Random House, 1969); Steven Bayme, ed., *Facing the Future: Essays on Contemporary Jewish Life* (New York: KTAV, 1989); and Seymour Martin Lipset, ed., *American Pluralism and the Jewish Community* (New Brunswick, N.J.: Transaction, 1990).

On Jewish migration patterns see Bruce A. Phillips, "Los Angeles Jewry: A Demographic Portrait," *American Jewish Year Book* (1986): 126–95; and Deborah Dash Moore, *To the Golden Cities: Pursuing the American Jewish Dream in Miami and L.A.* (New York: Free Press, 1994). Indispensable for Judaism in contemporary America is Jack Wertheimer, *A People Divided* (New York: Basic Books, 1993), which places changes in Jewish religious and communal life in the context of the wider society and offers an intriguing portrait of the vitality and diversity of American Judaism in the 1990s.

For good general studies of contemporary immigration and ethnicity with useful bibliographies for specific groups, see David Reimers, *Still the Golden Door: The Third World Comes to America* (New York: Columbia University Press, 1985); and Roger Daniels, *Coming to America: A History of Immigration and Ethnicity in American Life* (New York: Harper Collins, 1990). On the politics of identity and multiculturalism, see Darryl Gless and Barbara Hernstein Smith, *The Politics of Liberal Education* (Durham, N.C.: Duke University Press, 1991), for a positive assessment; and Arthur Schlesinger, *The Disuniting of America* (New York: W. W. Norton, 1991), for a much less sanguine view. The most insightful and persuasive works are David A. Hollinger, "How Wide the Circle of 'We'? American Intellectuals and the Problem of Ethnos since World War II," *American Historical Review* 98 (April 1993): 317–37; Charles Taylor, *Multiculturalism and "The Politics of Recognition"* (Princeton: Princeton University Press, 1992); Philip Gleason, *Speaking of Diversity: Essays on the Language of Ethnicity* (Baltimore: Johns Hopkins University Press, 1992); and Gleason, "Americans All: World War II and the Shaping of American Identity," *Review of Politics* 43 (October 1981): 483–518. Also useful is Lawrence Fuchs, *American Pluralism and Public Policy: Implications for the Jewish Community* (New York: American Jewish Committee, 1988).

Index

LIBRARY OF CONGRESS CATALOGING-IN-PUBLICATION DATA

Sorin, Gerald, 1940–
    Tradition transformed : the Jewish experience in America / Gerald
Sorin.
        p.   cm. — (American moment)
    Includes bibliographical references and index.
    ISBN 0-8018-5446-6 (alk. paper). — ISBN 0-8018-5447-4 (pbk. :
alk. paper)
    1. Jews—United States—History.   2. Judaism—United States—
History.   3. Jews—United States—Politics and government.
4. United States—Ethnic relations.   I. Title.   II. Series.
E184.J5S666   1997
973'.04924—dc20   96-28303
                                                                    CIP